DARK S**OUL** OF THE SOUTH

ALSO BY MEL AYTON FROM POTOMAC BOOKS, INC.

The Forgotten Terrorist:
Sirhan Sirhan and the Assassination of Robert F. Kennedy

DARK SOUL OF THE SOUTH

The Life and Crimes of Racist Killer Joseph Paul Franklin

Mel Ayton

Potomac Books, Inc.
Washington, D.C.

Library of Congress Cataloging-in-Publication Data
Ayton, Mel.
 Dark soul of the South : the life and crimes of racist killer Joseph Paul
Franklin / Mel Ayton.
     p. cm.
 Includes bibliographical references and index.
 ISBN 978-1-59797-543-8 (hardcover : alk. paper)
 1. Franklin, Joseph Paul. 2. Serial murderers—United States—Biography.
3. Hate crimes—United States. I. Title.
 HV6248.F6713A98 2010
 364.152'32092—dc22
 [B]
                                                          2010044685

Printed in the United States of America on acid-free paper that meets the American National Standards Institute Z39-48 Standard.

Potomac Books, Inc.
22841 Quicksilver Drive
Dulles, Virginia 20166

First Edition

10 9 8 7 6 5 4 3 2 1

CONTENTS

INTRODUCTION

Searching For Answers

It was clear from my interactions with him that Joe Franklin saw himself as sort of a one-man, heavenly-ordained, and racially motivated lynch squad.

—*Michael Watkiss, a former attorney for Joseph Paul Franklin*

Joseph Paul Franklin, the only racially motivated serial killer ever pursued by the Justice Department, left a tantalizing evidentiary trail, never before exhaustively explored.[1]

Franklin was, by his own admission, an "outlaw," a "racist," and "weird." He was a white supremacist, a Nazi, and a Ku Klux Klansman. He advocated and carried out violent enforcement of his views. He saw African Americans and Jews as subhuman, and he knew no moral obstacle to racial violence. Indeed, he invoked the Bible to support his criminal acts. As a lone-wolf terrorist in the 1970s, Franklin armed himself to the teeth for his mission, which he said had been condoned by God. He was already primed for it through his indoctrination by the American Nazi Party, the National States Rights Party, and the Ku Klux Klan.

Franklin's killing spree was contemporaneous with other racially charged incidents throughout the United States from 1977 to 1980, including the 1978 Klan rallies in Decatur, Alabama, which brought thousands of Klansmen into the streets for the first time in more than a decade; and an alliance of Klansmen and neo-Nazis that resulted in the killings of five labor organizers in Greensboro, North Carolina, in 1979. (The killers were later acquitted.) In 1980 Klan members shot five African

American women in Chattanooga, Tennessee. In 1981, shortly after Franklin's kill-ing spree ended, the Ku Klux Klan attacked Vietnamese shrimp boat owners and workers in Galveston, Texas.

Franklin had his defenders. There were, and still are, self-styled "patriots" of militia movements and white supremacist groups who believe he was a victim of the government, a hero who only put into practice the "duty of every white American to protect the white race." These groups characterize Franklin as a romantic, archetyp-al anti-hero, synonymous with John Dillinger, Jesse James, or Billy the Kid—men who committed daring deeds, outwitted the authorities, and were forced to commit their crimes because of an unjust system.

Well into the 1980s and 1990s, hate groups around the United States lauded Franklin's deeds. During this period, America saw an unprecedented level of racial hatred and publicity by white supremacist groups led by Richard Butler, host of the 1982 Aryan Nations Congress. In 1983 Robert Matthews founded "The Order" in Washington State, an armed group that would later be responsible for numer-ous bank robberies and racially charged murders. In 1984 The Order assassinated Denver talk show host Alan Berg because he was a Jew and an outspoken critic of racism. In the late 1980s William Pierce, who was inspired by Franklin and dedi-cated his book *Hunter* to him, hailed Franklin as a hero of the white supremacist movement. *Hunter,* a novel about an avenging white supremacist who guns down innocent Jews and African Americans, eventually became a best seller.[2]

What could possibly have caused Franklin to lose so much respect for other human beings that he would pick up a sniper rifle and end the lives of so many people? How could he have become so twisted, so cruel, and so unremorseful? How could he have embraced the notion that God dictated killing innocent human beings and faceless strangers on the street? Or that hatred was a virtue?

He was responsible for at least sixteen bank robberies, two bombings, the wounding of five people (including a famous civil rights leader), and the murder of many more. He was the most prolific racist killer of his age, and although his crimes have not been as well publicized as those of racist killers James Earl Ray or Byron De La Beckwith, they are nonetheless a vital part of American civil rights history.

The 1960s were a time when competing political ideologies tore apart families, towns, and countries. For many, including this author, it was a time for positive change in politics, human rights, and culture. To Franklin and many of his fellow Southerners, however, the 1960s represented a time when change invoked fear—fear of Jewish influence over American life, fear that the United States would no longer be a bastion of white supremacy after the landmark legislation of Lyndon Johnson's Great Society, and fear that equal rights for African Americans would lead to the destruction of the Southern way of life.

Writing the story of Joseph Paul Franklin's crimes has not been an easy task for a number of reasons. I accumulated a wealth of documentation, including the complete police murder files from the Salt Lake City Police Department, the summary report from the Cincinnati Police Department, numerous court records, Franklin's prison file, news agency articles, and transcripts of interviews with the subject. I compiled a dossier on Franklin's movements throughout the United States—the towns he visited, the aliases he adopted, the motels he stayed in, and the numerous banks he robbed as he embarked on his self-confessed mission from God to rid the world of African Americans and Jews.

I met pitfalls on the way. The task of teasing out truth from fiction in this case was not an easy one. Franklin was a notorious fabricator and manipulator. He was deceptive and cunning, and he lied repeatedly to extricate himself from the charges that were eventually leveled at him by law enforcement agencies, federal prosecutors, and state prosecutors. He also confessed to a number of crimes and then retracted his confessions. At one time he wrote to the district attorney of Gwinnett County, Georgia, confessing to the attempted murder of Larry Flynt. When officials went to the United States Penitentiary in Marion, Illinois, to interview him, he said it was all a hoax. Later, police became convinced he had been telling the truth all along.

Cincinnati police officer Michael O'Brien, who had investigated Franklin's crimes over a period of twenty years and was able to interview him by telephone in the late 1990s, once observed that "if Franklin said he did it, you can usually take it to the bank." That may be true in many instances but not all. After scrutinizing Franklin's statements to police and the media, his writings, his politics, and numerous witness statements, including those by family members, I discovered that Franklin was less than candid on a number of occasions. For example, one particular part of Franklin's story was especially difficult to adjudicate—the Rainbow murders, in which a West Virginia man was tried and convicted for the murders of two young women. There was no solid evidence to place Franklin at the scene of the crime. He eventually provided a detailed confession with drawings of the crime scene, but there remained puzzling aspects of the case, including the wealth of evidence that pointed to Jacob Beard as the killer of the two girls Franklin confessed to murdering. It was also difficult to determine whether Franklin's confessions concerning two murders committed in Atlanta were true or not. In order to find out, I have matched comments made by Franklin with the evidence accumulated by law enforcement agencies to gauge Franklin's veracity. Eventually, I believe I was able to establish the truth.

I also initially found it difficult to establish the facts regarding additional crimes Franklin confessed to but was never charged with. Like the Rainbow murders confession, we had Franklin's word and his word alone. Corroboratory evidence was sadly missing in the police investigation files.

Lack of sufficient evidence to prosecute Franklin was not the only reason various state authorities did not bring Franklin to justice for many of his murders. When he made his confessions, he had already been serving life sentences for other crimes and had been sentenced to death for one particular crime—the murder of Gerald Gordon outside a St. Louis synagogue. Many state prosecutors wondered if Franklin had confessed to certain crimes simply to have a furlough at the taxpayers' expense. Some authorities from Georgia and Oklahoma believed it would have been a waste of taxpayers' money to bring him to trial; therefore, many truths about some of his crimes would never be revealed fully as they would have been in a court of law.

This book is an examination of a vicious killer and a segment of an American society that nurtured his twisted ideals. It is also an indictment of the hate groups that poisoned his mind and led him on such an evil journey, including the American Nazi Party, the Ku Klux Klan, and the National States Rights Party. It is also the story of how an evil ideology warped the mind of an already seriously disturbed young man.

Franklin was not a serial killer as defined by many true crime writers on websites across the Internet. Even Franklin took issue with this characterization, at one time stating, "I just look at myself as an outlaw of the Wild West. They didn't go around killing innocent women [like serial killers]. I would never do that either . . . I like the term 'multiple slayer' better than 'serial killer.'" He was indeed something quite different from a serial killer who murders to fulfill a deviant personal need. Franklin committed his murders in the name of a "higher ideal," as he often stated. His acts of murder served political ends—to start a race war in the name of white supremacy and Nazi ideology.

In many ways Franklin's appalling crimes take a back seat to the underlying theme of this book—the damage that hate crimes and hate ideology have inflicted on American communities. Franklin did not suddenly invent his mission. He was tutored in it and provoked into it through the organizations he joined and the hate literature he studied. The hate ideologies he embraced became the kaleidoscope in which he viewed and understood the world in which he lived. In fact, the hate organizations Franklin joined were no less effective in indoctrinating their members in evil ways than the Muslim fundamentalist terror groups that have inspired a large number of young people to murder innocent citizens around the world.

When I began researching Franklin's crimes, I was intrigued by what was missing from other accounts of his life. As I researched the news stories and interviews Franklin had given over a twenty-year period, I found much the same thing—the real Franklin was missing. There were sketchy details here and there and quotations from people who knew the killer—but nothing that really explained why an allegedly sane individual who knew right from wrong, a man who professed to be a committed Christian, would embark on such a lethal mission to murder time and again.

During the period of my research, I knew that sooner or later I would have to correspond with Franklin. And I was aware that Franklin had a reputation for manipulating people. Cincinnati prosecutor Melissa Powers said of him, "The guy's very crafty, very manipulative. He's probably the ultimate of all manipulators."

I seriously doubted Franklin would cooperate with a writer who had no sympathy with Nazi or white supremacist ideologies and who had no intention of glorifying his acts. I made that quite plain in my initial letter to him and said that my objective was to write about his crimes in a way that explained his motives—personal and political—and that I had no intention of giving him a platform to espouse his philosophy. I also set out certain stipulations—there would be no money for his story, I would be checking his answers against other sources before I accepted them, and he would have no rights of censorship within the final narrative. Complete control of the project would rest with me.

Franklin's reply was favorable, and he agreed to be interviewed, initially by letter. There was also the possibility that he would allow me to visit Potosi Correctional Center, where I would interview him personally. However, as the months passed throughout 2008, Franklin stopped writing, and I could only guess he had been advised by his family or lawyers that the project was not in his best interests. In early December 2008 I telephoned his counselor at Potosi, and she said she would meet with him and ascertain his position. She later told me that Franklin often went through periods of paranoia, and this was probably the reason he had stopped writing. She also said he had been curious about my English accent and that he seemed quite amused when she told him it was "typically English."

Within a few weeks Franklin had resumed his correspondence. But he continued to balk at answering the many questions I had sent him and instead made repeated demands for reading materials, especially books and periodicals on spiritualism and psychic phenomena. To his credit, he did offer to speak with me by telephone. However, despite numerous solicitations to the Missouri Department of Corrections, I was unable to arrange a telephone interview, the reason being Franklin was held in long-term isolation. Accordingly, I made arrangements to send him the books and newspapers he had requested in the hope he would eventually come around to answering my questions about his life and crimes through written correspondence. But despite my many solicitations, he continued to stonewall, excusing himself by making reference to his obsessive-compulsive disorder, which he said had prevented him from putting pen to paper.

This turn of events may have been fortuitous. Franklin had initially lied throughout his trials and in many interviews he gave to the media. For example, the Cincinnati prosecutors believe Franklin was less than candid when he claimed he thought the two children he murdered in 1980 were "little men." Furthermore, there was little Franklin could say with regard to his crimes that had not already been established by law enforcement agencies, the court system, or the numerous interviews he has given in the past. Relying on his prior confessions; individuals who knew the killer; the numerous witnesses to his crimes; the voluminous police, prison, and court records was perhaps the only true path to chronicling his story.

— ONE —

The Shooting of Vernon Jordan

[The Jordan shooting] was all part of a plan to start a race war. I saw violence as the only way to accomplish things. I still believe that violence is good if it's directed toward the right people.

—*Joseph Paul Franklin*

[My life's greatest achievements were] I guess, the two shootings I did of high publicity celebrities, Vernon Jordan and Larry Flynt. It was just something to me that, it meant to me that I was able to beat the system . . . shoot them and get away with it.

—*Joseph Paul Franklin*

The thirty-year-old sniper assassin was born James Clayton Vaughn Jr. He grew up as a child of the South whose attitudes to the changing social and political landscape of the 1950s and 1960s and a new era of civil rights for African Americans would provoke him into carrying out his self-conceived mission to save white America by instigating a race war.

He grew up in Birdville, a low-income suburb of Mobile, Alabama. He always loved guns, hunting, and most of all the history and traditions of the Old South, as he was attracted to its romantic and violent tales of white supremacy. He was also caught up in the violence and lawlessness of the Old West, and he admired Confederate rebels like William Quantrill and outlaws like Jesse James and Billy the Kid.

1

He emulated his Western heroes by wearing cowboy hats and other Western regalia well into his twenties. "Quantrill, the guerrilla fighter. He was my biggest influence," Franklin said. "And I was a big fan of Jesse James."[1]

By 1976 he had become so obsessed with white supremacist ideology that he changed his name to Joseph Paul Franklin. He chose the name Joseph Paul to honor one of his heroes, Joseph Paul Goebbels, Hitler's propaganda minister. He chose the name Franklin to honor Benjamin Franklin, hero of the American Revolution. In 1977 he gave himself a CB handle—The Bushwhacker. He wanted to go to Rhodesia, a country that denied equal rights to its black citizens. He wanted to "kill blacks," he said.

In the spring and summer of 1980 racial tensions in city ghettos across America were growing, the result of rising inflation and unemployment, exacerbated by the summer heat. Each week the list of violent incidents grew. In Miami, riots claimed sixteen lives. In Wrightsville, Georgia, two months of racial conflict over African American demands for economic equality resulted in sixteen people being indicted, including two white men charged with the wounding of a nine-year-old African American girl. In Natchez, Mississippi, demonstrations and scattered vandalism occurred after a white woman shot a black man who had allegedly been shoplifting. At least ten African Americans were arrested on charges of carrying concealed weapons. In Muskegon, Michigan, African American leaders warned of a volatile situation because an arson investigation regarding a fire that burned the home of a civil rights leader was not conducted properly.[2]

Now, in the warm spring of 1980, thirty years into his poverty-stricken and tragic life, Franklin was ready to accomplish the most defining act of his three-year crime spree. He was preparing to assassinate civil rights leader Vernon Jordan. He would show America he was a man to be reckoned with. He lusted after infamy.

For three years Franklin had cruised around mixed-race neighborhoods in cities across America, living off the proceeds of his bank robberies and targeting African American males and their white female partners, whom he believed had committed the cardinal sin of associating with one another. During those three years he had also targeted Jewish places of worship. He believed Jews had been responsible for the civil rights movement and were also, as he often stated, the "children of the devil."[3] "I was on a holy war against evildoers," Franklin said. "Evildoers were interracial couples, blacks, and Jews. I was the executioner, the judge, and the jury."[4] Franklin added, "It was all part of a plan to start a race war. I saw violence as the only way to accomplish things."[5]

In 1976 Franklin had sent threatening letters to president-elect Jimmy Carter, accusing him of pandering to African Americans. However, by 1980, he claimed he had not been stalking the president and that he was "not interested at all in Jimmy Carter."[6] His first target of choice, he claimed, was Georgia state legislator and civil rights activist Julian Bond, but no one was ever home when Franklin went to Bond's house.[7]

Franklin chose as his next target Jesse Jackson, who had been an aide to Martin Luther King Jr. in the late 1960s. Jackson had been one of the last people to speak with King on the evening of April 4, 1968, in Memphis, Tennessee, just moments before James Earl Ray fired the fatal shot that struck King in the head. Franklin had gone to Jackson's hometown of Chicago to seek him out. However, Jackson was not in Illinois at the time, so Franklin decided to drive to Fort Wayne. "I was . . . stalking [Jackson]," Franklin said. "I went up to Chicago a couple of times but I never got a shot at him. I guess it just wasn't in the cards that I shoot Reverend Jackson."[8]

Franklin began looking for another "nigger bigwig" to assassinate, but, failing that, he would be satisfied hunting down mixed-race couples.[9] Driving through Indiana, the territory of Franklin's hero John Dillinger, he heard on the radio that Verndon Jordan would be speaking in Fort Wayne. Scouring newspapers and listening to the radio, he discovered Jackson was staying at the Marriott Hotel.[10]

Franklin had a dark side—a veiled, sad side. From the time he was a child growing up in an abusive household, he had a relationship with life and death he couldn't understand. He had crying bouts whenever his past caught up with him. In his short relationships with both his wives, in 1968 and 1978, his charm, wit, and good humor soon turned, within the year, into bitterness and disappointment, and he began to abuse each wife in the same way that his parents had abused him.

Franklin was five-feet, eleven inches tall, weighed 180 pounds, and had brown hair that he often dyed blonde and wore both long and short. He often dyed his hair so frequently that it was at risk of falling out. His right eye was green and his left blue. He had lost most of his vision in his right eye and he wore glasses as he had very limited eyesight in the left eye. Without his eyeglasses, which usually bore a dark tinge, he had a brooding and menacing look about him. He had his initials J. V. (James Vaughn) tattooed on his left upper arm and had five scars on his left leg and two scars on his right leg, as well as scars on his stomach, left arm, and right hip. Also appearing on his arms were tattoos, the left forearm bearing an eagle and the right forearm the Grim Reaper (skeleton and sickle), which he had tattooed on his arm after one of his frequent visits to Dallas, Texas.

Franklin had a sardonic wit and often told people, in his slow Southern drawl, that he was a white man and a Native American, which was his way of saying whites were the only *true* Americans. He listed his religion as Christian Scientist or Spiritualist and was fascinated by the occult and the idea that signs determined his fate.

Franklin suffered from what he called "minor neuroses," but he believed he was not "stark raving mad." He said that during all his acts of murder he "knew exactly" what he was doing.[11] He told one reporter he was "not insane. You can see that. I'm *weird*."[12] He had long been fascinated with the purported mystical elements within numbers, and the pseudoscience had guided him for years. He told one reporter he liked her first name because it had three letters. "That's a good number," he said. "It's all throughout the Bible, best book in the world. Jesus was thirty when he started his ministry. He was killed when he was thirty-three, and stayed in the tomb three days."[13] He was especially taken with the numbers 2, 3, and 5. He thought the number 13 was "a good number for me."[14] He also claimed he used his dreams for guidance.[15]

Franklin would frequently suffer mood swings. However, he was essentially an altogether innocuous-sounding and ordinary-looking individual, which was one of the reasons he was able to escape justice for so many years. He blended into his surroundings. Franklin also had the ability to slip in and out of murder scenes without detection or leave any forensics evidence that would link him to his crimes. For his main method of killing, he chose a sniper rifle because he knew that bystanders would not be able to tell where the shots came from or where he was positioned.

In the early morning hours of May 29, 1980, Franklin took up his sniper position across from the Marriot Hotel and lay in wait for his target. By his side he placed a police scanner to warn him of any police responses to the crime he was about to commit. He spread himself out in an area situated on a grassy embankment overlooking Jordan's first floor room. Although Franklin had, over the previous three years, placed himself in dangerous situations on his nationwide killing spree, this night he still felt fear. "It's scary, it's not easy, I assure you," he later said. According to Franklin he felt fear because he was "taking a gun and aiming it at somebody and knowing you are fixing to take a human life and you could get caught and spend the rest of your life in prison or get executed for what you did."[16]

A few hours earlier he had entered the hotel and requested information about accommodations. It was a ruse to find out more about Jordan's movements. During his time in the hotel Franklin saw Jordan sitting at the hotel's bar with a white woman. He did everything in his power to contain his rage.[17] A motel employee,

Mary Howell, spoke with Franklin. During their conversation he expressed his deep hatred for African Americans.[18]

By any stretch of the imagination, the assassin's shooting skills were remarkable. As he was blind in his right eye and nearsighted in the other, he required a strong lens to see out of his right eye. He also had difficulty in using a bolt-action rifle. He believed they were made for right-handed shooters, and he was left-handed. He said using his left hand came naturally to him, something he had been doing ever since boyhood when an accident on his bicycle robbed him of sight in his right eye and damaged his left eye. He therefore used an automatic or a slant-action pump or a lever-action rifle, preferring the "little Marlins or Winchesters."[19]

Franklin had a "standard procedure," as he described it, to destroy the weapons he used in his crimes. He would carry tools in the trunk of his car to dismantle them. He would use a Black & Decker drill to cut the barrel of the rifle in half and then scatter the parts in different places—usually a wooded area so the parts would eventually become so rusty that they could never be traced. He also believed that anyone who stumbled on to the gun parts would not realize the pieces were part of a pistol or rifle. He would put the wooden parts of the pistol or rifle in a paper bag then place them in a dumpster. Each time he carried out these acts, he would make sure no one was watching. He was an extremely methodical assassin.

Franklin was also careful not to sell any of the murder weapons, and contrary to later reports, he insisted he "didn't make [a] living. . . . by buying and selling guns." According to Franklin, he made the story up to cover up his involvement in numerous bank robberies.[20]

Before he took his sniper position, he visualized everything in his mind about what would happen, what he would be doing in the moment before he pulled the trigger, and what steps he would take to escape. "Very few people really have or are able to set up, or sit there and visualize things . . . like I am," Franklin said. "I'm really good at visualization and all . . . I can actually just look at a scene and figure out a real good place to ambush somebody." He also truly believed God "wanted me to do that stuff . . . it was the will of God."[21]

The assassin owned a metallic brown 1975 Camaro with extra-high gloss and red pinstripes. It had chrome mag wheels, four tires of the same make with white raised letters, plaid vinyl seat covers, dual exhausts, and a spoiler. He parked the car nearby on an exit ramp of I-69 that ran parallel to the Marriott Hotel so he would be able to make a swift escape. After parking his car on the side of the highway, he lifted the hood, pretending the vehicle had broken down, and took a high-powered 30.06 rifle from the trunk.

As he lay prone under grass cover on the knoll approximately 140 feet away from Jordan's room, Franklin prepared his rifle, checked the scope mechanism, then practiced his aim. There was no doubt in his mind he wanted to kill his victim. If he simply wounded Jordan he would feel like a "complete failure." He formed in his mind what his response would be if he were ever disturbed or if he were challenged by a police officer or citizen. He had decided that if ever a police officer approached him, he would "shoot him dead right on the spot." In all his sniping attacks, he would carry a powerful handgun in the waistband of his pants for just such an eventuality.[22]

Franklin was extremely fastidious in his behavior before the shootings. Before he carried out his sniper attacks, Franklin made sure he did not frequent any bars, stores, or restaurants in the areas of his intended killings. He frequently operated in racially mixed neighborhoods, cruising around, looking for his targets, and searching for places where he could safely shoot someone without being seen. He avoided purely African American neighborhoods because he thought he would be conspicuous in the crowd. If he ever accidentally drove into a black area, he would quickly look for an exit.

Franklin chose his clothing so he would blend in with his surroundings. At times he wore an Afro wig and blackened his face with charcoal.[23] He would not even stop his car to ask for directions, as he knew the people he stopped could eventually become eyewitnesses to his crimes. His method of escape was to flee as soon as his mission was accomplished, moving speedily and with purpose. As he took each step, he would concentrate his mind, always trying not to panic. The night before he committed his crimes, he would file off the serial numbers on his weapons. He would wipe everything down, being careful not to leave fingerprints. When handling potential evidence, he would wear gloves. Sometimes he would use stolen bicycles to take him from the scene of the murder or robbery to his car. The use of a bicycle gave Franklin the advantage of not having to steal cars, which would have been an additional risk in the commission of his crimes. He also used police scanners so he could keep track of police movements in the neighborhood.

During the commission of his every single crime, Franklin was always careful to throw away the clothes he wore and then buy new ones. Sometimes he would purchase a new pair of glasses or new shoes and then ditch them later. He was always conscious that law enforcement agencies could use the clothing to possibly identify him at a later date or match threads from the clothing to the crime scenes.

The assassin's meticulous way of doing things arose from an obsessive-compulsive urge to check and recheck that he had suffered from since he was a child.

He insisted people with his type of mental disorder "were not crazy. It's just an anxiety disorder that affects about 2 percent of the population. And people with it can function just as well as anyone else. The only problems they have are with various obsessions and compulsions that make them want to wash their hands and do other unnecessary things."[24] He was aware that his obsessive-compulsive disorder worked to his advantage as a killer. It forced him to visualize anything that could go wrong. Another key to his success was physical training. He eschewed cigarettes, drugs, and alcohol. He often ran wind sprints to keep in shape and even rejected coffee, as it could affect his aim."[25]

Most people experience the flight-or-fight danger detection system—scanning our surroundings and becoming hypervigilant for danger. Whereas most people take for granted that a situation is safe unless there are clear signs of danger, those suffering from OCD like Franklin obsessively assume that situations are dangerous unless they have a guarantee of safety. Franklin's compulsive rituals were undertaken as a natural safety-seeking response that reduced his distress. Only once did his fear and anxiety prevent him from committing a murder. "I was in Atlanta in a wooded lot," he said. "I got a bead on a dude with a shotgun but I didn't have the nerve to pull the trigger. Usually I'd feel fear and shoot anyway."[26]

Around 2:00 a.m., as he lay in wait on the grassy knoll, Franklin saw an African American man exit a car near the Jordan's room. A beautiful blonde woman accompanied the man. As the man stepped out of the car and into the lit parking lot, Franklin didn't know for sure whether or not it was Jordan, but since he was African American, Franklin decided there was a good chance it was. Franklin had also concluded that if it wasn't Jordan, then at least he had a mixed-race couple in his sights.

Vernon Jordan, who was becoming one of America's leading civil rights advocates, had gone to Fort Wayne, an industrial city of 175,000 people, as the guest of honor to deliver a speech at the the Urban League's annual Equal Opportunity Dinner, a lavish fund raising dinner for the local chapter. Jordan arrived in the city on Wednesday afternoon, May 28, 1980, and registered at the Marriott Hotel. He was assigned room 180, a ground floor room. That afternoon he held a press conference in which he criticized the Carter administration as one of "promises made and promises un-kept."[27] Later he attended a forty-five minute cocktail reception prior to his speech, which was given to an audience of 400, two-thirds of whom were African American.

During the speech Jordan expressed fear for the loss of African American freedoms in the 1970s and told his audience that he hoped for further advancement of race relations in the 1980s. His cautious speech reflected his philosophy. At forty-four years old, he had shied away from violence all his life in favor of healing the rift between the races. Like Martin Luther King Jr., Jordan was a moderate, a voice of reason, and a man who had recently been viewed by many African Americans as their senior spokesman in the nation.

Jordan criticized the blind enthusiasm of the country's move to the right, which would be exemplified later that year with the election of Ronald Reagan as the president of the United States. He criticized the move toward a balanced budget at the expense of social programs. He also criticized the candidacy of John Anderson because he would take votes away from President Carter. However, Jordan was especially critical of Carter and spoke of blacks always having the "choice between the lesser of two evils" in a presidential election. He accused the presidential candidates of having neglected social issues and said that blacks helped elect President Carter in 1976. "The Black vote in 1976," he said, "was absolutely decisive, and I think it's going to be more decisive in 1980 . . . ."[28]

Jordan said that after the speech he "stood around greeting people . . . then . . . I went to my room and called [my wife] Shirley to tell her how things had gone."[29] Jordan was feeling "drained and restless." Although tired, he knew that sleep would be impossible and decided to wander around the hotel. He spoke to a number of people about the evening's speech and eventually ended up with a group of Urban League members at the hotel bar, the Piper's Glen Room. Among them was an attractive blonde named Martha Coleman. Coleman and Jordan began discussing the Urban League and "racially mixed children."[30]

Martha Coleman had been married four times but had no children. Her fourth husband was Robert Coleman, an African American attorney who had children from a previous marriage. After the divorce, she kept in close contact with two of the children and assisted one of them financially as a college student. She had long been interested in racial issues and was on the board of the local chapter of the National Urban League. As a child, Martha Coleman had lived with her closest living relative, an aunt, Eva Braun, who was in her eighties and in poor health. They kept in touch weekly. Coleman lived in Huntingdon before moving to Fort Wayne and worked at International Harvester most of her life. At the time of the shooting, she was a scheduling supervisor at the plant. Friends described her as "striking and beautiful" and as a "warm person." One friend, speaking of allegations that Coleman had somehow been involved in the shooting, said the thirty-six-year-old was "not the kind of woman who would be involved in something like this. She wouldn't hurt a fly." Coleman, who had been taking a Women and Labor course at Indiana University-Purdue University at Fort Wayne, was described by one of her teachers as "a very bright woman and a very fine woman."[31]

Coleman said she spoke with the civil rights leader in the bar, and when the last call for drinks was made, Jordan said he wanted more coffee. "He indicated that he was tired of bars, restaurants, that type of thing," she said. Coleman drove Jordan to her two-story white frame house in her red Pontiac Grand Prix. The house was situated on tree-lined Lafayette Esplanade, which was in a racially mixed neighborhood in south central Fort Wayne. Jordan didn't believe his trip with Coleman was a "risky thing to do."[32]

Jordan had been scheduled to fly to Houston the following morning, and it was on his mind as Coleman drove him to her house. They sat around drinking coffee "for maybe half an hour" and "chatted," Coleman said. "He was just talking. I drove him to my home. I made coffee and that was that."[33]

During the twenty-five minute return journey, they stopped at a red light about two and a half miles from the Marriott. Three white youths in a car saw them at the light and began to shout racial slurs. According to Jordan, "They continued on and I thought nothing of the episode. This was Indiana. It was all very familiar to me. I had driven around the state as a college student—by myself or with friends, black and white, and was always comfortable doing so."[34]

According to Fort Wayne public relations director Dan Gibson, "[The youths] looked over and saw a black-on-white situation and made some racial overtones. As the light changed, they took off ahead of Mrs. Coleman." Gibson said the youths pulled into the parking lot of a fast food restaurant and would not have had time to get to the motel ahead of Jordan. FBI agents later concurred.[35]

Jordan and Coleman arrived back at the hotel around 2:00 a.m. Instead of dropping Jordan off at the entrance, Coleman took him around to the side entrance, which was closer to his room. Within seconds, as Jordan exited the car, a thundering shot from a high-powered rifle pierced the half-lit parking area and ripped through the back of Jordan's cotton jacket, exiting through his chest. Coleman said she was looking in her rearview mirror when she heard the shots. Jordan had gotten out of the car and was walking behind it when he was shot, she said.

In a state of shock, Coleman rushed to Jordan. She later told police she heard "a sound, which to me sounded like something breaking my car window." She also described the shot as a "thud, which sounded like a stone hitting the windshield."[36] According to Coleman, "Jordan screamed and said, 'I've been shot, call the police.' I jumped out of the car, I saw him lying on the pavement. I immediately ran into the Marriott and told them someone was shot and to please call the police."[37]

Other witnesses heard only one shot. Motel guest Patrick Gillespie of Chicago thought an M-80 grenade had exploded. "It rose me right up out of my bed," he said. From his fifth-floor room, Gillespie said he saw a man leaning on the back of the car and heard him yell, "Help me. Somebody shot me."[38]

Jordan had slumped against the trunk of the car and then collapsed on the pavement, his head resting near the left taillight. He was alive, but only just. He had been struck in the left side of his back by a bullet from a 30.06 hunting rifle commonly used to hunt deer, the impact lifting him off his feet and hurling him into the air. The bullet missed his spine by about a quarter of an inch. Jordan had a sensation of floating "as if I was in a dream and then I was on the ground."[39] One of his first thoughts was of his trip to Houston the next morning, which he thought was "a crazy notion under the circumstances."[40] When he felt blood soak through his shirt, he knew he would never make the trip. He was also aware that people in the rooms above him had come to their windows to look, but no one would come down, afraid, he believed, the shooter was still out there and that they would be targets too if they came to help.[41] "So I lay there alone," he said, "on the pavement all the while with a vivid sense that people were watching me from above."[42]

Jordan felt a pain in his abdomen that was "indescribable, beyond all measure." He remained wide-awake and could feel the blood draining from his body. After the bullet had entered the lower left side of his back it sliced through his intestines and exited from his chest. The ammunition had exploded upon impact, creating a wound the size of a man's fist and sending bullet fragments throughout Jordan's body, damaging his intestines in the process. The slug had also ricocheted, grazing his right leg. As he lay in the parking lot, Jordan began to hear his mother's voice telling him to trust in God.[43]

Jordan's spirits lifted when he heard a siren in the distance and flashing lights approaching. The paramedics placed him on a stretcher, and Jordan, knowing it could be fatal if he fell asleep, spoke with them on the way to Parkview Hospital. He was conscious enough to ask medics to call his deputy, John Jacob, and ask him to break the news to his wife, Shirley. On arrival at the hospital, Jordan began to protest when orderlies ripped his Brookes Brothers suit from his body as they prepared him for surgery.

Dr. Robert Stovall, a member of the board of the Fort Wayne Urban League, had been at the Marriot Hotel dinner that evening, and when he heard about the shooting, he rushed to the hospital. There was a debate about who should operate on Jordan. Stovall became insistent that African American Dr. Jeffrey Towles operate rather than the white surgeon on duty. However, Stovall insisted that race did not enter into his decision. He simply knew that Towles was the better surgeon. Initially, Towles had said he did not want to operate as it wasn't his turn, but Stovall insisted and Towles relented.

There would be five operations in a sixteen-hour period. The first lasted four hours. Towles discovered that the bullet had entered Jordan's middle back area between the chest cavities and the pelvis and found there were two or three small exit wounds. Jordan had some numbness in his left leg, but Towles thought it was unlikely this would lead to paralysis.[44] Towles believed he would never get Jordan off the operating table "because he was bleeding so profusely in so many places."[45] He said that Jordan would have been killed if the angle of the shot had been a centimeter different from its actual path. After surgery Jordan was listed in serious condition in the hospital's intensive care ward but was strong enough by Saturday to have a telephone installed in his room. However, he nearly died again following a second operation when he experienced kidney failure and developed pneumonia in the right lung.

Towles, speaking of Jordan's wounds, said, "There was an explosive effect like nothing I've ever seen before."[46] He also noted, "When I was at Detroit General and in Louisville, I saw all kinds of wounds. I've never seen a wound like [Jordan's]. And based on what I saw, [Jordan] was not supposed to make it."[47] The surgeon did not detect any bitterness or animosity in Jordan. He said the civil rights leader's reaction was one of "dismay." "Why?" Jordan asked Towles.[48]

Jordan's wife, Shirley, learned of the shooting, which became the first major news story for CNN, around 5:30 a.m. at the couple's New York City home on Fifth Avenue. After receiving the news, a friend, Don Thomas, arrived at the house to comfort her and offer assistance in traveling to Fort Wayne. They left New York on a private plane with a stop in Philadelphia to pick up their daughter Vickee, a twenty-year-old student at the University of Pennsylvania. After conferring with her daughter-in-law, Jordan's mother also traveled to Fort Wayne from her home in Atlanta.

At the scene of the shooting, police stumbled upon a trove of clues. A matted area in the brush opposite the motel suggested that the sniper had laid in wait for his victim. Police also found a spent shell case from a 30.06 copper-jacketed rifle bullet near the matted grass where Franklin had lain. The grassy mound was in a triangle formed by an exit ramp from I-69, about forty yards from where Jordan was shot. Fort Wayne police officer Nicholas Litwinko laid down in the sniper's lair and later told reporters, "I had a clear view of everything that took place in the shooting area and also a view of Mr. Jordan's room." Police scoured the area by helicopter and searched the area on hands and knees. Nearby trash cans and sewers were searched and guests of the hotel were interviewed. In a crack of the sidewalk near Jordan's room, police found the damaged 30.06 slug that had gone through Jordan.[49]

By the weekend police investigators had concluded that the shooting was a manifestation of racism, particularly the violent Ku Klux Klan activity that has often been part of Indiana's history. The FBI believed the shooting was the work of "apparently more than one person in a premeditated act."[50]

FBI Director William Webster, on receiving the news of the assassination attempt, immediately sent twenty agents to Fort Wayne to investigate whether there had been a conspiracy to "violate Jordan's civil rights." Webster had concluded there was evidence of a conspiracy, and "that gets us into the case."[51] Webster had been assuming it was a conspiracy because of reports of the three youths who had insulted Jordan and Coleman as they were returning to the hotel. Webster also believed the incident provided a legal mechanism by which the FBI could enter the case, as it was a federal crime to "injure, threaten, or intimidate" persons traveling on public highways.[52]

President Carter, who had used the word "assassination" in his response to the shooting, had also given Webster a green light. Webster's response was to send agents to investigate even though no motive had been discerned and therefore no federal crimes had been involved. The FBI director was relying on a wide interpretation of the crime to introduce federal involvement in the police investigation. Murder or attempted murder was the responsibility of individual states; the FBI only had jurisdiction when federal laws had been violated.

By June 4 the FBI had interviewed more than four hundred people, including a suspect in the case who had made abusive comments about Jordan at the Marriott bar the night of the shooting.[53] He was quickly eliminated from their inquiries. They also investigated forty-year-old John Thompson Douglas, a welder from Grabill, a small town approximately ten miles northeast of Fort Wayne. At 10:30 on the morning after the shooting, Douglas had been arrested by Allen County deputy sheriffs after he had been spotted riding a motorcycle while drunk. When he was arrested, officers confiscated three unloaded rifles, including a Remington 30.06, that were tied to his motorcycle. Douglas insisted he had "never even heard of Vernon Jordan" and that he had bought the rifles for a hundred dollars from another motorcyclist about 6:00 a.m. on Thursday, four hours after Jordan was shot. Police checked his alibi, which established that he had been home at the time of the shooting. They also examined the 30.06 and found that the barrel was dirty, indicating the rifle had not been fired recently. The FBI soon eliminated him from their inquiries after a ballistics test proved that Douglas's rifle had not been used in the shooting.[54]

The Fort Wayne police and FBI were puzzled by the wound in Jordan's back, which contained several bullet fragments. They wondered why the bullet fragmented, but later discovered it had first hit a metal fence then split, causing the wounds to the back and the graze on his leg.

Wayne Davis, who later became the first African American to become a Special Agent in Charge (SAC), headed the FBI investigation. Davis said he believed only one bullet had been fired at Jordan instead of the two or more shots investigators had initially believed. "Only one shell casing has been found," Davis said. "It's a very good possibility only one shot was fired."[55]

As with many famous shootings, an element of mystery had entered the case. "Martha Coleman said that after the shooting the desk clerk at the Marriott . . . showed me a message from a woman he [Jordan] had received. He asked me, 'did you leave this?' I said no. That message said, 'For your next chicken dinner call' something, a local Fort Wayne number. He said it was the third call from that particular woman that night."[56]

The FBI was also intrigued by reports that John Larry Ray, a brother of the man who killed Martin Luther King Jr., may have been the shooter. By late June they began looking for him; they wanted to know where he was on the night of the shooting. The FBI did not know it at the time, but John Ray had been heavily involved in King's assassination, a fact that was not established until many years after the Jordan shooting.[57] In May 1980 John Ray was a fugitive from justice as a federal escapee after failing to report to a St. Louis halfway house in February 1980 to finish a sentence for bank robbery. He was also wanted for questioning in a May 30, 1980, bank robbery in Liberty, Illinois, in which $15,000 was stolen.

The FBI's suspicions about Ray resulted from a statement by FBI Director William Webster, who said there were similarities between the shootings of King and Jordan that warranted the questioning of Ray. Both civil rights leaders had been stalked by assailants, and the King assassination was financed by bank robberies. Conrad "Pete" Baetz, a Madison County sheriff's deputy who recognized John Larry Ray in a shopping mall, eventually captured him in late June. Baetz had been involved in the House Select Committee on Assassinations (HSCA) investigation into the King assassination and knew the fugitive. He said the FBI had every reason to suspect Ray. "The circumstances with Jordan are almost identical," he said. "A 30.06 rifle was used. Jordan, leader of the National Urban League, was shot in front of his hotel. The first reports on Jordan sounded like the first reports on King. . . ."[58] However, the FBI was never able to link Ray to the Jordan shooting.

The reaction to the shooting from Fort Wayne residents, political leaders in the United States, and African American leaders was immediate. Political leaders expected the nation's ghettos to explode in a frenzy of violence. Most remembered how cities across America had flared up in major riots after the assassination of Martin Luther King Jr. in 1968. United States Judge Allen Sharp believed the city had come within a hair's breadth of rioting on a scale not seen since King's assassination. However, the nation's cities remained quiet partly because the shooter and his motives had not yet been determined. One of the reasons why African Americans had reacted violently to the assassination of Martin Luther King was the fact that initial police reports had described a white assailant fleeing the scene of the crime.

The assistant manager of a Fort Wayne pizza restaurant said, "It kind of puts us in the category like Memphis and Dallas." Other citizens, representative of the general population, told reporters the murder attempt stigmatized their city, which they now believed shared the shame of Memphis and Dallas. Sam Nelson, who held vigil with hundreds of citizens outside the Parkview Memorial Hospital, said, "It's a ridiculous crying shame." Many citizens agreed that, despite initial fears of African Americans responding with violence, the city would stay calm and that it was unlikely it would erupt in violence as it had after the King assassination.[59]

The motive remained unclear to investigators, but some speculated there was no racial element to the shooting. Some reporters and police investigators speculated that because a white woman had accompanied Jordan, personal motives might have been involved. Their musings led to newspaper stories suggesting that love triangle may have been the motive for the shooting. This may have been a well-intentioned effort to calm the community's fears, or police investigators may have harbored genuine concerns that Jordan and Coleman were not being fully candid about their relationship.

Fort Wayne police used euphemisms to promote their love triangle theory. Police public relations director Gibson, who had been informed by detectives that Jordan had been accompanied by a woman who was not his wife, suggested the shooting may have been a "domestic-type thing."[60] Investigators also said Martha Coleman had not been "fully cooperative" and that she refused to give them the name or the whereabouts of her "current boyfriend." Though Coleman told the police that she and Jordan had spent less than a half-hour at her house before the shooting, the circumstances were such, police investigators alleged, as to suggest that some disgruntled lover might have tried to kill Jordan. After answering questions for Fort Wayne police and later the FBI, Coleman went into seclusion under police protection.[61]

The police were also concerned Coleman had phoned a lawyer following the shooting. Apart from her concern about Jordan, she feared for her own safety. "I'm going to have to go back there and live alone," she said. "I'll be left to deal with the kooks and people who know I'm living alone." Coleman said that while she waited for the ambulance she phoned a lawyer because she "felt it the logical thing to do . . . I think anybody who is in the company of a nationally prominent person and that person is shot. . . . I don't believe they would be thinking clearly if they didn't call an attorney."[62]

After police interviewed her, Coleman said she had been willing to undergo hypnosis to reconfirm her lack of involvement in the shooting, which she felt was a "racial incident." "I am a very private person," she said. "I like to keep myself and the media has made it impossible for me to do that. I was never a suspect. I was in the wrong place at the wrong time."[63]

Despite their initial suspicions, by Friday police had changed their minds, and Dan Gibson, the police spokesman, said that the investigators had dropped the "domestic incident theory." They now believed Jordan had been shot from an ambush by a single white man who "probably acted on impulse."[64]

On Friday FBI agents interviewed Jordan, who by now had recovered enough to speak with agents. FBI spokesman Roger Young said, "He was able to give us some information that was helpful."[65] By Sunday, June 1, Fort Wayne police had concluded that a lone sniper had shot Jordan. The FBI had weakened in its resolve that the killing was part of a conspiracy but allowed that they were still checking out that possibility.[66] On June 8 Jordan underwent surgery for an abscess. He was listed "in serious but stable condition" at Parkview Memorial Hospital.

On Friday, June 6, Coleman voluntarily took a lie detector test administered by an FBI agent. She "passed with absolutely no question whatever. She now has been absolutely eliminated as having any involvement whatever," said her attorney, Charles P. Leonard. Leonard said that sending Coleman into seclusion after the shooting—a course of action he said was suggested by the police—had been the right thing to do. "She's concerned, as I have been concerned, for her well-being," he said.[67] Leonard also said Coleman had stayed in seclusion after the shooting not because she had been hiding anything but because she wanted to avoid becoming a "national figure."[68]

Martha Coleman was angry at the media's "innuendoes, the implied things, the half-truths" about her private life and said the publicity might undermine her effectiveness as a civil rights worker. "I have no regrets," she said. "I did nothing wrong."[69]

Franklin was also angry at the media but for different reasons. He was upset that newspaper reports of the shooting, especially those reports that implied Jordan had been shot as the result of a love triangle, had missed the real reason for the assassination attempt. "You know, they didn't even want to make that appear racially motivated," Franklin later said. "Jordan was involved with somebody else's wife. So that kinda pissed me off . . . because the media was just flat out then . . . I think they were deliberately doing it . . . the government basically controls the media in this country . . . to a large extent . . . they were pretty well suppressing the news . . . I guess they were afraid they'd start a race war . . . and that's what I was trying to do."[70]

Following the shooting Franklin dyed his hair a darker color and bought a new pair of glasses and new clothes. To reinforce his point about his determination to provoke a race war, Franklin "turned up the heat," as he described it, and drove to Cincinnati, where he would carry out more racially motivated murders, hoping this time the media would realize that a race war had indeed begun.[71]

— TWO —

The Early Years

It was torture to live at home. It was pure hell. Wake up in the middle of the night, someone get you out of bed and just beat the hell out of you. We just have bad memories of my mother because she fussed a lot and she hit a lot. My father . . . he had a cane. I know he hit Jimmy. He used to hit him with it all the time.

—*Joseph Paul Franklin's sister Carolyn*

Joseph Paul Franklin was born James Clayton Vaughn on April 13, 1950. He was the son of James Sr. and Helen, who was nine years older than her husband. The couple had three other children: Carolyn, Marilyn, and Gordon. James was the second of the four children. He also had a half brother and two half sisters.

Helen was the daughter of Otto and Elise Rau, who immigrated to the United States from Germany and bought forty acres in the rural Semmesa suburb of Mobile, Alabama, in western Mobile County. Her parents, who supported the Nazis during World War II, were stern and inflexible and brought Helen and her seven siblings up under strict guidelines and control. As a young woman Helen had a child born out of wedlock. One friend who lived with Helen and her husband for several months said she was "a full-blooded German, a real strict, perfectionist lady. I never saw her beat any of [the children], but they told me stories."[1]

James's father—who was from the Mobile, Alabama area—was a disabled Navy veteran and a butcher by trade. He returned from World War II as a battle-shattered epileptic, and soon after James Jr. was born, he lost his job. He left the house when James was eight years old. James Sr. seldom visited his children, but whenever he returned, he would beat them. Helen had her husband jailed for public drunkenness twice during two of his visits. Sometimes he would disappear for months and even years at a time.

When James's parents were together, they fought constantly. Franklin's older sister, Carolyn Luster, remembered an incident when the family was living in Dayton, Ohio, when she was six years old and young James was three. Her mother, who was eight months pregnant at the time, had given her father money to buy Carolyn a pair of shoes for school. However, James Sr. took off on an alcoholic binge, spending the money in bars and not returning for a week. When Helen asked him where he had been ("fussed," as Carolyn described it) and if he had Carolyn's shoes, he reacted by beating her up. She subsequently lost the baby.[2] "I was probably five years old. That's my first memory," she said.[3] Around this time, the family moved from Dayton to New Orleans, shifting from one lower class neighborhood to another, then eventually settled in Mobile, Alabama. Along with the move came the constant beatings. James's childhood directly influenced what he would become when he grew up.

By the 1950s the political climate in the South had become extremely volatile. Alabama during James's childhood was like living in a foreign country. Throughout its small cities and towns, cotton fields, cotton mills, and red clay roads, business sections and shopping centers were clearly segregated. Signs proliferated in every town and city—"White Waiting Room," "Colored Waiting Room," "Men, Women, Colored," "Drinking Fountain—Whites Only," "No Colored Need Apply." The general feeling of Alabamans was that African Americans should be taught to work in menial occupations. Those African Americans lucky enough to have had an education at one of the South's few black universities more often than not ended up as train porters or hotel doormen.

The Ku Klux Klan had grown in strength after World War II as black action and agitation for voting rights accelerated, spurred on by some progressive Southern white politicians. This resulted in an increasingly violent backlash from the forces of white supremacy, especially following the Supreme Court's 1954 ruling on African American rights. Alabama became the site of such landmark civil rights actions such as the Montgomery Bus Boycott (1955–1956), and Klan membership began to rise.

By the 1960s Alabama had been the scene of many conflicts in the civil rights movement, including the 1963 bombing of the Baptist church in Birmingham where four little girls were killed, and confrontations between African American students and whites at the University of Alabama, which was the last state-supported university to cling to racial segregation. It was also the home state of the most famous civil rights leader, Martin Luther King Jr., who called Birmingham "the most segregated city in the United States." In 1963 Birmingham was the scene of a demonstration in which police chief Bull O'Connor unleashed police dogs and fire hoses on demonstrating children. In 1965 the state hosted the famous "Freedom March" to Selma, where Sheriff Jim Clark's police officers charged the crowd.

Whites in Alabama were attracted to the Klan for a host of reasons. The Klan adhered to the paranoid style in American politics—especially the idea that Northern liberals had conspired with Jewish bankers to disenfranchise the whites in the South. The organization was steadfast in its beliefs about white supremacy. It had an image of mysterious and macabre white-hooded members and burning crosses. More importantly, the Klan appealed to uneducated poor white farmers and industrial workers because it used violence to protect Alabama's citizens from the growing sense in the 1960s that Black Power had provoked the South's African Americans to rise up against whites. The Klan offered comfort because it gave simple answers to complex questions and because it was a fraternal organization that gave its members a community of like-minded believers.

Mobile is the third most populous city in Alabama, and today it has a population of nearly half a million. In the Mobile of James's childhood, African American students were barred from attending public schools with white children and were not accepted at any of the state's universities. Throughout Mobile, the city parks, playgrounds, golf courses, and swimming pools were segregated, and African Americans were excluded from white churches, hotels, barbershops, cafes, and movie theaters. They were also barred from trying on clothes in stores.

The Vaughns moved into in a poor, all-white, housing project on the south side of Mobile called Birdville. The small suburban town's housing had expanded during World War II to accommodate the phenomenal influx of workers, which created a huge housing shortage. Thomas James Place was the proper name for Birdville, which was built just outside of Brookley Air Force Base to provide relief for the housing shortage. The development consisted of a series of interwoven curving concrete streets named after various birds, thus giving the town its nickname.

One side of the tracks was African American, the other side white. There was a considerable amount of racial tension in the area. According to Cincinnati detective Michael O'Brien, "Birdville is described as basically one side of the tracks is black and the other side is white, and so there was a lot of racial tension in [James's] upbringing. There was a lot of problems between whites and blacks in that area."[4] However, Franklin later insisted he was not a racist as a boy. "I didn't really hate blacks," he said. "I wasn't a black hater at the time. I really had no contact with them, quite honestly."[5] However, he had grown up hearing white men in authority advocate brutalizing black citizens.

The Vaughns often lived hand to mouth, and their houses were cramped and sparsely equipped. Their Mobile home was a red brick corner apartment made of cinder block walls and had three bedrooms, a small kitchen, and one bathroom with a sink, toilet, and bathtub, but no shower. James shared a bedroom with his younger brother Gordon. The Vaughn family was extremely poor by any relative standards. They lived on James Sr.'s Navy disability check and whatever social services would give them. Church friends and a local welfare worker took a special interest in the Vaughn children, often taking them to the movies and providing clothes, food, and toys for the children. An uncle would occasionally drop by with a bag full of groceries.

According to Carolyn, a typical day in the family home began with fighting and squabbling. James Sr. would have already started drinking, which upset young Carolyn so much she said it made her "sick."[6] Carolyn had no good memories growing up. It was evident the parents' attitude to their children mirrored that of their own parents. Helen frequently slapped her children for slight infringements of her rules. If the children ate their meals too slowly or spent too much time on the telephone, she would quickly administer physical punishment. "It was torture to live at home," Carolyn said. "It was pure hell. Wake up in the middle of the night, someone get [sic] you out of bed and just beat the hell out of you. We just have bad memories of my mother because she fussed a lot and she hit a lot. My father . . . he had a cane. I know he hit Jimmy. He used to hit him with it all the time."[7] The young James had the scars to prove it—a series of scars on his scalp were the result of the beatings his father inflicted.

Carolyn was an astute observer of the damage her parents were doing to their children, especially the boys. At one time, she remembered, the young James simply went outside the house to eat a bag of popcorn. James Sr., who used a cane due to his disability, followed James out of the house, knocked the bag of popcorn out of his hands, and started beating him mercilessly with the cane. He was relentless, Carolyn said.[8]

James's mother was very much a perfectionist and a taskmaster. She was also an alcoholic and abusive, not only to her own children but also to the neighbor's children. When James and Helen divorced, she babysat to earn extra money but would frequently administer the same harsh punishments to other people's children that she gave to her own. Many years later James blamed his father and his mother for the rage within him. When he was asked if some commentators were correct in saying his mother was the source of his murderous rages, James replied, "They're exactly right . . . cause I had a dream . . . while I was in Marion . . . and it said you're a prisoner right now because you killed your mother. That is *the* reason you're locked up. You killed your mother."[9] James also thought his mother was "so masculine and acted so much like a man."[10]

James, who got the worst of his parents' abuse, started hitting back at his mother and his sisters, and he used to imitate his mother's attitude towards animals. His pathology had already begun to take shape. "They [Jimmy and Gordon] used to torment cats, hang 'em up by their tails on the clothesline," Carolyn said, "and Jimmy just changed and we stopped talking."[11] Helen's attitude to animals was no better. If one of her children brought a stray animal home, she would physically abuse and injure it. Later James would remember that "my mom once poured hot, scalding water on a stray dog. That's cruel. Sadistic, isn't it?"[12]

James Jr. was also the target for his father's rage, a product of James Sr.'s alcoholism and violent tendencies. James Sr. was unable to hold down a job for long. He frequently left the household to go on drinking binges, and when he returned, he would beat his wife and children. The children went into a panic when he did come home because he would then launch into violent behavior, usually singling James and his mother out for the brunt of his rage. James recalled, "My father would abuse my mother and then she would call the police."[13] The young James dreamed of the day he could run away from his home life and away from his father's wrath.

The Vaughns separated in 1958 when Jimmy was eight years old and divorced in 1965. Helen managed to feed her children by social security checks and money she earned babysitting. By 1980 James Vaughn Sr. moved to Birmingham, Alabama. By 1980 he was undergoing treatment at a veteran's administration hospital in Mississippi, following a decline in his health brought on by wounds he suffered during the war and his longtime alcoholism.

During this period the South was experiencing a quiet period in the history of the civil rights movement. After World War II the introduction of air conditioning had conquered the lethargy-inducing climate of the Deep South, and workers from northern Rust Belt cities began immigrating to the Sun Belt. Although the past was still central to the Southern way of life, Southerners had more important things on their minds, including concentrating on work and business—that is, until the U.S. government in the mid-1950s intervened in the affairs of the South's social structures. It produced a reaction not seen since the days of Reconstruction, provoking citizens across the South into a renewed defense of their apartheid system. White animus toward African Americans took on a new dimension in working class areas like Birdville. During this period James was beginning to absorb the attitudes of the community around him and voiced concern that troops were being used to escort African American children to educational establishments.

At the time of his parents' divorce, James was enrolled in Arlington Elementary School. He excelled at good conduct and had a quiet nature; no doubt he had acquired a personality built around his fear of not wanting to say anything that would provoke a beating. School records indicate he was a promising student who became an avid reader, but gradually his grades declined. James's sister Carolyn described him as a loner at school.

Clearly affected by his parents' attitude towards him, James turned his simmering aggression towards his younger sisters, Marilyn and Carolyn. A distance grew up between them. In time, the coolness James expressed towards his sisters was repeated with his brother Gordon. Studies have shown that the inability of children to form close relationships with their siblings is an important factor in how the child eventually relates to and forms relationships in society. Sometimes the relationships with other family members make up for the distance the child feels from the parents. If the relationship with the siblings is cool, the child has no one to easily turn to when things go bad. The increasing loneliness and isolation is repeated in the world outside the family.

Both brothers turned violent during their teens according to the youngest sister, Marilyn Garzan, who was seven at the time. She said they frequently fought each other, tortured cats, and played with Mace and guns in their bedroom. Marilyn said, "[James and Gordon] would line up books against the wall—the wall was concrete, this was living in the projects—and they would shoot guns and there were bullet holes all over the wall, and if I came in and I was nice, and they were in a good mood, they'd let me shoot, too."[14]

Both Marilyn and Carolyn described their brother James as a person who had always been "strange and angry."[15] As a teenager James also developed food phobias and became obsessive about things. He refused to drink out of the same glass as his brother and sisters even if it had been washed. Whenever he sat down on a chair, he would cover it before sitting down simply because one of his siblings had sat on it.[16]

James always felt different from other children and considered himself to be "weird with a capital W."[17] He read fairytales partly to escape an abusive household, and he considered himself to be a bookworm. "I guess you'd call me a bookworm," Franklin said. "When I was like nine, ten, and eleven, I was living in those fantasies all the time."[18] Young James showed a flair for drawing, an ear for music, and a keen interest in religion. However, he rarely went to school. He later remembered he "made very low grades. The only thing I got As in was conduct, 'cause I was one of those really quiet kids."[19]

When he was eleven James stayed with an uncle in Georgia. He was already familiar with guns and loved to roam the woods near his uncle's place carrying a loaded rifle. "I was just pretending like I was shooting, but I wasn't really shooting it," he said. When he returned the following summer, he shot a pistol for the first time but said he did not enjoy the experience. At sixteen he was given a 16-gauge shotgun from his older brother Gordon, who taught him to hunt in the woods. From that day, according to James, he was never without a gun.[20]

An accident on his bicycle at the age of seven had left James with severely impaired eyesight. He became blind in his right eye and partially blind in his left, and this no doubt affected his learning. Many years later he described his disability as being "as close to blind as one can get. You know I just make use of what I've got . . . I mean I can see well enough to shoot, you know."[21] The injury also left him exempt from military conscription at a time when young men were being drafted to fight in Vietnam. To James, owning guns was a way of empowering him and compensating for his own emotional shortcomings and his eyesight disability. Guns allowed him to manipulate, dominate, and control.

As a young boy James was fascinated with television westerns that glamorized the harsh realities of the American West. James' favorite pastime was dressing up like a cowboy, emulating characters in such popular television shows as *Maverick, Cheyenne, Sugarfoot, Have Gun Will Travel, Wagon Train,* and *Bronco.* However, if he played with other boys, he would always choose to play the part of the outlaw.

He would dress in a black shirt, a black cowboy hat, black boots, and black jeans. The thrill of dressing up as a cowboy would remain with him until his late twenties, according to James, even after he had begun his murderous rampage.[22]

In the early 1960s James enrolled in the state's largest and oldest high school, Murphy, located on a sprawling forty-acre campus at 100 South Carlen Street near downtown Mobile. The fifteen-year-old James was appalled to witness the influx of African American students in the student body.

James was one of many Southerners who came of age in the thick of the turmoil that surrounded the battle for equal rights and who subsequently found the social upheaval difficult to understand or accept. Along with most white Alabama males, he believed that black children had their place. Throughout the 1950s whites were rarely found guilty of offenses against African Americans, lynching still existed, and James had grown up listening to white men in authority tell stories of how they treat "uppity niggers."

By the time he entered high school, young James had embarked on a search for spiritual meaning. He was also desperate to escape the clutches of his parents. By the time he was sixteen, he was reading the Bible constantly and became a health food faddist. He was also attracted to fringe religions and joined the Sun Myung Moon church. Unimpressed with the church's teachings, he began to attend other Christian churches in the Mobile area. He even became fascinated with British Israelism, a white supremacist ideology that originated in England in the late nineteenth century.[23] The ideology eventually became the foundation for the Christian Identity movement. Believers thought the lost tribes of Israel migrated north through the Caucasus Mountains (hence the term *Caucasian*) until they eventually settled in Scandinavia and the British Isles. According to J. Gordon Melton, author of the *Encyclopedia Handbook of Cults in America*, the Christian Identity faith is a "religion by sociopaths, for sociopaths."[24]

Like most Christian Identity followers, James completely misinterpreted the Bible. He became obsessed with its purported messages about racial integrity. He was fanatical about the Bible because he used it to prove his points about race. He could quote scripture word for word, but the bottom line was his belief that whites were the master race. According to Carolyn, when he was about sixteen James went through the Mobile phone book and made a list of every church: "He visited every church in Mobile . . . he would walk to church, from where he lived on Kellogg Street and carry a Bible. He had a Bible with him everywhere he went. He could tell you the Bible up and down."[25] She said James "was known because he walked down the street with his Bible like this, in his arms. We thought by him going to church that it would change him but it didn't seem to change him at all. It just seemed to make it worse."[26]

James's aunt, Evie Vaughn, said James became a follower of evangelist Garner Ted Armstrong in 1969, one year after Armstrong divorced his first wife. "Jimmy was a teenager and came by our house with a Bible in his hand," she said, "telling my husband how excited he was about joining evangelist Garner Ted Armstrong's church. The next thing I knew one of his sisters told me she had heard he joined the American Nazi Party and that she was scared to death of him."[27] His first wife said, "That just goes to show you how easily led he was. He never talked religion around me. A church was the last thing I would have expected him to join. But now it looks like he was anxious to join anything."[28]

The early years of constant criticism, punishment, and ridicule shaped the young James into a disruptive and delinquent teenager, and the hate literature he acquired had a profound impact on the way he saw the world. He became enraged when his all-white neighborhood began to integrate, and he began to develop ideas that the world would be better off without blacks, Jews, and "race-mixers."

In his quest to find direction and acceptance, James looked for answers in the local libraries. He became fascinated by the life of Hitler and stole *Mein Kampf* from the Mobile Public Library. *Mein Kampf* made sense to him and he thought Hitler's Final Solution for people of purported inferiority was the right idea. He was in awe of Hitler's intelligence. James knew then this is what he had been searching for, according to his sister Marilyn. "He worshipped Hitler," she said. "When I was a little girl he would tell me stories of how the different ways they killed Jews, because this was one of his obsessions, the Nazis and the Klan and all."[29] According to James, he joined the American Nazi Party when he was only thirteen years old. "I became really obsessed with the Nazi Party," he said.[30]

James didn't know any Jews, but he did have a construct in his head based on what he read about them and in the literature he studied—a medieval type of human being, a Fagan figure, duplicitous, always scheming and conspiring against the citizens of the host country. Jews were the evildoers in the bogus *Protocols of the Elders of Zion*, a fabricated Russian secret police document that told of rabbis meeting to invent a plan for world domination. Despite being utterly discredited for at least 100 years, belief in this document has proved remarkably resilient among hate groups. The text takes the form of an instruction manual to a new member of the elders, describing how they will run the world through control of the media and finance and replace the traditional social order with one based on mass manipulation. Scholars generally agree that the Okhrana, the secret police of the Russian Empire, fabricated the text in the late 1890s or early 1900s, but belief in it still persists, particularly within far-right groups like the KKK, Christian Identity, and other militia organizations in the western states of America. It is also popular with jihadists in the Middle East.

In 1967, at the end of his junior year at Murphy, James dropped out of high school despite having average to above average intelligence. He was ineligible for the draft because of the loss of vision in his right eye. His violent tendencies became worse, resulting in violent attacks on his mother followed by questioning by Mobile police officers.[31]

Around Valentine's Day 1968 he met a new girl in the neighborhood, sixteen-year-old Bobbie Louise Dorman. Two weeks later they were married. It was another way of leaving the family he so detested. James was kind and gentle with Bobbie at first, but after a few weeks, he changed, "like night and day," she said, and he became "cruel and violent." She believed something was bothering him a great deal, but he never told her what. Several times James beat his wife so hard she thought he was going to kill her. She said he had crying spells and headaches. The beatings were a clear sign that James was emulating the father he hated. Twice Bobbie found him huddled in the corner of the room crying about his father.[32]

According to Bobbie, James had "fantasies about being a motorcycle gang member."[33] He dressed in boots, blue jeans, a denim vest with a swastika crudely sown on it, and a heavy chain fastened to his belt. While his sixteen-year-old wife looked on, James would stand rigid in front of a mirror, snap his heels, throw the infamous Nazi salute and exclaim, "Heil Hitler!" "He had a lot of fantasies," she said. "He used to fantasize that he was a Hell's Angel—you know, he had the jeans and the jacket and he carried a knife. But he never owned a bike. It was like James just wanted something to belong to, something different. I guess the Nazis were about as different as you could get."[34]

James and Bobbie had a daughter, and the couple formed a life of quiet domesticity but the marriage was destined for failure. Following apologies to Bobbie for his violent behavior, James would soon lapse into his old ways. In fact, James's personality had not changed at all, as his young wife had initially believed. Even before his marriage, Mobile police had begun to take an interest in him for minor disturbances. He had several arrests for disorderly conduct, assault, and carrying a concealed weapon. The marriage lasted only four months after Bobbie became convinced her husband was "mentally unstable."[35]

Federal open housing legislation passed in 1967 and 1968, and the subsidized project where James and Bobbie lived had until then been a white enclave in a predominantly black neighborhood. After the passing of the Great Society legislation, the project was integrated for the first time. Like most civil rights reforms in Alabama, this one brought with it a notable upsurge in Klan and other segregationist sentiment. Soon an older friend of James began bringing racist literature for him to study, trying to convert him. James later recalled, "Once you consciously go over the stuff [Nazi hate literature] over and over again, it just goes down in your conscience and you begin to think that blacks and Jews aren't even people at all."[36]

For the next several years James was a stranger to his sisters and his mother. They were unaware he had moved to Washington, D.C., to become an active member of the American Nazi Party. "Jimmy was gone, we didn't know where, when our mother died in 1972," Carolyn said. "A year later he went back to our house and asked where the lady was who had lived there, and a little boy told him she was dead." James was upset at the news and sought out Carolyn, who had a family of her own in Mobile. "He was really changed," she said. "He was wearing a white karate suit, and he got real upset when he saw I had a black maid. We fought about it, and I told him he could leave if that was how he felt."[37] She never saw him again.

THREE

Longing to Belong

That's one great trouble with our movement. Ninety percent of the people in the movement are lunatics.

—*George Lincoln Rockwell, founder of the American Nazi Party*

Within a year of meeting her James divorced Bobbie. Following the divorce, he moved to Arlington, Virginia, home of the American Nazi Party headquarters. He offered his services to the movement and at first enjoyed associating with like-minded members. The organization had, by this time, reinvented itself following the assassination of its founder, George Lincoln Rockwell, in 1967. James said, "I was just eighteen when I first got into the movement, you know, just started reading *Mein Kampf* and getting into Nazi philosophy . . . and as time went on I just became more . . . into it . . . I took it seriously whereas a lot of other people . . . just talked about it."[1]

James had been attracted to the images of Hitler's Third Reich, and he identified with the unusually powerful armed force that took over most of Europe in the name of the white race. As a powerless and poor young white man he was also attracted to a Germany which brought all classes together in an effort to restore the honor they had lost during World War I and rid the world of "lesser peoples." James had adopted the belief that the white people of America had lost control of their democracy and that the government had given too much to African Americans, including special privileges denied the white worker. He also believed blacks were lazy, were ugly, and bred recklessly, fueling an angry army of misfits who were ready to riot at the drop of a hat. The inner cities, he believed, were the result of the black man's character.

To James, Jews were conspiring with African Americans to take over America. Growing within him was an intense desire to act out the Nazi ideology—the enemy is evil, therefore it must be destroyed. It was the only way he could express his newly discovered ideology. He began to fantasize about killing Jews and blacks.

James had joined the American Nazis at a time when the sniper killing of American Nazi Party leader George Lincoln Rockwell and the subsequent trial of his assassin had been receiving a lot of national news media exposure. Rockwell had founded the American Nazi Party in 1959 and established his headquarters in Arlington, Virginia, across the Potomac River from Washington, D.C., At the time of Rockwell's death, the membership of the American Nazi Party was believed to have only 200 members.[2]

Following Rockwell's assassination, some followers split from the party, giving their allegiance to other racist organizations like Christian Identity. Others joined former Nazi Party member Frank Collin's National Socialist Party of America, which later became famous after they organized a march through the largely Jewish town of Skokie, Illinois, and enraged community leaders.

The party now came under the new leadership of Matt Koehl, Rockwell's deputy. A year after Rockwell's death, the same year James joined the party, Koehl set out his leadership ideas in an interview for the press. Koehl told reporters, "I was born a racist. I never could see the sense of mixing of blacks and whites. It's highly indecent. I've always believed in the establishment of an all-white America. . . . What we know is coming is race war. Race war is just around the corner in historical terms. We expect there will be a serious American defeat in Vietnam because of the administration's no-win policy . . . there's going to be chaos in America . . . we will hold out at that time the only alternative."[3]

The new leadership spurned theatrics and advocated a less activist image. They began by changing the party's name, which included the infamous term *Nazi,* and renamed it the National Socialist White People's Party (NSWPP), which they considered to be less offensive. They were moving away from the more outrageous and provocative tactics, like the demonstration in 1965 when a Rockwell trooper put on black and white minstrel garb, slipped past Capitol Police officers, and made a dramatic entrance in the well of the House of Representatives to protest civil rights legislation.

Despite these new changes, the party still urged members to proclaim their white supremacist views, stand their ground by ignoring gun registration laws, and acquire a minimum of 100 rounds of ammunition for each weapon they owned. However, party regulars felt their new leaders were trying to soft sell the traditional hard-line views of white supremacists and, disappointed the new leadership had abandoned the cherished swastika insignia, began leaving. Consequently, between 1967 and 1970, the organization was silent and therefore received very little publicity. By 1970 most leaders across the movement had left or were on the verge of leaving.

James joined the Nazis in the faint hope of giving his bitterness and anger some purpose in his life. However, he was by nature a loner. He was intelligent but lacked the capacity to be either a leader or a follower of men, or the ability to connect in any meaningful way with his fellow members. His personal physical disability seemed to be intertwined with his worldview—a view that was conspiracy-oriented, resentful of others, bitter, and paranoid.

Unable to channel his intelligence into a career or a profession, and unable to accept authority in a place of work, James directed his skills and energies to negative outlets. African Americans and Jews became the focus for his purpose in life and his hatred. To James, the Jews were responsible for all the ailments of society. It was self-loathing writ large, no doubt stimulated by the recognition that he was uneducated, unskilled, and on the bottom rung of the social and employment ladder. James believed he had found a niche in life with the American Nazis, and he became more convinced that the majority of the American people would one day accept his fanaticism and extremist views.[4] "I just started hanging out with other people with similar beliefs," he said, "and when you hang out with people . . . who believe what you do you are constantly reinforced. . . . Once you consciously go over the stuff over and over again, it just goes down in your conscience and you begin to think that blacks and Jews are not even people at all."[5] His sister Carolyn said, "When he moved [to Arlington] . . . he met these people and got involved with them because he felt like they were his family. He didn't have a family but they were for him, they helped him."[6]

During 1968 and 1969, James made his mark on his new adopted family by showing he had the guts to practice what he preached. The NSWPP exploit for which James was best remembered concerned the November 1969 New Mobilization Committee to End the War in Vietnam (Mobe) demonstrations in Washington, D.C., The demonstration was nicknamed "The March Against Death." Mobe leadership came from a broad range of peace groups ranging from the Communist Party and Socialist Workers Party to the Quakers, radical pacifists, and liberals. Many of them had learned their organizing skills in the civil rights movement of the preceding decade. Mobe programs were simple, calling for an end of the war and withdrawal of American troops.

The March Against Death was a solemn, single-file march from Arlington Cemetery, past the White House, and to the Capitol. Marchers congregated at Arlington Cemetery at 6:00 p.m. on November 13, 1969. Each of the more than 46,000 participants carried a placard with the name of an American soldier killed in the war or a destroyed Vietnamese village. At 10:00 a.m. on Saturday November 15, a memorial service at the west side of the Capitol was held, followed by the mass march, which proceeded down Pennsylvania Avenue, past the White House, and to the Ellipse. The march was followed by a five-hour rally featuring prominent speakers and a cultural festival. Among the numerous Americans who endorsed the New Mobilization Committee's activities were Martin Luther King Jr.'s widow, Coretta Scott King, and antiwar activists Dr. Benjamin Spock and Rev. William Sloane Coffin.

In an effort to oppose the New Mobe and also to garner some publicity for the party members, the NSWPP decided to attack the New Mobe's headquarters. The operation seemed unlikely, as the Nazis were vastly outnumbered and their uniforms made them stand out from the crowd. The leader of the operation, James Mason, asked James to organize the attack. However, there was a problem—James had not been popular among members, and no one else volunteered to assist him. James had never really fit in with the Nazi Party regulars because he had made no effort to adopt the authoritarian Third Reich look of the other members. He was scruffy and unkempt and looked more like the enemy ranks of hippies and radicals than his fellow party members. There were other problems with James. The new member had a predilection for direct action, a tactic the party was moving away from. (It was not until the dramatic break of Joseph Tommasi's National Socialist Liberation Front from the NSWPP that there would be an organizational vehicle for revolutionary violence in the world of explicit national socialism in America.)[7]

After some cajoling, Mason was successful in persuading some members to help provide a diversion while James carried out the operation against the New Mobe's headquarters. Alone, James stormed the small building, setting off tear gas grenades that forced an evacuation. To Nazi supporters he became a hero for the cause.[8]

Not all the violence at the demonstration was initiated by rightwing crazies, however. A small group of radical street fighters shouting, "War, war, one more war," and "Revolution now!" tried to break through police lines to storm the White House, which had been encircled by empty buses. This same group had tried to storm the Justice Department the day before, stoning the building and breaking windows. Demonstrators had torn down the Stars and Stripes and replaced it with a Vietcong flag, while others rioted and had to be subdued with tear gas.[9]

James was creating a name for himself in the American Nazi Party. He became fascinated with Charles Manson, the crazed white supremacist who murdered Hollywood actress Sharon Tate, among others. Cinncinati prosecutor Melissa Powers believed that James "kind of drew off of Charlie Manson . . . he's kind of a copycat."[10]

However, James had a notion of sparking racial warfare that didn't involve killing rich white people. He would instead target interracial couples. It became an enduring fantasy that never left him. He later said he was angry at rising black crime and was on a mission from God to put an end to "race-mixing," but his crimes served a larger purpose. "That was all part of a plan to start a race war," he said. "I saw violence as the only way to accomplish things. I still believe that violence is good if it's directed toward the right people . . . I felt the jungle will prevail. Gangs of blacks will be running all over the place, doing robberies, raping women. . . . I could see this stuff coming. It was the logical conclusion of race-mixing."[11] He also described his mission as "trying to create an actual, full-scale race war. . . . Once enough people get involved . . . it would create enough tension that eventually the blacks and whites would . . . be going at it."[12] "I thought it was my duty," he said. "It was what God wanted me to do . . . I really think God was with me, protecting me."[13]

The year following his "heroic" efforts at the anti–Vietnam War demonstration in 1970, James was photographed in a Nazi uniform outside the White House. He was protesting a visit by Israeli prime minister Golda Meir. For the next three years he became involved in similar ugly racial incidents and was occasionally arrested for carrying concealed weapons. He also began insulting mixed-race couples he saw on the streets of Washington, D.C., and neighboring towns. James began to develop a philosophy that his race-hate message would be taken seriously only if he spread mayhem and bloodshed throughout the United States. He developed a plan to assassinate as many blacks as he could while always holding close to his chest his prospective bombing campaign against Jews. "I always used to talk about it," James later recalled. "I remember telling a girl I knew . . . in Silver Spring, Maryland. I said . . . it's not *if* I'm gonna kill some niggers, it's *when*, the only question is *when*.

I mean, I remember telling her that and I used to talk about it all the time [and] to anybody who would listen but they didn't take me seriously."[14]

James remained essentially a loner within the American Nazi Party. He did not believe most of the members were serious while he was ready to start acting for the cause. He thought most of the members simply wanted to talk about changing the world. He began to see the Nazis as an organization that wasn't violent enough to assist him in what was quickly becoming his divine mission—the elimination of African Americans and Jews in America, or "cleaning up America" as he put it.

On October 25, 1972, James was convicted of carrying a concealed weapon in Fairfax, Virginia.[15] Two days after his arrest, his mother died. Relatives tried to contact him without success. In 1973 he returned to his hometown. When he arrived at his mother's house he was shocked to learn from a neighbor that she had died the previous year.

After a visit with his sister, James returned to the Washington, D.C., area. He secured a job as a maintenance man and lived in Hyattsville, Maryland, but moved to Atlanta in 1974 where he earned a high school equivalency diploma and studied at a junior college. Although the city had a liberal white population that adopted a more sophisticated attitude following the progressive civil rights measures of the 1960s, it was nevertheless a center of racial conflict. Former Atlanta mayor Ivan Allen Jr. believed that the city "still had more than our share of racists and bigots in Atlanta and the rest of the South, and not all of them were blue-collar Wallaceites living with their hatred and bitterness on the fringes of town. Many of these people made up the privileged Southern class of people who belong to the exclusive country clubs and work in air-conditioned skyscrapers and go home every evening to expensive lily-white suburbs so they can carry on their tirade against the Negro in smug isolation."[16]

As soon as James arrived in Atlanta, he joined the National States Rights Party (NSRP), a racist organization that was led by Jesse Benjamin (J. B.) Stoner. James was welcomed as a member and met Stoner "in 1973 and also [Stoner's aide and brother of James Earl Ray] Jerry, too."[17] The politics of the NSRP were described by Martin Durham as "[combining] veneration for the defeated Confederacy [and the original Klan] with an enthusiasm for Der Sturmer and the Waffen SS."[18] Stoner was so racist and extreme he advocated killing Jews and said his neo-Nazi Party would eliminate them with gas chambers, electric chairs, and firing squads. "The only thing I find wrong with Hitler," Stoner told his followers, "[is] that he didn't exterminate all those six million Jews he's credited with."[19] In 1969 Stoner joined a team of lawyers working for Martin Luther King Jr.'s assassin, James Earl Ray. He frequently referred to the civil rights leader as "Martin Lucifer King."

Throughout the 1960s the NSRP played a major role in racial strife throughout the South. In January 1965 a party member, Jimmy George Robinson, violently attacked Martin Luther King Jr. in a Selma, Alabama, hotel lobby. Five party members were arrested in Atlanta in 1958 and charged with dynamiting a synagogue. Eight party members were indicted in Birmingham in 1963 and charged with interfering with court-ordered school desegregation.[20]

James was welcomed as a member. Stoner remembered meeting him but could only recall that "he wore thick glasses." James was given the responsibility of selling the organization's newspaper, *The Thunderbolt—The White Man's Viewpoint*, on the streets of Atlanta. The NSRP adopted the thunderbolt insignia as its emblem. It was a symbol that originated with Hitler's storm troopers. Party literature was circulated that originated with the Nazi editor Julius Streicher. One pamphlet depicted Jewish men sucking blood through straws from the body of a dead gentile child, while rabbis were depicted as catching blood flowing from the wounds inflicted upon a gentile woman.[21]

According to his sister Marilyn, James moved once more from Atlanta to College Park, Maryland, just outside Washington, D.C. He earned a blue belt in karate and lived alone in an abandoned office building that he was hired to maintain. Marilyn moved in for a while and saw his racism develop into an obsessive hate. "If he ever saw a white and a black together," she said, "he'd go right up and say, 'That's disgusting,' or something like that. Lots of people don't like the colored, but he was one to let you know it."[22]

James also became enraged when Marilyn looked at any African Americans. If they visited a restaurant, he would tell her they weren't allowed to touch the door handles in case an African American had touched them. Instead, he would use a napkin to open doors. If the restaurant had African American employees, they would leave and look for a different place to eat. James also told his sister she could not listen to certain types of music if a Jew had produced the record.[23]

Marilyn finally left James's house when he became angry over letters she had received from a Hispanic boyfriend who lived in Montgomery. She lost touch with her brother until 1978. One night Marilyn had visited a mall in her hometown of Montgomery. It became one of the most frightening nights of her life. James walked up to her in a shopping mall and said, out of the blue, "You still dating spics?" By this time Marilyn had married her Hispanic boyfriend, and they had a six-month-old baby. James had already embarked on his cross-country killing spree and had admitted to her in a telephone conversation or letter that he had murdered someone. Although she did not know in which state the murder was committed, she knew the victim was a black man, and her brother had described the murder in detail. By the time James had confronted his sister, he already had the Grim Reaper tattooed on his right arm. Marilyn became afraid James would kill her baby and think "he was doing [me] a favor."[24]

During one of Marilyn's visits, James became so aggressive that she simply did not want to be near him. Marilyn has characterized this period in James' life as the time of his transition into a serial killer.[25] During this period he listened to and admired the white power radio broadcasts of Dr. William Pierce, author of *The Turner Diaries*, which would become the Bible for antigovernment white supremacists in the 1980s and 1990s and would inspire Timothy McVeigh to blow up an Oklahoma City federal building in 1995.[26]

During his time in the Washington area, James's fixation with mixed-race couples was fast becoming an obsession, and he insulted them at every opportunity. On Labor Day 1976 he tailed a black man and his white date for ten miles by car to a dead end and then sprayed them with Mace. He was also angry that year when Georgia's Jimmy Carter beating President Ford in the November election. James sent Carter a letter threatening his life. "In 1976 I found one of his [Carter's] campaign promises and he was talking real race mixing," Franklin said. "I just grabbed an envelope and scribbled on it 'You rich politicians. You're selling out white kids!'" The letter also said that Carter "wasn't worth the cost of a rope it would take to hang you with."[27]

By the time he joined an Atlanta branch of the United Klans of America in the spring of 1976, the hate organization was in rapid decline. The FBI's COINTEL-PRO (Counter Intelligence Program) targeted the KKK and the NSRP. As a result the Klan's membership was reduced from 14,000 in 1964 to 4,300 in 1971. Accordingly, the power of the Klan had been severely diminished.[28] The Klan would not garner any real nationwide publicity until the infamous march in Greenwood, North Carolina, in 1979, when Klansmen and socialists fought in the streets, resulting in the deaths of five people. However, during the early to mid-1970s, what the modern Klan lacked in numbers it made up for in fanatical recruits like James.

James was impressed by the way the Klan portrayed the civil rights movement as a Communist-Jewish conspiracy. He was also impressed with the way the Klan engaged in acts of terrorism to further its cause. KKK members had been responsible for numerous acts of firebombing homes, synagogues, and the offices of organizations that opposed them. Sam Bowers, the Imperial Wizard of Mississippi's White Knights of the Ku Klux Klan, led an organization that was responsible for more than 300 acts of violence in the mid-1960s.[29] The organization was responsible for the murders of three civil rights workers in Meridian, Mississippi, in 1964, as well as the Birmingham church bombing of 1963 in which four young girls were killed. And James still believed in the Klan's tradition of racial bigotry and hatred and the central theme of the organization: race war.

James volunteered as an organizer for the United Klans and eventually was promoted to the supervisory position of Kleagle, an assignment that made him responsible for recruiting new members. The Klan had hidden training camps across the Southern states, and James wanted to learn survival training, which often included building booby traps, bombs, Molotov cocktails, and other incendiary devices. He also became familiar with the camps' caches of weapons. Klan terrorists had arsenals that included automatic weapons, hand grenades, Thompson machine guns, mortars, bazookas, rifles and shotguns, dynamite and other explosives, and large quantities of ammunition. Bombings were a favorite tactic of Klansmen because, if properly planted, a bomb would destroy itself and leave no traceable evidence. According to Delmar Dennis, a former Klan member who became an informant for the FBI, "[Klan members would] think of themselves as being soldiers in a war, and therefore it was right to kill."[30]

It was around this time that James joined the Alabama National Guard's 161st Medical Battalion. "It was during the spring of 1977," he said, "however, I can't remember the exact dates, I think it was April of 1977."[31] The short period of time he spent in the National Guard unit provided him with further opportunities to practice his weapons skills.

James was also interested in receiving Klan training to learn how to accomplish a mission that had been building in his mind about how to eliminate the African Americans and Jews he hated so much. He became familiar with the literature the Klan exposed its members to, including *We Will Survive,* a how-to book that listed detailed instructions for making bombs and using firearms. The book not only advocated violent action against Jews but provided the necessary instruction to create bombs to achieve that end. James was also involved in Klan debates about dealing with their "nigger problem." They centered on tactics any particular Klan group would use to further their cause. The tactics included threatening telephone calls, cross burning, beatings, church bombings, and the ultimate Klan sanction—murder.

In *The Racist Mind,* Raphael Ezekiel, a University of Michigan social psychologist, divided white racists into four categories—leaders, ordinary members, loose cannons, and potential terrorists, all joined by the belief in the superiority of the white race and the efficacy of violence.[32] As a Klan member, James began to exhibit features recognizable in two of these categories. His violent responses and his willingness to act on them at every turn placed him on the level of potential terrorist and loose cannon.

By the autumn of 1976, James had had enough and considered the Klan to be a joke, so he left. Alone, but still harboring a racist mission, he started to teach himself advanced sniper skills and began acquiring his own arsenal of weapons.[33]

Although James had often insulted interracial couples, his first violent act occurred on September 21, 1976, when he sprayed a mixed-race couple with Mace. Aaron Miles, an African American who had been to a play one evening with white female friend Carol Eastwood, would be Franklin's first victim. James drove behind Aaron and Carol's car for about fifteen minutes, finally following them into a dead end street. Aaron approached James and asked if he had been following them. James replied "Following you? No one's following you, boy. This is a free country. I can go where I want."[34] James then approached the couple and sprayed Mace in their faces. When questioned after the incident by a Montgomery County, Maryland, police officer, James told him that he thought interracial dating was wrong.[35] James was arrested and given bail, but he jumped bail and never stood trial.[36] His actions suggested he was now beginning to put his ideas into practice. He had finally expressed his rage.

James had crossed the line, impelled by everything that had gone on in his past, and there was no going back. He was fearful but also excited that he had taken a bold act on behalf of the ideology he adopted as his own. And he was determined to act alone because he felt the American Nazis and the KKK were not professional or violent enough to assist him in what he believed was his divine mission—the elimination of African Americans and Jews from American society. A year later, when he was just twenty-seven, he would commit his first murder.

James knew he was wrong when he attacked Miles and Eastwood with Mace, and he believed it would eventually bring him grief if he were caught. But things had been building up inside him. He had embraced the notion that if he were to be successful in his life as a radical rightwing activist, he had to take the chance. Days after the attack he expected some kind of retribution from the police but nothing happened. Following the incident James began to believe he was invincible, that he would never be caught. The stress of committing a risky and unlawful act had diminished, and in subsequent crimes he would not feel the same fear and anxiety he had felt when he crossed the line of violent action in support of his ideals.

On September 21, 1976, thirteen days after he sprayed Miles and Eastwood with Mace, the twenty-six year-old signed a petition to change his name to Joseph Paul Franklin in Upper Marlboro County, Prince George, Maryland. He told people that he had just discovered who his father was and wanted to adopt his father's name. [37] But according to his sister Carolyn, "He didn't like his daddy's name . . . his father was drunk, him [sic] mean, him [sic] beating my mother."[38]

The petition was approved, and his name legally became Joseph Paul Franklin. He later cited the reason for the name change as a desire to emigrate to Rhodesia to join the Rhodesian armed forces. Franklin believed that if he enlisted, he would be given legal sanction to kill blacks as a member of Ian Smith's rebel white supremacist army. He knew that his real name, which appeared on his criminal record, would have kept him out. According to fellow convict Frank Sweeney, whom he later met in prison, Franklin had incredible ideas about wanting to kill blacks. Sweeney had lived in Zimbabwe and had been drafted into the Rhodesian Army some years previous. Sweeney said Franklin had wanted to go to Rhodesia to "waste niggers" and believed he "could just walk down the street and kill blacks with impunity."[39]

A new passport in the name of Joseph Paul Franklin was issued on November 24, 1976, in Birmingham, Alabama, with an expiration date of November 23, 1981. The would-be mercenary did not go to Africa, but he did decide to keep his new name.

Franklin's plot for a nationwide crime spree began to take shape in the mid-1970s as he became increasingly angered by what he calls "black crime." The idea of shooting Jews and African Americans had first come to Franklin one day in 1975 when he walked past a synagogue in Maryland. "I remember thinking," he said, "I could just sit there with a rifle and pick off Jews. I could get a whole lot of Jews at one time."[40] He had also been asked to leave a rooming house in the winter of 1975 and decided to "do some killing . . . couldn't get a job . . . [I] was going to pay some Jews back for it."[41] It marked the beginning of his emotional unraveling.

He was also becoming frustrated with Klan and NSRP members who, he believed, were not taking their ideology seriously and were afraid to act on their convictions. He believed the organizations were heavily infiltrated by the FBI. "I found out that most of the organizations are often infiltrated," he said, "so I had to take a different course of action."[42] His action was to abandon his memberships in the Klan and NSRP and take off on his own, restlessly roaming the country from state to state, acting on his beliefs.

And he was not too far out in his thinking that he could act with impunity. Franklin committed one violent act after another and remained anonymous. Feeling safe, he began to think of other ways to attack the system and started to plan more "propagandas of the deed." Franklin eschewed the type of attack favored by other criminal snipers like Texas Tower sniper Charles Whitman, who initiated one single uninterrupted orgy of violence that eventually killed sixteen residents of Austin. Franklin's idea centered on hit-and-run shootings and bombings. Eventually he would desperately crave acknowledgment for his crimes or at least acknowledgment that a racist sniper was attempting to incite a race war.

During his three-year murder spree, Franklin chose ordinary, faceless people for his victims, people who had been doing the most ordinary things—a restaurant manager taking a break outside his restaurant, a football star on a date, a couple going shopping, or a group of young people out for a jog. The victims were carrying out the banal tasks of everyday life, their last unremarkable moments juxtaposed with the murderer's swift brutality. And it was almost impossible to connect him to the crimes. Investigations were hampered by multiple jurisdictions and the way Franklin invented novel ways to disguise himself, including "blackening up" his face and wearing Afro wigs.

Franklin got away with his crimes for years because he had the right looks and adopted sniping as a method of killing. He never stopped moving and usually killed from a distance, picking victims he had never met as targets for his racist mission that he believed was ordained by God. "It was my mission," he said. "I just felt like I was engaged in war with the world. My mission was to get rid of as many evildoers as I could. If I did not, then I would be punished. I felt that God instructed me to kill people."[43] He decided to fund his mission by robbing banks, developing his bank robbery skills by reading books about his heroes Jesse James and John Dillinger.

FOUR

Targeting Jews

Everybody in America is free to hate. Hate is natural. It's not anti-American to hate. Why does the Jew think that he alone is above criticism and hate?
— *Homer L. Loomis, co-founder of the pro-Nazi Columbians, November 1946*

The only propaganda that finally awakens a people is the propaganda of the deed.
— *Robert Miles, Grand Dragon, The United Klans of America*

Anti-Semitism did not originate in the United States or Nazi Germany. Anti-Jewish sentiment was part of the effort by the newly established Christian faith to show that the death of Jesus was not an accident of history, but something that was preordained. During the Middle Ages, the blood libel, as it was called, took hold and provoked many Christians into believing Jews were less than human and engaged in ritual murders of innocent boys. Throughout history, the Jews bore this image and became a pariah people who were not allowed to intermingle with Christians. It was not until 1965 that the Vatican finally conceded that the Jews were not, after all, responsible for the death of Christ. It is also true that centuries of vilification of Jews enabled the Holocaust, clearing a path for irrational loathing in the hearts of men and burdening Jews with a mythic guilt.

Jews had migrated to North America since the colonial era. However, as waves of immigrants entered the United States in the nineteenth and early twentieth centuries, fear born of resentment and ignorance began to take hold in many American communities.

Southern Jews were a people within a people. Being Jewish in the South was to live as a minority in a majority culture. Southern Jews were fundamentally different from their northern cousins mainly because they assimilated more quickly and intermarried more frequently. As lawyer Herbert Elsas said, "[Jews in the South in the 1950s] wanted to be Rotarians. They wanted their religious activities to be closely related to those of their Christian neighbors. The longer [they] had been here, the more they wanted that kind of identification. They didn't want to say, 'I'm not Jewish,' but, 'I'm Jewish, but it's not so different.'"[1]

For the most part Jews in the South were left alone by their non-Jewish neighbors, though life was far from easy for those who wished to maintain an orthodox lifestyle. The sting of anti-Semitic sentiments among the majority Protestant population of the South was always something to be reckoned with. There was the vulgar anti-Semitism of the George Lincoln Rockwells and the J. B. Stoners but there was also the "civil" anti-Semitism of Southern law firms, corporations, dining clubs, and golf clubs, and the exclusion of Jews from prestigious white hotels, resorts, and country clubs. These sentiments had arisen through the dissemination of anti-Semitic propaganda throughout the United States throughout the late 1800s and until recent times.

The peak of anti-Semitism in the United States was the period between World Wars I and II as discrimination against Jews spread throughout universities, banks, manufacturing industries, advertising agencies, social clubs, and resorts. In the postwar years, anti-Semitism abated due in part to the disgust many Americans felt towards Nazi treatment of the Jews and the horrific circumstances of the Holocaust. However, in the South, as the Cold War became a reality and civil rights legislation was debated in the North, many Southerners began to equate the preservation of white supremacy with anti-communism. Southern white politicians promoted the idea that communists were stirring up discontent among African Americans, and they claimed that, since many of the most famous anarchists and Communists were Jewish, the Jews must be part of the conspiracy to foment rebellion.

Violence against Jews was never as large a problem in the South as violence used against African Americans, but it caused great suffering nonetheless. Attacks on Southern Jews and Jewish property in the 1950s and early 1960s were notable for their frequency. Yet the phenomenon of "non-violent" white racists harboring a relatively benign attitude when it came to Jews was typified by Eugene "Bull" O'Connor, the Birmingham, Alabama, commissioner of public safety whose dogs and fire hoses became internationally recognized symbols of Southern racism in the 1960s. At a law enforcement conference organized after the first wave of synagogue bombings, O'Connor expressed surprise that Jews would be targeted.

And, for most white Southerners in the 1950s, it was their fundamentalist, Bible-based religion that played a major role in the South's embrace of Israel and the acceptance of Jews in their communities. However, the extreme elements within white Southern society—including Joseph Paul Franklin and his fellow extremists in the Ku Klux Klan, the National States Rights Party, and the American Nazi Party—had a different way of looking at things. In the late 1960s J. B. Stoner's newspaper *Thunderbolt* announced the republication of the classic text *The Negro A Beast*. The book contained a new introduction by Stoner in which he stated that while the Christian religion was a religion of whites the Jewish religion was Satan's religion and that Satan's forces included "his children, the Jews' and the black beasts."[2] Not only did this fringe group of extremists in the South see the Jew as fundamentally evil, but they also believed Jews were responsible for the civil rights movement—a movement that most white Southerners abhorred. All the leading Klan groups in the South adopted the belief that the Supreme Court's *Brown v. Board of Education* decision was made by "a Jew-dominated federal government [that] instituted a revolution to dispossess the majority." Klan leaders frequently denounced the "synagogue of Satan," a phrase Franklin would repeat time and again during his trials.[3]

As 1977 opened Joseph Paul Franklin was taking steps to learn as much as he could about how to develop weapons skills for his coming mission to rid the United States of blacks and Jews. In the spring of that year Franklin joined the Alabama National Guard, the 161st Medical Battalion. During his time in the guard he attended regular meetings and was given training in weapons and armaments. However, by the summer his interest had waned.

In the summer of 1977 Franklin, believing God was protecting him, began what would become a three-year journey across America on his God-given mission. In 1976 he had set his mind on a bombing campaign against Jews after having spent some time learning the rudiments of bomb-making from his time in the Klan. But he still kept in mind the attractive idea of instigating a race war between blacks and whites. Franklin's first acts of extreme violence were two bombings, committed only a few days apart.

Bombing was not a new phenomenon in the South, but it took on a new virulence following the *Brown v. Board of Education* decision integrating schools in the South. Throughout the 1950s and 1960s, hundreds of African American and Jewish homes, schools, and houses of worship had been targeted by extremists. Bombs were going off on an alomost basis throughout the states of Florida, Tennessee, Alabama, and North and South Carolina. Homemade bombs, stacks of dynamite, and suitcases filled with gunpowder killed or injured hundreds of people and destroyed millions of dollars worth of property. Between 1954 and 1959, 105 of the bombings were of Jewish synagogues, houses, and community centers. Racist bombers struck synagogues in Charlotte, Atlanta, Miami, Nashville, Gastonia, Jacksonville, Birmingham, and a host of other cities across the Southern states.[4] In 1962 journalist James Graham Cook wrote, "The assault mounted by the white South to repel the forces of integration has been accompanied by an outburst of anti-Jewish propaganda perhaps unmatched in the history of the region . . . only since the Supreme Court's school integration decision of 1954 have the masses of the white South been introduced in any really significant way to the rather more Northern notion that the source of America's troubles is the 'Jewish conspiracy.'"[5]

It was during this period that Franklin purchased a CB radio, finding it helped him keep track of police movements. He used several handles but found the bushwhacker handle most appropriate. He also thought the handle was very amusing when he heard "some other people on my CB one time when I was giving them my handle . . . they were talking about it. They said, "Bushwhacker? Isn't that one of those people who waits behind bushes and shoots people? " However, he discovered the benefits of owning a CB radio did not outweigh the risks, as he had one stolen, which resulted in his car's alarm going off. "I know [that] had [someone] called the cops . . . I [would have] to discuss with them somebody breaking into my car [and] they would've wanted to see my ID and I always usually registered in motels under different names . . . and that would have attracted suspicion on me which might mean they would start investigating me. So anything that might cause a brush with the law I avoided."[6]

Although Franklin had left the Klan, he did not abandon the Klan's ideas of how bombing campaigns could publicize the white supremacist cause or how bombings could instill fear in Jews who were purportedly promoting and aiding the civil rights movement. He saw Jews as being "the cause of all the troubles in the world . . . and I wanted to kill as many as I could . . ."[7] And although he did not know it then, Franklin was slowly defining himself as the embodiment of the white lone-hunter terrorist of the future—the fictional killer later described in the novel *Hunter*, written by white supremacist William Pierce. *Hunter*'s fictional protagonist is the lone white racist whose murders of interracial couples and integrationist leaders set an example so dramatic that hundreds of other whites carry out spontaneous acts of assassination along the same lines without the need for a leader or organization to show the way.

However, Franklin needed funds to begin his campaign of killing. To prepare himself for his career as a bank robber, he read biographies of his heroes, William Quantrill and Jesse James, and drew especially from John Dillinger's methods of robbing banks.

Dillinger had learned his methods from two members of Herman K. Lamm's gang when he was serving a prison sentence in Indiana. Lamm was a German émigré who was famous for being the first bank robber to use professional methods to rob banks. Around 1917, when Lamm was serving a sentence in a Utah prison, he developed his own system for robbing banks. He was the first to case a bank, carefully taking note of the numbers of guards, alarms, and bank clerks, and the type of weapon a bank guard was armed with. He gave each member of his gang a role in the robbery, including lookout, driver, vault man, and lobby man, and used stopwatches to time each part of the robbery plan. Lamm also became the first robber to use well-designed plans and maps to exit the scene of the crime and planned the journey to be taken to avoid police roadblocks. He would also attach his maps of back roads to the dashboard of the getaway car.[8]

Franklin romanticized his bank robberies, believing he was an incarnation of famous outlaws he had worshipped. "I'm Jesse James or Billy the Kid," he said.[9] "I just look at myself as an outlaw of the Wild West."[10] His first major bank robbery was in an Atlanta suburb on June 16, 1977. It was well thought out, and he spent a long time planning it. After the robbery, he cut and dyed his hair from brown to black to blonde in order to change his appearance.

In the three years Franklin spent crossing the United States on his self-styled mission, he adopted numerous aliases—including his birth name, James Clayton Vaughn Jr.—and also invented names like Joseph Hart, William Quantros, Joe Price, Charles Pitts, William R. Jackson, Joe Dunn, Michael Larsen, Eddie Logan, Joseph Morrow Stewart, George William Stewart Jr., Francis Nickles, Bill Bradley, Edward O. Garland, Joseph R. Taylor, Joe Anderson, and Joseph Nickles. It is also likely Franklin took the alias Joseph R. Hagman from the 1970s most popular soap opera, *Dallas*, combining his first name with the initials of the leading character in the series, J. R., and the surname of the actor who played him, Larry Hagman.

Franklin felt he had to be in complete control of the dangerous situations he got himself into. He also believed he possessed a sense of honor as a bank robber. In fact, according to Franklin, during one of his many bank robberies over the period of his three-year killing spree, he was appalled at his own behavior when he robbed a bank in Oklahoma. He was so disgusted, he said, that he never repeated it. According to Franklin, "I pulled out my sawed-off shotgun and the teller, a woman . . . it scared the living daylights out of her. I never again pointed a gun at a woman. I'd just pull it out of my pants or coat and show it to them, but not point it."[11]

On July 5, 1977, Franklin purchased fifty pounds of explosives from an explosives distributor in the Charleston, South Carolina, area. Later, ATF agents would discover Franklin's fingerprints on the forms he was required to fill out.

Franklin chose as his first Jewish target Morris Amitay, a Jewish leader and lobbyist he had first read about when he lived in the Washington, D.C., area.

Amitay was the executive director of the American Israel Public Affairs Committee, a Jewish lobbying group funded by the Israeli government. It was the only pro-Israel group registered with Congress. For the previous two decades, Amitay helped raise more than two million dollars for congressional candidates and had been an aide to Senator Abraham Ribicoff. He had previously held various jobs at the State Department as a foreign service officer in Italy and South America. In his role as the director of the American Israel Public Affairs Committee, he frequently testified at congressional hearings on foreign policy and national security issues and led successful lobbying efforts on behalf of United States–Israeli relations. The publicity Amitay received in the national press made him a prime target for anti-Semitic groups.

Amitay lived in Rockville, Maryland, a suburb of Washington, D.C. Franklin decided to bomb Amitay's home using a homemade dynamite bomb. At 3:00 a.m. on Monday, July 25, 1977, Franklin arrived at the brick split-level house, situated at 4710 Sunflower Drive in the affluent Flower Valley subdivision of Rockville. Amitay had lived there with his wife Sybil and their three children (Michael, Steven, and Cheryl) for eight years.

Franklin took his homemade dynamite bomb from his car and walked up to the Amitay house. Under cover of darkness he placed the bomb directly outside the family room, directly below the bedrooms. On this night the Amitays had all been upstairs asleep in their bedrooms. Morris and Sybil were in the master bedroom situated at the front of the house, while the children in the side bedrooms were closest to the explosion.

Franklin ran a 400-foot yellow extension cord from the side of the house to nearby Bittersweet Lane, a side street, and attached the wire to a detonator. At 3:20 a.m., Franklin ignited the bomb, producing a huge thundering blast that residents in the region heard from three miles away. The explosion nearly tore away a wall of the Amitay house, which had taken the full force of the blast. Glass, bricks, and shingles were strewn across their yard. The force of the explosion lifted the roof off the next-door neighbor's colonial house and smashed windows. Insulation from the Amitay house was blown out into the yard and hung from an evergreen's bare branches. Damage to the Amitay's house was later estimated at fifty thousand dollars. The explosion also cracked windowpanes in neighborhood houses and tore siding loose in homes as far away as five blocks. Fortunately, the bomb did not ignite a fire.

Sheila Snipes, a neighbor, ran to the house following the blast and saw the Amitays, who looked calm except for Sybil, who cried out, "My house just exploded!"[12] Fortunately, the Amitays had emerged from the rubble unharmed. However, among the debris lay their beagle puppy, Bingo, who had been killed in the blast. The dog had been a birthday gift for one of the children. It was found dead in the family room below the children's bedroom.

When emergency services arrived, fire department spokesman Lt. Leonard King said, "This is the worst explosion I've ever been involved with." Another fireman couldn't understand "how any of the family had gotten out alive."[13] Soon after the bombing, the ATF, the FBI, and the county's fire marshall arrived and examined the scene of the crime. They immediately initiated an investigation but were soon stymied as no vital clues had been left. Philip Caldwell, the spokesman for the Montgomery County police, believed it was the work of "a professional, but there are different degrees of professionalism in something like this." ATF agents disagreed, believing "professionals would have leveled [the] house."[14]

Agents and police sifted through the rubble, placing items in plastic bags for laboratory analysis, but none were found to be useful. Later, police questioned witnesses who had caught sight of a car speeding away from the area just after the blast. However, they had spotted the wrong car, and when police found the vehicle that was identified, the three occupants were interviewed, but police concluded they had nothing to do with the bombing.

Investigators were puzzled as to whether or not the bomber had intended to kill the Amitay family or simply frighten them. The explosives were sufficient, but the placement of the device prevented the entire house from receiving the full force of the blast. However, Franklin had simply gotten it wrong. "I blew most of that house to smithereens," he later said. "But I put the bomb on the wrong side, away from where the people were sleeping."[15]

Franklin was now caught up in the excitement of his self-appointed mission. A few days later he drove to Chattanooga, Tennessee, looking for a synagogue where he could safely plant another bomb. This time he was determined to succeed in killing the occupants of his chosen building.

―――――――――

Chattanooga had long had a Jewish presence in the city. A few Jewish settlers, facing religious persecution, came to upper east Tennessee in the 1770s and to middle Tennessee by the 1820s. By 1870 groups in Nashville, Memphis, Knoxville, and Chattanooga had purchased land for cemeteries—a first concern of new Jewish communities—and founded congregations for worship. Some of these Jews were merchants and craftsmen from central Europe who fled the pogroms of eastern Europe. Later waves of Jewish immigration to Tennessee included Holocaust survivors and Russian Jews fleeing anti-Semitism. Today more than 20,000 Jews live in Tennessee. The Jews who lived in the South in the eighteenth and nineteenth centuries were almost without exception peddlers and merchants and their importance to the region's economic well being was such that in the decades immediately following the Civil War, they played an increasingly prominent role in the South's political and social life as well.

The Jews' success provoked intense feelings of resentment in men like Franklin who believed these alien people had built their wealth "on the backs of decent poor Southern white men." However, by 1977 most Jewish congregants had come to believe that the virulent strain of anti-Semitism that had occurred in previous decades had subsided. Accordingly, what occurred on the night of July 29 would shock them into believing that the bigotry of the past had not really gone away.

When Franklin arrived in Chattanooga, he registered at the Airport Inn Motel. After reconnoitering the area around the airport, he chose as his target the Beth Shalom synagogue that was in Chattanooga's Brainerd district, a short distance from the Airport Inn. He felt that the building was a synagogue of Satan, as he would later describe it. He was also convinced he was doing the right thing, as his evangelical Christian interpretations of the Bible had led him to believe that killing Jews was condoned in passages from the Book of Revelations.[16]

The Beth Shalom synagogue (at 20 Pisgah Avenue, Chattanooga) had been built in 1958 and was made of wood with a brick front. It was the only synagogue for Orthodox Jews in the city. The congregation was led by Rabbi Meir Stimler and had a membership of approximately one hundred worshippers, an assembly of businessmen, retailers, pharmacists, doctors, and many other Jews who were financially successful.

On Friday, July 29, Franklin constructed his dynamite bomb, later characterized by ATF agents as "high grade and highly sophisticated," and walked the short distance to the synagogue.[17] He placed the explosives under the floor by way of a crawl space situated underneath the building. He placed the bomb near the center. It was attached to several extension cords that led to the Airport Inn, 200 feet away. The cord had been plugged into a socket next to an ice machine in the hallway of the motel.

As Franklin waited for the timed bomb to explode, eight members of the congregation, who had been attending a meeting in the synagogue, decided to leave as they did not have a quorum—ten persons were required to be present, but on this day only eight attended. It was a stroke of luck—when Franklin's bomb finally detonated shortly before 9:00 p.m., an hour after the members left, the blast blew out the inner sanctuary, collapsed much of the walls of the frame building, and blew the roof off. No one was injured. The blast dug a two-foot crater and collapsed the synagogue's walls into twin mounds of rubble. The bomb left a strong smell of exploded dynamite. Franklin later expressed disappointment that he had "got mixed on times and [I] set it to go off at the wrong time. If I would have set it an hour earlier, I would have killed them all. And I was trying to kill them all."[18]

Franklin's bomb was designed to strike terror, panic, and confusion into the hearts of the Chattanooga Jews. He wanted his message to resonate—Jews are an alien race and were God killers who were marked for destruction. Jews in the South had seen it all before in bombing campaigns of the 1950s. However, many Jews in Chattanooga had come to believe that by the 1970s, hate campaigns against them had subsided. Rabbi Stimler could only wonder why his synagogue had been attacked. The rabbi, who lived in a separate building behind the synagogue, was overjoyed that no one had been inside the building when the bomb ignited. He was, however, puzzled because "there had been no threats, nothing of the kind. I just don't understand it. I have no idea what caused it. One minute there is a synagogue, then *boom*, it is no more."[19]

The majority of the citizens of Chattanooga did not condone the bombing. After all, they had lived side by side with the Jewish community for generations as neighbors and business associates, and they understood all too well that since the 1950s, the extremist fringe in their midst was trying to separate the Jews from the wider community. The Chattanooga media's reaction to the bombing reflected the shock and horror felt by the majority of the citizens of the Southern city.

Investigators attempted to recover chemicals, gunpowder, fuse fragments, footprints, and possible tire markings that may have been linked to the bombings. The ATF's computers soon identified technical similarities between the Amitay and Beth Shalom bombings, and both investigations were coordinated by the ATF's explosives enforcement branch. An ATF spokesman said, "A computer scans all our bomb cases and flags similarities. Then we immediately begin working on the two together."[20] Investigators in Maryland and Tennessee held meetings and compared notes, but there was little to go on.[21] All they could conclude from the evidence they collected was that the two bombings were similar—similar materials had been used, and the crimes resembled the racist bombings of the past. But the bombings yielded no physical clues about the identity of the bomber or his motives.

Had Franklin's bomb failed to detonate, investigators would have had more clues to work with. They may have discovered the type of dynamite used in the bombings, where it had been bought, and who purchased it.

However, because the bomb went off, agents had a more difficult task. The emphasis of the investigation was solely on being able to compare lists of likely suspects, questioning potential witnesses, fingerprinting suspects, and taking casts of tire tracks and footprints. Eventually, the ATF and the local police concluded that they had exhausted all their leads, and the case was closed in November 1979. It would be another five years before agents learned the true identity of the Chattanooga bomber after two ATF agents paid a visit to Marion in 1984.

Franklin appeared to be home free. Nearly a week after the Beth Shalom synagogue bombing, he drove to Wisconsin, bent on striking out at a judge who he believed had been lenient when sentencing African Americans convicted on rape charges.

— FIVE —

Stalking MRCs

[Biological integrity] is absolute, total, and uncompromising loyalty to one's own racial group and absolute, uncompromising hatred for outsiders who intrude and threaten to mix their genes with those of the females of the group.

—George Lincoln Rockwell, leader of the American Nazi Party

I felt the jungle will prevail ... gangs of blacks will be running all over the place, doing robberies, raping women. I could see this stuff coming. It was the logical conclusion of race-mixing.

—Joseph Paul Franklin, speaking about "black crime" in the 1970s.

Madison is the capital of Wisconsin and the county seat. It is also home to the University of Wisconsin–Madison. The Midwestern city is located in the center of Dane County in south central Wisconsin, 77 miles west of Milwaukee and 122 miles northwest of Chicago. Madison rarely experienced outbursts of anti-Semitism or racial violence in its history and was always known for its liberalism, even though one of the city's famous characters, Republican mayor Bill Dyke (a one-time personality on WISC-TV) once ran for vice-president with the notorious segregationist Lester Maddox. At the time that Franklin visited Madison, the city had a black population of around 6 percent.

Franklin's trip to Madison occurred one week after the Chattanooga bombing on August 7, 1977. His journey was financed by bank robberies he had committed in DeKalb County, Georgia, on June 16 and in Columbus, Ohio, shortly after. He arrived in Madison in his dark green 1972 GM Capri, carrying a stolen weapon. Emulating his outlaw heroes, he was dressed in dark clothes and a dark cowboy hat.[1]

Franklin chose the town because he had read about a judge, Archie Simonson, who had been lenient towards black defendants in a juvenile rape case. There may also have been an anti-Semitic motive for choosing the Jewish judge as a target. When he arrived in town on August 6, 1977, Franklin registered at a Madison motel using the name of a famous outlaw, John Wesley Hardin. He planned to kill Simonson, a "Jewish bastard" as Franklin described him, the next day. He may also have been aware that Wisconsin abolished the death penalty in 1853 and had the longest-running prohibition on capital punishment of any state in the country.

On the way to the judge's house, however, Franklin became involved in an altercation with an interracial couple, Alphonse Manning Jr. and his white girl-friend, Toni Schwenn. They were both twenty-three years of age. Franklin had lusted after the opportunity to kill interracial couples, or "MRCs" as he labeled them, especially those involving a white woman and an African American man. Franklin believed that "the only good interracial couple was a dead interracial couple . . ."[2]

The couple had no inkling they were about to confront a man who had harbored an obsessive rage towards mixed-race couples, or that he was a man who believed they were nothing more than beasts ready for the slaughter. In fact, he was so taken with the idea that blacks were inferior that he believed there were physical changes in a woman after she had been with a black man. According to Cincinnati prosecutor Melissa Powers, Franklin told her that women changed in appearance after being with an African American man, "like their ass gets real saggy and their boobs get different." Franklin just couldn't stand the thought.[3]

As Franklin entered Madison's East Towne shopping mall, he thought Manning's car had blocked him in, and he became agitated. Franklin noticed that the driver was black and accompanied by a white woman. When the couple stopped, they noticed Franklin yelling at them from a short distance away. Manning opened his car door and approached Franklin. According to Franklin, he became nervous as Manning approached his car and was concerned the African American might report him for a stolen gun and the explosives that were visible on the backseat of his car. There are some indications that Franklin may also have spotted a police car at this time, which invoked panic.

As Manning approached, Franklin decided he was going to kill the couple. As soon as Manning got within distance, Franklin began firing his pistol. He "just whipped out that pistol, *boom*, you know, got him right there in the midsection." He then ran over to the car where Toni Schwenn was sitting just as Manning was collapsing in a heap. As Franklin darted to the couple's car, he raised his pistol and shot Toni Schwenn, who had been sitting in the passenger seat. "There she was," Franklin said, "she was staring right at me in the face looking like she was trying to recognize me, you know, so I just put the big barrel up there again with one hand, you know, and went 'pow,' shot her right in the back."[4] Both Manning and Schwenn died instantly of their wounds.

As Franklin ran back to his car, his cowboy hat blew off. He did not have time to reclaim it and it would later be used as evidence against him. Franklin then "threw [the car] into reverse and pulled alongside" the couple's car. The killer sped out of the shopping mall and onto the highway. He didn't know that he had been spotted as he fled the scene, and a witness would later pick him out of a photographic lineup.

Franklin said the murders were committed "on the spur of the moment. I hadn't planned it. I just whipped out my pistol and shot him right there."[5] However, he did not have any remorse and never regretted shooting the couple, who he believed had been breaking God's purported laws against racial mixing. Franklin said, "It just happened to be two people that I totally hated, so I didn't dislike it. Once [whites] began having sex with blacks, in my mind—as steeped as I was in that—they weren't even human."[6] He also believed "it was the will of God that I should do it, just as it was the will of God that Samson kill all the people he killed. You know, God wanted him to kill those Philistines, that to me, the blacks were Philistines." Franklin also claimed his act was part of his plan to start a race war, even though he had killed the couple on the spur of the moment.[7]

In the Deep South, African Americans had been victimized by many petty indignities, including prohibitions against sexual relations between black men and white women. From the time of the Civil War, the fear that black men would marry white women if they were given their freedom was a core political tenet of many Southern politicians and community leaders even up to the 1950s and 1960s and beyond. The legacy Franklin and his fellow Southerners inherited was exacerbated by the courts' failure to suppress violence against African Americans. Judges and lawyers accepted white arguments that violence was necessary to preserve the white way of life in the South.

The accusations that blacks were naturally inclined to white rape escalated after the Civil War, when white Southerners smeared all blacks as rapists. Especially worrisome were African Americans who drifted from town to town in search of work. Frequently the fears of the white community resulted in white hostility leading to lynchings. And the justification for lynchings resided in the common belief that it was a legitimate expression of popular sovereignty and that the law was nothing more than the will of the people, therefore individuals who did not conform to that will could be popularly executed outside the law. There was a precedent that seemed, at first glance, to support this idea—American colonists had unseated British authority by asserting their popular sovereignty in the streets. The idea spread that when the government refused to exercise the popular will, the people mobilized.

Before the Civil War, Southern politicians had warned that if the slaves were freed, Southern women would be socializing with black men and the white race would thus be in peril. Following the war there was a fear that white women would not be able to walk down the street without being accosted by a black man. It was for this reason, Southerners argued, the war had been fought in the first place, and that once the war had ended, it was necessary now more than ever for the white Southerner to preserve the integrity of white womanhood. "Such is the explanation," Southern historian W. J. Cash wrote, "of the fact that from the beginning, they justified—and sincerely justified—violence towards the Negro as demanded in defense of women."[8]

The idea of "Southern black rape" was nationally popularized at the beginning of the twentieth century through movies like D. W. Griffith's *The Birth of a Nation,* released in cinemas in 1915, and in books like Thomas Dixon's *The Clansman.* Griffith's movie romanticized the Ku Klux Klan as "freedom fighters" protecting the Southern way of life from greedy and licentious Northerners and Southern "scalawags." The movie frightened Southern audiences into believing that equal rights for African Americans would result in race-mixing. One particular scene presented a black man attempting to rape a white woman who eventually rescued her honor by taking her own life. A contemporary account of the movie stated: "Soon the newfound freedom of the former slaves leads to rude insolence. Black militiamen take over the streets in a reign of terror. Flashes are shown of helpless white virgins being whisked indoors by lusty black bucks. At a carpetbaggers' rally, wildly animated blacks carry placards proclaiming 'Equal rights—Equal marriage.'" The central theme of Thomas Dixon's *The Clansman* was the "Southern rape complex," and he described blacks as "thick-lipped, flat-nosed, spindle-shanked . . . exuding . . .

[a] nauseous animal odor." In Dixon's view the decision to award African Americans the vote amounted to every Southern woman being at risk of "barbaric violation."[9]

In the 1950s Southerners were exposed to hate literature that reinforced the idea that if black men gained their freedom, they would eventually socialize with and perhaps marry white women, turning their offspring into a "mongrelized race." When Franklin was five years old, lynchings and beatings were occurring all across the South as a result of the Supreme Court's 1954 decision to desegregate schools. Polls taken in the region found 90 percent of whites disapproved of the idea that schools should be integrated. Other polls found that most whites saw African Americans as inferior.[10] In the 1950s Southerners also became fearful of rock and roll music. The rightwing magazine *The American Nationalist* warned its readers that white girls were "squealing and drooling over Negroidal crooners."[11] In 1955 a popular radio station in Columbus, Ohio (WDAK) warned its listeners that African Americans were pushing to integrate kindergartens so that when the children grew up, "they will be accustomed to each other and intermarriage will result."[12]

In 1955 the case of Emmett Till was also making headlines across America. Till was a fourteen-year-old boy who was murdered for allegedly making a sexually implicit statement (a wolf whistle) to a young white woman in a store in the town of Money, Mississippi. The man arrested for killing Till told reporters, "As long as I live and can do anything about it, niggers are going to stay in their place. Niggers ain't gonna vote where I live. If they did, they'd control the government. They ain't gonna go to school with my kids. And when a nigger even gets close to mention sex with a white woman, he's tired of living."[13] Those Southerners who were disinclined to join a lynch mob or engage in violence usually gave their support to politicians of the time who railed against "the sexual appetite of black males for white women."[14]

Many newspapers in the South promoted the idea that the stereotypical white Southern belle was in danger if African Americans attained equal rights. Georgia state attorney General Eugene Cook told reporters after the U.S. Supreme Court handed down its *Brown v. Board Of Education* ruling which outlawed segregation in the classroom, "As I view it. the scope of [the Supreme Court decision] goes directly to our miscegenation laws. . . . Once [our laws] are struck down, I foresee a [racial] amalgamation stampede."[15]

Many Christian churches throughout the South invoked the word of God to support the miscegenation laws. Oft quoted were two particular passages from the Bible that purportedly supported both the idea that races should not mix and that African Americans should be deported to Africa. Numbers, chapter 25, chronicles the story of Phineas, who, acting alone but with the "mind of God," stayed God's plague on Israel by ramming a javelin through an Israelite man and a Midianite woman, killing them both. Their crime was race-mixing. Matthew 18:8, which says, "Wherefore if thy hand or thy foot offend thee, cut them off, and cast them from thee. It is better for thee to enter into life halt or maimed, rather than having two hands or two feet to be cast into everlasting fire," was frequently invoked as an argument to ship African Americans to a state of their own where they could govern themselves.

Two of Franklin's heroes also voiced their disapproval of mixed-race marriages. In one of his speeches, J. B. Stoner said, "The main reason why niggers want integration is because niggers want our white women . . . you cannot have law and order and niggers, too."[16] In 1972 his *Thunderbolt* newspaper carried an article entitled "Daily Press Suppresses News of Nation Wide Rape Epidemic of White Women." The newspaper also declared that the African American male was a "sex-oriented creature" who sought to "indulge in his favorite crime: RAPE." The organization encouraged its members to use a poster, "The Black Plague," that depicted a knife-wielding African American man and a prostrate white woman and warned its readers, "every thirty minutes a woman is raped in the United States." In 1976 the paper declared that it would take only a minority of white women to "drown our race in a sea of color." White men had a duty to discourage interracial marriages, the newspaper exhorted its readers, and such couples should be "shamed into disgrace." In October 1978, in the midst of Franklin's crime spree, the newspaper printed a comic strip in which the hero sprays tear gas in the faces of an African American man and his white female companion.[17] It is not known if the cartoon strip was inspired by Franklin's 1976 assaults.

George Lincoln Rockwell would often blame Jews for promoting communism that led to black rebellion. He also charged Jews with "scheming" to "mongrelize" the American racial stock by promoting racial integration and "interbreeding" with blacks. Biological integrity, said Rockwell, is the "absolute, total, and uncompromising loyalty to one's own racial group and absolute, uncompromising hatred for outsiders who intrude and threaten to mix their genes with those of the females of the group."[18]

The Klan was especially hostile to white women who dated or socialized with African American men. As early as the 1870s, Nathan Bedford Forrest told Congress that one of the reasons for the rise of the Ku Klux Klan had been black rape of white women. In the 1920s the Klan claimed that the NAACP's advocacy of social equality was provoking black men to "lust upon women of the white race."[19] In March 1965, Klansmen shot and killed a white civil rights worker, Viola Luizzo, on a highway in Selma, Alabama, because she had rode in a car with African American men. And as late as 1970, Alabama Governor George Wallace was distributing campaign leaflets that featured photographs of seven young African American boys crowded around a white girl. To many Southerners the message was clear—whites should protect their children from black rapists.

Franklin leaned on the experience of killing Manning and Schwenn when he targeted other mixed race-couples. He learned to shoot the black man first, because "if you shot the black man first, the woman would just stay by his side like a dumb fucking idiot. It's the funniest thing, it happened every time."[20]

Although Franklin had assaulted mixed-race couples before this was the first time he had actually committed murder, and he realized he had defeated the odds and gotten away with it. From this experience he drew the conclusion that God would protect him when he carried out further killings. In fact, he held the bizarre idea that God would make him invisible when he committed his murders. "That's why he got so bold," said Cincinnati prosecutor Melissa Powers.[21]

Powers also believed there may have been a sexual component to Franklin's MRC murders and asked him if he committed the crimes because of a sexual urge. He denied it, but she noticed he became very "weird" when it came to talking about sex. Despite Franklin's denials, Powers believed killing mixed-race couples "turned him on."[22]

The incident in Madison had not been planned. Although he had no regrets about killing an interracial couple, he still wanted to kill as many Jews as he could by bombing their homes and places of worship. Franklin was itching to find a place to strike where he would be able to carry out his attacks as a sniper or bomber undetected.

Short of funds, he drove to Little Rock, Arkansas, on September 7, and calm and cool as always, he walked into a bank and ordered the cashier to hand over money. His getaway went unhindered, and he drove to Dallas looking for new weapons. After registering at a motel, Franklin scoured the newspaper ads looking for a 30.06

rifle. An ad for a Remington 30.06—which had been placed by a man in Irving, Texas—attracted his attention, and he bought the rifle for $200 before heading to a rifle range to practice his skills and adjust the telescopic site.

The task of acquiring new weapons was fairly easy for Franklin. In the 1970s most states had weak gun laws, and although Congress had attempted to pass stronger laws after the 1968 assassination of Senator Robert F. Kennedy, the results were desultory. Most criminals had no difficulty in acquiring any type of weapon they desired. Franklin used newspaper ads to buy and sell guns and rifles and frequented flea markets where few questions were asked about the purchaser's identity, but he also purchased weapons from legal gun dealers. For many states there were no mandatory background checks and no waiting period. All that was required of Franklin was for him to answer no to all the questions on the purchase form: "Have you been convicted in any court of a crime punishable by imprisonment for a term exceeding one year?" "Are you a fugitive from justice?" "Are you an unlawful user of, or addicted to, marijuana, or a depressant, stimulant, or narcotic drug?" "Have you ever been adjudicated mentally defective or have you ever been committed to a mental institution?" Naturally, Franklin answered no to all the above.

Franklin spent a week in Dallas, always moving around and registering at local motels, then drove to Oklahoma City, looking for a synagogue to bomb. However, when he arrived, Franklin changed his mind. He went to St. Louis, where he knew he had a better chance of finding a suitable venue with good cover, since St. Louis had a much larger Jewish population and therefore many more synagogues to choose from. Although Franklin originally thought he would use a bomb, he later changed his mind and decided he would hide in the bushes of a nearby synagogue and pick off the congregants with his sniper rifle as they exited.

On Friday, October 7, Franklin drove to St. Louis and registered at the Holiday Inn under an assumed name. Using the local telephone directory, Franklin considered a number of synagogues. After reconnoitering, he chose the Brith Shalom Kneseth Israel Congregation situated at 1107 Linden Avenue in the St. Louis suburb of Richmond Heights because he thought the knoll across the street was a good place for a sniper's perch.

The Richmond Heights synagogue Franklin targeted was an egalitarian, conservative Jewish congregation, committed to the study of Torah (education) and the practices of T'fillah (worship) and Tikun Olam (social action). It was part of the larger community of Jews who lived in the suburbs around St. Louis. BSKI, as it was known, was centrally located, with close access to Highway 40 (I-64), I-170, and the St. Louis suburbs of Clayton, University City, Olivette, Ladue, and Creve Coeur.

Franklin's pre-murder planning was, as always, meticulous. When he scouted the area around the synagogue, he thought the bushes nearby gave him excellent cover for his sniper attack. It was a good place for an ambush, he decided. He bought a box of ten-inch nails, a guitar case to conceal his rifle, and a bicycle that he would use so potential witnesses would not be able to identify his car. He ground the serial numbers off the rifle and cleaned the weapon thoroughly, even wiping the cartridges and bullets down. He also wiped his newly purchased guitar case clean. Wearing gloves, Franklin placed the rifle in the guitar case and checked his CB radio to ensure he would be able to monitor police calls.

The evening before the shooting, Franklin rode his bicycle to the synagogue to ensure it would carry him swiftly away from the scene of the crime. He then hammered two nails into a nearby telephone pole situated one hundred yards from the synagogue to serve as a gun rest. He wrapped a sock around the nails and hid the guitar case, which contained his rifle, in nearby bushes.

The next morning (Saturday October 8) around 9:00 a.m., Franklin drove to the parking lot near the synagogue, rode a bicycle to his sniper's nest, and collected his rifle from the bushes. He had researched the service times and knew the worshippers would leave the synagogue sometime around 1:00 p.m. following an event organized by Maxine and Merwyn Kalina, who had invited about 200 guests to their eldest son Ricky's bar mitzvah. Checking and rechecking his rifle and ammunition he lay in wait. The telephone pole and a strand of six-foot saplings provided cover.

Shortly after 1:00 p.m., as the congregants began to leave the synagogue through the front door, Franklin began firing, expending all his ammunition. "As soon as they came out," he said, "I opened fire. I hit two . . . I wanted to kill at least two of them. After the first two shots I fired three quick shots randomly at the synagogue."[23]

As Ricky Kalina was saying good-bye to his guests outside the synagogue and showing a friend his brand new digital watch, he heard what sounded like firecrackers.

Connie Lincons was standing at her front door near the synagogue when Franklin fired. "It sounded like a canon going off," she said. "I saw one man fall, then another. People were dropping to the ground and screaming. It was terrible."[24]

Two wounded men lay outside the Brith Shalom synagogue. A few kids came into the auditorium, according to one witness. They were shouting, "They're shooting people, they're killing people."[25] Gerald Gordon, who was forty-two years old and lived in nearby Chesterfield, had been shot in the left side of his chest as his two young daughters stood nearby. A bullet had pierced his left arm and lodged in his chest, destroying his internal organs.

One of the bullets Franklin had fired passed through a suit coat worn by thirty-seven year-old Steven Goldman, but he wasn't injured, although he felt what he thought was some sort of bug bite his shoulder. Goldman swooped up Gordon's little girl and held her tight as they ducked between parked cars to avoid more bullets. Thirty-year-old William Lee Ash of Akron, Ohio, lost his left pinkie finger, which got embedded in his hip when he was struck. He was treated and released from County Hospital.

Mitt Rossner, executive director of the synagogue, said Gordon had been getting into his car in the synagogue parking lot to the north of the building when he was hit. Rossner said the second shot rang out a split second later and the bullet passed through Steven Goldman's coat as Goldman was getting into his car a few feet away.

A congregant quickly called for an ambulance and, when it arrived, it took Gordon to St. Louis County Hospital. Two hours later, at 3:00 p.m., Gerald Gordon died of blood loss resulting from damage to his lung, stomach, spleen, and other internal organs.

Rabbi Emeritus Benson Skoff said he did not know about the shooting until later. He did not wait around after the Shabbat services and headed for home. "Somebody who was at the service knocked on my door," he said, "and when I opened it, she was crying and her husband was standing next to her, silent. She told me what happened. It was a terrible shock. Things like that just don't happen."[26]

As Gordon was being transported to the hospital, Franklin was fleeing the scene of the crime. He had managed to squeeze off five shots, hitting three men. He placed the rifle in the guitar case, threw it into the bushes, then jumped onto his bicycle, riding a block to the parking lot where he had hidden it only hours before. Franklin hid the bicycle, got into his car, and headed south out of St. Louis on I-55 to Memphis. He left the five spent cartridges at the scene. Franklin became angry and disappointed that his attack had not resulted in more casualties. He had wanted to "kill five Jews with five bullets," he said, and he still believed his criminal acts were not hate crimes.[27] Later, in response to a journalist's suggestion they were, he said, "Every murder is committed out of hate."[28]

STALKING MRCS — 61

Police lieutenant Thomas Boulich headed the murder investigation. Police officers, who had arrived on the scene almost immediately after the shooting, cordoned off the area and began to question potential witnesses. They also collected evidence and searched the surrounding area. They found the Remington 30.06 rifle at the foot of the telegraph pole, the five spent cartridges, and the guitar case. Police found the getaway bicycle in the nearby parking lot.

Lieutenant Boulich told the media, "We are working on a lot of angles beating the bushes to try and come up with something. At this point we have nothing concrete, no suspects."[29] Richmond Heights detective Capt. Lee Lankford said, "It was a very carefully planned, highly premeditated attack. He obviously came here and got set up. He laid in wait."[30] Although there was little to go on, police were able to acquire a description of the assailant—white male, nineteen- to twenty-five years old, five-feet, six inches, with a medium to thin build, high cheekbones, acne, wearing blue jeans with frayed cuffs and a green army fatigue jacket, and carrying a black guitar case.[31] A reward of $4,000 was issued for any information leading to the arrest of the shooter.

Within a week police had used a chemical process to restore the serial number of the rifle that Franklin had filed down. They traced the rifle to its former owner. Two St. Louis County detectives traveled to Texas to interview him and found he had sold it four weeks before. His description of the buyer closely matched Franklin's.

The murder of Gerald Gordon was a watershed for Franklin. After fleeing the scene of the crime, he began to worry that the rifle he left behind could be traced. He decided there and then to change tactics so as to confuse police who were looking for a rabidly anti-Semitic bomber and sniper. He would now concentrate on killing African Americans instead of Jews, although he had no remorse in shooting Gordon. "I can't say that I have [any remorse]," he later said. "The only thing I'm sorry about, I'm not sorry about what I did, I'm just sorry, you know, it's not legal . . . " When Franklin was asked, "What's not legal?" He replied, "Killing Jews."[32]

In February 1978 Franklin put his new plans into action. He drove to a neighborhood he was familiar with in northeast Atlanta, looking for mixed-race couples. When he saw twenty-two-year-old African American Johnny Brookshire walking down the street with his twenty-three-year-old white girlfriend, Joy Williams, he became enraged and fired his rifle. Brookshire died instantly from his wounds. Joy, who had been shot in the stomach, survived but was paralyzed from the waist down.

Police had no witnesses and no leads to go on.[33] Once again, Franklin had gotten away with an outrageous hate crime—another notch in his belt on his mission to rid the world of people he considered to be less than human.

For the next three years, Franklin would act as a ghost, stalking and killing innocent people as they went about their business and always remaining anonymous to his victims. He always killed outdoors, which made the task of investigating his crimes that much more difficult. While police officers could successfully investigate a homicide without any apparent motive, they could not carry out a proper investigation without physical evidence or witnesses. Witnesses might lie, but physical evidence rarely did. Investigators believed that the ideal murder scene is a "body in a house," meaning that discoveries about a murder can be kept away from curious onlookers or journalists. A murder indoors provides the police with some knowledge about the ownership of the house or a rental agreement or a utility bill that may lead them to possible suspects. A body in a house or building means the murderer has used some means of entry——if there is no forced entry, police may assume the victim and perpetrator knew one another. A killer may also leave fingerprints, bullets, fibers, a blood spatter, or other traces of evidence in a house. However, bodies found outdoors cause difficulties for the investigator in that the exigencies of the weather, wild animals, or curious passersby may disturb the crime scene. If a person is shot outdoors, particularly in a forest or wildlife area, it is likely some bullets may never be recovered or a blood spatter pattern may be more difficult to discern. A murder in a wooded area also makes it less likely witnesses will be found. Additionally, Franklin had now begun to use a sniper rifle in his attacks on African Americans, making it much less likely he would be identified, even though some attacks took place in crowded areas.

Although Franklin had abandoned his plans to kill Jews, he was still more determined than ever to continue with his mission. Believing God was on his side and that God made him invisible, he continued on his killing spree, confident he would never be caught. There was also a personal motive in Franklin's mission. "My main [aim] at the time," he later confessed, "I was trying to get rid of all the ugly people in the world . . . I considered blacks the ugliest people of all, you know."[34]

However, he first had to find and eliminate the one man he thought had been promoting racial mixing more than any other individual in America—the publisher of *Hustler* magazine, Larry Flynt.

SIX

Lawrenceville, Georgia

[My grandfather] . . . showed me the evils of racial mongrelization and he taught me how whites should fight it.

—*J. B. Stoner, leader of the National States Rights Party*

Larry Flynt was born in Lakeville, in Magoffin County, Kentucky, on November 1, 1942, to Larry Claxton Flynt and Edith Arnett. He was the oldest of three, but his sister Judy died in 1951 of leukemia at the age of four. Soon after her death, relations between Flynt's parents worsened. After his mother divorced his alcoholic father in 1952, Flynt moved to Hamlet, Indiana, with his mother and his brother Jimmy, where they stayed with their maternal grandparents.

After having spent his childhood in poverty, Flynt's financial situation did not improve in his adolescence. It was a difficult time for him—he didn't feel comfortable in Indiana with his newly remarried mother or in Kentucky with his alcoholic father. At the age of fifteen, he became a bootlegger in the mountains of Kentucky, and shortly afterward, in 1958, he joined the U.S. Army, though he was discharged for low test scores after barely a year. Flynt returned to his mother's home in Dayton, Ohio, and worked at the General Motors assembly plant.

He was determined to reenlist in the military, and in 1959, Flynt was accepted into the U.S. Navy. He served as a radio operator aboard the USS *Enterprise*. Flynt left the navy in 1964 and began working in a General Motors factory in Dayton, during which time he studied for and passed his high school equivalency exam.

The navy provided Flynt with a stability he didn't find at home, and his tours of duty expanded his experiences outside the confined world he was born in. After a short courtship, he married then shortly divorced his first wife, Mary. Soon after, he met Peggy, whom he married while she was pregnant with another man's baby. Soon into their marriage, Flynt discovered that she was being unfaithful and blamed Peggy's mother, Ernestine. In a fit of rage, he shot at Peggy's mother, and she fell down a flight of stairs. Following his arrest, Flynt claimed temporary insanity and entered a psychiatric center in Dayton, Ohio. Peggy and Larry were divorced not long after.

Newly single, Flynt purchased a bar in Cincinnati from his mother in 1970, which he turned into a strip club, believing it was a thriving market for working-class men. Flynt's club proved an immediate success, and within the next few years, he expanded his business, opening similar clubs that he named Hustler Clubs in Columbus, Cleveland, Toledo, and Akron.

After his Hustler Clubs gained popularity, Flynt bought into a vending-machine business, but he was soon in debt. He eventually abandoned the business to focus entirely on promoting his clubs. Flynt started a membership program, publishing a two-page newsletter that featured pictures and facts about his strippers. The newsletter was such a success that he was persuaded to produce a magazine connected to his business. He studied the editorial content and pictures in *Playboy* and *Penthouse* and concluded that they were targeted toward middle-class males. Flynt started *Hustler* in July 1974, and directed it to working-class men who Flynt believed wanted a different kind of pornography.

Flynt hired a pornography editor to help him improve *Hustler*'s content and look, and by April of 1975, Flynt was grossing over $500,000 an issue. However, many people considered it offensive and extremely vulgar. Some critics objected to the magazine's portrayal of women being beaten, burned, chained, and raped. Flynt also came under attack for publishing nude vacation photographs of Jacqueline Kennedy Onassis in the August 1975 issue of the magazine. The pictures, which Flynt purchased from an Italian paparazzo, made him a millionaire.

Flynt also provoked many racists, especially in the South, when he published a photo of a naked mixed-race couple. The explicit photographs of the interracial couple were titled "Butch: A Black Stud And His Georgia Peach." When Joseph Franklin flipped through the magazine and came across the photos, he flew into a rage and "saw blood."[1] He said, "It just showed a black male and a white female together and when I closed [the magazine] up I just thought to myself, 'I'm gonna kill [Flynt].'"[2] He later said, "I just got very incensed because of photos that they published in *Hustler*, you know, mixed-race, you know, white women with black men so this made me sick, you know, grossed me out and still does."[3]

In July 1976, Flynt was arrested on charges of pandering, obscenity, and having links to organized crime. The central theme of the trial was the disputed notion of whether or not a publication was obscene. Flynt's initial loss in court and subsequent jail sentence established the legal point that individual communities had the right to define what is obscene and could legislate what local stores could sell. Ultimately, he won this case on appeal, but his battles in court had just begun.

The trial provided Flynt with a great deal of publicity, since the free speech debate was an issue that was important to the media. He met a lot of famous people, including President Jimmy Carter's evangelist sister, Ruth Carter Stapleton, who convinced Flynt to visit her, telling him they had many common beliefs about sexual repression. The two connected immediately and established a friendship. A few weeks later, Flynt claimed he had a vision of God while flying in his jet with Stapleton on his way to Los Angeles. Out of this experience he became a born-again Christian and vowed he would change the content of his magazine and avoid portraying women in such a vulgar manner. According to Flynt, he was with "Jimmy Carter's sister, Ruth Carter Stapleton. I just started seeing visions. And hearing voices. And talking in tongues. It was some weird experience. I knew that I wanted to hear from a good shrink what had happened. That's who I sought out. I've been fine ever since."[4] Although his wife Althea opposed it, Flynt was determined to change his magazine into a Christian publication.

Flynt's views about the First Amendment had not been altered by his conversion to Christianity. On March 6, 1978, Flynt was faced with another charge in Lawrenceville, Georgia, regarding whether or not the August 1977 issue of *Hustler* was obscene. Flynt had hired a local lawyer, Gene Reeves, to represent him. Reeves, who was known locally for his tenacity and dramatic flair in the courtroom, told Flynt he thought *Hustler* was "filth," but he agreed that Flynt had a constitutional right to publish it. Flynt laughed at Reeves's honesty and said, "You're the first honest lawyer I've met. You're hired."[5]

President Carter's sister, Ruth, had offered to testify on Flynt's behalf, but the magazine proprietor dissuaded her, insisting it was God's will and might hurt her or President Carter if she took the stand. A few hours after speaking to Ruth on the telephone, Flynt and Reeves took a break from the trial's proceedings to have lunch and left Lawrenceville's county courthouse to walk to a nearby cafeteria. Across the street in an abandoned building, Joseph Franklin was perched in the window, waiting for Flynt to leave the restaurant.

In the days before the shooting, Joseph Franklin drove to Gwinnett County and registered at a motel near Lawrenceville. His anger at Flynt had not abated, and he was determined to stop the publisher. He believed that by killing Flynt, the magazine would stop publication altogether. "I figured the whole magazine would fold once I got rid of Flynt," Franklin later said.[6]

On March 6, 1978, Sara Hutchins, a part-time worker for the Records Section of the Gwinnett County Surveyor's Office in Lawrenceville, took a telephone call at 12:20 p.m. It was lunchtime, and no one was around the office, nor was anyone in the office of the solicitor county attorney, so Hutchins had taken it upon herself to answer their phone. "Tell Solicitor Gary Davis he doesn't have to worry about Larry Flynt anymore. Jesus has taken a hand in it," the caller told her. Hutchins was upset by the call and put the caller on hold before attempting to find Gary Davis's secretary, but it was too late. The caller had hung up.[7] As Hutchins put the telephone down, she heard the sounds of sirens coming from just a few blocks away. An ambulance was speeding towards the scene of a shooting.

Larry Flynt had always taken precautions for his safety in light of the fact that he had become a controversial figure in the United States. He was also aware that many people who voiced their displeasure at his magazine had threatened his life. Flynt was moreover involved in disseminating controversial stories about the Kennedy and King assassinations—activities that would inevitably attract the attention of conspiracy-minded fanatics. Flynt had launched a new magazine earlier in the year, the *Los Angeles Free Press*, and the first issue included charges that the CIA coordinated the assassination of President Kennedy and that the FBI conspired to cover it up. Flynt believed the charges could prove dangerous. The notorious conspiracy-mongerer lawyer Mark Lane was a coeditor, which guaranteed that the publication would receive a lot of controversial publicity. Incredibly, Flynt believed the CIA had been trying to poison him during a recent visit to Washington, D.C., and said that at one of the city's airports, which he would not name, "something besides gas" was nearly pumped into his private jet before one of his staff members "smelled something."[8]

Flynt had hired bodyguards for his personal protection, and the previous year, he had asked officials in Columbus, Ohio, for a zoning variance so he could install a six-foot fence around his suburban mansion. His attorney at the time, David S. Bloomfield, said the fence was needed because Flynt had received several bomb threats. Carol Trimble, his publicity director, said Flynt had received three or four death threats a week by mail or telephone.[9]

However, on this day, as he entered the restaurant in Lawrenceville, Flynt felt he had no need for his bodyguards because the people of the town were "so friendly" and he felt very relaxed. Being shot was the last thing on his mind.[10] Unknown to Flynt, Joseph Paul Franklin had been stalking him and had followed him to Columbus, Ohio, on at least two occasions.[11]

Flynt and Gene Reeves both ate a lunch of salad and a grapefruit drink in the popular V and J Cafeteria, which catered to around 150 customers per day. Joseph Franklin read in the newspaper that Flynt ate in the same cafeteria everyday.

Within seconds after Flynt and Reeves exited the cafeteria, shots rang out from what police later concluded was a Magnum .44 caliber Marlin deer rifle. Flynt collapsed on the sidewalk, having been struck twice, once in the stomach and again in his side. One of Flynt's lawyers, Herald Price Fahringer, said he had "a terrible, ugly hole in his stomach." Reeves ran down the street, fleeing for safety, but collapsed after running ten yards, having been hit in the arm and stomach. No one could tell where the shots came from, but later suspicions centered on the abandoned hotel building where Franklin had been hiding. It was about twenty-five yards from the spot where Flynt and Reeves fell. A witness, Sandra Collins, said, "All I seen was one man who was hollering, 'Help me.'"[12] Reeves had felt a bullet tearing through his insides. He glanced down at his dress shirt and saw blood. A bullet that grazed Flynt's side had entered Reeves's arm, ricocheting and traveling through his spleen and liver and into his pancreas. The two critically injured men were rushed to the Button Gwinnett Hospital, where both underwent emergency surgery.

The judge had indicated the previous week that the trial would end on Friday afternoon, and no one knew that the session would run over until Monday. Once again, Franklin seemed to have luck on his side.[13]

Reeves spent twenty days in a coma. After he came to, he ripped a breathing tube out of his throat in a panic when he couldn't breathe. That required surgery to repair damage to his esophagus. But eventually, Reeves made a full recovery and later resumed his law practice.

Flynt did not fare so well. At Button Hospital, he underwent two surgeries. In one four-hour operation, half of his stomach and his spleen were removed and his liver repaired. He also had almost two feet of his small intestine and one foot of his large intestine removed. One of the bullets had struck the cauda equina area of the spine, and the prognosis was not good. A second operation on Tuesday was scheduled to stop bleeding from the bullet wounds. Flynt had received twenty pints of blood to keep him alive. The initial prognosis gave him a 2 percent chance of survival.[14]

Despite his condition, Flynt met with reporters the following day and said from his hospital bed, "I'm going to walk again. They're giving me a fifty-fifty chance but I'm going to walk again. They gave me a 2 percent chance to live when I was shot. I could walk out of here tomorrow, if it wasn't for my legs." He described his pain as "like someone clawing the meat off your legs and setting them on fire. . . . I have some feeling in my legs. They say that's a good sign. But I can't move them."[15] His wife, who was only twenty-four, said she believed in miracles and that "it's very important to pray at this time. I just thank God he's alive."[16]

On the Wednesday evening following Monday's shooting, Flynt was moved to Emory Hospital in Atlanta, accompanied by his surgeon, Dr. Tehri Bagheri. Dr. John T. Galambos, who first examined Flynt on his arrival at Emory, placed Flynt back on the critical list and began treating him for the internal infection that had been caused by the contents of his torn intestines. Galambos had disagreed with Button Gwinnett Hospital's diagnosis of "stable and improving." Galambos told reporters, "I would not have taken him off the critical list. He is still critical and will be for the next several days until the danger of infection is over."[17]

Dr. George Tindall, chief of neurosurgery at Emory, examined X-rays of Flynt's spine and immediately scheduled a two-hour surgery to relieve pressure on his spine from bone and bullet fragments of a .44 caliber slug. Following the operation, Flynt was taken off the critical list. However, the odds were never in Flynt's favor, and he would be confined to a wheelchair permanently. Throughout his ordeal, he had undergone three operations and suffered internal infection, pneumonia, and gastro-intestinal bleeding.

———————————

Flynt blamed the CIA or the FBI or some "elements within" for the shooting. He thought he was shot because of articles he published on the Kennedy assassination.[18] Flynt's aides were convinced the attempt his life was to prevent him from investigating the assassination of President Kennedy and Martin Luther King Jr. A reward was offered for any information that would lead to the apprehension of the conspirators and it was publicized in Flynt's *Los Angeles Free Press* and newspapers across the country. Flynt aide Andrew Jaffe said the police should check out the purported link between the Kennedy assassination and the shooting. Gwinnett County police humored him and said they would investigate the charges.[19]

The idea that Flynt had been a victim of conspiracy was promoted by many conspiracy buffs who had been trying for years to prove that JFK, Robert Kennedy, and Martin Luther King Jr. had been assassinated by the CIA or the Mafia or a rightwing cabal of the "military-industrial complex." Chief among them was leftwing activist Dick Gregory, who said that blame for the Flynt shooting should rest with him because he asked Flynt to offer a $1 million reward for information on the assassination of President Kennedy. "I felt kind of responsible for him getting shot," Gregory said, and that the shooting was not a "surprise" for him. "I told him 'They're going to get you.' It was the same kind of hit they used on Dr. Martin Luther King," he told reporters.[20]

From the beginning, the attempt to find the sniper was hampered by false starts and misleading information. Police at first believed the shots had been fired from a car and issued an alert for a 1974 or 1975 Silver Camaro. Hours later this lead was discarded, and they began to concentrate the investigation on the abandoned hotel building. Police had also issued composite pictures of a couple that had been seen in the area of the shooting. They suspected the couple might have been involved after investigators questioned several people who had been in the vicinity of the courthouse. Police eventually concluded the couple might have been involved or at the very least they may have witnessed the shooting. Police investigators also questioned Flynt employees. Acting on a statement made by Althea Flynt that 25 percent of the employees of Flynt's magazines had been fired about a week prior to the shooting, local police at first considered that a disgruntled employee might have been responsible.

Police were hampered in their investigation by Althea. She refused to let police talk to her husband even though Capt. Burt Blanott, who headed up a team of eight investigators assisted by an agent from the Georgia Bureau of Investigation, called to interview Flynt "at least a half dozen times" about the shooting. Blanott had asked to see Flynt only after being told by doctors at Emory University Hospital "that there was no medical reason why [they] couldn't question him." Blanott and Gwinnett County police chief John Crunkleton said Althea had also refused to offer a reward for information in the case. "We asked the Flynts, since they offered a $1 million reward for information about the Kennedy assassination, if they would offer say

$90,000 for information in this case. They won't put up a penny," Crunkleton said.[21] However, a few months later Larry Flynt relented and offered a $100,000 reward for information that would lead police to the culprit.

But the Flynt family was taking steps on their own to find out who was responsible. They asked the seven-man team of investigators they had hired to investigate the Kennedy assassination to also look at the Flynt shooting. The team concluded that the attempt on Flynt's life was a "very well-planned effort," but they could not find either any evidence about who shot Flynt or any evidence to link the shooting with the Kennedy case.[22] Flynt told a local television station from his hospital bed that he "personally [believed], and I think I'll be able to prove it before too long, that this was done by the CIA or the FBI or elements within. I'm not accusing the leaders of any of these organizations but the network of the spying we had going on, the corruption in Washington, it's still there."[23]

In an effort to find clues, police removed a door and window from the abandoned hotel building and sent them to the Georgia state crime laboratory. For several days the building was kept under guard. The state lab also said they had concluded that bullet fragments taken from the shooting scene came from a .44 caliber rifle.[24]

By April the police were still flummoxed. Chief Crunkleton said, "If we could come up with a motive it would narrow the field greatly but at this point we don't have a motive. There's so many angles to it, anybody's theory is as good as the next." Nearly 500 witnesses had been questioned and almost 2,000 staff hours were expended in the search for the sniper. Six county investigators worked full-time on the case with the assistance from the Georgia Bureau of Investigation and Lawrenceville police.[25]

By April 14 Flynt had been moved to Ohio State University Hospital. He had a private room that was protected by Ohio State University Police and Franklin County sheriff's deputies. At times Flynt thought he experienced some feeling in his legs, but the doctors had warned him of ghost pains. Joanne Fairchild, a spokeswoman for Flynt, said her boss did not really care who shot him. When asked by reporters if he was curious about the shooter, Flynt said, "I don't want to know who shot me. I want to know what shot me. People like that represent an element in society that must be changed."[26] However, he was still determined to investigate the Kennedy assassination. He became convinced he had been shot because he was on the trail of

JFK's assassins. Flynt insisted he knew that Lee Harvey Oswald did not assassinate President Kennedy and that he knew exactly who did. He planned his exposé for the October, November, and December issues of *Hustler* magazine. He told reporters, "I know my life may be in jeopardy. If they kill me, they kill me, but I must give the public the facts."[27]

Flynt's stoic façade after the shooting was an image he wanted to show the world. In fact, he was a physical and emotional wreck. Newspaper columnist Bob Greene, who visited Flynt at Emory Hospital in April, saw Flynt strapped into a sitting position with tubes running in and out of his body, feeding him medicines and removing wastes. Flynt's eyes could not focus, and the morphine and barbiturates had turned his eyes into cue balls. Greene became upset when his friend began to weep and sob. According to Greene, Flynt was so strung out on drugs that he thought he had been in a car accident. At other times he thought he knew who had shot him. In his more conscious moments, he cried out "I know I've done some wrong things . . . Oh God!"[28]

By May 1978 Gwinnett County police still had no concrete evidence that would lead them to a credible suspect in the shooting. But they did concentrate their energies on what later turned out to be a false lead. Gwinnett County district attorney Bryant Huff said, "There are several persons involved," and they were possibly linked to Flynt's Ohio-based publishing empire or to organized crime. He said the possible motives were "internal business problems within his company, business problems across the country, and the role of organized crime in pornography." He added that an interview with Flynt in May "confirmed the truth of a lot of stories we had heard which were possible motives."[29]

By March 1980 the $1 million reward for information had not been claimed. A team of detectives was still assigned to the case, but they admitted they simply had no hope in catching Flynt's shooter. Gwinnett County police sergeant Terry Johnson said, "There are no new developments. Nobody has been picked up. All leads have virtually been exhausted." Flynt's staff was more critical of the police investigation, accusing the police department of not expending sufficient energy in finding the assailant. Flynt's own investigators were still on the case, but they too failed to find any new leads.

After the Lawrenceville shooting, a mistrial was declared, and prosecutors dropped the charges against Flynt. However, one year later, in March 1979, Flynt was convicted in Fulton County Superior Court on eleven counts of distributing obscene materials. He received a sentence of eleven years in jail, to be served consecutively, and was fined $27,500. Judge Nick Lambros said the jail terms would be suspended on payment of the fine and if Flynt ceased the distribution of pornography in Georgia.[30]

In the months following the shooting, painkillers kept Flynt in a constant stupor that, he believed, only added to his paranoia about being gunned down. "Before the operation the pain was so great," he told reporters, "I became a drug addict trying to control it. I OD'd three times. It's hard to relate the agony I went through . . . it was like standing in scalding hot water up to my thighs." Althea said, "It was terrible. Larry was on so many drugs he didn't know where he was. He couldn't make decisions or anything. He was totally out of it all the time."[31]

However, five years later he felt like a new man. In 1982, after four years of constant pain, the nerves leading to his legs were cauterized to stop all sensation. By 1983 he was lifting weights and exercising, and his spirits were raised. The faith he had embraced in 1977, however, had left him, and he confessed he "was back to being an atheist."[32]

By 1983 the wheelchair-bound Flynt had come to the conclusion that his attacker or attackers were still targeting him. He took precautions by hiring the best-equipped private security forces money could buy. He was living in a gray stone mansion, once owned by the pop singers Sonny and Cher, in the Bel Air section of Los Angeles behind a ten-foot-high wall that encircled the house. His remote controlled gates were monitored twenty-four hours a day. Within the house, armed bodyguards protected Flynt. Althea Flynt told reporters, "What else can we do? There's somebody out there who wants to murder my husband."[33] The Flynts began to believe the police themselves had something to do with the shooting and claimed there was a possibility the CIA and the KKK conspired together.

After Franklin fled the scene of the crime, he felt like a "complete failure." He was "very upset" about not killing Flynt.[34] Franklin said, "I was wishing later that I had actually fired, you know, emptied the gun . . . actually fired all six or seven rounds at him. But I thought at the time he was already dead. It was one of the first snipings I had committed so I was not that good then but if I'd done that two or three years later I would've just . . . he would have been history."[35]

Franklin's disappointment at not killing Flynt did not prevent him from seeking out other targets. He was still looking for personal and ideological satisfaction and to make a name for himself. As the years followed and the press did not characterize his efforts as instigating a race war, he became extremely frustrated. Curiously, Franklin made no effort to claim responsibility for the assassination attempt on Flynt or the reasons behind it, and it is likely his sense of failure prevented him from making some kind of approach to the media. However, because Franklin had failed in his attempt, he became determined that in the future he would make sure he fired multiple shots to ensure he killed his victims. Meanwhile, it would be another six years until Gwinnett prosecutors discovered the real identity of Flynt's shooter. Leaving Georgia's law enforcement agencies perplexed, Franklin returned to Chattanooga, the city where he had carried out his second bombing.

— SEVEN —

Mrcs Redux

Question: Which cases do you think you were doing God's work?

Joseph Paul Franklin: Well, the mixed-race couples, you know . . . so . . . when that's carried to its ultimate conclusion what's that going to be? The complete mixing of the races, you know.

Following his attempted assassination of Larry Flynt, Franklin was running short of funds. On April 11, 1978, a month after his attempt on Flynt's life, he robbed a bank in Louisville, Kentucky. By the summer he had ran out of funds, so he robbed two more banks within a two week period—one in Atlanta, Georgia, on July 25, and a bank in Montgomery, Alabama, on August 12.

On July 29, four days after he robbed the Atlanta bank, Franklin drove to Chattanooga, the city where he had bombed a synagogue in 1977. He had acquired a 12-gauge shotgun and prowled the streets looking for a suitable target. He did not have to wait long. When he drove to a Pizza Hut restaurant, he spotted an African American man with a white woman. With his 12-gauge shotgun clasped securely to his chest, he hid in tall grass in the parking lot of the restaurant and waited for the couple to finish their meal. As Bryant Tatum exited the restaurant with his girl-friend, eighteen-year-old Nancy Diane Hilton, Franklin fired once, killing Tatum instantly. He then turned the gun on Hilton and fired. Luckily, Hilton survived her wounds. A Chattanooga police team led by Inspector Tim Carroll launched an intensive investigation of the shootings, but they had nothing to go on. Franklin had left no clues as to the identity or the motive of the shooter.[1]

Franklin returned to his home state, renting an apartment under the name James A. Cooper, situated at 118 Clanton Street, Montgomery, Alabama. By that time he had exchanged his car and bought a 1972 Plymouth Satellite with a Tennessee tag. During his time in Montgomery, Franklin met sixteen-year-old Anita Carden in an ice cream parlor. They began dating; however, his relationship with Anita did nothing to stem his racial hatred.

After he left the Clanton Street apartment in late September, Franklin stayed at the Travel Lodge Motel on Federal Drive, and Anita visited him there on several occasions. During October, after spending two or three weeks at the motel, he left for a week and came back with money that police believe he acquired in yet another bank robbery. On October 11 he surrendered his Tennessee driver's license, number 5238668, in Marenco County, Alabama, and on November 9, he requested a duplicate Tennessee driver's license in the name of J. A. Cooper. Anita and Franklin spent Christmas together in Montgomery, but he left shortly afterward for a week and returned with a large sum of money he had acquired through yet another bank robbery.

Over the Christmas period Franklin had asked Anita to marry him, and in January 1979 they drove to Atlanta and were married in the DeKalb County Courthouse. They spent the honeymoon period of January and February traveling around the South visiting Birmingham, Phoenix City, and Knoxville, during which time Anita discovered she was pregnant. But their honeymoon period was not always cozy. Franklin had to use different IDs at each motel they visited because of his frequent tantrums that often resulted in smashed motel furniture.

Anita knew nothing about her husband's mission, and there is no evidence to suggest she knew about his numerous bank robberies. In fact, for the next three years, Anita believed she was married to a plumber named James A. Cooper who went away on contracting jobs only to return with large sums of money.[2]

From the beginning Anita's life with Joseph Paul Franklin had been fraught with violence. She also had to listen to her husband's constant racist ravings. However, Anita's brother Don said Franklin was generous "when times were good." According to Don, Franklin bought him a motorcycle and often treated Anita to expensive gifts.

Between February and July of 1979, Franklin and his wife rented a duplex at 601 Ann Street in Montgomery. He tended a garden and grew alfalfa sprouts. On

April 3, once again running out of funds, he drove to Nashville and robbed two banks.[3] In May he had been gone for most of the month in unexplained but profitable absences. In July he left his wife in Montgomery and continued his mission. "He acted like he was a secret agent," one police officer said, "always moving, always having to avoid capture by enemy agents. He was like a soldier on a mission, but for whom? Or was it all in his head?"[4]

Following the shootings of Tatum and Hilton in July 1978, another year passed before Franklin struck again. On July 29, 1979, he drove to Doraville, Georgia, seeking out more victims. Doraville, a small town in DeKalb County, is part of the Atlanta metropolitan area. The town's racial makeup in the late 1970s was 46 percent white and 15 percent African American.

Cruising through town Franklin noticed an African American man in a Taco Bell restaurant who he believed had been flirting with white women. He parked his car nearby, retrieved his 30.30 Savage rifle from the trunk, and lay in wait in a wooded area 150 feet from the parking area. A short time later Franklin saw the same man leave the restaurant and walk toward his parked car. The man he observed was, in fact, the manager, twenty-nine-year-old Harold McIver, and the white women he had been talking to were members of his staff. As McIver walked from the restaurant toward his car, an explosion came from the wooded area nearby. Franklin had fired two shots from his rifle. Both bullets hit McIver. He died from his wounds.[5] Once more, police investigators had little to go on, and the murder remained unsolved for two decades.

Nine days later, on August 8, Franklin drove to Falls Church, Virginia, not far from the Washington, D.C., suburbs he lived in and frequented after he left Mobile in the late 1960s. He pulled up outside a Burger King restaurant and saw African American Raymond Taylor sitting at a table eating his dinner. At 9:50 p.m., customers heard an explosion of breaking glass throughout the restaurant. Franklin had fired a high velocity 30.30 rifle bullet that passed through a large plate-glass window on the east side of the building. According to Franklin, he "decided [Taylor] would be a good target because of where he was sitting at. There wasn't anyone else around. I had him right in the crosshairs and I just slowly squeezed the trigger. Evidently, I dropped him right on the first shot."[6] Taylor was taken to Arlington County Hospital, where he was pronounced dead. Franklin fled the scene in his car unhindered.[7]

As the investigation into the sniper murders progressed, the police became convinced the murderer had no apparent personal motive. Law enforcement officials remained extremely concerned about the killer on the loose—no matter how affluent the neighborhood and no matter how comfortable the surroundings, anyone could be a target. And they had good reason to believe the task of capturing the sniper would be extremely difficult. Throughout cities across America, among the endless supermarkets, stores, and gas stations, Franklin had taken up his sniper position in the natural habitat of ordinary Americans. And each time, he carried out his act of sniping, and despite busy, well-lit streets, witnesses were sparse.

On August 25 Franklin telephoned his wife to learn that he had become a father. Several days later he visited Anita and their newborn baby in a Montgomery hospital, but he had no intention of settling down to married life, and within seven months, the couple separated. Apart from infrequent visits when Franklin was in town, he did not live with Anita again. Anita brought up his daughter, who later made contact with her father and visited him in prison.

On Sunday, October 21, Franklin drove to Oklahoma City in search of more targets. He arrived at a shopping center situated near the Oklahoma State Fairgrounds sometime in the afternoon and began looking for a hiding place to carry out a sniper attack. He soon found an ideal site: a clump of shrubbery hidden among evergreen and cedar trees on the north side of the fairgrounds. After checking and rechecking his rifle and ammunition and going over in his mind the escape route he had planned, he laid in wait for his intended victims.

At 5:00 p.m. that warm afternoon, forty-two-year-old African American Jesse Taylor was on his way home after taking his three children to a hula-hoop competition. He was accompanied by his wife, thirty-one-year-old Marian Vera Bressette (a nurse's aide who was white), and their three children, ages twelve, ten, and nine. They had decided to stop off at a supermarket to buy groceries.

As Taylor walked toward his car with grocery bags in hand, Franklin fired his rifle from his sniper's nest, 195 feet across the street. Taylor was hit, and he slumped against the car. Then two more shots rang out. A witness, sixteen-year-old supermarket employee Charles Hopkins, said, "He was yelling 'No, no, no.' [Taylor] went up against the car and he got shot again." The shots threw the victim to the ground.[8] As his wife knelt over him screaming, Franklin fired again, hitting her in the chest. Both victims died instantly. Watching from the car windows were their three children, hysterical and distraught at what they had just witnessed.

Franklin had fired five shots; four took effect. He had also damaged several cars during his shooting spree. A shopping center patron, Vince Allen, witnessed the shooting. He later said, "I just turned around and saw a man fall. He was catching bullets. I couldn't see where they were coming from."[9]

Police officers arrived approximately four minutes after the shooting. Oklahoma City police officer McLaughlin was the first to observe Taylor slumped up against his white Ford LTD and Bressette face down on the ground next to him. They were both lying at the driver's side rear of the car. Officer J. M. Martin said that when they arrived, neither of the victims showed any vital signs. Police later recovered three bullets from the shopping center parking lot and shell casings from the grove of trees. Police sergeant Tom Mundy said the shooter was "obviously well-versed in the use of a high powered rifle."[10] Police questioned the children and six other witnesses, but no leads were forthcoming as to the identity of the shooter.

Franklin returned to DeKalb County, Georgia, in his 1969 blue two-door Ford Custom. On the way he picked up a hitchhiker, fifteen-year-old prostitute Mercedes Lynn Masters, and their friendship quickly developed into a relationship. She lived in Sandy Springs, Georgia's sixth largest city and the second largest suburb in the metro Atlanta area, a place Franklin knew well. He moved in with her for a short period of time, and they frequented cinemas and bars together.

However, in an ill-considered moment of candor, Masters unwittingly sealed her fate. She confessed that she had had sexual relations with several African American men. On December 5, 1979, Franklin drove out to a desolate wooded area and shot Masters in the head with a 12-gauge shotgun. Franklin later confessed, "Maybe it had something to do with the fact that I had sex with her first. And when she told me she had sex with a black dude then . . . things changed . . . then I decided to kill her. . . . If I found any woman who had dated blacks [I would want] to kill 'em. You know, if I had any woman in the car who told me she had dated blacks she was history." After he shot Masters, he thought it was "real gruesome . . . you can imagine what damage [a 12-gauge shotgun] will do."[11]

Cincinnati prosecutor Melissa Powers believes Franklin may have killed many more women than he has confessed to. "I think there's a lot of dead prostitutes around," she said. "He shot one of them in a park, he told me, because she wouldn't shut up. She kept mouthing off to him and he knew she was dating a black man. There was a scrapbook of Polaroid pictures. When they caught him . . . a scrapbook was one of the things that was taken from him. He was really surprised when it didn't show up in discovery when he was defending himself . . . And nobody knows where that scrapbook is. . . . There were pictures of prostitutes posing naked with his gun, that's what he told me. I'd be willing to bet the women in that book are dead."[12]

The beginning of a new year and a new decade would be Franklin's most prolific period as a killer. During the following nine months, he would travel the nation, committing murder after murder then fleeing; he was always on the move and staying at numerous hotels and motels on the way using a string of false identities. In 1980 Franklin would start to kill for reasons other than his political convictions. His motives for these crimes would not be political or ideological. He had developed an urge to kill.

On January 1 Franklin registered at a hotel in Indianapolis. At the time, the population was 25 percent African American. Race relations had deteriorated during the 1960s as a result of poor housing and employment opportunities for blacks, white flight, and urban decay. Court-ordered desegregated school busing was also a controversial change.

"That was the first time I had ever been in Indianapolis," Franklin said. "I had my CB then . . . "[13] Franklin spent a week or so reconnoitering the city, choosing his target areas carefully. On Saturday, January 12, at 11:10 p.m., he spotted his first victim, a mentally retarded nineteen-year-old African American man, Lawrence Reese. Reese had been in a Church's Fried Chicken restaurant as he waited for the store to close so he could begin his cleanup chores. The fast food restaurant was only four blocks away from the expressway. From 150 yards away, Franklin fired one shot with his 30.30 rifle. The bullet smashed the plate-glass window and continued on, hitting Reese in the chest and killing him instantly.

On Monday evening, January 14, around 10:50 p.m., Franklin struck again in the city. This time he saw nineteen-year-old African American Leo Thomas Watkins, who was standing inside a convenience store, the Qwic Pic Market, located in a small shopping mall. Watkins and his father, Tom, had been waiting to start an exterminating job in the food market when Franklin spotted them. Getting a bead on the son, Franklin fired his sniper's rifle through the plate-glass window of the store.

Leo was hit once in the chest and died instantly. "I just stood there," said Leo's father, "and watched my boy die."[14]

Once again Franklin had chosen his victims carefully. The Qwic Pic was only eight blocks from the freeway, where he could make a swift exit from the scene of the crime. Franklin said he liked to "get out of the area as soon as possible . . . move fast, you know what I'm saying? As soon as you do something like that you get out and put as much space between you and that scene as possible . . . I mean I just tried to put distance between me and that area. It's just the way I operated, you know. I didn't believe in sticking around in the area. . . . Bank robberies, all that too, you know, bombings, whatever."[15]

Det. Donald Patton, who investigated both Indianapolis murders, matched both recovered bullets to the same rifle but he was at a loss to discover any hard evidence that would give him any real leads as to the identity of the killer.[16]

By Wednesday January 16, Indianapolis police captain E. Timothy Foley, commander of the Indianapolis Police Department's homicide branch, thought the killer may have targeted a third victim, twenty-one-year-old Rita Hatchett. She had been attending a birthday party with friends and relatives on Tuesday evening, January 15, when several shots were fired through a window of the house. Hatchett was hit in the chest but survived her wounds. Foley said, "Frankly, it worries me whenever we have a murder without an apparent motive . . . the [Reese and Watkins murders] are particularly worrisome." Foley drew conclusions about the Hatchett shooting by making reference to the fact that "in all three cases, the victim was in a well-illuminated room, at about 11:00 p.m., and was shot through a window."[17] Although Franklin later took responsibility for the Reese and Watkins shootings, he has never confessed to the attack on Hatchett.

Franklin was driving a 1971 dark green Chevy Nova with a CB antenna at the time of the Indianapolis sniper attacks. The car had a black interior and mag wheels, and the back end was jacked up, making it look like a souped-up racing car. Initially light blue when he bought it in Georgia, he had painted it black after the Indianapolis shootings. By June of that year, witnesses were describing it by that color. He also changed his look. He dyed and cut his hair and bought new glasses and new clothes.

On January 20 Franklin drove through Milledgeville, Georgia, and called his ex-wife Anita collect. He was on his way to New Orleans, where he would stay between January 24 and 31. It was during his stay in New Orleans that Franklin was arrested for carrying a concealed weapon, a .41 Magnum handgun. He used his false Tennessee driver's license, carrying the name James A. Cooper, for identification.

He spent a week in jail. After his release he continued on his travels, and on March 1, he was stopped for speeding in Iowa.

By April he had returned to the Deep South, clocking up yet another traffic ticket in Lynn-Haven, Florida. In mid-April he traveled to Cincinnati and purchased a 30.06 Model 742 Remington rifle. From Cincinnati he drove to Indianapolis to obtain a driver's license. He was accompanied by a man he met during his travels, B. J. Gann, who police believed had no knowledge of Franklin's murders.

By late April Franklin continued on his quest to find new prey. He drove to the state of Wisconsin, a place he had visited in 1977 where he had committed his first MRC murders.

Rebecca Bergstrom was one of four daughters of Lester and Virginia Bergstrom. She lived on the family farm in Frederic, Wisconsin, before moving to Madison to continue her education. The Village of Frederic is a rural community located in western Wisconsin, north of the Twin Cities and south of the Duluth-Superior area on State Highway 35. Farms, forests, and lakes characterize the area.

In 1977 Rebecca graduated from Frederic High School. She had been editor of the school newspaper and was also active in church activities, and she liked to work with young people. Her family and friends described her as "real friendly" and a loving, warm person. She attended vocational school in Rice Lake before deciding to enroll as a secretarial student at a school in Madison. She had planned on spending the summer of 1980 helping her parents on their 200-acre farm and working at Farmer's and Merchant's Bank in Frederic, where she had recently been hired. She had last been home on February 8.

In May 1980 Rebecca, who lived in student accommodation with four other girls, had just returned from a ten-day spring vacation to Jamaica. During the Jamaica trip, Rebecca was in the habit of carrying her passport around her neck as a precaution against it being stolen. When she returned home, she continued to carry it that way.

Rebecca had telephoned her father on Tuesday, April 29, telling him she was very excited about going home for the summer. On Thursday afternoon, May 1, she met her boyfriend, Tim Boehmer, at a Madison restaurant. At 9:30 on the morning of May 2, Rebecca—dressed in a tank top, blouse, and a denim skirt and, carrying $300 that her parents had sent to her—phoned her friend Linda Knuf, a student at the University of Wisconsin at Eau Claire. Rebecca had called to ask if she could stay the weekend at Linda's house. Linda, a friend of Rebecca's since childhood, shared the house with other students. Linda and Rebecca had met a number of times since the previous summer, when they spent a couple of weeks together in their hometown of Frederic.

Linda said Rebecca had planned to hitchhike to Linda's place from Madison. Linda had planned on going to a party from 4:00 p.m. until 10:00 p.m. that night, and she told Rebecca that if she could not find the party, she would meet Rebecca back at the house later that evening. However, Rebecca evidently changed her mind about visiting Linda or going to the party and, instead, decided to go home to Frederic, planning to stop off at her uncle's house in Tomah first. Apparently, Rebecca's parents were aware of her change of plans and later told police their daughter had definitely hitchhiked to Tomah. Lester Bergstrom also told police he had warned his daughter about the dangers of hitchhiking, and as far as he knew, she had heeded his warnings. However, she had told her parents there were so many students in Madison who came from Frederic that she never had to worry about a ride home.[18]

Rebecca never arrived at her uncle's house in Tomah. Friends last saw her in a Madison restaurant at 2:30 p.m. on Friday afternoon, May 2. On Saturday, May 3, Scott Tormoen and Steve Caucutt had been hiking in the 1,300-acre Mill Bluff State Park about five miles from Tomah. Straddling the Monroe-Juneau county line near Camp Douglas, Wisconsin, and in extreme eastern Monroe County, Mill Bluff State Park is situated on both sides of Interstate 90/94 and is a popular venue for swimming, camping, and hiking. The park's sandstone buttes were islands in glacial Lake Wisconsin during the Ice Age 12,000 years ago. Travelers passing through the park area are intrigued by the unusual, tall bluffs rising abruptly from the flat plain.

Around 4:40 in the afternoon, Tormoen and Caucutt were continuing their hike in the sweltering heat when they stumbled on the body of a young woman lying facedown near their trail. One hundred dollars in small bills was scattered near the body. Her shoes were found some distance away. She had been shot three times with a .44 caliber handgun, a large gun that was twelve or thirteen inches long with a seven-and-a-half inch barrel. The girl had been shot once in the lower back, once in the upper right shoulder, and once in the head. The bullet to the head created a hole three inches in diameter.

The two youths ran to a ranger station about a mile away and told Camp Douglas ranger Neil Ziegler what they had discovered. Ziegler returned to the scene with Tormoen and Caucutt in a truck and notified the local sheriff's office. According to coroner Gary Winningham, the girl had been dead for one to two days, and any one of the three bullets would have been fatal.[19]

When townspeople heard the news, many senior citizens remembered the last time the park had seen a murder—in 1942 an AWOL soldier killed two social workers who had given him a ride.[20]

Monroe County sheriff Ray Harris and his deputy, Ronald Pearson, soon determined the body was Rebecca's. When she was found, she still had her passport around her neck. Her parents took the news of her death very badly, according to police, and they were at a loss to understand why their daughter had been murdered. Grief-stricken, Rebecca's parents tried their best to give the police as much information about their daughter as they possibly could.[21]

When police arrived on the scene, they soon found a tire track nearby and a piece of chrome and taillight lens they deduced had come from the same car. However, Monroe County sheriff Ray Harris and his team of investigators could not trace the car they believed the killer had been driving. They also determined the young woman had been shot at the scene of the crime, and dismissed a theory that Rebecca had been killed elsewhere and then her body dumped. Harris said, "There was $2 here and $10 there and so on," near the scene of the murder, and a knapsack had been found lying nearby containing some clothing. He also concluded that whoever killed Rebecca had been familiar with the state park area. However, Sheriff Harris and his officers were unable to understand what motive could have been involved. An autopsy was performed at the state crime laboratory in Madison. There were no signs of rape or a beating, and a motive of robbery appeared to be ruled out, as money had been left at the scene of the crime. The Sheriff and his team interviewed over fifty people connected with the case without success. "I've been all over [Polk] county," Harris said. "We are also checking with some people out of state. She knows a lot of people."[22]

At first police thought they had solved the case when they located a man who had bragged to a bartender that he had killed Rebecca. However, their investigation revealed the suspect was a former mental patient who had merely read about the murder in a newspaper and decided to confess. Police officers soon traced the purported murderer's movements on the day of the murder and concluded he could not possibly have been involved.

Without the establishment of a motive or any indication from the police that an arrest was imminent, local residents began to live in fear that a killer was on the loose. Their fears were exacerbated when another young woman—Marie McClellan of East Bend, North Carolina—was found murdered in the state park on May 28. She had died from a stab wound in the throat, and a jackknife was found at the scene.[23] David Shudlick, the Monroe County district attorney, urged residents to take precautions and advised that local women should not be alone or with strangers near wooded areas whether during the day or at night. He also advised that no one should hitchhike and that homes should be locked at night.[24]

Police investigators kept the Rebecca Bergstrom murder case open, but their inquiries led nowhere. The case would not be solved for another four years. Because Rebecca's money had been left at the scene of the crime and there had been no evidence of sexual assault, investigators ruled out robbery and rape. However, years later, Justice Department officials discovered that Franklin had picked Rebecca up hitchhiking. When they struck up a conversation, she told him about her spring vacation and admitted she had dated a Jamaican man. In a fit of rage, Franklin shot her.[25]

Once again Franklin had managed to evade capture in the commission of his murders. But his latest killings were not giving him the satisfaction he craved. He was gradually becoming obsessed with the idea that the infamy he sought and the race war he desired could not be fulfilled until he did something that would really get attention, like the assassinating a famous civil rights leader.

The attempted assassination of Vernon Jordan shocked a nation that still recalled the tragic murders of JFK, RFK, and Malcolm X. Senator Edward M. Kennedy, who had been campaigning for the presidency in nearby Ohio, called the shooting "another reminder of the senseless violence that stalks our land."[26] Kennedy immediately cancelled plans for campaign speeches and hurried to Fort Wayne. President Carter phoned the hospital and made plans to visit Jordan on Sunday. Carter said the shooting was "an assassination effort" and added, "It is ironic that this life would be attacked, because he has spent it fighting against the causes of violence."[27] When Carter visited Jordan, he reaffirmed his belief that Jordan was the target of an assassination attempt, which he defined as "the attempted murder of a prominent person."[28]

When civil rights activist Jesse Jackson arrived at Jordan's hospital, he immediately assumed the shooting was the result of a conspiracy and that Jordan may have been the first of the assassin's targets. Jackson spoke of a "hit list of people who took a strong stand on civil rights." He also said the bullet that hit Jordan was "seemingly well-placed by a professional, which is a political statement."[29]

Frank Heyman, the Fort Wayne city controller, in a naive effort to calm the situation, said he believed the incident "was not a racially motivated incident. In fact, there is really no racial tension in Fort Wayne." Allen County prosecutor Arnold Duemling exacerbated the situation by saying he thought the shooting might have stemmed from Black Nationalism rather than the views of a "racist redneck."[30] Fort Wayne mayor Winfield Moses Jr. cryptically stated, "Anyone who is an expert with guns could have done this."[31] The local press, after speaking to city officials, introduced the idea that the attempted assassination of Jordan may have resulted from a domestic motive.

Following the attempt on Vernon Jordan's life, Franklin was quickly becoming incensed that the news media were not covering his crimes in the sensational way he felt they deserved. He believed the media were suppressing the news about the Jordan shooting and the murders of the mixed-race couples in order to avert conflict in the African American communities. Of course, this is what Franklin desperately wanted to happen. He decided to "turn up the heat . . . just start committing more killings . . . just try to force them to get me publicity because they didn't want to publicize what I was doing."[32] Cincinnati prosecutor Joseph Deters said Franklin was "perturbed that the media didn't pick up on this [the Jordan shooting] as a racial incident . . . and he was hell-bent on making a statement in that fashion. He went there [to Cincinnati] to kill, preferably a racially mixed couple, but in that absence, he was there to kill blacks. . . . Joseph Paul Franklin fancies himself as this white supremacist, racial purist, and he would like to go down in history as that. The sad truth is he enjoys killing people."[33]

EIGHT

The Triangle Murders

June [1980] was the most prolific, I mean . . . was most prolific as far as murders go
in that month. I committed six murders. A big chunk of all the ones that I eventually committed in the whole three years . . . I committed right there in those three
months you know.

—Joseph Paul Franklin

Joseph Franklin's idea of turning up the heat, after news organizations had
avoided categorizing the Jordan shooting as a racial crime, was to head for
Cincinnati, where he thought further bouts of mayhem and carnage would this
time spark national interest in his deeds. He was also heading for a city that had a
history of poor race relations. It was a tinderbox primed to ignite with one act of
extreme racial violence.

According to Franklin, "I was just getting very upset because the news media,
the national news media, wasn't covering what I was doing. They were pretty well
suppressing the news. I don't know, I guess they were afraid they'd start a race war
or something. And that's what I was trying to do. I just decided to just turn up the
heat a little bit. Just start committing more killings and . . . just try to force them to
get me publicity because they didn't want to publicize what I was doing."[1]

By June 3, 1980, Joseph Franklin had arrived in Florence, Kentucky (about
twenty miles from Cincinnati), where he registered at the Florence Motel, 7111
Dixie Highway, using the alias Eddie R. Logan. Franklin had been eager to sell one

of his guns, a Remington 700 30.06 rifle, since he realized that he could not shoot it because of his disability. He placed an ad in the *Cincinnati Enquirer* that read, "Remington 700, 30.06 rifle $225. Only fired 5 times. Must sell. Tel: 371-5304 Ext. 21." The advertisement ran June 7 and 8. He also ran another advertisement to sell his electric guitar and amplifier, which he had bought at Wilking's Music in Greenwood, Indiana, giving the Florence Motel room as his address. Franklin did not sell the rifle, but he did have an inquiry about the guitar and amplifier from a Harrison, Ohio, woman, Susan K. Taylor, who Franklin described as a "kind of a housewife-looking type lady."[2]

On June 7 Taylor telephoned the number listed in the advertisement and spoke to the hotel switchboard. She left a message for Franklin to call her back. Taylor had bought a guitar on that day and wanted an amplifier to go with it. Franklin called her back around four or five o'clock the following afternoon, June 8. He told her he needed to sell both the guitar and amplifier because he didn't have time to take lessons. Taylor told him she would think about the sale and call him the next day.

Around 10:00 a.m. on June 7, thirty-three-year-old Thelma Bryant had been driving her car around Cincinnati trying to contact her girlfriend on her CB radio when Franklin came on the air asking for directions to the nearest gas station. Bryant directed him to the Shell station on North Bend and West Fork Road. As she was giving Franklin directions, she was pulling into the gas station. Five minutes later Franklin approached Bryant's car and said, "You're the girl I was talking to on the CB aren't you?" Franklin had noticed her CB radio aerial.[3] According to Bryant, Franklin appeared to be acting very strangely. She noticed his eyes were bloodshot and glassy as he struck up a conversation. She also noticed Franklin had dyed blonde hair and wore it collar length.

Franklin told Bryant he was originally from Florida, where he had left his girlfriend because of a fight, and that he had driven up from Florida on June 6 and was staying in a Florence, Kentucky motel. He also told Bryant he was on his way to see his sister who lived in Indianapolis. Bryant thought it quite strange he would tell this to a "perfect stranger" and she began to feel "uncomfortable." As she was about to leave the gas station Franklin asked her out. Bryant begged off, claiming she had a jealous husband. She had been so taken aback by Franklin's demeanor she drove off in the wrong direction from her home because she was afraid he would follow her.[4]

On June 7 Franklin drove around Cincinnati's mixed-race neighborhoods looking for his next target. He hoped it would be a mixed-race couple. He chose Bond

Hill, one of the neighborhoods in Cincinnati lining the Mill Creek, an urban stream in southwestern Ohio. Bond Hill began as a commuter suburb connected to Cincinnati via the Marietta-Cincinnati Railroad. Beginning in the 1960s, redlining by the Federal Housing Authority and blockbusting by Hamilton County realtors rapidly changed the demographic makeup of the community. The first African American family moved to Bond Hill in 1964, but by 1978 nearly 70 percent of the community was black.

Explaining his choice, Franklin said, "I didn't want a totally black neighborhood because then I would be really conspicuous, you know."[5] He spotted an area suitable for a sniper's position, a hill next to railroad tracks, and parked his black Chevy Nova in a parking lot next to a business that faced the street. The car had "mag wheels, you know," Franklin said. He wore an Afro wig and his face was blackened with charcoal. Parking his car, front facing outward for a quick exit, he walked to a store, the Big Brothers III Carry Out, located on the corner of Tennessee and Reading Road. He began reconnoitering the area, on the lookout for a suitable sniper's perch, but he noticed someone else was around and considered aborting his plans. Franklin ducked in the bushes and hoped whoever it was would not remember him. His chosen lair was in the midst of dense shrubbery, so he placed a large piece of paper on the ground to identify the spot when he returned later.[6]

According to police files, Franklin picked up a woman, Kathy Sewell, later that day in Cincinnati after contacting her on his CB radio.[7] However, he denied meeting her on this date. According to Franklin, "That bimbo said that she saw me with a CB you know in that Chevy. She used to pick men up on the interstate with her CBs, you know. She had that wrong also, you know. But . . . why she would lie about that I don't know . . . but she said that she had saw me in a gas station, but it was a shopping center parking lot. . . . She was just . . . a bimbo used to go around picking up men. She was married too . . . stepping out on her husband on the freeway and I was just one of the men that she had . . . stopped . . . and met. You know what I'm saying? It was around January 1980."[8]

On the morning of June 8, Franklin again reconnoitred the area he had chosen and once more visited the Big Brothers III store, according to a witness, Paul Jacobs, a store employee. Jacobs, who saw Franklin's face on television months later, told police the killer had entered the store on the afternoon of June 7 and the morning of June 8. Jacobs said he waited on Franklin both times.[9] Franklin's actions, if true, contradicted his own methods of being careful not to speak to anyone or allow himself to be seen at the scenes of his crimes. For his part Franklin denied he went to any businesses in the Reading Road area. He told Melissa Powers, "[That would be] a security breach . . . I would never have done that . . . I would . . . never even [talk] to anybody even so much as to ask them for directions in the area of the sniping because I knew what that could lead to . . . with potential witnesses . . . eyewitnesses."[10]

On the evening of June 8, Franklin returned to the sniper's nest at the railroad trestle dressed in a military camouflage jacket and beach hat, the type of hat he wore when he committed his bank robberies. From the trunk of his car he took out a .44 caliber Ruger Magnum Carbine. The rifle had a tubular magazine located in the fore end and held a capacity of four rounds with an additional round in the chamber. It was gas operated and semiautomatic and could be fired very rapidly. Franklin had bought the rifle in Louisville through a newspaper ad and had a telescopic sight fitted in Huntsville, Alabama. According to Franklin, "It's just amazing. I remember [I bought it] in Louisville because most places I bought so many guns I would forget where I bought them, you know."[11]

The streets were deserted, and Franklin did not observe any cars or people on Reading Lane. But he was concerned that his car was parked near a local business late at night and police might arrive and examine it. For that eventuality he prepared himself for a shoot out and convinced himself he would kill anyone who interfered with his sniping. He would "[shoot] him dead right on the spot." For that eventuality, Franklin said, he carried his " . . . .357 [pistol] . . . loaded . . . in my waist band."[12]

"It seemed like I had to sit there for at least an hour or two," Franklin said.[13] During the stakeout he would hear voices from a distance and the sounds of people walking in his direction, but he was unable to see anyone around. He was looking for mixed-race couples but this night he was out of luck. "That would have been ideal," Franklin said. "I preferred those."[14] Franklin had considered giving up and returning to his motel room when he heard someone shouting, "sounding like blacks," he said, and as he raised his head to look down the hill, he heard someone yelling and spotted "two dudes coming down the sidewalk."[15] He thought one of them was "about my height, taller than the other one." The other person was "two or three inches" shorter.[16]

Franklin, tired of waiting for a mixed-race couple to appear and getting ready to leave the area, changed his mind "and decided these kids would be good enough."[17] "I just decided to just go ahead and split," Franklin said, "when all of a sudden they walked up, you know. And I wouldn't even know they were coming, but they were yelling on their way down the street, you know, yelling to somebody or seem like they might have been going to meet some other people," Franklin remembered.[18]

The "two dudes" Franklin had spotted were two cousins, fourteen-year-old Darrell Lane and thirteen-year-old Dante Evans Brown, who were spending the weekend at their grandmother's house. LaVon Evans, who was seven at the time and used to sleep in a bunk bed above him, described his brother Dante as an athletic boy who smiled a lot, loved his five-speed bicycle, and took him under his wing. The cousins, Dante and Darrell, were born on the same day a year apart.

Around 11:30 p.m., the boys' grandmother, Carol Brown, had fallen asleep, so the two boys decided to sneak out the house and head to the Brothers III Carry Out to buy candy. On the way they met Linda Lane, Darrell's big sister, and asked her to go along with them, but she declined the offer. Linda continued on to her grandmother's house to change clothes, and as she did so, she heard noises that sounded like cars backfiring.

A local boy, thirteen-year-old Anthony Jones, saw the boys coming out of the motel parking lot and walking northbound on Reading Road on the west side of the street just below the railroad trestle.

To Franklin, the fact that Darrell and Dante were children was of no consequence. To him, the boys were simply "baby niggers" and "baby boogies."[19] As the boys approached the store, Franklin aimed for the tallest boy, Darrell, and fired one shot from his Ruger .44 Magnum rifle. He heard Darrell fall and make a sound. As soon as Dante started to run away, sprinting across the street, Franklin fired again "without really aiming" and shot him in the back. He then shot Darrell again in a signature move—shoot one, then the other, then shoot the first one again. If he had time he would "shoot the second one again."[20] It was a method he vowed to follow after his failure to kill Larry Flynt.

The angles of the boys' wounds showed the bullets were fired from well above the victims, who were walking north toward the trestle. Darrell had been shot twice. The first shot entered his upper left chest; damaged his heart, liver, pancreas, the largest artery in the abdomen, and the spinal column; and severed the spinal cord before lodging in his back. The bullet was later recovered. A second bullet grazed his right finger, went through his right hip, and exited through his right thigh. It was fired when Darrell was on the ground, paralyzed and near death. Dante had been shot in the back and the bullet exited from the front of his abdomen, showing he had been shot from behind and from a higher point. It perforated his liver, right kidney, and intestine. A second bullet hit him in the right knee. Franklin thought his second shot was lucky. He said he did not have time to aim properly and "just shot randomly" and never looked back to make sure he had shot both boys.[21]

Twenty-seven-year-old African American Priscilla Richardson was driving northbound on Reading Road with her passengers, twenty-three year-old Bertha McKibben in the front passenger seat and eighteen year-old Delores Hatcher in the back, when they heard four very loud shots ring out from the direction of the parking lot. Anthony Jones, who was approaching Duff's Restaurant at the time the shots rang out, also heard the sounds of four shots. The volume of the sounds indicated a large-caliber weapon. The three women in the northbound car saw Darrell and Dante fall as they were shot. Richardson heard Dante call out "help me, please, help me."[22]

The noise of the gunshots had awoken the grandmother, Carol Brown. When she discovered the boys had broken the rules and gone out after dark, she quickly dressed and began looking for them. Her granddaughter, Linda, sprinted after her. As Linda walked towards the convenience store, she saw a scene of "unspeakable horror." Her grandmother was holding Darrell's hand. The boy was still clutching the dollar bill he had planned to spend at the store. He was mortally wounded.

As soon as Priscilla Richardson saw the shooting, she pulled into a driveway next to the railroad trestle near Franklin's sniper's perch, then turned around, heading southbound on Reading Road to go to the District 4 police station. When Richardson arrived, she informed police officer Charles Weinschelbaum of the shooting. He reacted immediately and drove to the scene of the crime.

When Weinschelbaum arrived at Reading Road, he saw the two boys lying on the sidewalk. Dante was lying on his side, holding his abdomen. He was unconscious and lying in the grassy area between the sidewalk and the street. He appeared to be dead.[23] The officer attended to Darrell first, rolled him onto his back, and unzipped his jacket, and then attended to Dante who appeared to have no carotid pulse and, whose pupils were fixed and dilated. Nevertheless, Weinschelbaum performed CPR on him, but there was no response.

Weinschelbaum grabbed his radio and requested rescue units for the boys. Officers Jerry Ernst and Denise Rousseau arrived in Car 416 and took Dante to the hospital. During the journey the boy became conscious and managed to speak to Officer Ernst about the shooting. Dante said he did not see who shot him. He simply heard gunfire. He was alive but only just. Soon after arriving at the hospital, he lapsed into unconsciousness once more. He lingered for two days in the intensive care unit of University Hospital without ever gaining consciousness again and died from acute peritonitis at 8:03 a.m. on June 11. The county coroner, Dr. Charles S. Hirsch, determined that Dante Evans Brown had died from "hemorrhage and shock caused by a gunshot wound to the chest and abdomen with perforations of heart, liver, pancreas, and aorta."[24]

Rescue 38, Engine Company 9, and a Norwood paramedic unit all responded to the call for assistance. Medics attended to Darrell but without success. Officers Ernst and Rousseau took him to the hospital, where Dr. Kitty Connor officially pronounced the boy dead at 1:32 a.m. on June 9.

Ten minutes before midnight, specialist Gerry Gramke and Sgt. Dan Steers also responded to the police bulletins and drove to Reading Road. Gramke and Steers interviewed witnesses, took photographs of the area, and made diagrams of the scene of the shooting. Following the postmortem examination of Darrell, Dr. Hirsch drove to the shooting scene to assist detectives in determining the direction of the shots. Responding to Hirsch's opinion that the shots had come from the west side of the railroad trestle, specialist Clarence Cesar of the homicide unit recovered four cartridge cases. Like a spent slug, a casing can help narrow down the type of gun that may have been used. The cartridge cases were later identified as .44 caliber Remington Mag Federal brand. Police determined the casings were fired from a .44 caliber Ruger Magnum Carbine rifle.

Detectives photographed the entire scene, took soil samples, photographed a partial footprint in the soil, measured the distance from the train trestle to the positions of the boys, recovered a beer bottle, and processed the casings and bottle for latent fingerprints. The results of the fingerprint tests were later found to be negative. Police also used metal detectors in the area around the trestle.

On hearing news of the shooting the next day, frantic Bond Hill parents kept their children home from area schools. As protective police helicopters hovered over the suburb, residents shut themselves inside. Myron J. Leistler, the Cincinnati police chief, formed a task force. All fourteen investigators from the city's homicide squad were assigned, as were two officers from each of the city's five police districts. In all, nearly thirty officers worked on the case over the years. They worked twelve-hour shifts with no days off for four months. However, all investigative leads led nowhere. By September 1980 police were at a loss in determining the motive or identity of the killer. In total, over $100,000 was spent on the investigation.[25]

Det. Michael O'Brien spent three weeks combing the region for Ruger .44s. O'Brien said "We were unsuccessful, but hundreds of weapons were test-fired, hundreds. . . . The investigation of Darrell Lane and Dante Evans Brown was my first case . . . this was a rare case with a sniper-type shooting and no clues involved and no motive that we knew of at the time, especially with two young kids. What type of motive are you going to have there?"[26] Years later O'Brien would remember the shock and horror the community felt on hearing the news of the boys' murders. "This wasn't the typical homicide," O'Brien said, "when you have two children, thirteen, fourteen years old, little children who were shot in a sniper shooting with no clear motive—two children on their way to the candy store! It obviously had the city and the neighborhood in an uproar."[27]

———————————————

After he fired the shots, Franklin "didn't stick around that area at all. I mean I just tried to put distance between me and that area."[28] Franklin returned to his motel room in Florence and "stayed a couple of days" until he was sure the police did not have any suspects. He also intended on getting "rid of that gun as soon as possible." He cut the rifle up into small parts, put the wood parts into a paper bag, and threw it into a dumpster. He scattered the metal parts in a wooded area around Florence. He said there had been "a lot of wood on that particular model, which looked like a small M-1 or M-2."[29] According to Franklin, when he read about the shooting in the newspaper, he was surprised he had killed both boys.[30] But he was also pleased. "I just considered that if it was just wounded I was a complete failure," he said.[31]

Franklin returned to the Florence Motel. When he awoke early the next morning, he called Susan Taylor and asked her if she had decided to buy his amplifier and guitar. Taylor said she did not need the guitar but might be interested in the amplifier. She told him she would like to get back to him on Tuesday or Wednesday, but Franklin said he had to leave town. Eventually, Taylor was persuaded to accept Franklin's invitation to see the amplifier before he left town. They agreed to meet at his motel later that afternoon.

When Taylor arrived around 5:00 p.m., Franklin asked her if she had trouble finding the motel. "I guess I could have told you to look for my car," he told her. "It's right here." Franklin pointed to his Chevy Nova with Indiana license plates.[32] Franklin said he would sell the guitar for ten dollars, so she bought both the guitar and amplifier for sixty dollars. He took the goods to her car and on the way asked her if she wanted to buy a gun. She declined but did write down the car's license number because she felt "he was strange."

Franklin left Cincinnati and drove to Columbus, Ohio, a city he had visited previously when stalking Larry Flynt. He had also robbed a bank near Columbus's

High Street in 1977. When he arrived in town, Franklin looked up the names of gun stores and took his rifle to one particular store and sold it. According to Franklin, "It was scratched so I did not sell it for very much."[33]

Franklin did not stay around for too long and decided he would go to Johnstown in Cumbria County, Pennsylvania, a mountainous area in the Appalachian chain, famous for three great floods in 1889, 1936, and 1977, and situated some sixty miles from Pittsburgh.

According to Franklin, he had "spent a lot of time in Johnstown" over the past three years, so he knew the area well and had given some consideration as to how he would exit the city once he committed his intended murders.[34] Disappointed that he hadn't found a mixed-race couple in Cincinnati, he thought this time he would be lucky. On June 15, 1980, Franklin scouted the area near Johnstown's Washington Street Bridge and found an ideal place that would give adequate cover for his sniper's perch while providing him with an excellent view of the city. He took his "really big weapon, a .35 caliber Remington" out of the trunk of his car and walked to the hillside, a wooded area near a railroad overpass, fifty-five yards from the bridge. Settling down in a clump of trees and brush, he waited for his prey. He rested the rifle on his knee in "you know, that typical . . . military-type stance."[35]

Before long a couple passed by the area. Franklin thought they spotted him and his car, so he squatted on the ground when they looked in his direction and pretended to write something in the dirt. However, the couple didn't take any notice of him and continued on their walk. Franklin soon grew impatient. Every now and again he would lift the rifle to look through the telescopic sights. His preferred target was a mixed-race couple, but by now he felt he would be satisfied with any black man who happened to walk by within distance.

At 12:10 p.m, as Franklin glanced through the scope of his rifle, he was surprised to see a mixed-race couple about to walk across the Washington Street Bridge toward downtown Johnstown. It was twenty-two year-old Arthur Smothers and his sixteen year-old white girlfriend, Kathleen Mikula. Franklin remembered that Smothers was wearing a baseball cap and that Mikula looked "a blonde haired kind of a dumb looking broad . . . goofy-looking."[36] The couple had recently talked about getting married. They had known each other for about a year.

Franklin could hardly believe his eyes. He became excited at the prospect of killing the couple. "Lo and behold," he said, "I was so glad to see them." Franklin made sure the two were together. He saw they were at first separate from one another as they strolled across the street, but as soon as they started to cross the bridge, he knew they were together. He acted quickly before they had a chance to walk outside the range of his rifle.

Franklin aimed for Smothers first. His sniping method had been perfected by experience. He knew that if he shot the woman first, "the black would usually run off and I wouldn't get a chance to get him . . . this is what I found out starting out. So I changed from then on and always shot the black guy first because when she was standing there she would always stay with him to try to help but he would always run off when she was shot."[37]

When the wounded Smothers collapsed, he rolled over off the sidewalk onto the tile gutter. Franklin saw Mikula shouting at passing traffic and racked the slide action of his rifle, firing a quick shot before she could get away. He missed, but his shot took a large chunk of concrete out of the bridge. Kathleen was in shock and became immobile. "She didn't even run, which is fortunate for me," Franklin said. "I just racked the action and put it on her again and this time I got her. And she dropped right there. . . . I racked the action one more time and shot [Smothers] again and then one more time and shot her again."[38] Both died instantly. Franklin was "glad a mixed-race couple [had been] eliminated."[39]

Traffic had by now become stationary on the bridge as Franklin sat on the hill that was at a major intersection for the bridge road. People on the bridge had no idea where the shots were coming from, and no one looked in his direction. "That's the thing," he later said, "they never tell where the shots are coming from, where you're at . . . so that's one reason it's so easy to get away with . . . that type of murder . . . "[40]

Franklin ran down the hill towards his Chevy Nova, jumped in, and followed the escape route he had planned to exit the city. "Once I saw I got both of them," Franklin said, "I just started running . . . I just took off trucking, jumped in my car, you know, [I] had an escape route already planned . . . so I took that right out and left."[41]

Franklin drove to Washington, D.C., but did not stay there long. He had run out of money, and the nation's capital was not a propitious venue for a bank robbery, since a good escape route from town was vital. He took off for Burlington, North Carolina, where he robbed a bank and laid low for a few days before going to Virginia Beach. However, he left after a couple of hours as "it wasn't the place" for him. He decided to drive to Kentucky.

Franklin may also have made a detour to Nashville, Tennessee, before driving to Kentucky. According to Nashville man Robert Cassidy, Franklin bought a

Browning 30.06 rifle from him on June 24 or 25. Cassidy said he recalled the date because Tuesday and Wednesday were his only days off from the CSX Railroad. Cassidy said he had advertised four guns separately in the Trader's Post between June 16 and June 23, and he knew he sold the Browning 30.06 after the advertisement ran out. Cassidy said he got a phone call from a man in a nearby town and gave him directions. He recalled the man as being six feet tall and weighing around 180 pounds with reddish hair and spectacles with one thick lens. Cassidy said the man never smiled. "I couldn't break that personality," Cassidy recalled.[42] By June 25, however, Franklin was in West Virginia.

Driving through Pocahontas County in his black Chevy Nova, Franklin picked up nineteen-year-old Nancy Santomero and twenty-six-year-old Vickie Durian. Nancy came from Huntington, a small town in New York State. Her sister, Mary Kauffman, described her as a "loving, caring person."[43] Vickie was from Wellman, Iowa. Both women had been traveling with a friend, Elizabeth Johndrow. However, when the three women were in Richmond, Virginia, Johndrow decided to stay, while the other two women made plans to travel to the Rainbow Festival, a counterculture gathering in the Monongahela National Forest in Pocahontas County in the southeast part of West Virginia. In order to save money, they decided to hitchhike.

The first Rainbow gathering was a four-day event in Colorado in 1972, and the festival has been held annually in the United States from July 1–7 every year since. The festival was originally organized by youth counterculture tribes based in Northern California and the Pacific Northwest.

The culture of the Rainbow festival and the lifestyle of the participants was not something that was likely to solicit empathy from Joseph Franklin. From the time he spent as a member of the American Nazi Party, he loathed left-leaning "hippie types" almost as much as he loathed Jews and African Americans. So from the moment Nancy and Vickie entered Franklin's car, they were destined to become victims of his hatred and rage. Both girls were, to Franklin, "hippie-type looking broads."

During their car journey with him on June 25, 1980, all three struck up a conversation, and Franklin did not take long to ask them their opinions of African Americans. As soon as one of the young women mentioned she had dated African American men, Franklin reacted violently. "One of them told me she was into race-mixing, you know," Franklin said.[44] "The other one told me she would [date African Americans] if she had the chance . . . I had no choice but to kill them."[45]

John Blake, a local Pocahontas County man, was driving home from work when he saw Vickie and Nancy headed north on Route 219 just above Lewisburg. Blake stopped at the little general store in Maxwelton and saw Vickie and Nancy entering. Blake positively identified the girls because of Nancy's red University of Iowa Athletic Department sweatshirt. It would be the last time they were seen alive.

Franklin had planned to kill the girls at the convenience store where he had stopped to buy gas. Instead, he decided to drive to a remote rural area where he thought there would be no witnesses. He drove the girls to Briery Knob, about seven miles from Droop Mountain Battlefield State Park and thirty miles from the interstate. As Franklin approached the road leading to Briery Knob, he turned off onto a smaller road surrounded by trees. He told the girls that he was going to rape them. Both Nancy and Vickie resisted his advances, and Franklin, realizing further attempts were futile, ordered the women out of his car. When they refused, he shot both of them with his pistol, a foreign-made .44 Magnum with a seven-and-a-half inch barrel. "First words [Vickie] said was 'Oh, my God,'" Franklin remembered. "Second one didn't say anything. It was very quick. I shot the one in the front, one in the back, shot her again . . . I was so psyched up, I didn't hear the gun fire, really."[46] After Franklin shot Vickie, he aimed his gun at Nancy, this time firing wildly. He "whirled around and shot, aimed more carefully with both hands at [Nancy] and shot her in the head."[47]

Vickie had been hit twice in the chest, and Nancy was hit once in the head and twice in the chest. Franklin pulled the young women out of his car and laid them beside the dirt road. Driving off along the same route he took to enter the wooded area, he passed a car coming towards him. He averted his head so the driver would not see his face. Franklin drove to a dump near Hico, almost sixty miles away, to get rid of the girls' duffel bags, hiding them under a bush thicket.

Police officials later characterized the murders as "an execution." The young women were shot at such close range, investigators discovered, that Nancy had powder burns on her chin. During the police investigation, West Virginia State Police Sgt. Clarence "Rocky" Layne told the media the bullets were reloads, or used shell casings refilled with powder and capped with new bullet tips. Those bullets, he said, were likely .41 or .44 Magnum. Layne also said the weapon was more likely a revolver than a rifle but could have been a Ruger .44 Magnum carbine.

The families identified the bodies two weeks later. They also examined Nancy Santomero's missing sandal and the girls' missing backpacks that had been found at the end of the deer season. Vickie's sister, Mary, would for years deliberate on the circumstances of her sister's death and about the "fear and terror" Vickie would have suffered during "her last hours on earth" that day on Briery Knob.[48]

In the space of one month Franklin had committed six murders in three states. The murders in Cincinnati, Johnstown, and Pocahontas County would, in Franklin's mind, form a triangle on a map. He would later refer to these killings as "The Triangle Murders."

After Franklin shot Nancy and Vickie, he was desperate to rid himself of the Chevy Nova, which he thought may have held forensics clues tying him to the murders. His suspicions turned out to be well founded. The car had been light blue before he painted it, and the paint pattern matched vehicle paint chips found on one of the girl's bodies.

By June 27 he had arrived in Lexington, Kentucky, and using the alias Edward O. Garland, Franklin bought a 1975 brown Chevrolet Camaro for $2,300 from a local man, William Embry Jr. A notary and a friend of Embry's, Gary Barkley, witnessed the sale. The Camaro was a metallic brown 1975 model with extra high gloss and red pinstripes. It had chrome mag wheels, four tires of the same make with white raised letters, plaid vinyl seat covers, dual exhausts, and a spoiler. Kentucky law provides that the license plate remain with the car when it is sold. It is then the responsibility of the new owner to reregister the car in his name. Franklin never notified the Kentucky Department of Motor Vehicles of the new ownership.

By June 28 Franklin had returned to Lexington, where he bought two BP radial tires. A few days later he took the car to Paint Master to have the car repainted. By July 26 he was in Florence, Kentucky, where a hotelkeeper noticed a large sum of money in his room, which police later learned was the proceeds of his bank robberies. On July 30 Franklin turned in his Indiana license for a Kentucky license at the Kenton County Circuit Court in Covington. He listed an address in Erlanger, Kentucky. Terry Hellmann, the deputy clerk, issued a driver's license to Franklin on September 24, 1980, in Covington. On August 7, Franklin registered at a hotel in Erlanger. His wife received birthday cards postmarked this date.[49]

The following day, August 8, Franklin traveled to Montgomery, Alabama, to visit with his wife. She later said that she noticed a rifle in the trunk of his car. The visit didn't last long, and by August 10 he was back in Johnstown, where he bought a wig. From there he traveled to Salt Lake City, Utah. According to Melissa Powers, Franklin thought God had rendered him invisible to carry out his missions. "That's why he got so bold and ended up doing the Salt Lake City ones in broad daylight," she said.[50]

NINE

The Salt Lake City Murders

I didn't do it, but whoever did it was justified. [Fields and Martin] were race-mixing and that should be punishable by death. Race-mixing should be a capital crime.

—*Joseph Paul Franklin*

In the 1970s and 1980s, Salt Lake City, Utah, had experienced more serial murders than what might be considered typical for an American city. According to Salt Lake Police Detective Jim Bell, "a lot of the people arrested for serial murders around the country have spent time in Salt Lake City." Utah, and particularly Salt Lake, Bell said, holds the strange distinction of being host to more serial killing cases than any other state. Bell, who had investigated many serial killings in his time on the force, said he was not quite sure why this was the case, but he opined it may have had something to do with the confluence of two major national freeways, I-80 and I-15, both of which pass through the city. With these two major freeways forming a big X, it is a crossroads and, according to Bell, "a good town to get lost in." Bell said there may have been other reasons why serial killers visited the city. "It sounds weird," he said, "but some of them even told us they like Salt Lake City for the same reason everybody else likes it. It's clean, it's a nice place, they like the mountains and they like the people."[1]

When Franklin drove into Salt Lake City, he found it difficult to spot a racially mixed couple on the streets, which was hardly surprising considering the small numbers of African Americans who lived in the city. But within a matter of days he had found suitable targets for his intense rage at whites and blacks that had "broken God's laws" about racial mixing.

Using the alias Joseph Hart, a favorite false identity used by his hero William Quantrill, Franklin first registered at the Evergreen Motel on August 19, but after a short examination of his assigned room, he returned to the front desk and confronted the manager, Viola Bowles, about "'nigger hairs" on his bed. Franklin told Bowles he could not stay there and immediately checked out.[2]

He went instead to the World Motor Hotel, where he stayed for two nights before moving to the Siesta Motel on August 12. He left still owing for the second night. He was later described by the staff of the motels as having shoulder-length, blond, curly hair and wearing thick, tinted prescription glasses and a leather wrist-band with silver spikes.

During the following week, Franklin moved around, registering at different motels, including the Country Club Motel (August 14), the Sandman Motel (August 15), the Regal Inn Motel (August 16 and 17), the Se Rancho Motel (August 19), and the Scenic Motel (August 20). Franklin used various aliases to register including Charles Pitts, Joseph R. Hagman, William R. Jackson, and Joseph R. Hart. When Franklin registered at the Sandman Motel on the fifteenth, the motel's manager, Mary Rushton, was at the reception desk with her daughter Sherrie. Rushton thought Franklin had been on drugs, and when she checked his room, she discovered a handgun.[3]

During the early morning hours of August 13, the manager of the Siesta Motel, Reed Newburger, walked across the motel's parking lot to check if the license number Franklin (using the alias Charles Pitts) had written down was correct. It wasn't. Newburger wrote the correct license number on the registration slip. He thought nothing of it and did not challenge Franklin. However, Franklin had made a fatal mistake by not replacing the original licence plates with one of the false plates he kept in the trunk of his car. The mistake would eventually become an important link to his crimes.

A guest of the Country Club Motel, twenty-year-old Diana Luker spoke with Franklin during his stay there. He told her he had been traveling for three or four weeks, having come from New York, and that he liked to travel, sometimes sleeping out in his car, and that he jogged to stay in good condition. Franklin invited her out for dinner or a show, but she made an excuse and told him to call her the following week.[4]

On the morning of August 9, a seventeen-year-old girl, Gene Cox, had been walking near the Salt Lake City Palace—an indoor arena used for hockey, basketball, and musical events—with her friend Shaun Jones when Franklin pulled up and began talking to her. He introduced himself as "Joe Hart" and asked Cox for her phone number, which she readily gave to him. He phoned her the next day and asked her out. She agreed and he picked her up around 11:00 a.m. They spent the day together in Bountiful, a small community a few miles north of Salt Lake City. Franklin took her to the Lagoon Amusement Park, where she worked. During their conversations, Franklin spoke to her about blacks, although she could not remember much of what was said. She did recall he commented about how blacks and whites intermixed in the city. She also saw he had a handgun in the glove compartment of his car. After Franklin took Gene home, she never saw him again, although they did speak on the phone when he phoned later that night. During the conversation, she told him she did not want to see him again.[5]

On August 10, under the alias Joe Price, Franklin took his car to the Gordon Wilson Chevrolet dealership and requested that the turn signals on his Camaro be repaired and a front body panel replaced. He returned to the dealership two days later to collect his car.

On Sunday evening, August 17, around 10:00 p.m., two prostitutes, Mickie McHenry and Cindy (Sparkle) Taylor, were sitting on a wall at their usual place of business, 400 South State Street, when a man who introduced himself as Joe pulled up driving a brown Camaro. Joseph Franklin asked Mickie if she would like to go get a drink. She had not planned on picking up clients that day, but she agreed, and Franklin did not at first appear to be threatening. As she got in his car, she confessed that she was not old enough to drink and that she charged forty dollars for sexual favors. Franklin and Mickie rode around for a while, stopping to eat sandwiches at the Whataburger Restaurant before checking into Franklin's motel.[6]

Det. Don Bell, who had been with the Salt Lake City police department since 1971 and worked on every major case since 1979, described the eighteen-year-old Mickie as "a struggling college student . . . so she would go out two days a week on one of the streets that a lot of prostitutes worked on."[7] As Franklin and the girl drove around town he began to ask her if she had ever been with "a nigger or anything like that." Franklin told her that all African Americans were like "apes, not very intelligent," and "all of them should be killed." He also told Mickie that his animus towards African Americans also extended to those who associated with them, including "white girls" who even "spoke to a black man."[8] He said his favorite subject was "killing" and that he had "killed niggers" before. He then offered to kill Mickie's pimp if she so desired and went on to describe the best way to kill—"wait until they were in a crowd and shoot them."[9] Later, they again discussed killing the two black pimps. Mickie warned Franklin that he would be caught. He disagreed and told her, "You follow them and you pick out the right time [and] even if it's in a crowd you can just shoot them, and if there's enough cars or something hiding you . . . you can get away with it."[10]

Franklin also told her he was a member of the Ku Klux Klan, he had extensive knowledge of the organization, and he knew all the different groups and who their leaders were. He also told her he had killed blacks in the past and asked her to make a list of black pimps in the area so he could come back and kill them.

Mickie saw that Franklin was armed with two handguns, and he offered her one of them so she could kill an African American man who had been standing on the street as they pulled up at a stop sign. When she declined the offer, Franklin told her he was a contract hit man for the Ku Klux Klan and asked her if she wanted him to "kill those niggers." Mickie said no. She told him to put the gun away and became very concerned about what he was going to do. Franklin then told her, "It's real easy. I've done work like this before. You just walk up, you shoot 'em, and everybody is concerned with them falling, no one pays any attention to you." While driving past Liberty Park, Mickie told Franklin that the east side of the park was predominantly white, the west side was predominantly Mexican, and the middle was where "the blacks and the pimps all hang out . . . to pick up the girls."[11]

Franklin took Mickie to Room 208 of the Regal Inn. Before having sex, Franklin insisted on taking nude photos of her holding his rifles and pistols. He asked her for a list of all the black pimps in town so he could kill them, and when a black bellhop went by the room, he tossed a gun into her lap and invited her to shoot the man and "watch him squirm."[12] Later, after she was picked up for questioning by police officers, Mickie was shown an album of Franklin's photos. She recognized one girl, another prostitute, who worked in Salt Lake City and went by the name of Susan.

During the time she spent with Franklin, Mickie noticed two rifles that were standing in the corner of the room. One of them had a black rubber pad on the butt and "some type of carving" on the stock. She also noticed a silver handgun. Franklin did not talk about them, and Mickie was afraid to ask. She also noticed Franklin's tattoos, an eagle and the Grim Reaper. After having sex with Mickie, Franklin took her to her apartment. She introduced him to her roommate Cindy Taylor, and all three made small talk until Franklin left.[13]

The following day Lori Jacobs was walking south on 500 East at 400 South at around 10:00 a.m., when Franklin pulled into a parking lot near the sidewalk and began talking to her. He told her his name was Joe, that he was from Bowling Green, Kentucky, and that he was on his way to California. According to Jacobs, he began talking about blacks and started ranting, expressing his hatred towards African Americans. Franklin said there were "too many niggers in Bowling Green." He also told her that he "didn't go around Liberty Park because there were too many niggers [there]." Jacobs made the mistake of telling Franklin she worked as a lifeguard at a Liberty park swimming pool. Franklin told her that he would return to see her but would not go swimming in Liberty Park as there were "niggers that swim there."[14] Two or three days later he drove by the pool looking for her, but she had been disturbed by Franklin's racist rants and hid from him.

Around this time, Franklin tried to pick up another girl, Sylvia Webb, whom he had seen standing at a bus stop. He offered her a ride home. According to Webb, "around the time of the homicides," Franklin asked her if she wanted a lift. Webb accepted, and Franklin drove her home. During the journey, Franklin asked her if she had dated blacks. She told him she hadn't. Franklin praised her and told her it made him angry to see blacks and whites together.[15]

Around 5:30 p.m. on August 20, Franklin picked up two more girls, Sandy Vigil and Rhonda Rainwaters, who were hitchhiking in the vicinity of 445 East 800 South to downtown. The girls wanted to cash a check before the banks closed at 6:00 p.m. During the short ride, Franklin, who called himself Herb, asked if both girls would "go out with him." Even though they both admitted they were "frightened" of him, they gave him their names and addresses. Franklin told them "that he hated to see white girls with niggers because it wasn't right." He also told the girls of his intense hatred of African Americans and asked whether the girls had "gone out with blacks." When they told him they never dated African American men, he asked to see them again later in the evening. The girls begged off, and as they exited his car, he gave them a calling card with the initials FIB printed on it. Later that evening, between 9:00 and 9:20 p.m., Vigil and Rainwaters spotted Franklin in his car in the downtown area.[16]

By 10:00 p.m. Franklin had arrived at Liberty Park. Gary Spicer, who lived nearby, saw a brown Camaro turn into his driveway then drive down the sidewalk and into a vacant lot next to his house. Spicer saw Franklin exit his car, walk to the trunk, and lift something out.

At 9:00 p.m. on Wednesday, August 20, twenty-year-old African American Theodore T. Fields telephoned fifteen-year-old Karma Ingersol, who was white, and asked her if she would like to go jogging. Ted was the son of Rev. Theodore Fields, and he had two sisters, eighteen-year-old Linda and seventeen-year-old Martha. Karma and Ted had dated between December 1979 and May 1980, when they broke up. Karma's parents had been opposed to the relationship, as they did not believe their daughter should "date blacks." However, the couple still remained friends.

During the telephone conversation, Karma asked her friend Terry Elrod, who was also fifteen and white, if she wanted to join them, and she reluctantly agreed. Unknown to Karma, Ted had also invited his friend, eighteen-year-old African American David L. Martin (a friend with whom he boxed at the Police Athletic League Gym), to join them. Ted and David's parents described the two young men as "sociable, clean cut . . . without any known enemies."[17]

The foursome decided on a route through Liberty Park that Ted and Karma had used the night before. It was an opportunity to enjoy the last days of summer in their favorite urban park. Terry and Karma walked to 700 West and 900 South where Ted and David picked the girls up and drove to David's home. They parked the car and began jogging towards Liberty Park. When they passed the 7-Eleven at 900 South 500 East, Terry remembered someone yelling Martin's and Ingersol's names, but the group did not stop to talk. It was a friend of Ingersol's, Earl Burnett, who was standing in the parking lot nearby.[18]

A neighborhood resident, Sefo Manu, saw a man in a Camaro drive northbound on the west loop of Liberty Park at a high rate of speed before jumping a curb and continuing northbound on 500 East. Manu described the driver as five-eleven, with shoulder-length hair. He said that the car was newer than his own 1974 Camaro, was dark maroon with red trim, and had mag wheels with writing on all four tires, a spoiler, and a dual exhaust. When the driver reached 900 South, Manu said, he ran a red light and then made a U-turn, finally pulling into a field on the northwest corner of 500 East 900 South. Gary Spicer and John Fellows, who both lived near the park, also noticed a dark Camaro with mag wheels. Spicer saw the car park in the lot between his house and an intersection and saw a man about six feet tall get out of the car.[19]

Once inside the park, the Ted and his friends began jogging south along the west loop until they reached the tennis courts where Karma and Terry became winded, unable to run any farther for the moment. When the girls reached 600 East and 1300 South, still inside the park, Ted and David joined them once again. As the group walked along they were met by two other joggers, a young couple, and exchanged greetings. The group continued jogging and exited the park at 600 East and 900 South and headed west toward 500 East and 900 South.

Around 10:15 p.m. the four were within a crosswalk about halfway across the road intersection of 500 East and 900 South Street. As they continued jogging, Ted was in front with Karma, while Terry and David were behind him when the first shots were fired. Franklin had positioned himself in the midst of tall weeds in the vacant lot near Gary Spicer's house. No one observed him fire his rifle. As Terry heard the sound of the shot, she felt her arm burn, and it began to bleed. Karma thought the first shot sounded like a firecracker. Terry then heard a second shot, and David started to fall. Ted caught him in his arms as David cried out, "Oh, my God, Ted, they've got me." All three began pulling David to the curb as Ted told the girls to run.[20]

Karma knew that Ted was right and both girls had to escape. They ran west on 900 South until they encountered Mary Biddlecomb, who was outside her home. As she looked behind her, Karma saw David in a sitting position with Ted trying to pull him to the curb. Within moments Ted had been hit and collapsed. A total of six shots had been fired.

A single bullet had entered the outside of David's upper right arm between the elbow and the shoulder. The bullet made two exit wounds on the inside of the arm but did not enter the body. A second bullet entered the left part of his chest near the left nipple and exited at the right shoulder near the neck, leaving three exit wounds. The bullet remained on the outside of the rib cage beneath the skin. A third bullet had entered the back approximately two inches to the right of the spine and twenty-three inches below the top of the head. The bullet entered the chest cavity, causing extensive injury especially to the right kidney and liver. The bullet then exited through the right upper chest at a position near the right nipple.

Ted had been shot in the back below the right shoulder blade. The bullet entered the chest cavity, perforating his aorta. A second bullet had entered the top of his right shoulder, traveling downward in the body, perforating the right lung, diaphragm, and the liver.

Gary Lamar Snow was standing with Mary Biddlecomb outside her apartment at 447 East Ninth South when he saw the four joggers. As he was leaving in his car and backing out of Biddlecomb's driveway, he heard a shot and then a second shot. He said he heard six shots in total. Snow ran back inside the apartment to phone the police. Twelve year-old Michelle Spicer had been with her friend Carrie Beauchaine when she heard rifle shots. They both looked out of a kitchen window, and Carrie saw the shooter getting up from a kneeling position in the field.[21]

Thirty-eight year-old Clarence Albert Levinston Jr. saw David Martin stumble while the other three gave him assistance. As he heard further shots, he knew immediately it was a sniper attack. He also knew the direction the shots were coming from, so he drove his car in front of the victims to give them some cover, blocking the crosswalk. The shots continued even as David and Ted lay mortally wounded.

Cindy Taylor, who had met Franklin the previous Sunday, was also in the area when the shooting started. She was approximately half a block north of the shooting when she heard the shots and saw David and Ted fall. Because Cindy was a prostitute, she did not want to get involved so she returned home. Neither Cindy nor Mickie connected Franklin with the shootings until days later, when Mickie discovered the victims were African American, and she remembered Franklin's statements about hating blacks. However, they chose not to inform the police, as they feared they would be arrested on charges of prostitution.[22]

Gary Spicer came out of his house once more when he heard shots fired. Spicer looked across to the field where he had observed the Camaro and saw a man he had observed earlier standing in the field firing his rifle then "crouching and running." He also saw him throw his rifle into the trunk of his car and drive away westbound on 900 South. Spicer said the man was wearing a flat-topped, wide-rimmed hat and a waist-length jacket.[23]

Marilyn Diane Wilson had been inside the nearby 7-Eleven when she heard shots fired. The third shot directed her attention to the crosswalk outside, where she saw a man lying on the ground and another falling to the ground. When she reached Ted and David, Clarence Levinston was already there standing over the two men. Wilson tried to assist the young men since she had some medical training. Wilson rolled both men over in her attempts to render aid. She found a pulse on both victims.

Police and rescue units raced to the scene. David, barely alive, was rushed to the hospital but died hours later. Ted was already dead by the time the ambulances arrived.

Shortly after the shooting, Karma made a hysterical phone call to her father, Lee Ingersol, telling him that Terry had been shot. Lee and his brother Mel immediately got into Lee's truck and drove to the scene of the shooting, arriving shortly after the police patrol units. Lee had been under the impression that his daughter had been planning on jogging with Terry that night and had no idea she was meeting Ted and David. Police later received several tips that Lee had harbored hatred towards African Americans, and he was questioned about it. He was quite open about his views and told police investigators that he held no particular prejudice against blacks but felt because of the social stigma attached to racial couples, it was in his daughter's best interests if she did not date blacks. He took a polygraph test that exonerated him from the crime.[24]

Detectives spoke to Terry, who was being treated at the nearby trauma center for her superficial wounds. She was still badly shaken but managed to tell police about the shooting. Salt Lake City detective Don Bell was unable to detect a motive for the attack. "These were two young boys," he said. "They'd never been in trouble with the police. We didn't have an outstanding motive. We didn't know whether it was something related to the girls, whether it was something related to the boys or simply just a case of mistaken identity. . . . We'd never had a homicide like this in Salt Lake City. We'd never had people just gunned down, especially young people gunned down in the middle of an intersection."[25]

The following morning, police investigators returned to the crime scene to conduct a more thorough search. In the field across from the park, they found tire tracks. Technicians photographed and measured them. Near the tracks police found six 30.30 bullet casings. Because some witnesses said they had heard shots coming from an abandoned building nearby, detectives concluded they simply heard the echo of shots.

Investigators retrieved the bullet slugs from the victims and sent them to the ATF Laboratory in San Francisco along with the casings to determine the type of gun the assassin used. ATF expert Ed Peterson concluded the six casings were all fired from the same rifle and the slugs were fired from the same rifle. Peterson identified the rifle involved as a Marlin manufactured with a Microgroove barrel, a gun that could fire seven shots and only eject six cartridges. Police also determined that the rifle could have been a Glenfield 30.30.[26]

Police searched gun shops and classified ads for recent purchases, and investigators assembled 150 weapons that matched the descriptions. They tested each one, but none had fired the bullets found at the scene.[27] The doctor who performed the autopsy on Fields and Martin concluded their wounds were consistent with seven shots being fired from the field where Gary Spicer and John Fellows had seen a white man acting suspiciously. When a $5,000 reward was posted for information about the rifle, dozens of people handed in similar rifles to police claiming to have purchased the weapon from a man resembling Franklin.[28]

The four young joggers all belonged to the same Protestant church, but the killings were seen by many in the African American community as a consequence of Mormon hatred for blacks. The assumption was based on the notion that Mormons had always "hated black folks," and given the history of black exclusion from the Mormon hierarchy, there appeared to be some truth in the matter.[29] Accordingly, in the immediate aftermath of the shootings and in an effort to calm the black community's fears, police chief Bud Willoughby, a huge man who acted like a typical hard-nosed cop, announced that the shootings were not racially motivated. It was a serious error and allowed the police investigators to concentrate their efforts on what turned out to be false leads.

The first suspect in the case was African American George Phillip Moore, who had allegedly raped Terry Elrod some months before the shooting. Moore had been on bail awaiting trial. Terry thought she might have been the intended victim in the shooting because Moore was allegedly trying to silence her.[30] Other suspects included Brian Price, who Ted had once fought with in Dec's Restaurant. Salt Lake City police investigated the case, but no charges were made.

Meanwhile, detectives followed up other leads and interviewed family members, including Terry Elrod's father, Ralph "Teach" Elrod, who appeared to be a likely suspect as he was the leader of a biker gang, The Barons, and reputedly a member of the Ku Klux Klan. Police spent three days tracking him down. When they found him, he agreed to come in for questioning. Investigators were thorough with him. He said he had been on a whitewater-rafting trip at the time of the shootings and friends could support his story. Police also suspected he may have been aided in the shooting by his cousin, Mel "Caesar" Boswell, also a member of the gang. It was common knowledge that Ralph was upset by his daughter's relationship with an African American man. Police initially thought that because a black man had raped Terry, her father might have taken steps to put an end to the relationship. However, Terry insisted her father did not object to her dating African Americans. She also told police that her father had met Ted Fields at one time and told her he liked him.[31] Both Ralph Elrod and Mel Boswell were given polygraph tests along with other members of the gang, and all were eventually eliminated as suspects.

Police investigators also had to consider the possibility that the shootings were the result of a drug connection because Karma told police that Ted Fields had been dealing drugs—mostly marijuana. She told them that a week before the shootings, Ted had been trying to raise $300 to buy drugs to sell. Karma offered to put up half the money.[32] Nineteen year-old Troy Harris corroborated Karma's story, telling police that on August 19, 1980, he had been approached by Ted and asked if he wanted to put up seventy-five dollars to buy some speed to resell for profit.[33]

When Earl Burnett was interviewed, he told investigators he was a close friend of Ted Fields, and that the only reason David Martin had been shot was because he resembled Burnett. According to Burnett, he and Fields were dating two prostitutes, nineteen-year-old Tamara Borden and nineteen-year-old Stephanie Peck, between May and July 1980. During the period they were going out with the girls, they tried to persuade them to give up prostitution. Burnett said the girls' pimps made no direct threats, although Karma thought the girls may have arranged the shooting. Terry said she heard from Earl Burnett that the pimps had made threats towards Ted. Police received information that Borden's pimp, twenty-three-year-old Earl Anthony Lee, had threatened Fields by telling him, "If I ever see you alone on the street I'll get you." Lee denied making the statement. The police questioned the girls and their pimps but could find no evidence that would link them to the shootings.[34]

When police investigators ran out of suspects to question, they returned to the crime scene and began to canvass the neighborhood. When they finally got around to interviewing Gary Spicer, they knew they had their important lead. Spicer told police that he had seen a slender white man packing or unpacking something in the trunk of his car, and when Spicer spoke to him, the man jumped in his Camaro and drove away. The detectives wondered if this car could be linked to the tire tracks found at the scene of the shooting.

Meanwhile, Salt Lake City authorities were concerned the killings may have been race-related, which was the opinion of the Fields and Martin families. "The general public wanted to know about the killings," Det. Don Bell said. "They wanted to know if they were race-related."[35] The U.S. Department of Justice in Washington, D.C., was concerned that civil rights violations may have been committed. Assistant attorney Steve Snarr was brought in to monitor the case. "Members of the black community were particularly concerned," Snarr said, "and were somewhat vocal about whether this was racially motivated but at the time there were no clear answers."[36]

FBI Special Agent Curtis Jensen from the Salt Lake City FBI Office was assigned to assist the Salt Lake City police. "When I first heard about this case," Jensen said, "I was incensed. It caused a great deal of concern among not just the black community, but all the community in Salt Lake City. They felt there was an assassin loose and it could happen again."[37]

The FBI and the Salt Lake City police began to believe the assassin had fled the area, so the FBI sent out nationwide teletypes to local and federal agencies describing details of the crime, including the weapon and shell casings. A reward of $50,000 was offered to promote the public's help, and calls flooded in. However, most informants who came forward were judged to be fantasists or were simply after the reward money.[38]

However, police did find one other important lead. It was Mickie, the prostitute who had met Franklin under the assumed name Bill Hagman. Although Mickie was at first reluctant to cooperate because she was a prostitute, Don Bell persuaded her to tell her story, and she agreed to be interviewed. At first Bell thought Mickie may have been an unreliable witness or she may have been just another false witness who was looking for the reward money. And even if Mickie's story was true, the role Hagman played was unclear. "Did it have anything to do with the killings," Bell wondered, "or was this just a bad guy who was blowing through town and was trying to [impress] this part-time hooker?"[39] Bell thought that if Mickie could identify the weapons she saw in the suspect's motel room, her story would have more weight. However, after looking at a picture display of the suspected types of weapons, Mickie failed to identify them, and her story appeared to be yet another dead end.

But Detective Bell, despite his doubts, continued to work with Mickie and Cindy, asking them to work with a police artist to make a composite sketch of Hagman. Salt Lake City detectives also used a psychic to help in their investigation. Many years later, anonymous detectives confirmed to the *Deseret News* that the department had used paranormal help in the past, including the investigation into the murders of Ted Fields and David Martin. Although police knew Franklin had been driving a Chevy, a psychic was able to accurately describe the car's black and white checked seat covers and a cigarette burn on the right armrest. "When your leads peter out, you use what you can," a former police official said.[40]

The investigation took an unexpected turn when Salt Lake City police received a response from the telex that had been sent out by the FBI after the shooting. Police in Cincinnati were investigating a similar unsolved double murder that happened two months earlier.

Franklin had no remorse in killing Ted Fields and David Martin, and he later confessed the two young men "had it coming" because they had "no business race-mixing."[41]

When Franklin fled from Liberty Park, he was prepared for any eventuality. He "actually had two rifles, another loaded with a Remington loaded in the back, in case any cops were chasing."[42] According to Det. Don Bell, Franklin "left here. He went north to a town, north of Salt Lake City, Ogden. He took the freeway across Nevada to Winnenaka, Battle Mountain, and Reno into San Francisco and he sold the rifle that he killed the kids [with] at a flea market outside of the Bay area." Detective Bell sent his team to the flea market outside San Francisco and they interviewed gun dealers and other witnesses. "They saturated the flea market," Bell said, "and they came up with witnesses who remembered Joseph Paul Franklin and remembered that he was selling guns but we could never find the gun [that killed Fields and Martin]."[43]

Whether Franklin drove to San Francisco after the shootings is unclear. Franklin denies it. However, by August 27, he had returned to Johnstown and stayed there for a few weeks, buying wigs on two occasions. By September 23 he was in Florence, Kentucky, unaware that law enforcement agencies were closing in on him. However, it was Franklin's arrogance, not police investigatory skills, that eventually led to his own demise.

— TEN —

Manhunt

I found out later through an article in the *Washington Post* that they . . . finally
. . . began to connect the Vernon Jordan shooting, the Cincinnati shooting, and the
Johnstown, Pennsylvania shooting . . . because they happened within such a short
period.

—*Joseph Paul Franklin*

om Gardner, who worked for the Cincinnati Police Homicide Unit, had been
monitoring information from around the United States that matched similar
shootings to the Evans Brown and Layne murders. On August 21, 1980, he
read in the news about a double homicide in Salt Lake City that occurred the previous day. Alarm bells rang. Gardner contacted the Salt Lake City Police Homicide
Unit and spoke with Sgt. Robert Nievaard, one of the investigating officers. Both
police officers decided to stay in touch and exchange details of the Salt Lake City
and Cincinnati murders.

On August 26 Gardner and Nievaard came to the conclusion that the murders
were similar, and the modus operandi fit other shootings that had occurred in Indianapolis, Oklahoma City, and Johnstown. They began to think they might have
a serial killer on their hands. The officers planned a meeting to bring in representatives from the city police forces that had unsolved sniper-shooting cases, along with
representatives of any other interested agencies, including the FBI. The meeting was
planned for September 15, 1980.[1]

Salt Lake City detective Don Bell had few doubts that the same individual had committed both sets of murders in Cincinnati and Salt Lake City and that it was the kind of killer they not encountered before 1980. "Once we were made aware of this information," Bell said, "we were pretty much convinced we were dealing with the same killer from back east, and this was actually our first real involvement with what is commonly now referred to as a traveling serial killer. This was a new concept to everybody not just out in Salt Lake. It was a new concept anywhere in the country, that killers would just travel across the country."[2]

While police in both states met in Cincinnati to compare the two shootings, Detective Bell went to work on the slim lead provided by Mickie, the prostitute Franklin had picked up. He checked out the motel she had visited with Franklin and found a registration card dated August 16, 1980, in the name of Bill Hagman, four days before the murders. Bell asked the FBI to search their database, but nothing came up, so Bell decided the name was an alias.

The FBI laboratory in Washington, D.C., dusted the motel registration card for latent fingerprints but found none. They also analyzed the signature on the card and noticed some unique characteristics that would make it easy to identify. Meanwhile the Salt Lake City team of investigators combed other areas of the city and questioned motel managers. "They conducted a search of all motel rooms from Ogden, which is thirty miles north [of Salt Lake City] to Provo which is thirty miles south," FBI agent Curtis Jensen said, "and they located about eight motels where this individual had stayed using false names each one different, using phoney addresses and using false license numbers for his car."[3]

Investigators also discovered that the suspect had stayed at the Scenic Motel on August 20, which was only nine blocks from Liberty Park. Though Franklin used different names at the motels, the FBI confirmed that the handwriting was the same. They also discovered that one of the cards yielded a fingerprint, but a check of the national fingerprint database showed no matches.

At the Sandman Motel, investigators found a registration card that listed a Camaro with two license numbers. It was the break detectives were looking for, and after they questioned the owner of the motel, they discovered that Reed Newburger had written the correct license number after checking the vehicles in the motel's parking lot. "[Newburger] must have been in his late seventies or early eighties,"

Bell said. "He went out every night around three o'clock in the morning and would take all of these motel registration slips and walk by all the cars and check their license plate numbers against what was put on the cards because he was so sure that his guests were going to steal a pillow or pillow case."[4]

Salt Lake City detectives Wagaman and Leary tracked down the history of the brown Camaro and found it had been registered to a member of a prominent Kentucky family, William Embry Jr. of 2129 Lakeside Drive, Lexington. "[Detectives] made contact with the police agency there," Bell said, "and tracked down the actual registered owner of this car. He had in fact sold the car to another person some months before."[5] Although the buyer had used a false name, police were able to build a composite sketch of him from the owner and one of his friends, Gary Barkley. Barkley remembered Franklin well and was able to provide the Louisville police artist with a composite. Additionally, one of the prostitutes who had met Franklin in Salt Lake City, Cindy Taylor, had been a part-time artist and was able to draw her own sketch of the suspect before working with the police artist. When the two sketches were compared, there was a remarkable similarity.

The police now had a car license number and a sketch of the suspect. On September 15, police representatives from the homicide units of Oklahoma City, Indianapolis, Cincinnati, Johnstown, and Salt Lake City police departments met at the Hamilton County coroner's office in Cincinnati. During the meeting, patterns and similarities began to emerge from the discussions. During the conference each police department presented its particular sniper case for review and open discussion.

Attendees at the conference agreed that although there were similarities in each homicide, sufficient evidence did not exist to link one with another. However, Salt Lake City officers revealed that a witness at the scene of the Salt Lake murders had observed a 1975 Chevrolet Camaro driven by a white man exit an empty lot near the shooting. The officers also told the others about Reed Newburger's license plate story and how they found the car's original through the help of the Kentucky State Police.

Detective Wagaman had entered the license plate and all the aliases used in the Salt Lake City area into the National Crime Information Center (NCIC)—a computer database that links over 57,000 law agencies nationwide. Wagaman's entry stated that the wanted vehicle was involved in a double homicide. On September 25, over a month after the Salt Lake City murders and ten days after the police conference, the FBI database produced results when an incident in Florence, Kentucky, led to the identification of the killer. When the conference attendees were contacted, they all now agreed the same killer was probably responsible for all the sniper shootings.

When Joseph Franklin had arrived in Florence, Kentucky, from Johnstown on September 23, he registered at the Scottish Inn, room 138, using his real name. On September 24 he drove to a nearby town, Covington, where he picked up a duplicate driver's license at the courthouse.

On the evening of September 25, Florence police officers and Boone County sheriff's deputies went to the Scottish Inn to arrest Gary Kirk, a nineteen-year-old Indiana native who was responsible, police believed, for armed robbery, possession of marijuana, and possession of a stolen car. Kirk had been staying in the room next to Franklin's.[6] When police arrived, there were seven or eight police cars in the parking lot with red lights flashing and radios blaring. Franklin contacted the manager of the motel and complained about the noise. "What are the cops doing," Franklin said, "and how come it is so noisy? I'm going to leave if you don't quiet down."[7]

According to Florence police officer Jim Riley, Franklin even rang the police dispatcher to complain. "This gentleman was quite upset," Riley said. "He wanted to know what the police were doing outside his door. How come so many police-men were there? Why is his car blocked in and that kind of stuff. He kept calling the dispatcher and after about the fourth or fifth call the chief said 'They're not looking for you sir, we've got a robbery.'"[8]

When the manager of the motel spoke to Florence patrolman Dennis Collins he informed Collins about "one of his guests" who was complaining about the police presence and the fact that his car was blocked in. The officers became suspicious of Franklin's complaints, so Collins ran a check on the station computer. At the same time, Collins saw a revolver on the seat of the Camaro.[9] When the results were returned, he knew Franklin's car was a wanted vehicle for a double homicide. When officers went to room 138, they spoke with Franklin, who they described as a slender white man with a slow Southern drawl. Inside officers saw two shotguns on the bed. They immediately handcuffed him and took him to the Florence police station for questioning. Franklin offered no resistance.[10] Cincinnati detective Capt. Donald Slaughter also said Franklin had a "multiplicity of identification cards" on him when he was arrested.[11]

When questioned at the police station, he at first denied ever having been to Utah, then said he had been there five years before, and then conceded he had been there in August. He became nervous when the interrogating officer began to ask about a "double homicide" involving his Camaro.

Florence police impounded the Camaro and informed the Salt Lake City police. Detective Bell and one of his colleagues took the next flight to Kentucky. The latent prints police removed from the Camaro matched those on file with the Mobile Police Department. According to Salt Lake City assistant attorney Steve Snarr, the Camaro was crucial to the case. "The car that Mr. Franklin was driving," Snarr said, "was unique. It had a unique color. It had red pinstriping that was the custom type of striping. It also had unique interior features and non-standard tires and other features that were noticeable to various witnesses who had observed the car in the Salt Lake area."[12]

In Florence, evidence technicians scoured the Camaro for clues. They took photos of its tires, hoping to match them with the tread marks found near the crime scene in Salt Lake City. According to Detective Bell, it was a major breakthrough for his case. "The tires were sort of a new prototype that were only being released east of the Mississippi," he said, " so for tires to show in a dirt field in Salt Lake City they would have to have been purchased at that time east of the Mississippi. That placed that car with that man in our city."[13]

Franklin was taken to a room in the police station to be interviewed by Det. Jesse Baker. "He would keep repeating questions," Baker said. "He would take a long time to respond to the questions and it was just very apparent that this gentleman had a lot to hide."[14] Baker said Franklin appeared unperturbed by questions concerning the stolen vehicle charge but became emotional when he was questioned about the Utah murders.[15] Thirty or forty minutes into the interview, Baker left the room, leaving Franklin with Officer Jim Riley. After Riley heard a knock on the door, he "opened [it] and there was an officer coming to let me know about the search warrant." Just as Baker returned to the room and began speaking to Riley he "heard a noise and saw [Franklin] going out the window."[16]

Franklin believed God had assisted in his escape. "The Lord didn't think my time had come to be caught," he said. "I was handcuffed to a chair. I prayed to the Lord. An hour later this blonde guy took the handcuffs off and left the room. I already knew where the window was because earlier that night a guy had rapped at the window and wanted to know how to get into the Florence police headquarters and I told him."[17]

Franklin jumped out the window, ran to the street, and began hitchhiking. Elza Harrell of Erlanger, Kentucky, picked Franklin up in front of Booth Hospital around

9:00 a.m., and he asked her if she could drop him off in Cincinnati. However, Harrell said it was too far and instead dropped him off at Frisch's Restaurant on Dixie Highway. Harrell later told police Franklin had been carrying a "large wad of money." After she dropped him off, Franklin gave her five dollars.

At Frisch's Restaurant Franklin approached Mark Gaunt and asked him if he would drive him to Over the Rhine, a downtown Cincinnati neighbourhood established by German immigrants who were reminded of the famous German river. Franklin offered Gaunt ten dollars to take him. The young man agreed and dropped Franklin off near Lunkenheimers, near Harrison Avenue Viaduct. At the nearby Western Hills Shopping Mall in Cincinnati, Franklin had his hair dyed by Debra Warner at Asimus Hair Center and later walked to Woolworth's and bought new clothes from sales assistant Patrick Cruse. Franklin's next stop in the shopping mall was McAlpine's, where he bought Hush Puppy shoes from Linda Hunter. According to a statement Hunter made to police, Franklin made a racial comment during the purchase.[18]

After shopping at the mall, Franklin caught a bus to Columbus, Ohio.[19] He spent the next day "sightseeing" at Ohio State University before taking a bus to Charleston, West Virginia; Winston-Salem, North Carolina; and finally to Atlanta, where he visited the home of Joseph Kitts in Camblee sometime around September 27. He then drove to Montgomery on October 5 to obtain a birth certificate for Joseph Kitts from the Bureau of Vital Statistics.[20] It is not known if the real Joseph Kitts knew Franklin. More likely Franklin had been simply researching a stranger's background to construct a new identity.

Though Franklin had escaped from police custody, the police still had his wallet containing his driver's license and photo. Detective Bell recalled how closely the photo resembled the two composite sketches. "Looking at that license," Bell said, "it was almost eerie. It almost looked like the composite that had been built up in Kentucky and the composite that I built out here in Salt Lake City [and] that we had done it using Joseph Paul Franklin's driver's license."[21]

Outside the Florence police station, trained dogs followed Franklin's scent for a few blocks then lost his trail. Det. Clay Newman of the Boone-Florence Felony Squad carried out a door-to-door search. Having no luck in recapturing Franklin, police filed charges of first degree escape and possession of stolen property.[22] The FBI issued a federal warrant for "unlawful flight to avoid prosecution." Investigators hoped the resources of the FBI could stop Franklin before he killed again.

Agents tracked Franklin's movements over the previous year and discovered they had coincided with several bank robberies. They showed his photo to bank tellers, who identified him.

On October 4 the United States Attorney's Office in Salt Lake issued a complaint charging Franklin with a civil rights violation. Bail on the warrant was set at $50,000. Before the complaint was issued, Salt Lake City authorities had discussed the case with federal authorities and decided not to go ahead with a state charge for the present time, as the evidence against Franklin was still too flimsy and a federal charge would more likely stick.[23]

The FBI also asked all field offices to assist in the manhunt for Franklin. FBI spokesmen told the media their interest stemmed from their conclusions that he had become a prime suspect in the wounding of Vernon Jordan. Although ballistics tests on the two 30.06 caliber rifles found in Franklin's car showed that the weapons were not used to shoot Jordan or Fields and Martin, they were aware Franklin probably owned many other guns.[24] On October 4 federal agent Steve McVey said the bureau was forced to assume a high powered rifle used to shoot Vernon Jordan could have been used in attacks on African Americans in five other cities—and the attacks "could all have been the work of Joseph Paul Franklin." McVey also said the FBI was proceeding on the assumption that a 30.06 caliber rifle for sale in a Cincinnati newspaper ad on June 7 was the weapon with which Jordan was shot and that police in Oklahoma, Salt Lake City, and Cincinnati were also assuming the same killer had struck in their cities.[25] "The shootings could be linked," McVey said, "but then again they may not be. We don't know if [Franklin] is involved in the [Jordan] shooting but we're looking at it on that basis. We think there was a rifle being sold in Cincinnati around the time Jordan was shot and so far it hasn't checked out with a legitimate address. The circumstances pique our interest but there's no way to pin any of these things down to Franklin."[26]

The fugitive's face and description were handed to the media nationwide. FBI special agent Curtis Jensen of the Salt Lake City FBI office, who headed the manhunt, said, "He was almost immediately put on the Ten Most Wanted list because of the notoriety and because of the seriousness of the crime—the fact that he was a suspect not only in this crime [the Jordan shooting] but in the assassinations of a number of black people all across the United States. These were cases that hadn't been solved."[27] To make the Most Wanted list, Franklin's files had been reviewed among hundreds of others. The FBI Washington headquarters chose the ten most wanted criminals based on a suspect's immediate danger to society and the probability that the suspect would not stop killing until caught.

On October 15 FBI Civil Rights Section Chief David Kohl asked John Douglas, an FBI profiler, to do a "fugitive assessment on Franklin." Douglas visited the FBI Department in Washington, D.C., to review Franklin's file. He concluded that Franklin would brag about his crimes at some point. Douglas also believed there was a good chance Franklin would return to Mobile, his hometown, "where he would feel comfortable." The profiler said Franklin was "pretty sophisticated at this point about police matters and knew he was a very wanted man." Douglas guessed Franklin would probably stay somewhere along the Gulf Coast, "particularly while it was cold up north."[28]

FBI agents also learned that Franklin had written a threatening letter to President Jimmy Carter because of the president's pro–civil rights views. Carter was currently campaigning in the South, where Franklin had last been spotted. The 1980 presidential election was only weeks away, and if Franklin was going to carry out his earlier threats, Carter would be a prime target. FBI agents and Secret Service agents worked together to find Franklin before he could strike at the president. "[The Secret Service and FBI] decided that Joseph Paul Franklin, also known as James Clayton Vaughn, was definitely a threat to President Carter," Det. Don Bell said, "because he had written that he would like to kill him so they passed pictures of Joseph Paul Franklin in every city that the president was going to visit."[29]

When the two rifles and two handguns taken from Franklin's car were examined in the FBI laboratory in Washington, D.C., analysts could not find any link with the Salt Lake City or Cincinnati murders. The FBI also researched Franklin's background and discovered he had legally changed his name and that his birth name was James Clayton Vaughn. Delving deeply into his past, agents discovered that Franklin had a criminal record and outstanding warrants to his name.

In late August or early September, before his arrest in Florence, Franklin had visited his former wife, Anita Cooper, in Birmingham, Alabama, driving his brown Camaro. In late September or early October, he visited Cooper again. This time he was on foot. His hair was dyed and styled differently, and he was wearing new glasses. When she failed to recognize him, he laughed and said, "Well, if I could fool you, I could fool anyone." During their conversation, Franklin "was just talking about Salt Lake City and two joggers and all. And he said it would be funny, you know, 'it would be funny if I did it' . . ."[30]

Meanwhile, the FBI, Cincinnati police, and Salt Lake City investigators were assembling evidence against Franklin. On September 28 Cincinnati police received a phone call from thirty-three year-old Thelma Bryant, who had recognized Franklin as the person who approached her on Saturday June 7 at a Cincinnati gas station, struck up a conversation with her, and asked her for a date. On October 12 Paul Jacobs came forward to relate to police how Franklin had visited the Brothers III store in Bond Hill at the time of the shootings. After they learned how Franklin would often use classified ads to sell his rifles, police investigators checked local paper ads and discovered an ad in the *Cincinnati Enquirer* advertising a Remington 700 30.06 rifle for sale for $225. The ad asked potential buyers to call 371-5304 extension 21, which was the phone number and extension for room 21 of the Florence Motel, 7111 Dixie Highway. When police checked the motel records they found that the room was rented to "Eddie R. Logan," a Franklin alias. The motel card retained Franklin's fingerprints. Cincinnati police could now place Franklin in the Cincinnati area at the time of the Evans Brown and Layne shooting.[31]

FBI agents had discovered that Franklin was raising money by selling his blood. They guessed that the suspect felt safer selling blood than robbing banks when he was on the run. In October Franklin was spotted selling a pint of blood for seven dollars in a blood bank in Birmingham, Alabama, in a section of town frequented by transients and derelicts.[32] Birmingham police chief Bill Meyers had been tipped by the FBI that Mayor Richard Arrington could be a target. Following the report Birmingham police tightened security around the city's mayor.[33] The FBI sent information packs about Franklin to blood banks in cities across the South.

In October President Carter was campaigning in the South, including New Orleans, and the FBI was concerned Franklin might go there. The president was also due to make a campaign stop in Lakeland, a region situated in central Florida, thirty miles from Walt Disney World. Carter planned to attend a political rally on October 31 at Florida Southern College, which would also be attended by Sen. Lawton Chiles, Gov. Bob Graham, and former governor Reuben Askew. Philip McNiff was the special agent in charge of the Tampa FBI office, situated some thirty miles from Lakeland. McNiff told reporters, "[Franklin] is the type of person you do not want around during a presidential campaign. Also, we know he sent a threatening letter to President Carter in 1976. We wanted to make sure he was not down here when [the presidential candidates] were. We [would] feel much better knowing where he is at this time."[34]

Franklin was actually staying in a gospel mission flophouse in Tampa, Florida, where he spent three nights before traveling to Lakeland on Tuesday morning, October 28. He had recklessly used his birth name, James Clayton Vaughn, to check in. He was in Tampa prior to the announcement that Carter was to visit Lakeland. McNiff said their investigation revealed Franklin attempted to buy a gun. "He tried to buy a gun in this area," McNiff said. "He definitely was interested in buying a gun. I believe from looking at his MO [modus operandi or method of operation] he would have been buying a gun and then holding up a bank to get money. He would be mobile again."[35]

FBI agent Fernando Rivero visited Sera-Tec Biologicals, a plasma donation center in Lakeland, and gave the manager, twenty-five-year-old Allen Lee, a copy of Franklin's Wanted flyer. The blood bank had 18 employees and around 120 visitors a day. The FBI believed it was a likely place for Franklin to show up if he was in town. Rivero also mentioned the impending visit by President Carter and that Franklin was "very dangerous." Lee said it was not at all unusual for an FBI agent to ask him to keep a lookout for someone. He had seen all kinds of drifters, down-and-outs, and wanted criminals trying to make ends meet by giving blood for five dollars.[36]

At 3:00 p.m. on Tuesday, four hours after the FBI visit, Franklin entered the Sera-Tec clinic to sell his blood. Claudette Mallard looked up from the receptionist's desk to see a man walk in the door wearing brown cowboy boots and a long-sleeved shirt open to the waist. He was carrying a suitcase. When she asked him his name, Franklin replied "Thomas Alan Bohnert" and began filling out forms. Franklin was then examined by Dr E. C. Wright, a friendly sixty-six-year-old man who began working at Sera-Tec after thirty years in general practice in Waynesville, Ohio. He was unaware of the FBI visit. "Any past diseases? Tuberculosis? Do you have any allergies?" Wright asked, running down the usual check list for donors. "Franklin wouldn't say he had and he wouldn't say he hadn't . . . asking this man questions was like pulling teeth . . . he acted as if he was doing a favor to be there." Wright thought Franklin was "strangely quiet," and after he completed the examination, he gave Franklin an urinanalysis that was negative. Wright also took Franklin's blood pressure, which was normal. The examination was complete in eight minutes.[37]

Franklin walked to the donation room, which was filled with twenty-four imitation leather orange and brown contour beds and a cartoon of Sleepy the Dwarf that warned, "No sleeping while donating." He was hooked up to an IV as his blood was spun through a centrifuge. He remained on couch number sixteen until after the red blood cells had been returned to his body. The technicians noted Franklin's Grim Reaper and eagle tattoos. One of them quietly walked to Allen Lee's office and told him the donor seemed to fit the description on the FBI's Wanted flyer. After looking at Franklin, Lee thought he appeared nervous and his behavior erratic. Lee called the FBI office, which was only five blocks away, at 4:30 p.m. Agent Bruce Dando told Lee to try to keep him there.[38]

Dando and Agent Brooke Roberts decided to call Lakeland Police for assistance and Detectives Gerald Barlow and Ray Talman Jr. met them at the blood bank. They agreed to wait outside for Franklin to leave. Inside the blood bank Franklin was told to rest for fifteen minutes after he had finished giving his pint of blood. Franklin became surly and asked, "What if I refuse to stay?" However, he relented and decided to wait the fifteen minutes. Claudette Mallard noticed it was 5:00 p.m., nearly time to go home, when Franklin signed a receipt and she gave him a check for five dollars. "Where can I cash this?" he asked, and Mallard told him the banks were closed but he could cash it at the Little Lost Diner around the corner.

As Franklin walked out of the blood bank clutching his suitcase, two cars stopped abruptly behind him. Agent Roberts jumped out of his vehicle and told Franklin he was being arrested. He put up no resistance. The officers allowed Franklin to cash his check at the diner before driving him to the police station for a fingerprint check. Robert also noticed Franklin had tried to obliterate his tattoos.

Joseph Paul Franklin's arrest followed a nationwide manhunt that involved the federal government and authorities from numerous states. "That made me feel very important," Franklin later said, "I was kind of flattered, really."[39]

At the Lakeland police station, Edgar T. Pickett, a Lakeland police officer who had been named the FBI's Officer of the Year in 1975, compared the FBI fingerprints with Franklin's and confirmed his identity, particularly the right thumb, which had a scar and an enclosure to the core.[40] Police officers concluded that they "could not rule out" the possibility that Franklin's presence in Lakeland at the same time as President Carter was "more than coincidence." [41]

Franklin was detained in Tampa at the FBI office. At first he denied he was Franklin and continued trying to scrape his tattoos from his arms. The ink was too deep to erase them. When Franklin was told he could make a phone call, he decided to call his ex-wife, Anita. During the conversation, which occurred around 1:00 a.m. on October 29, she learned Franklin's real name. She had known him as Jim Anthony Cooper. The FBI taped the telephone call, and during the conversation, Franklin told Anita and her mother that he had been arrested and accused of racial killings. During the conversation, he admitted the charges were true. Franklin told Anita, "They got me for twelve homicides down here and four bank robberies and the funny thing is it's true." Near the beginning of the conversation he said, "Have you heard about the two joggers in Salt Lake? . . . I did that."[42]

Before Salt Lake City detectives arrived in Tampa, FBI agent Robert H. Dwyer conducted a five-hour interview with Franklin. Secret Service agents joined him. However, Franklin would not admit to any of the murders. But he did reveal his racism to agents. He told Dwyer that he had owned several weapons, particularly handguns and high-powered rifles, and that he considered himself to be an expert in their use. Dwyer said he, "specifically talked about the mixing of the black and white races, and expressed with very strong emotion his disapproval of such mixing." Dwyer said Franklin considered himself a racist, "and he expressed a very strong dislike for the black people and for Jews. And he specifically also stated that he had no remorseful feelings at all at the deaths of these people."[43]

During his interrogation, agents asked Franklin if he wanted anything to eat or drink. He replied that he would like to have a hamburger but only if the officers made sure it had not been prepared by "niggers."[44] Franklin refused a hamburger an agent offered him because the agent could not "guarantee [him] that that hamburger [was] not cooked by a nigger." During the interrogation, Franklin acknowledged having been in Salt Lake City from August 15 to August 22, 1980, and described four guns that he had had with him. He said that he had been to Liberty Park but had stopped going because he had seen a lot of racial mixing there. Franklin denied having been involved in the murders.

Following the FBI interview, Franklin was handed over to U.S. Marshals and taken to the U.S. Marshals' holding cell at the federal court building in Tampa. A small group of African Americans stood watching across the street as two FBI agents led Franklin one block through downtown Tampa to the courthouse.[45] At the arraignment, an attorney, James Whittemore, was appointed to represent Franklin. His attorney expressly forbade any further questioning of the suspect by either the FBI or Salt Lake City detectives. Efforts were made through the United States Attorney's Office in Tampa to question Franklin with his attorney present, but the offer was rejected.

Franklin was held on a $1 million bond. He also faced a hearing on whether he should be transferred to Salt Lake City where he would be indicted for violating the civil rights of Ted Fields and David Martin.[46] He appeared in court on Wednesday,

October 29, and later told reporters, "I'm innocent . . . [the charges are] all trumped up . . . because of my white racist views." Asked if he really held racist views he replied, "Oh, definitely, I'm against race-mixing and communism."[47] Asked if he intended to be on hand for President Carter's visit to Lakeland, Franklin replied, "No, I'm not interested at all in Jimmy Carter."[48] However, years later, Franklin said that if he had not been caught he "might have just started after government leaders . . . I would have got a lot more publicity that way and it would have made them look weak because . . . here's a guy who can actually commit assassinations and get away with 'em."[49]

FBI director William Webster announced Franklin would be charged with violating the civil rights of the Salt Lake City joggers. In Salt Lake City, U.S. Attorney Ron Rencher said Franklin killed the two joggers because of "their race" and that his office "will immediately seek to have Franklin returned here to face the federal civil rights charges."[50] Although Franklin had denied his guilt to FBI agents, he did confess his crimes to another inmate on October 29. On October 31 FBI agents in Tampa contacted Henry Bradford, a federal prisoner who shared a holding cell with Franklin. Bradford told agents that Franklin had admitted killing Fields and Martin.[51]

On November 2 FBI agents transported Franklin's Camaro to Salt Lake City. Special Agent Jensen and Salt Lake City police conducted a through search of the car, including the interior and undercarriage, and items found were handed over to Jensen for processing at the FBI laboratory in Washington. A few weeks later Jensen received all the motel registration cards that linked Franklin with his crimes along with the spent cartridges, slugs, and bullet fragments.[52]

On November 5 U.S. Magistrate Paul Game was satisfied that Franklin was the man indicted in Salt Lake City on federal charges of depriving Fields and Martin of their civil rights by killing them. He ordered that Franklin be extradited to Utah. Game ordered the paperwork be prepared to transport Franklin to Utah, and he granted a government motion to take handwriting samples because prosecutors claimed he used eighteen aliases.

During the brief removal hearing, Assistant U.S. Attorney Lynn Cole called FBI arresting agent Fernando Rivero to the stand. Rivero testified that he identified Franklin through fingerprints and a photo on a driver's license left behind when Franklin escaped from police custody in Kentucky in September of 1980. The fingerprints matched those found on a brown Camaro, Rivero said, which witnesses identified at the scene of the Salt Lake City murders. U.S. Attorney Gary Betz told

Game that Franklin was wanted for questioning in the May 29 shooting of Vernon Jordan. Betz added that authorities also wanted to talk to Franklin about ten sniper slayings in four other cities, the alleged defrauding of a Utah hotel, a Georgia bank robbery, and the fraudulent use of identification to obtain a firearm. Game was also told of an escape warrant from police in Florence, Kentucky, and federal warrants charging Franklin with robbing two banks in Nashville, Tennessee. He added that Franklin was a drifter who had not held a job for three years and had used twelve wigs and other disguises to avoid authorities.[53]

On November 5 Salt Lake City detectives made another attempt at finding the rifle used in the Salt Lake City shootings. A team sent to southern Wyoming and northern Colorado was assisted by local law enforcement agencies. The detectives scoured newspaper ads, motels, and gun shops for the weapon and traces of Franklin, but the search proved fruitless.[54]

The same day Salt Lake City deputy county attorney Robert Stott prepared a complaint. Stott had been assigned to the case from the beginning and was familiar with the circumstances surrounding the shooting. The complaint and warrant charged Franklin with two counts of first degree murder. It was signed by a judge, who stated that Franklin would not be eligible for bail. Stott also prepared an affidavit and court order requesting that the probable cause statement and list of witnesses be sealed because of the potential danger to witnesses. However, state charges of murder were held in abeyance in favor of the government's civil rights case against Franklin.

On November 7 Franklin was transported to Salt Lake City to stand trial for the murders of Ted Fields and David Martin. He was flown by private jet with FBI special agent Robert H. Dwyer.

On the plane Franklin began talking to Agent Dwyer, who recorded the conversation after reading him his Miranda rights and receiving his consent. John Douglas had advised Agent Dwyer that if Franklin were extradited by private plane rather than a commercial flight, agents would be able to use the opportunity to elicit a confession from Franklin. Douglas knew that Franklin was afraid of flying, therefore the suspect would "look for emotional support to whoever was accompanying him."[55] During the flight Franklin began to act exactly as Douglas had suggested, and before they had landed at Salt Lake City airport, the killer had revealed numerous details of his three-year murder spree. However, Salt Lake City police and FBI agents were not at all convinced they had sufficient evidence to charge Franklin with the Salt Lake City sniper shootings.

ELEVEN

Denials and Confessions

I was on a holy war against evildoers. Evildoers were interracial couples, blacks, and Jews. I was the executioner, the judge, and the jury.

—Joseph Paul Franklin

D uring the plane flight to Salt Lake City Franklin began to give FBI special agent Robert H. Dwyer "chapter and verse" on his techniques and the disguises he had used to commit his crimes. Dwyer had taken John Douglas's advice and initiated a conversation with Franklin during the flight. With his mouth running off in various directions, Franklin even placed himself in various cities at times when sniping murders had occurred. The only crime Franklin would not admit to was the shooting of Vernon Jordan. Douglas believed this was because Franklin was ashamed he had not succeeded in killing the civil rights leader and believed "his place in history was suspect."[1]

During the flight Dwyer enacted another ploy to get Franklin to be more forthcoming about his crimes. Dwyer asked the pilot to fly over the Utah State Penitentiary. Dwyer pointed the prison out to Franklin and told him that this was the place where Gary Gilmore had been executed and that the convicted murderer's autopsy showed four bullets had exploded in his heart. The agent reminded Franklin that if he was found guilty of the murders of Ted Fields and David Martin and given the death sentence, this was the place the execution would be carried out.[2]

According to Franklin, Dwyer told him during the flight, "Man, they ought to give you a medal . . . you sure fixed those two niggers out there in Salt Lake. They ought to give you a medal for cleaning up the streets."[3] Courts call this interrogation technique "reasonable deception."

Franklin and the group of law enforcement agents escorting him arrived at Salt Lake City airport on Saturday, November 8, 1980, to face federal and state murder charges. He was escorted from the airport to the city center in a motorcade of three vans, five police motorcycles, and several police squad cars. Franklin was shackled and wearing a bulletproof vest. As federal marshals whisked him from a van into the Salt Lake City County jail, he shouted to reporters, "The communist federal government is trying to frame me."[4]

On Monday, November 10, at his arraignment before U.S. Magistrate Daniel Alsup, who set a hearing before U.S. District Judge Bruce Jenkins, Franklin pleaded innocent to the federal civil rights charges in the slayings of Fields and Martin and was held on a $1 million cash bond. Franklin was also ordered to supply handwriting samples for comparison with credit card receipts. County attorney Ted Cannon told Alsup the state would wait until after the federal case was completed before proceeding with their own prosecution. As Franklin was led away, he told reporters the charges were "trumped up" because of his racist views.[5]

Although Salt Lake City prosecutors wanted to try Franklin on state charges of murder, they did not have enough evidence, and what they did have was mostly circumstantial. Four eyewitnesses placed him in the Salt Lake City area between August 17 and 20, and Franklin and his Chevrolet Camaro had been spotted at the murder scene less than an hour before Fields and Martin were shot. In early October, Ted Cannon had told reporters, "Although evidence in the case continues to accumulate, it is at this time premature to file state homicide charges against the prime suspect in the case, Joseph Paul Franklin. However, both prosecutors and police are hopeful that sufficient evidence upon which an appropriate homicide charge can be based will soon be developed. The federal charges are a separate and distinct matter from the local murder charges. The federal complaint supports the theory that the individual so charged did violate the civil rights of both Martin and Fields because of their race and color."[6]

After Franklin's extradition from Florida, however, state prosecutors had changed their minds and decided to charge Franklin after all. They came to their decision after police informed them that the evidence had been accumulating since Franklin's arrest, and police now felt secure they had a viable case. Franklin was charged with two counts of murder, which were filed by the Salt Lake City County Attorney's Office on November 8. However, both federal and state prosecutors agreed that the federal government should try Franklin first.

Following Franklin's arrest the FBI had issued a statement in which they stated they wanted to question Franklin about the attempted assassinations of Vernon Jordan and Larry Flynt. However, U.S. Attorney Ronald Rencher issued a contradictory statement. "I don't think he is now considered by federal authorities to be a suspect in the Vernon Jordan shooting," he said. But an FBI spokesman in Indianapolis disagreed with Rencher. He said the bureau was "at this point uncertain of where it stood on the Jordan connection."[7]

Before the trial began, Franklin told a local television reporter, "I didn't do it, but whoever did it was justified. [Fields and Martin] were race-mixing, and that should be punishable by death. Race-mixing should be a capital crime."[8] On November 25 Franklin gave an interview with the *Cincinnati Enquirer* in which he discussed the allegations that he had stalked President Carter. Franklin said Secret Service agents traced him because of a letter he wrote President Carter in 1976. He said he wrote that President Carter "wasn't worth the cost of a rope it would take to hang you with." Franklin asked the reporters, "Is that a threat? That's not a threat." "In 1976, I found one of his campaign promises and he was talking real race-mixing. I just grabbed an envelope and scribbled on it, 'You rich politicians. You're selling out those white kids.'"[9]

On December 16, 1980, Franklin's lawyer, Stephen R. McCaughey, filed a defense motion in district court asking that Franklin be tried on state murder charges before being tried on federal civil rights charges in the deaths of Fields and Martin. On January 6, 1981, when Franklin appeared before Judge Bruce S. Jenkins, the motion was denied.[10]

The federal civil rights trial began in February 1981 and was presided over by Judge Jenkins. The particular statute Franklin was charged under states: "Whoever, whether or not acting under color of law, by force or threat of force willfully injures, intimidates, or interferes with, or attempts to injure, intimidate, or interfere with . . . any person because of his race, color, religion, or national origin and because he is or has been . . . participating in or enjoying any benefit service, privilege, program, facility, or activity provided or administered by any State or subdivision thereof . . . shall be fined not more than $1,000, or imprisoned not more than one year, or both; and if bodily injury results shall be fined not more than $10,000, or imprisoned not more than ten years, or both; and if death results shall be subject to imprisonment for any term of years or for life."

Robert Van Sciver led Franklin's team of lawyers, and the prosecuting team was led by U.S. Attorney Steven Snarr, with assistance from Richard Roberts, an African American civil rights lawyer from the Justice Department. Testimony in the case began on February 23.

Before the trial began, Franklin had been telling other inmates about his crimes. At the Salt Lake City county jail, Franklin was held in a double lockup, meaning that while he could not leave his cell, other prisoners could approach him and talk with him when they were on job breaks. He became friendly with nineteen year-old Robert Lee Herrera, who had been serving time for burglary. Herrera had been moved into tier G-2, where Franklin and other prisoners were held awaiting trial. Herrera was moved from his original tier A-2 cell because he had been involved in a fight with a black inmate.

On February 9, 1981, Herrera was talking to another prisoner about the poor security in the jail when Franklin, overhearing the conversation, asked Herrera if it was true there was a way to escape. Herrera told him there was "definitely a way out." During the conversation Franklin asked why Herrera was in a double lockup. Herrera told him it was because he had been in a fight with a "nigger." Although the fight had not been racially motivated, Franklin thought Herrera hated African Americans. He was clearly impressed by Herrera's apparent racist comments and his alleged knowledge of the jail's security. He continued to elicit more information from Herrera. When he asked Herrera why he had been in prison in the first place, Herrera, hoping to impress, lied that it was for "armed robbery." Both inmates began to share details about their crimes and Franklin confided to Herrera "he hated blacks."[11]

In particular, Franklin told Herrera how he had shot "two little niggers in Cincinnati." According to Herrera, Franklin described how he had observed the two boys walking to a store and that they appeared to be around thirteen or fourteen years old. Franklin said he had shot them at approximately ten or eleven o'clock in the evening from a railroad crossing and that he parked his car alongside the tracks. Franklin also told Herrera he had used a rifle with a scope and fired it left-handed because his "right eye was messed up."[12]

Herrera was housed with Franklin from February 9 to 19, and during this period Franklin repeatedly bragged about his murders and bank robberies. Franklin told Herrera it did not make any difference to him who he killed or how old they were as long as they were "black." He also told Herrera why he shot at the couples in Liberty Park. Franklin said he believed that people of different races should never mix and that when he saw the black men walking with the white girls in the park, he felt they should die. He told Herrera that he did not like seeing "a lot of blacks and whites together" in the park, and so drove around to find a place to park and a place "where it would be best to get a good shot at somebody."[13] Herrera said Franklin threw his rifle in his trunk and drove away after the shooting and later sold the rifle at a flea market in San Rafael, California. Additionally, Franklin told Herrera about the shooting of Larry Flynt in 1977 for portraying white women with black men and his involvement in the Vernon Jordan shooting.[14] He also told Herrera that after the shootings, he would usually get rid of the weapons by selling them at flea markets or pawn shops. He said he got rid of his Chevy Nova by dumping it in Tennessee.

Herrera arranged meetings with the FBI and local investigators and told them he had a proposition—he would become a federal witness against Franklin if the state would guarantee him an early release date. He contacted the FBI on February 17, 1981, six days before Franklin's trial began on February 23. Herrera told an agent that he was in the same cellblock as Franklin and that he had admitted shooting the two joggers in Liberty Park. The FBI agent passed on this information to the U.S. Attorney's office the next day, February 18. In order to determine Herrera's value as a witness, the government attorneys arranged to interview him the following day. During the interview, Herrera revealed further information, including Franklin's plans to escape from the jail. Herrera also told the attorneys that Franklin himself had suggested that he go to the FBI with the story and then later recant it on the witness stand.

The government attorneys did not make their final decision to use Herrera as a witness until Monday, February 23, the first day of trial, when they learned the results of a polygraph test he had been given the previous Friday. Herrera's name was then included on the government's formal witness list.[15]

Unfortunately, U.S. federal prosecutors were presented with a problem when they questioned Herrera—the difficulty of persuading a jury that a jailhouse informant (or snitch, as convicts describe them), was credible. The key questions prosecutors formulated were, "What does he know that every reader of a U.S. newspaper or television viewer does not know?" and "Has Franklin confessed to new material or only to the facts as already established in the news media? And if there is new material, can it be verified?" For Franklin's part, he denied confessing anything to

Herrera and called him a "liar, you know, a pathological liar . . . even his Hispanic friends don't like him now because he's a rat."[16]

Prosecutors knew that Franklin's confession could not stand alone. It was certainly a crucial piece of probative evidence—evidence that gave rise to an inference of Franklin's guilt. But his confession was not sufficient enough to build a case on, because a man like Franklin could have made the confession for a thrill, a laugh, or simple jailhouse bragging. However, they did believe that Herrera was a credible witness after he told them of Franklin's whereabouts following the Liberty Park shooting, and their investigation confirmed Herrera's accounts. Accordingly, prosecutors decided to use Herrera's sworn statement in the forthcoming federal trial.

Prosecutors were also convinced by Herrera's polygraph test, which he passed, and hoped the jury would agree that the jailhouse informant was telling the truth.[17] They were also certain they had a strong case when they discovered Franklin had confessed to the Salt Lake City murders to another inmate, Richard Hawley. Franklin purportedly told Hawley "that he had gone out to a park . . . and noticed that there were people out there, blacks and whites associating together, and that he had decided that he was going to do something about it."[18] According to FBI agent Curtis Jensen, "He confessed to Herrera that he had shot the two joggers in Salt Lake City and also confessed to a homicide in Oklahoma City."[19]

As the federal trial proceeded, prosecutors argued that Franklin was a fanatical racist who could explode into violence at the sight of blacks associating with whites. They also attempted to show that Franklin was near the scene of the killings and had a motive—a deep hatred of African Americans.[20]

The prosecution took a week to present its case. They called sixty witnesses, but they were never able to produce a murder weapon or a witness who could identify Franklin when he gunned down Fields and Martin. But they did produce witnesses who saw a "dark-colored Chevrolet Camaro" near "Liberty Park the night of the shootings," and witnesses who saw a man pump at least six bullets into Fields and Martin and who continued firing even after the two joggers had fallen to the ground.

The prosecution lawyers presented evidence that Franklin's 1975 Camaro matched the killer's car in nearly every detail—including the tire treads, brown metallic paint, and plaid seats. A number of witnesses identified Franklin as a man who often cruised through Liberty Park the week before the killings, speaking with disgust about the number of interracial couples he saw. A key prosecution witness was Gary Spicer, who testified he saw a man drive a dark-colored Camaro into a vacant lot next to his house and take "a long object" from the trunk of the car. Spicer said he heard gunshots, and when he looked outside, he saw a man firing a rifle toward the street, but he was unable to identify Franklin as the man he saw.[21]

Franklin's defense argued that Franklin could not have accurately fired the shots that killed the joggers and that witnesses had testified the gunman at Liberty Park had not been wearing glasses. Defense lawyers seized on Spicer's testimony, arguing that Franklin could not have been the killer because of his poor eyesight. They called an ophthalmologist, Randall Olson, to testify at the trial. Olson said that Franklin was totally blind in one eye and had extremely poor vision in the other. "Without glasses," Olson said, "[Franklin] would have a hard time distinguishing people from a trash can." The defense also called a sniper expert, Henry Tillman from the John F. Kennedy Center for Military Assistance in North Carolina, who testified that even a good marksman would have difficulty firing six or seven bullets accurately from a standing position with the rifle unsupported—the position Spicer described.[22]

During the trial, two of Franklin's cellmates and Franklin's ex-wife Anita Cooper told the court that the defendant had confessed to the sniper murders of Fields and Martin. Robert Herrera told the court how Franklin had confessed to him, and Anita Cooper testified that her former husband had told her in a telephone conversation that he hid in a field of weeds and shot the two joggers as they were leaving Liberty Park.[23] Former cellmate Richard Hawley told the court that Franklin had admitted killing the two joggers when he and Franklin were both incarcerated in the Salt Lake City county jail. Hawley said, "[Franklin] talked about going there [the park] the night of the shootings. He said he had quite a bit of excitement or joy at the time he pulled the trigger." Hawley added that Franklin "had gone out to a park . . . and noticed that there were people out there, blacks and whites associating together, and that he had decided that he was going to do something about it."[24] As Hawley testified on the stand, Franklin shouted out, "How long did it take you to make that up, Hawley, you liar!" Following his outburst, Franklin lapsed into silence after a warning from Judge Jenkins.[25]

However, Franklin was not finished openly declaring his contempt for the prosecution's witnesses. He repeatedly shouted "liars and snitches" when his ex-wife and his two former cellmates were mentioned in the courtroom.[26] On Tuesday, March 3, Franklin reacted in anger again as prosecutor Steve Snarr delivered his final statement and mentioned the testimony of Franklin's two former cellmates and his ex-wife. Snarr said they had acted courageously by testifying. "That's a lie," Franklin shouted. "They're liars, too." When Franklin refused to end his protest,

Jenkins removed him from the courtroom. He was allowed to listen to the proceedings in a nearby room via an audio linkup.[27]

On Tuesday, March 3, the jury began its deliberations. Judge Jenkins gave the cue to the jury, which consisted of ten women and two men, at 4:15 p.m. following closing arguments. On Wednesday, March 4, after nearly fourteen hours of deliberation over two days, the jury found Franklin guilty on both counts of the federal civil rights indictment. As Franklin left the courtroom, he told reporters, "I didn't do it. It's a government frame-up. That's what I've said all along."[28] His twenty-three-year-old sister Marilyn Garzan—who had traveled from Montgomery, Alabama, for the trial—sobbed as she heard the verdict. Later she told reporters, "It's not over. There's no way it's over."[29] She said her brother had made the decision not to testify. She was the only member of the family present for the trial.

At the trial's conclusion the Fields family expressed their joy at the verdict. Reverend Fields, Ted's father, said he believed "from the very beginning" that Franklin was guilty. "I feel justice has been done," he said, "and I feel happy about it."[30]

On March 12 Robert Van Sciver told the press his client might have had a better chance if he had taken the stand. Sciver asked for a new trial on the grounds that they had discovered new evidence that could discredit the testimony of key witness Robert Herrera. The motion stated that, as the trial progressed, defense attorneys had received information regarding two other jail inmates whose cells had been near Herrera's before Herrera had been moved to Franklin's jail area. The lawyers suggested that Herrera had told the two inmates that he planned to fabricate a story about Franklin to try to obtain lenience in his own case.[31]

On March 18 Franklin's attorneys said four new murder charges against Franklin in Oklahoma and Indiana were part of a government plan to force him to confess to the attempted assassination of Vernon Jordan.[32] Oklahoma City authorities had filed murder charges against Franklin accusing him of the October 1979 shootings of Jesse Taylor and Marilyn Bressette. Following the Salt Lake City trial, Oklahoma prosecutors now believed they had enough proof that Franklin had information about the Bressette and Taylor murders "only the killer would have known." They based their judgment partly on the evidence that prosecutors had presented at the trial and the witnesses who related to the court how Franklin had made a number of confessions about his murders. Oklahoma County district attorney Hob Macy said they had a "poor case" until the cellmates testified. Indianapolis authorities had also filed charges against Franklin for the murders of Lawrence Reese and Leo Watkins.

"We're in a long line," officials in Indiana told reporters after charges were filed.[33] The Indiana and Oklahoma prosecutors said they decided to file the complaints after talking with Herrera and Hawley. Oklahoma prosecutors said the Justice Department had given them additional evidence.[34]

At the conclusion of the federal trial, Robert Van Sciver said he would immediately file an appeal against Franklin's conviction. He also told reporters that two Justice Department officials from Washington, D.C., had called him since the trial ended offering a deal. The Justice Department would, allegedly, persuade state prosecutors in Oklahoma and Indiana to drop the state charges against Franklin if the accused would confess to the Jordan shooting and also take a polygraph examination.[35] Van Sciver called the new charges and the deal "absurd" and suggested they were politically motivated. He also said federal attorneys told him that if Franklin did not accept the deal they would encourage his prosecution in states that had the death penalty. Federal attorneys also reminded Van Sciver that the Jordan shooting federal charges only carried a maximum sentence of life imprisonment.[36]

On Monday, March 23, Salt Lake City judge Bruce Jenkins denied a motion by defense lawyers for a new trial. When Steve Snarr told the court the killings had scarred the lives of the two white women who were with the victims and that the judge should consider in his sentencing the fearsome nature of the crimes, Franklin erupted and shouted to Snarr, "Got any more lies about me, you little faggot?" And, in reference to African American prosecutor Richard Roberts, Franklin shouted, "You and that trained ape you've got lying for you."[37]

Franklin next turned his rage on Judge Jenkins. "You are nothing but an agent of the communist government, you bastard," Franklin shouted. "This whole thing is a farce." He didn't care what anyone thought of his racist views, and he didn't care what anyone in the courtroom thought of him. This was not the killer who had killed someone in a rage. Franklin was the type of killer, the jury soon realized, who could kill you because you gave him a dirty look.

Franklin left his seat and charged across the room towards Snarr and Roberts, knocking a pitcher of water into the air and dumping ice into the lap of FBI agent Jensen. Ten U.S. marshals immediately intervened and wrestled Franklin to the floor. "Put him in irons," Jenkins instructed. The marshals handcuffed and shackled Franklin and stood him at attention facing the judge. Franklin then began to complain the handcuffs had been fastened too tightly and were cutting into his wrists.

As Franklin stood before the judge, Jenkins recalled Franklin's youth, noting that he left home at fifteen, dropped out of school, and didn't have the opportunities available to many teenagers. "I suppose that's an explanation," Jenkins said, "but not an excuse for what happened here." Jenkins told Franklin it was not too late to change the course of his life while in prison.[38] He sentenced Franklin to two consecutive life terms, the maximum penalty under the law. Judge Jenkins told Franklin, "This whole tragic affair is something that needn't have happened shouldn't have happened and must not happen again."[39] Franklin responded by telling the judge, "I don't think I should be sentenced for something I didn't do."[40] Reporters noted that Franklin would be eligible for parole from federal prison in ten years.

Franklin appealed the case on the grounds that the district court erred in admitting evidence of a prior act. He said that evidence of the 1976 Mace incident involving a mixed-race couple, Aaron Miles and Carol Eastwood, should have been excluded because the incident was too remote in time from the charged offenses. His lawyers argued that the evidence should not have been admitted to show motive because "Franklin's racial motivation was not an issue at trial, but rather admitted throughout the trial. Instead Franklin denied participation in the acts which constitute the crime." They also argued that the court abused its discretion in allowing a government witness to testify despite the government's disregard of its open-file discovery policy and that the court erred in denying his motion for a new trial.

However, the appeals court ruled against Franklin, stating the trial court was right in its procedures with respect to Franklin's constitutional rights. In particular, the appeals court ruled that allowing the government to introduce evidence of the Mace incident was probative of motive. Before admitting the evidence, they concluded, the trial court properly heard Aaron Miles's testimony out of the presence of the jury. Both before Miles testified and again in the final jury instructions, the court cautioned the jury that the testimony was offered on the question of motive only.[41]

Franklin was furious he was going to prison because of an African American prosecutor. For his part, Richard Roberts told reporters the case was a victory for civil rights. "I hope it proves the Justice Department intends to vigorously pursue civil rights violations, no matter where in the country they occur," he said.[42] Roberts, who received a special commendation from the U.S. attorney general for his work on the case, also said the government was aiding and encouraging Franklin's prosecution on the local murder charges and said the government had dropped federal bank robbery charges against Franklin in Little Rock and Louisville so that he could be turned over to state officials.[43]

Following Franklin's conviction of civil rights violations for the murders of Ted Fields and David Martin, he was sent to the Medical Center for Federal Prisoners in Springfield, Missouri. His later appeal for the federal conviction was rejected. In a ruling the United States Court of Appeals stated that the appeal "argued that the evidence was insufficient to support the verdict. . . . In particular, Franklin suggests the government failed to establish that Fields and Martin were killed because they were or had been enjoying a public facility. We disagree. Several witnesses testified that Franklin had disapproved of the racial-mixing at Liberty Park. Hawley and Herrera both testified that he told them he shot two black joggers 'to do something about it.' The jury could well have inferred that he intended to deprive the victims of the opportunity to enjoy public facilities. The record reflects that the government presented sufficient evidence, as discussed above, from which the jury could find Franklin guilty."[44]

Immediately following the trial, Federal Marshal William Pitt turned Franklin over to the custody of Salt Lake County. When reporters asked whether or not the state was going to go ahead with their trial, county attorney Ted Cannon told them that Franklin would be tried and that he would demand the death penalty. In fact, the only reason Franklin faced state charges was because state authorities wanted Franklin executed for his crimes since the federal government did not have capital punishment at the time. Chief prosecutor John T. Nielsen said Franklin would be arraigned as quickly as possible in state court. However, there were fears that Franklin's lawyers might raise the question of double jeopardy when the state charges came to trial.

The prosecution team was led by thirty-seven-year-old veteran prosecutor Robert Stott, who knew what he was up against in seeking the death penalty for Franklin—"There were no eyewitnesses, no fingerprints, no smoking gun," Stott later said. "It was a circumstantial case.[45]

By the time the state trial began, Franklin had already gone through three sets of attorneys. He had fought with them or there was some conflict that made a working relationship unfeasible.[46] One of his appointed attorneys, Tom Jones, said Franklin had spat at him and threatened to kill him.[47] Franklin supporters had also made threats to prosecutors. Robert Stott said that members of his team had received death threats from white supremacist groups.

The killings had tested Utah's ability to deliver racially neutral justice in an overwhelmingly white, conservative, and Mormon state where blacks numbered only 12,000 in a population of 1.7 million and where a now-repudiated Mormon prohibition against blacks had left a legacy of antagonism. Historically, the Mormon Church had also taught the concept of "blood atonement" for sins. Although the concept was waning, Utah still permitted execution by firing squad for this reason—if the condemned person so chose it. The alternative form of execution was lethal injection.

In June 1981 Third District Court Judge Jay Banks ruled that Salt Lake County could try Franklin even though he had already been found guilty of federal civil rights violations in the killings. Banks said the county's first-degree murder charges against Franklin would not subject the defendant to "double jeopardy."[48]

At a pretrial hearing, Banks also denied Franklin's request to serve as his own counsel and said the defense attorney assigned to the case, Tom Jones, would continue to represent the defendant despite apparent conflicts between lawyer and client. Jones had asked to be removed from the case because he had "contempt and loathing" for Franklin. However, before the trial began, Judge Banks reversed his decision and ruled that Franklin had a constitutional right to participate in his own defense. He also allowed Jones to be replaced by Salt Lake City attorneys David Yocum and D. Frank Williams, a former Utah Supreme Court justice. Greg Skordas assisted Yocum.

Franklin believed he was well suited to represent himself in the state trial. Many years later he told Cincinnati detective Michael O'Brien, "I prefer to act as my own attorney . . . the place where I really learned a lot [was] when I was out in Salt Lake City, man, I used to study out there . . . early in the morning till late in the evening . . . that's when I first kinda learned the procedures and all that."[49] Franklin told reporters he was representing himself because "Jesus Christ" was helping him out. In an interview for local media, Franklin said he "sure ain't afraid. I have the feeling that Jesus Christ is helping me out. Jesus Christ was executed by the system. He was tried and convicted by false witnesses just like me."[50] Banks warned Franklin that he would not tolerate profanity or improper conduct, making reference to Franklin's removal from the courtroom during his federal trial when he repeatedly called a prosecution witness a liar.

Yocum's relationship with his client was less than convivial. "He was an interesting client to represent," Yocum said. "He could be as friendly and pleasant as can be or as intimidating as can be. He always wanted to test you to make sure you were tough enough to represent him. He pinned me up against the bars once. From then on, I always had a police investigator with me in case he got mad at me."[51]

In late August 1981, as the state trial was underway, Franklin had other murder charges hanging over his head in Oklahoma City and Indianapolis. The FBI told the media that Franklin was definitely a major suspect in the shooting of Vernon Jordan as well.

The state trial began on Monday, August 31. It took three days to seat the jury, and opening arguments did not begin until Thursday, September 3. In the first day all but one of nearly ninety potential jurors admitted to Judge Banks that they had read or heard news accounts of charges that Franklin ambushed and killed Fields and Martin. The judge also asked the potential jurors whether they had qualms about imposing a possible death sentence in the case, if interracial dating upset them, or if they were members of white supremacist organizations. Four said they had already formed an opinion as to Franklin's guilt or innocence. A few said they knew lawyers or witnesses in the case and two said it would take direct evidence to convince them of Franklin's involvement in the sniper shootings. Banks did not ask the jurors whether the publicity about Franklin tainted their ability to render an impartial verdict, but he pursued the point during individual questioning later in his chambers. The final jury selection was made up of five women and seven men. All the jurors were white.

Franklin denied killing Fields and Martin and argued that because he was a racist, the government was trying to connect him with a number of shootings of blacks, including the wounding of Vernon Jordan. Later in the day Franklin, wearing a black three-piece suit, shared in a conference with other lawyers at the judge's bench and read a list of twelve witnesses he planned to call. Deputy Salt Lake City Attorney Robert Stott said the prosecution would call about sixty witnesses during the trial.

Franklin delivered a five-minute opening statement to the jury. He said he was a victim of circumstances and sensationalized news reporting. "The evidence will show," he said, "that I was just passing through the Salt Lake City area on my way to San Francisco and I was just in the wrong place at the wrong time."[52]

On Thursday, September 3, the court heard the testimony of Mickie Farman-Ara (née McHenry), the prostitute whom Franklin picked up shortly before he committed the Liberty Park murders. She was one of sixteen witnesses called to the stand that day.[53]

On Tuesday, September 8, Franklin said he "definitely" planned to testify, and his list of witnesses included himself and his two sisters. The same day, Terry Elrod and Karma Ingersol took the stand and related to the court their stories about the sniper shooting. Sixteen-year-old Terry Elrod said she thought the shots that killed

Fields and Martin were intended for her because she was scheduled to testify as the victim in an unrelated rape case. Elrod told the court she was spending the night with her friend Karma. They agreed to go jogging with Ted, and since David had been with Ted at the time, he was persuaded to join them. As the four were leaving Liberty Park during their short jog, shots rang out, Terry said, and Martin fell. Terry told the court, "I looked around to see if there were cars or anything and I saw Dave—he looked like he couldn't talk and he was in really bad pain. There was another shot and Dave said something like 'Oh, my God! They got me.'" When Karma Ingersol testified, she related the story of the shooting and said she at first thought David Martin had been joking but realized he had been shot when she saw his blood.[54]

During the trial the prosecution called Det. Jesse Baker as a witness. Baker testified that he had interviewed Franklin in Florence, Kentucky, after Franklin's arrest on suspicion of possessing a stolen vehicle. Baker said that during the interview he appeared unperturbed by questions concerning the stolen car but became emotional when he was questioned about the Salt Lake City murders. Franklin immediately complained of the court's decision to admit Baker's evidence and wanted his testimony excluded. Instead the judge merely instructed the jury not to give too much weight to the fact that Franklin fled from the Florence jail.

On Friday, September 18, jurors left the courtroom for deliberations after both prosecuting and defense attorneys presented their closing arguments. During prosecutor Robert Stott's closing argument, he summed up the state's case against Franklin. "Take this man with his built-in hatred of blacks," Stott said, "and take this man with his hair-trigger hostility and his small arsenal in his car—put that man in the intersection forty-five minutes before the shootings and do you have a mere coincidence?"

The jury debated for around six hours before convicting Franklin. Franklin sat impassively when the verdict was read on Friday, September 18. However, Yocum was less composed and put his head on the table in a gesture of despair.[55] The sentencing phase of the trial came the following Wednesday. Under Utah law the jury would decide the verdict. When Franklin returned to the court for sentencing, he said he wasn't afraid of dying.

During a recess, Franklin once again tried to escape from police custody. He had been left unattended in a holding room, and before the court officer returned, he had freed himself and pried the holding room door off its hinges. He concluded that the elevator was his only way out of the building, but it was only operable with a guard's key. However, Franklin had acquired a six-inch screwdriver with the handle removed, probably supplied by a fellow inmate, which he used to pry open a control panel on the holding cell elevator. Franklin hot-wired the electronics using a paper-clip and a dime and called the lift to his floor.

Police closed off the streets, and jailers searched the courthouse when Franklin was discovered missing. Every available police officer was brought in to scour the downtown area. Courtroom artist Scott Snow, who witnessed the chaos in the court-house, later recalled, "One day after a break during the Franklin murder trial we had been waiting longer than usual for court to reconvene, when a marshal runs into the courtroom and gets another marshal and they both run out together. That was unusual. Then another marshal ran out. Apparently, they had 'misplaced' the defen-dant. When we all stepped into the hall to see what was going on, we saw police and marshals fanning out all over the court complex in search of him. Everything was a potential hiding place—trash bins, cars; they were looking everywhere."[56]

Minutes later one of the guards realized that the top handle on the elevator had been loosened, so he climbed up on top and noticed there was some movement in the shaft. He began to crawl in the air ducts looking for the escapee. When the guard spotted him, Franklin scurried away, always remaining out of the guard's reach. However, when Franklin came to the end of the air duct, another guard was wait-ing for him. They had found him in the shaft near the top of the five-story Hall of Justice. According to Salt Lake City detective Don Bell, "We cleaned him off and combed his hair and the jury was none the wiser. They just got an extra hour for lunch."[57]

The escape attempt came as David Yocum had finished telling the jury that the state had no more right to impose the death penalty on Franklin "than the person you think killed Ted Fields and David Martin had to kill them." Yocum told the court that Franklin still maintained his innocence and had instructed his attorneys not to beg for mercy. "He is an intelligent, religious, humorous, useful human being," Yo-cum said, "who could make a contribution to the improvement of the world and so-ciety." Robert Stott responded by telling the jury, "There's nothing romantic about this case. Nothing to sympathize with, nothing to pity—except those two young men shot by a cowardly sniper. The moment the defendant stepped onto that hill with a rifle, he made the decision to subject himself to the death penalty. You weren't there and you didn't force him. You've looked him in the face, something he never did to Ted Fields and David Martin. The question is what punishment fits the crime."[58]

Clearly angered by Stott's passionate advocacy for the death penalty, Franklin blurted out, "The question is, what evidence was used?" Judge Banks told Franklin to remain quiet, saying he would have an opportunity to address the jury later. Stott continued by reminding the jury that the victims were killed "for the most meaningless reason in the world—they were black and were jogging with two white girls. Joseph Franklin did not know them, he knew nothing about them." Reminding the jury of Franklin's statements of his own innocence, Stott said, "The victim of circumstance in this case is not Joseph Paul Franklin; it's each of the victims—who were in the wrong place at the wrong time."[59]

The verdict came at 10:00 a.m. on Wednesday, September 23. Jurors had deliberated for two hours and returned to the courtroom to tell the judge they could not reach the required unanimous verdict on the death sentence for Franklin. Four jurors had opposed imposing the death penalty. Under Utah law, Banks had to impose life sentences.

Franklin stared at the jury but showed no emotion as the clerk read the verdict. He mouthed the words "thank you" to the jury. Yocum put his arms around Franklin's shoulders as they both grinned. However, his sisters, Marilyn and Carolyn, began sobbing softly. Yocum said Franklin was "very happy, obviously" that the jury failed to agree on the death penalty. "I'm very gratified they returned the verdict of life," Yocum said, "but I still disagree with their guilty verdict."[60] Yocum said he would appeal Franklin's conviction and said he was convinced "the evidence [did] not show his guilt."

However, Franklin's demeanor changed when Judge Banks described Franklin as a man who did not accept society's "moral rules or religious rules." The judge told Franklin, "It will be my recommendation to the [state] Board of Pardons that you never get out of prison." Franklin responded with a string of obscenities and an ethnic slur to the judge as he was taken from the court. "That's a lie," Franklin shouted. "You're the one who ain't got no morals."[61] Later, Franklin asked Judge Banks to declare the conviction "illegal and void."[62]

Following the trial, Robert Stott, who was frustrated by the jury's decision, asked the four jurors who had dissented from the others when it came to imposing the death penalty why they made that decision. They replied they were not "absolutely certain" Franklin was guilty, as no one had seen him commit the murders.[63] Stott said "we've never had a . . . case that we spent as much effort in trying to obtain the death penalty . . . in the Franklin case . . . we vigorously sought the death penalty because we felt that Franklin should receive the most severe punishment for his crime. It was a cold-blooded sniper murder of two innocent victims."[64]

TWELVE

The Stabbing

Vengeance is mine, saith the Lord.

—FBI director William Webster, in a telephone call to Vernon Jordan, after Joseph Paul Franklin had been critically injured by Marion prison inmates.

In May 1981, a few months after the Salt Lake City federal trial and four months before the Salt Lake City state trial, FBI officials were still telling the media they did not have a suspect in the Jordan shooting. Steve McVey, an FBI spokesman said, "We're making progress. We're still hopeful. All the normal clichés are applicable. We have leads every week all over the U.S. We're still looking for a weapon."[1]

However, Fort Wayne mayor Winfield Moses said he believed the police had their man. "I feel very confident [Franklin] is probably the one," Moses told reporters. "We've followed literally thousands of leads and this is by far the best one. The FBI has told me they feel 99 percent sure it's Franklin. But until an arrest is made there will continue to be frustration." McVey was more circumspect and told the media, "Franklin has not been eliminated as a suspect. But neither have we isolated him as a prime suspect. We need something significant to develop to solve this thing. It's like finding your way in the dark."[2]

Following Franklin's state trial in Salt Lake City, he was sent back to the Medical Center for Federal Prisoners in Springfield, Missouri. He had arrived there months earlier for psychiatric tests after he had been found guilty of civil rights violations in his federal trial. In December 1981 he met Frank Sweeney, a fellow inmate who was housed on the same floor as Franklin. They would exercise together during breaks, and they built up a friendship.

Sweeney had much in common with Franklin. Both men admired the white supremacist regime in Rhodesia, and both harbored intense racist beliefs. In fact, Sweeney had at one time served in the Rhodesian Army. During one conversation Franklin told Sweeney he had always wanted to go to Rhodesia because he wanted to "waste niggers." Sweeney became incredulous at Franklin's ignorance of the situation in Rhodesia. He told FBI agents Franklin wrongly believed a white man could simply walk down any street in a Rhodesian town and begin shooting black people with impunity.

When Sweeney explained to Franklin that he could not kill blacks at will, the former Klansman began to tell Sweeney he was responsible for several murders of blacks in the United States that he had never been charged with.[3] Specifically, Franklin told Sweeney he had killed "two blacks" in Indianapolis before driving to Cincinnati. He confessed that he had killed the "baby boogies" and "baby niggers" there. Franklin also explained how he would roam the country looking for blacks to kill. According to Sweeney, Franklin said he would often go to black neighborhoods wearing Afro wigs and blacken his face with charcoal when he reconnoitered the areas. Franklin added that he would then return to the black neighborhoods and wait for a target.[4]

During his friendship with Franklin, Sweeney decided he should be cautious in his dealings with his new friend. He decided to not ask too many questions, as it might make him suspicious. Sweeney would return to his cell at the end of the day and write down what Franklin had told him. Following his release from prison, Sweeney contacted the Cincinnati police. As he was also on parole, he appeared to be a credible witness, as he was not in a position to ask police to persuade the courts to reduce his sentence. In fact, Sweeney said he wanted nothing in return from the Cincinnati authorities for supplying his information. Cincinnati police investigators concluded, "He had scruples, and although he wasn't crazy about blacks, he thought it wrong to kill two kids for nothing." Sweeney had also informed the FBI of what he knew but complained, "They were more interested in prosecuting Franklin for the Vernon Jordan shooting than anything else."[5]

The FBI and local police investigators soon realized they had a problem with the information supplied by Sweeney and Herrera. Sweeney told the FBI he thought Robert Herrera was a liar and a perjurer. Sweeney said that a man he met in the Witness Protection Program had told him Herrera had gotten all the information about Franklin from the newspapers and that, as Franklin was an obsessive racist, he would never have taken Herrera, who was Hispanic, into his confidence. Sweeney said Franklin often characterized Latinos as "grease balls" and "spics," and that he hated them. Sweeney was given a polygraph test by an FBI agent, who described Sweeney as one of the worst subjects he had ever ran and that he could not "get any results on him."[6]

However, this did not prevent the FBI from accepting Frank Sweeney as a key witness in their impending charges against Franklin for the attempted murder of Vernon Jordan. And FBI agents were convinced that Lawrence Hollingsworth, another of Franklin's jailmates in Salt Lake City, was telling the truth when he told them Franklin had confessed to the Jordan shooting.

Following the Salt Lake City state and federal trials, the FBI and the Justice Department believed the trials had given them sufficient evidence to charge Franklin with the Jordan murder attempt. They said motel registration slips indicated Franklin had stayed in Fort Wayne "immediately prior" to the shooting, and they were able to place Franklin in Fort Wayne by an analysis of handwriting samples on the motel slips.[7]

On January 31, 1982, Franklin was transferred to the United States Penitentiary in Marion, Illinois. Apart from furloughs to other states, where he would stand trial for his sniper attacks and bombings, he would remain there until the mid-1990s. He was put in a non-segregated section of the prison.

Inmates were sent to Marion when they caused problems at other federal institutions or were security risks at state prisons. The "worst of the worst" prisoners were not sent to Marion until 1979, when it was designated as the Federal Prison Bureau's only level six prison. Prior to that, the prison had housed younger offenders, and even after the worst prisoners in the system began to arrive, the institution was characterized as open in that inmates were not overly controlled and could roam the compound unrestricted. It was a recipe for disaster, officials would learn in the years that followed. According to one corrections officer, "Every warden in the entire system suddenly had an opportunity to get rid of his worst inmates by sending them to us and that is exactly what they did. I'm not certain that anyone in Washington [Bureau of Prisons headquarters] really understood just how many bad apples we had streaming in here."[8]

When Franklin arrived at Marion, the thirty-one-year-old racist killer instantly became a prime target for African American prisoners. Franklin's Salt Lake City trial lawyer David Yocum believed Franklin was "a marked man the minute he got there."[9] It did not take long for Franklin to figure our where he stood among the black prison population, who openly showed contempt for the white supremacist. As soon as he arrived in the prison, he made it known to other white prisoners he wanted a knife to defend himself. Franklin also knew that maintaining his image and the necessity of not showing weakness were a thousand times more important in prison than on the streets.

The Aryan Brotherhood offered Franklin a weapon on the condition he join the organization. However, Franklin refused. He thought the AB was apolitical and antithetical to his beliefs since they had abandoned their Nazi philosophy in favor of Norse and Viking symbolism and their primary orientation was drug trafficking. The Brotherhood was the dominant gang at the time of Franklin's transfer to the prison. They spent most of their time dealing and using drugs. In the 1960s the gang was formed as a means of bringing the race war from the streets of America into the prison system. However, by the 1970s, the raison d'être for the gang had changed. Bureau official Michael Lee Caltabiano described the change as "[developing] during the 1970s into an organized predatory gang [whose] main interest became protection, extortion, and narcotics in prison."[10]

In what appeared to be a curious move on Franklin's part, he befriended an African American man when he arrived at the prison. The two were housed in cellblock F, which was occupied by seventy-two inmates. Free time spent out of cell was one and a half hours per day, and the prisoners usually spent that time in a small hallway. Recreation was one hour per week in winter and two hours during the summer. After the black convict had spent some weeks gaining Franklin's confidence, he asked the racist killer if he had shot Vernon Jordan. Franklin, in an obvious attempt to gain some credibility in convict circles as a man not to be crossed, told the black inmate, "Yeah, I shot him."[11]

On February 3, a few nights later, Franklin returned from supper around 6:40 p.m. All the cellblock doors were open, and the prisoners were able to meander around. As Franklin entered the cell of another inmate, a group of black convicts cornered him and, using a knife made out of cans, stabbed him fifteen times in the neck and abdomen. Two or three guards in charge of the cellblock were nearby but did not see the attack. Following the stabbing Franklin stumbled out of the cell, blood oozing from his wounds. A guard saw him and came to his aid. Prison staff telephoned emergency services, and Franklin was taken to Marion Memorial Hospital, where he underwent surgery for his wounds.

Prison officials found the weapon that was used in the attack lying in the cell of the inmate Franklin had visited. It was a "homemade ice pick-type instrument," prison officials told the press.[12] After investigating the stabbing attack, the FBI decided not to prosecute. Springfield FBI agent Robert Davenport said results of the investigation had been given to the U.S. Attorney's office in East St. Louis, but the prosecution was declined because Franklin could not, or would not, identify his attackers and there were no witnesses.[13]

The following morning in Washington, D.C., FBI director William Webster telephoned Vernon Jordan and told him about the stabbing incident. Webster told him, "Vengeance is mine, saith the Lord . . . I want to report to you that last night in the Marion prison, Joseph Paul Franklin was stabbed . . . they're putting him by himself from now on." According to Vernon Jordan, this was "really my last extended thought about Joseph Paul Franklin."[14]

When Franklin returned to Marion from the hospital, he was immediately placed in K Unit, which was considered reserved for an elite category of prisoners. K Unit prisoners were even more isolated than Control Unit prisoners. The unit was a cluster of seven cells situated in the basement of the prison under the hospital and completely isolated from the rest of the institution. The cells, which measured nine by eleven feet, were larger than those in the other prison wings. Prisoners in the unit had their own showers and toilets, spent about twenty-two hours confined to their cells, and were not allowed to leave them at the same time. The unit also banned visitors, including journalists.

Franklin's fellow cell block inmates were some of the most infamous criminals in America, including Christopher Boyce, who had been convicted in 1977 of selling satellite secrets to the Soviet Union and who was serving a forty year sentence (with an extra twenty-five years from when he escaped from California's Lompoc Prison and spent ten months robbing banks as a fugitive). The unit also housed another traitor, Edwin Wilson, a former CIA agent who had been convicted of illegally shipping twenty tons of explosives to Libya and plotting the murders of two prosecutors, five witnesses, and an inmate who told the FBI of his plans. In later years the unit also became the home to notorious Gambino family mafia boss John Gotti.

Other famous inmates at Marion included Leonard Peltier, a leader of the American Indian Movement who had been convicted of murdering two FBI agents; Jonathan Pollard, a former U.S. navy intelligence officer who spied for Israel; and Jack Henry Abbott, a murderer and friend of author Norman Mailer who went on to kill again after Mailer and other New York literati were successful in persuading the parole board to release him.

Franklin detested the years he spent in Marion. Although he thought the prison looked "fairly new" and the administration "kept the halls clean," the cell blocks had "broken out windows, unpainted walls . . . you could . . . have to sleep next to a window . . . these lubbered windows . . . and they break out and when they do they don't fix 'em. You got a cold even when it gets ten to fifteen below zero; you got that air blowing right in on you. I've actually had to take stacks of newspapers and put 'em in with blankets . . . freezing to death, man."[15]

Franklin was an inmate at Marion during the famous 1983 lockdown. Two guards, Merle E. Clutts and Robert L. Hoffman, who were accompanying inmates through the prison, and an inmate were killed in separate incidents. One guard was stabbed forty times. It was the culmination of a violent outbreak that had lasted for three years from 1980 to 1983, partly because the warden, Harold Miller, refused to implement a total lockdown. During that period eight inmates were killed by other prisoners, and there were fourteen attempted escapes, ten group disturbances, and eighty-two serious assaults on inmates or staff. The disturbances were the result of relatively lax security procedures, including allowing escorted prisoners to approach other inmates in cells. The other inmates sometimes unlocked their handcuffs with a stolen key then handed them a knife.

After the deaths of the guards there were numerous assaults on staff and cell searches turned up hundreds of homemade weapons. A group of inmates would later claim, in a class action lawsuit against the Bureau of Prisons, that Marion's guards beat and tortured them in retaliation for the murders. However, after listening to testimony in an eight-day trial, a federal magistrate concluded there was no credible evidence to support the charges, but he did agree that isolated incidents of abuse may have occurred. Magistrate Kenneth J. Meyers said that, given the circumstances at Marion, "an extra push or shove would be understandable," he and said the guards had been put under extreme stress because they had been physically attacked and had been doused with feces and urine. Additionally, "fires were being set by inmates, cells were being destroyed, and officers were being told they would be killed."[16]

Following the murders of the guards, sixty veteran prison officers were brought in from nine other federal prisons, and new procedures were instituted, including three guard-escorts whenever a prisoner was moved from one part of the prison to another. Additionally, prisoners were confined to their cells for meals.

In September 1980, at his first news conference since the attempt on his life, Vernon Jordan said he was "confident" the FBI had been doing all it could "to bring my assailant to justice." He "never had any doubts" the FBI was doing its utmost. When asked about FBI director William Webster's assessment that the shooting had been a politically motivated assassination attempt and possibly a conspiracy, Jordan said, "I have to accept Webster's evaluation of the situation. In the dark, I could not know who was behind the trigger."[17]

In November 1980 Webster said Franklin's arrest was "significant," and that he had not been eliminated as a possible suspect in the shooting of Vernon Jordan.[18] In March 1981 the *Los Angeles Times* reported that the FBI had collected motel registration cards that showed that Franklin was in Fort Wayne "at about the time" Jordan was shot. The *Times* quoted unnamed law enforcement officials as saying there was still insufficient evidence to seek an indictment, but they believed that some of the information the Salt Lake City inmates supplied to authorities was so detailed that only the killer could have known about it.[19]

The government felt they had to act quickly because of the corrosive social element involved in the crime. The public was becoming convinced that Jordan had been shot as the result of a conspiracy, perhaps linked to the alleged conspiracies surrounding the assassinations of Martin Luther King Jr., President Kennedy, and Robert Kennedy. In July 1980, two months after the shooting, a Louis Harris poll showed 45 percent of the American public polled believed the shooting was not the work of one person, but instead "part of a broader conspiracy." Sixty-one percent of African Americans nationwide were sure the Jordan shooting was an attempted assassination that was planned well in advance, and 85 percent of Americans polled agreed with the statement, "It makes you wonder what's going on in this country when leaders such as John and Robert Kennedy, Martin Luther King, and now Vernon Jordan are all victims of assassination attempts." Nearly 91 percent of African Americans shared this view, and 80 percent agreed "there are groups in this country who are so racist that they would like to assassinate effective black leaders such as Vernon Jordan." Nearly 89 percent of African Americans shared this view. Eighty-three percent of Americans polled believed it was "so easy to commit assassinations in this country that any public figure that takes controversial stands will find his life in danger." Among African Americans, about 90 percent felt the same way.[20]

However, by June 1982, government lawyers were convinced that Joseph Franklin's attempt to kill Vernon Jordan was the act of a lone gunman that resulted from the "ex-Klansman's rage at seeing Jordan with a white woman." Federal attorneys, under the leadership of Assistant Attorney General William Bradford Reynolds (head of the Justice Department's Civil Rights Division), sent a brief to federal judge Allen Sharp in which the government asserted they would prove the wounding of Jordan fit a pattern of violence by Franklin. "He has admitted observing a black man and a white woman drinking at a bar," the brief stated, "becoming enraged by that fact, following them, setting up an ambush, and shooting the man with a rifle as he exited the car in which the two had been driving." The brief alluded to confessions Franklin had made to Herrera and Hawley in the Salt Lake City jail in which Franklin allegedly stated that he had shot a political figure in Fort Wayne, Indiana.[21]

Government lawyers also believed important pieces of evidence they had collected supported Hawley's and Herrera's statements, including a signature on a Fort Wayne motel registration card and the fact Franklin tried to sell a 30.06 rifle, the same type of weapon that fired the bullets that wounded Jordan. Government lawyers cited the testimony of a motel employee, Mary Howell, who said she spoke with Franklin in Fort Wayne about the time of the shooting and that Franklin had expressed a deep hatred of African Americans.[22]

Shortly before Franklin was tried and convicted of murder in the Salt Lake City trials, he was secretly photographed in jail after he refused to participate in a police lineup. The FBI showed the film to witness Mary Howell, who identified Franklin as a man she saw in Fort Wayne the day before Jordan was shot. According to Sheriff N. D. Hayward, the FBI filming occurred while Franklin was being held in the Salt Lake County City jail, and jail personnel cooperated with the FBI but did not actually participate. The FBI had asked Franklin to sit at a table in the jail dispensary and sign some legal documents and filmed him as he signed them. The FBI selected inmates and jail personnel who resembled Franklin to participate in the filming to simulate typical police lineup procedures.

Franklin's defense attorney, David Yocum, said the "picture-taking" violated Franklin's constitutional rights. Yocum said he was asked by the FBI to view the pictures near the end of Franklin's state trial in late September. "I refused," Yocum said. "It was a blatant violation of his civil rights. It was illegal and improper."[23]

The FBI would not confirm the truth of the allegations, and Justice Department lawyers in Washington refused to comment on the filming of Franklin in the jail or an alleged offer of a plea-bargain arrangement. "That's evidentiary and we cannot discuss that," said Special Agent Lane Bonner, supervisor of the FBI's press office in Washington, D.C. Justice Department lawyers suggested offering Franklin a plea-bargain arrangement if he would confess to shooting Jordan, newspaper reports alleged. The reports also said federal authorities were prepared to promise Franklin that local prosecutors would not seek the death penalty in the to shootings of Ted Fields and David Martin if Franklin admitted shooting Jordan. Allegedly, the FBI told Franklin that he would be sent to a "more comfortable" federal prison if he cooperated.[24]

The Salt Lake prosecutors had balked at the purported plea bargain, as they were determined to seek capital punishment for the murders. Additionally, they did not use the film of Franklin. Deputy Salt Lake County Attorney Robert L. Stott, who prosecuted Franklin, said witnesses who testified in the trial were not asked to view the film.[25]

Justice Department lawyer Barry Kowalski, described by his peers as a "pit bull of a prosecutor," was chosen to head the federal prosecution team for the Jordan shooting trial. Daniel Rinzel assisted him. The Justice Department chose Kowalski based on the prosecutor's reputation as a fierce defender of civil rights legislation and his commitment in prosecuting hate crimes.[26]

The grand jury was presented with a civil rights indictment instead of a murder indictment because Justice Department lawyers were hesitant about charging Franklin with murder based on the evidence they had. The grand jury returned their civil rights indictment on Wednesday, June 2, 1982, in the U.S. District Court in South Bend, Indiana. There had been concern among government lawyers that trying Franklin in Fort Wayne would attract criticism that a Fort Wayne jury would be prejudicial against Franklin. Franklin was indicted under the 1968 Civil Rights Act that had been signed into law on April 11, 1968, one week after Martin Luther Ling Jr. was assassinated in Memphis, Tennessee. The indictment charged Franklin with violating Jordan's constitutional rights to enjoy the accommodations of an establishment that provides lodging to transient guests.[27]

Fort Wayne mayor Winfield Moses, on learning of Franklin's indictment, said, "I think it's fantastic. Our evidence all indicates that [Franklin] was the most likely person. The evidence was pretty thorough even though there was no one flying overhead with a motion picture camera."[28]

Vernon Jordan was not so convinced the government had an airtight case. "The state of Indiana declined to prosecute Franklin," Jordan wrote, "saying there was not enough evidence to prove beyond a reasonable doubt that he had shot me, but the federal government moved forward with its case. I was not much involved in the legal proceedings surrounding Franklin. That was for law enforcement to deal with . . . Section 245 [of the civil rights law] was a very weak basis on which to have proceeded because the prosecution had to show that I had been shot because my attacker was trying to prevent me from using a public accommodation. That was never the issue. I was shot because I was black and in the company of a white woman."[29]

Franklin's lawyer, David Yocum, was incensed that the government had sought to try his client for the Jordan shooting. "It's ridiculous that a man serving four consecutive life sentences," he said, "would even be considered for being prosecuted for a maximum ten year [sentence]. The Justice Department must really be looking for points with the black people."[30]

By July 1982 Franklin had been transferred to the Metropolitan Correction Center in Chicago. Later that month, in a letter filed in federal district court, he said his life had been threatened by staff and other inmates in the Chicago jail and wanted a transfer to the county jail in South Bend, the venue for the Jordan federal trial.[31] The expedited transfer was unnecessary, since Franklin's trial was scheduled for early August.

The Jordan trial was presided over by federal district judge Allen Sharp and began on Monday, August 9, 1982, with Judge Sharp spending an hour discussing the judicial system with the eighty prospective jurors, all of whom had been selected at random from eleven Indiana counties. Judge Sharp was not convinced government charges against Franklin were solid. He believed that trying the matter as a civil rights case in federal court instead of as an attempted murder case in state court was "pushing federal court jurisdiction close to its constitutional limits." The judge also refused to allow the prosecution to introduce evidence about Franklin's conviction for murdering Ted Fields and David Martin.[32]

Franklin's court-appointed attorney was J. Frank Kimbrough. As Franklin sat passively, dressed in a long-sleeved white shirt, blue vest, and blue trousers, Kimbrough began his opening statement by reminding the jury that his client's previous convictions and alleged racism did not mean he shot Jordan. "The evidence will show," Kimbrough told the court, "we don't know who shot Vernon Jordan and that is a hard pill for the government to swallow." Kimbrough said the government was frantic to provide a solution to the shooting and was using Franklin as a "convenient solution."[33]

Because it was a civil rights case, the jury had to be convinced not only that Franklin, who was blind in one eye, was the gunman, but that he shot Jordan because he was black. Barry Kowalski told the jury at the trial's outset that he did not have any eyewitnesses to the shooting, nor did he have the gun used to wound Vernon Jordan. Instead, Kowalski said, they had a piled up a mass of circumstantial evidence. Kowalski said two prison inmates would testify they heard Franklin bragging about the shooting. He said one inmate would testify he saw Franklin pretending to point a rifle at a television set during a show about blacks and exclaim, "I'm going to shoot him just like I shot Jordan." Kowalski said another inmate, Lawrence Hollingsworth, was watching television with Franklin when he heard him express approval of the killings of black children in Atlanta and brag about shooting Jordan.[34]

The following day Vernon Jordan and the surgeon who saved his life gave testimony to the court. Jordan said he never saw the person who shot him and never heard the shot, just felt the impact and felt his body getting wet with blood. Jordan described the speech he made to the Fort Wayne chapter of the National Urban League, drinking coffee with Martha Coleman, and driving to the motel with her. Jordan later wrote about the trial in his memoirs. "I did go to South Bend, Indiana, to testify at Franklin's trial, although there was not much for me to add, because I had not seen who shot me. For the most part, I was there to establish for the record my activities and whereabouts during the evening."[35]

A series of police officers and FBI agents were called to testify and described searching the Marriott Inn and finding a dark, matted-down area where a sniper apparently lay in wait on a grassy knoll overlooking the door to Jordan's first-floor room. Another witness swore under oath that Franklin came into his grocery store after the shooting and graphically detailed the attempted murder. The witness told of how Franklin had said, "It was perfect. If it had been a little different it would have gotten him just right."[36]

On Friday, August 13, the prosecution rested its case after four days of testimony from more than forty witnesses. One of the two final witnesses prosecutors presented was Lawrence Hollingsworth, who denied he was planted in the jail by the FBI and denied he expected any special treatment in exchange for his testimony. Judge Sharp denied a request by Kimbrough to acquit Franklin of the charges that he shot Jordan. Sharp held up a hand with thumb and forefinger almost touching and asked prosecutor Daniel Rinzel, "Isn't it true that we came that close to having a Martin Luther King incident here?" "That's right, your honor," Rinzel replied. "That's one of the reasons we believe this case needs to be fully and completely prosecuted." In denying Kimbrough's request, Sharp said, "It is not the job of a trial judge to sort through and weigh the evidence. The jurors are the judges of the facts."[37]

On Monday, August 16, the defense presented their case over the course of a day. Franklin took the stand and was asked by Kimbrough if he shot Vernon Jordan. "No, I did not," Franklin replied. When Franklin was asked to expand on his racist views, he said, "I don't hate every individual. I hate the [black] race as a whole. I don't believe in race-mixing and things like that." Franklin also admitted his convictions on state and federal charges for the Salt Lake City murders. Twice he denied shooting Jordan, once under questioning from Kimbrough and again when he was cross-examined by Kowalski. When Kimbrough asked Franklin if he had ever used the words, "I shot Vernon Jordan," Franklin replied, "No, I haven't. If I had they would have recorded it." Franklin said prisoners had lied when they testified that he had bragged about shooting a "nigger bigwig" and they had all been government plants that deliberately set out to make him confess to the crime. Testifying for almost one hour, Franklin admitted there was a similarity between his handwriting and signatures on motel registration cards in Fort Wayne but denied ever staying at the hotels or being in Fort Wayne in May 1980. He said he could not recall where he was when Jordan was shot.[38]

The all-white eight-man, four-woman jury retired to consider their verdict on Tuesday, August 17, after two hours of final arguments by the defense and prosecution. Kimbrough insisted the government's case was a "square peg jammed into a round hole. It doesn't fit." He said the evidence showed not that Franklin shot Jordan but that "the government wants so badly to put this case on Mr. Franklin. The evidence shows the government subtly and not so subtly will do that which is necessary to tailor a witness's testimony and recollection to try to make it fit."[39]

Before the jury retired at 12:30 p.m., Judge Sharp informed them that they must decide not only whether Franklin shot Jordan but also whether he committed the crime in order to prevent Jordan from using the facilities of the Fort Wayne Marriott Inn. Because of the special nature of the 1968 Civil Rights Act, the jury had to decide whether Franklin shot Jordan because he was black.

The jurors returned at 8:55 p.m. to give their verdict. As they pronounced Franklin innocent of the crime, the convicted killer smiled and raised his right hand in a gesture of victory. "All right," he said in a very satisfied voice. The judge told the jurors, "Your decision, while a controversial one, is well within the law and well within the evidence." He then announced he was enjoining anyone, including the news media, from talking to members of the jury. The media soon challenged the judge's decision. Richard Cardwell, who represented eight news organizations, said, "First Amendment rights are disintegrating every minute."[40] The judge later retracted his decision and allowed the news media access to the jurors. Explaining his reasoning for his initial decision, Sharp told the jurors, "My main purpose was to prevent lawyers . . . and overzealous news reporters from interfering with your private lives."[41]

A dozen U.S. marshals guarded the table where attorneys sat and sealed off the court exits while the jury was released. Prosecutor Daniel Rinzel told reporters outside the courthouse, "The decision of Franklin's guilt or innocence was up to the jury and we accept what they did." He told reporters the government did not plan to reopen the case. "This case is finished," he said. The director of the NAACP told the media, "I just hope that at some time the perpetrator can be found and appropriately punished. We have to accept the jury's decision."[42] Franklin's lawyer J. Frank Kimbrough left the courtroom hurriedly without comment. Franklin was taken away in a van, the windows covered with cardboard and newspapers.

In interviews with the media, two jurors said that most of the jurors believed that Franklin shot Vernon Jordan. However, they said, the decision was made to acquit because the government failed to prove its civil rights case. One of the jurors, who asked to remain anonymous, told reporters, "I think most of us—our gut feeling—was that he did it. But we could not go by gut feeling. . . . We had to go on evidence and there really wasn't enough evidence to prove [Franklin's guilt]." A second anonymous juror said, "The indictment was not proven on all points." The juror added that, despite the vote for acquittal, jurors thought the testimony of Frank Sweeney was credible.[43]

Following Franklin's federal trial for the shooting of Vernon Jordan, Fort Wayne County prosecutor Arnold H. Duemling said he would not go ahead with state charges against Franklin, as he did not have enough evidence to convict. In Indianapolis, prosecutor Stephen Goldsmith said he saw "very little useful purpose to be served" in trying Franklin for the murders of Leo Thomas Watkins and Lawrence Reese. He said he would have to call some of the same witnesses who testified in the Jordan case. He allowed he would contact District Attorney Robert Macy in Oklahoma City, where Franklin was charged in the murders of Jesse Taylor and

Marian Bressette.[44] However, as time passed, both cities abandoned any hope that they would have sufficient evidence to bring Franklin to trial.

Franklin blamed Robert Herrera for losing the government's case against him. "He testified [at the Jordan trial]," Franklin said, "he got an additional five grand for that . . . I think he deliberately threw a monkey wrench in their whole case in . . . South Bend, Indiana . . . he messed up the whole case for them cause he was so . . . obviously a liar . . . he's the one that messed [the] case up."[45]

Following the Jordan trial and later prosecutions of members of hate groups, Barry Kowalski became the "number one enemy" of white supremacist groups, according to Morris Dees, executive director of the Southern Poverty Law Center in Alabama, which monitors racist groups. Dees said that for years afterward, Kowalski was frequently disparaged in white supremacist newsletters.[46]

It would take another thirteen years for the whole truth of the Vernon Jordan shooting to be revealed. Meanwhile, Jordan never allowed himself to dwell on either Franklin or the shooting. "The pain was such," he said at his first news conference six months after the shooting, "[and] I was sufficiently sick—that I did not spend much time thinking of how I was shot, but rather just on getting well. . . . [I am] not nervous, not jittery and I have no fear. I never was and I'm not now." Many years later when he came to write his memoirs, he remembered the circumstances of the shooting and the trial of Joseph Franklin. "It was useless for me to be embroiled in Franklin's fate," he wrote. "[Franklin] was an avowed racist who believed that the mixing of races was abhorrent. So, in the end, there was no conspiracy, grand or small—just a corrosive belief in white supremacy that led to a hate crime."[47]

THIRTEEN

Going After Franklin

He'll kill you because you are Jewish. He'll kill you if you walk into a synagogue. He'll kill you if you are a black person and walk down the street with a white person.

—Chattanooga assistant district attorney Stan Lanzo

The defendant's history of violence, terror, murder prompts this court to do all it can so that he will never kill again.

—Wisconsin judge William D. Byrne

I am opposed to capital punishment but Mr. Franklin puts those beliefs to a sore test. Mr. Franklin is a pathetic creature who will be dangerous until the day he dies.

—Dane County, Wisconsin, district attorney Hal Harlowe

F ranklin's luck was still holding up, and he had thus far escaped the death penalty. But his time in Marion was anything but comfortable. Attempts had already been made on his life, and he was under constant threat of repeat attacks. Even though he was now held in the prison's protective wing, he knew that sooner or later he would be killed because of his notoriety. He was also being investigated by numerous state law enforcement agencies for the crimes he was suspected of but never tried for. Feeling the pressure of living in a hostile environment, Franklin began to reveal details of his unsolved crimes in the hope he would be transferred to a less dangerous prison.

In August 1983 Franklin had written to Gwinnett Police saying he wanted to talk to them. Lawrenceville police officers Capt. L.D. McKelvey and Sgt. John M. Cowart visited Franklin at Marion the following September and said he indicated a "good bit of knowledge about the [Larry Flynt] case."[1] Franklin had also telephoned Monroe County chief deputy Ron Pearson in February 1984 and confessed to the murder of Rebecca Bergstrom. However, Monroe County district attorney David Shudlick said more information was needed before charges could be filed. Shudlick told reporters that the FBI was involved in the investigation and he was awaiting confirmation they had discovered corroborative evidence in which to charge Franklin.[2] Shudlick, like all law enforcement officers investigating murders, knew that confessions were worthless without some corroboration, particularly details of the crimes no one else could have known. Corroboration separated the serial confessors from the serial killers.

It appeared to law enforcement officials that Franklin was desperate to find some way out of Marion, and his apparent ploy was to confess to his crimes so he would be extradited to other states to stand trial. It also became evident to many investigators that trial furloughs would also provide Franklin with opportunities to escape.

All leads in the 1977 bombing of the Beth Shalom temple in Chattanooga had been pursued without any success by the federal Bureau of Alcohol, Tobacco, and Firearms. The ATF had closed the case in 1979. However, five years later the Chattanooga Police Department was alerted to an interview Franklin had given to the media in Marion in which he confessed to the bombing. Police contacted the ATF investigator assigned to the case, and the investigation was reopened.

On February 29, 1984, at Marion, and in the presence of a ATF agent and a Chattanooga police officer, Franklin, having waived his Miranda rights, voluntarily confessed to the bombing and possession of explosives. Franklin told the investigating officers he had intended for the Beth Shalom synagogue explosion to be timed with an evening service when the building would be full. During the interview Franklin openly voiced his racist political and religious beliefs that motivated the bombing.

In March 1984 Franklin was indicted. The indictment was announced as prosecutors in Georgia and Wisconsin and a Justice Department official disclosed that Franklin was also a suspect in at least thirteen homicides in seven states as well as the attempted assassination of Larry Flynt. Franklin was taken from Marion to the Chattanooga jail for the trial, which was held July 10–12, 1984. Judge Doug Meyer was the presiding judge, and an eight-man, four-woman jury was empanelled. The jury included two African Americans. Two prominent local attorneys, Hugh Moore Jr. and Jerry Summers, represented Franklin. However, the lawyers' task of representing Franklin was made difficult by his behavior. Minutes after entering the courtroom, Franklin began shouting out anti-Semitic remarks.

During the trial it was revealed that Franklin had obtained the explosives (dynamite and Tovex) by using his birth name to purchase dynamite from a Chattanooga supply store in late June 1977, and the Tovex from a Charleston, West Virginia, supplier in early July 1977. Franklin's fingerprints on the ATF Explosives Transaction Records of these sales were compared to known prints and identified as Franklin's by an expert. Additionally, a handwriting analysis was made of Franklin's signature of his alias on the forms. The signatures were determined to be Franklin's.

The defense strategy was to show that Franklin had confessed to numerous crimes throughout the country to obtain a transfer from Marion, where he lived with restricted privileges because his life was threatened. The defense was highly unusual in that it informed the jury of Franklin's political and religious beliefs, and his prior offenses, as well as crimes to which he had only confessed to but not yet been tried or convicted of. The tactical problem was to get the jury to believe that Franklin was lying when he confessed to the details of the bombing in Chattanooga as part of his ulterior motive to get out of Marion.

The prosecution strategy was also unusual in that they wanted to corroborate the confession carefully to ensure that the jury would find Franklin credible. Both defense and prosecution recognized the unique positions in which their strategies placed them. In their opening statements, prosecuting attorneys noted that this was a different type of case in which the defense would ask the jury to believe that Franklin, characterized as a well-read person, gathered the details of the bombing from various media accounts but didn't actually commit the crime. For the most part, prosecutors would repeatedly refer to Franklin's personality and radical beliefs as a way of convincing the jury Franklin was the likely perpetrator of the crime.

Over the course of the trial, Franklin's lawyers questioned the state's witnesses regarding the extent of media coverage and the details of the bombing so they could demonstrate contradictions between Franklin's confession and the actual events. The defense attempted to show that the circumstantial evidence that pointed to Franklin was insufficient without his confession, which was to be discredited by revealing his ulterior motive for confessing and his purported superficial familiarity with the facts surrounding the bombing. Another aspect of the defense effort to discredit the confession was to show that the investigating officers led Franklin through many of the details of the bombing to establish corroboration for his confession. Franklin did not testify on his own behalf during the trial.

The only witness called for the defense was John M. Cowart, the Lawrenceville, Georgia, police officer who had been assigned to investigate the ambush shooting of Larry Flynt. In Franklin's confession to the Chattanooga bombing in February 1984, he specifically denied being involved in the shooting of Larry Flynt. Officer Cowart told the court of another previous confession in December 1983. At that time Franklin expressed his desire to be removed from Marion and stated that he would cooperate with Officer Cowart if Cowart would try to facilitate a move to another prison. Franklin then confessed to the Larry Flynt shooting. In this statement to Officer Cowart, Franklin allegedly remarked, "I'll tell you I'm getting to a point now where I'd say anything just to get out of here for awhile."[3]

Franklin also told Officer Cowart he had bombed the house of the Washington, D.C., Israeli lobbyist Morris Amitay. During the direct examination of Cowart by Franklin's counsel, not only were some of the general conditions at Marion brought out, but Franklin's lawyers also specifically inquired about his stabbing, alleging it was proof that his life had been in danger. Franklin's lawyers asked Cowart whether they had discussed an alleged attempt by prisoners to assault Franklin sexually during the stabbing incident. At this point in the examination, Franklin reacted, denying that any such attempt had been made. The terse exchange between Franklin and his lawyers ended when they withdrew the question after their client adamantly denied it.

State and defense lawyers made closing arguments on July 12, 1984. Prosecutors emphasized Franklin's political and religious beliefs as his motive and asked the jury to find his confession credible. Assistant District Attorney Stan Lanzo told the jury that Franklin had bombed the synagogue because of his intense hatred of Jews. "He'll kill you because you are Jewish," Lanzo said. "He'll kill you if you walk into a synagogue. He'll kill you if you are a black person and walk down the street with a white person."[4]

In his summation Lanzo told the jury that Franklin was housed in a special control unit at Marion to protect him from black convicts. "He ought to be in the general population," Lanzo said, "where they can test him to see if he's a real man." The sneer from Lanzo provoked Franklin into demanding his right of reply. Over his lawyers' objections, the judge ruled that Franklin had the right to make such a statement. When the jury returned, the judge instructed the jury, "Mr. Franklin has requested that he be allowed to represent himself as far as a closing statement to the jury. I caution you that his statement is a statement. It is not testimony. It is not sworn testimony. He is merely acting as his own attorney, which he has the right to do, in making a closing statement to you. It is not evidence."[5]

Franklin then began his statement, telling the jury that it was unrehearsed and that he had "just recently decided to make this statement, within the hour." After a preliminary comment regarding the stabbing incident at Marion, Franklin said, "[The prosecutors] are jealous because I'm a man. They're nothing but punk boys compared to me." He continued, "I want to make your job a little easier here, as far as your deliberations go. You know, I admit to you I bombed the synagogue. You know, I did it. You know, and I'll tell it to anybody around. It was a synagogue of Satan."[6]

He had carried his Bible to the attorney's lectern and quoted passages from it to support his hatred of Jews. In fact he had been reading the Bible throughout the trial without losing track of the trial's proceedings. Looking at his attorneys, who contended Franklin had lied about the bombing in hopes of getting transferred out of Marion, Franklin told the jurors they had been given "slander and lies." His argument continued, as he attempted to explain why he planted the bomb, basing his position on his interpretation of the Bible. He particularly quoted passages from the Book of Revelations. He expounded on the purported Jewish conspiracy, claiming that "they control the American government. They control the news media. Control all different branches of the U.S. government. The communist nations are all controlled by Jews, and all the western democracies are controlled by Jews." According to Franklin, the "Kahzar Jews are trying to destroy [the white race] through race-mixing and through communism." He said, "This country was founded by white men who were believers in Jesus Christ. They've been taken over by atheists. I'd just like to tell you this—the only way for the white man to survive is to get on their knees and pray to the Lord and accept Jesus Christ as their personal savior."[7]

Following Franklin's statement, Jerry Summers made his closing argument. He reminded the jury that Franklin was not on trial for his beliefs. Summers never contested Franklin's possession of explosives but instead attempted to show that Franklin confessed to the bombing as a part of his scheme to obtain a transfer from Marion. The defense also tried to show how investigating officers had put words in Franklin's mouth when they interviewed him in February 1984. Summers stressed

that, given Franklin's beliefs, affording him a fair trial was of paramount importance. He asked that the jury "put aside any feelings that [they] have in regard to
whether [they] agreed or disagreed with him . . . and . . . make [the] decision on the
facts of this case." He continued, "I don't think you're ever [going to] see any two
lawyers in the position probably . . . where really we're asking you to not believe our
client and the DA's asking you to believe him." He argued that without Franklin's
confession, the defendant would never have been a suspect in the bombing, and
that, given his already substantial prison sentences, Franklin had nothing to lose
in confessing. Summers argued that understanding Franklin's ulterior motive for
the confession was crucial to determining his credibility. Summers also noted that
Franklin had used the trial as a forum to express his political and religious views,
which was part of what he wanted from his trial. After Summers finished but before
the district attorney gave his final argument, Franklin left the courtroom for the
second time at his own request.

In his final argument, Assistant District Attorney Lanzo stated that he had
thought the trial would be "kind of a low-key trial," and he apologized for "misin-
terpreting what actually became quite dramatic." He argued that Franklin did indeed
want to use the trial as an opportunity to publicize his political and religious beliefs.
Nevertheless, despite Franklin's desire to get out of Marion, Lanzo said the prosecutors had not promised him anything at any time to obtain his confession. Remarking
that Franklin was a credible person, he said that "the motive for being here in this
trial is the same motive for the explosion of the synagogue. . . . He wants attention for his attitudes and his feelings, his warped, demented thinking about races of
people."[8]

The jury's job had been made a little easier with Franklin's last minute confession. The jury returned a guilty verdict in forty-five minutes, and Judge Meyer
sentenced Franklin to fifteen to twenty-one years for the bombing and six to ten
years for possession of explosives. Meyer ordered the sentences served consecutively after Franklin had completed four life sentences for the murders of Fields and
Martin in Salt Lake City. Franklin showed no emotion as the sentences were read.
He simply said, "Thank you, your honor," before being led away by two marshals.

Franklin's lawyers, Jerry Summers and Hugh Moore, appealed the conviction and had some success with lower courts. The U.S. Court of Criminal Appeals
held that Franklin had "not knowingly and intelligently waived his right to the assistance of counsel and that the trial court had abused its discretion in allowing
[Franklin] to participate in closing argument." However, in 1986, the case was
finally decided by the State Supreme Court, which stated that "although the trial

Franklin, indicted in the shooting of civil rights leader Vernon Jordan, is shown following his conviction on June 2, 1981, of two counts of first degree murder. Thirty-one-year-
old Franklin (whose hometown was Mobile, Alabama) was sentenced to life in prison for
shooting two black joggers in Salt Lake City in 1980. (AP/Wide World Photos.)

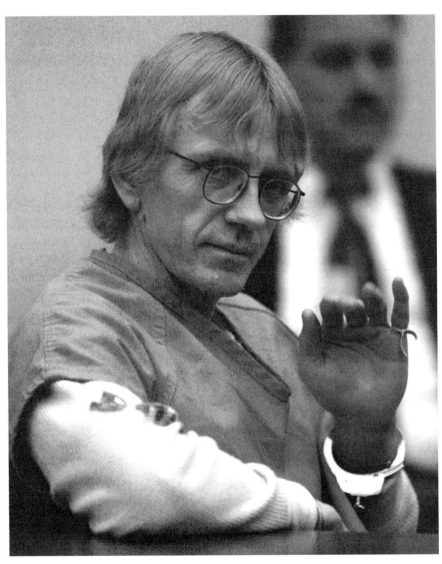

Franklin gestures while seated in the courtroom in Clayton, Missouri, on February 27, 1997. Franklin, who threatened to kill again if allowed to live, was sentenced to death for killing a man in a sniper shooting at a Richmond Heights, Missouri, synagogue in 1977. The forty-six-year-old represented himself during the trial and asked the all-white, all-male jury for the death sentence, thanking the court for a fair trial after the sentencing. (AP/Wide World Photos.)

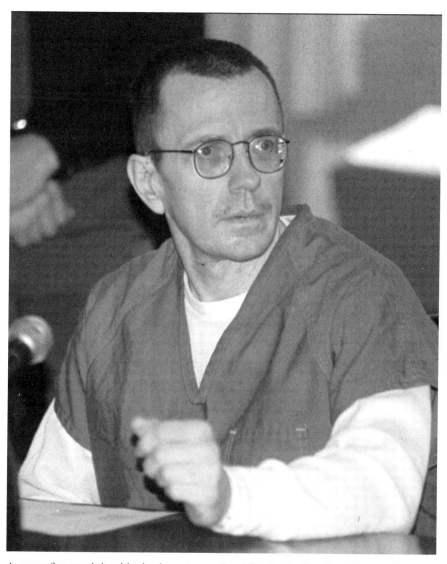

A year after receiving his death sentence, Franklin sits in Hamilton County Common Pleas Court on October 19, 1998, in Cincinnati, Ohio, where jury selection was set to begin in his trial for the murder of two African American boys. (AP/Wide World Photos.)

President Jimmy Carter, left, shakes hands with Vernon Jordan, president of the Urban League, in a hospital room in New York on August 6, 1980. Jordan was recovering from gunshot wounds he suffered after he addressed the Convention of the National Urban League in Fort Wayne, Indiana. Jordan's would-be assassin was never captured, but many years later Joseph Paul Franklin confessed that he had tried to assassinate Jordan after stalking and then failing to shoot civil rights leader Jesse Jackson. (AP/Wide World Photos.)

President Carter presides over a meeting of black leaders, including Vernon Jordan of the National Urban League, at the White House on December 4, 1978. Jordan is seated to Carter's right. (AP/Wide World Photos.)

Publisher Larry Flynt lies on a stretcher in Atlanta, on April 14, 1978, as attendants prepare to load him on board a hospital plane to Ohio State University Hospital. Franklin targeted Flynt, founder and owner of *Hustler* magazine, after Flynt published photos of a mixed-race couple. Franklin shot Flynt and his attorney with a sniper rifle in Lawrenceville, Georgia, on March 6, 1978. Both men survived their injuries, but Flynt was left paralyzed from the waist down. (AP/Wide World Photos.)

George Linoln Rockwell, founder of the American Nazi Party. Franklin worshipped Rockwell and believed in the Nazi leader's warnings that racial integration and mixed-race marriages would destroy America. His fellow Klansmen constantly reinforced Franklin's sense of mission, which he repeated to anyone who would listen in the early days of his murder spree. An anti-Semite and racial bigot, Rockwell would often blame Jews for promoting communism that led to black rebellion. He also charged Jews with "scheming" to "mongrelize" the American racial stock by promoting racial integration and "interbreeding" with blacks. (AP/Wide World Photos.)

Lawyer J. B. Stoner, center, on May 27, 1969. Stoner represented James Earl Ray, Martin Luther King Jr.'s assassin. Stoner is pictured with Ray's brothers John Larry Ray and Jerry Ray. Stoner was the founder of the racist National States Rights Party that Franklin joined in the early 1970s. Both men also held membership in the Ku Klux Klan. Stoner frequently voiced his disapproval of mixed-race marriages and was an important influence on Franklin. (AP/Wide World Photos.)

court was incorrect, that [Franklin] had a right to make the statement to the jury in this case, that court did not err in the circumstances of the trial in exercising his discretion to allow [Franklin] to make a statement to the jury. The judgment of the Court of Criminal Appeals is, therefore, reversed and that of the trial court is reinstated."[9]

———————

Gwinnett County, Georgia, district attorney Bryant Huff said he planned to seek an indictment against Franklin for the shooting of Larry Flynt by mid-April of 1984, and that a grand jury had been impaneled for a two-month term. He said he would probably seek charges of aggravated battery. "The evidence is both interesting and intriguing," Huff said. "We will try to present it in the most neutral manner that we can because we realize the case is six years old."[10]

Huff said racism would be a motive to consider and that Franklin had reacted to a *Hustler* magazine spread showed a sexually explicit pictorial of a racially mixed couple. Huff said they had evidence that Franklin stayed in a motel near Lawrenceville and bought a car in Gwinnett County around the time of the shooting. Capt. McKelvey told reporters that Franklin had been a suspect since 1980 after he and Sgt. Cowart went to Illinois for a conference with law enforcement officials who believed Franklin might have been responsible for shootings in their cities. Franklin was considered a viable suspect all along, McKelvey stated, but "emerged a much better suspect than before" after McKelvey and Cowart interviewed him for four hours in Marion.[11] In August 1983 Franklin had written to Gwinnett Police, saying he wanted to talk to them. McKelvey and Cowart visited him the following September. "He indicated a good bit of knowledge about the case," Cowart said, "and he gave us enough leads that we felt we had probable cause to seek an indictment. The more we checked his background the more of a suspect he became."[12]

What McKelvey did not tell reporters, however, was that Franklin retracted his confession once the law enforcement officers arrived at Marion and that the killer had been playing games with them. Franklin's letter to Gwinnett authorities stated, "My name is Joseph Paul Franklin. I shot Larry Flynt. If you bring me to Gwinnett County, I'll tell you about it." Franklin was making yet another desperate attempt to get out of Marion. When officers could not guarantee Franklin's transfer, he told them the letter was only a hoax. However, Franklin did supply the police with enough information to persuade them he was, indeed, the shooter. Franklin described the interior of the two-story abandoned storefront building where the shots came from. He described his escape route, the vehicle he used, and where he drove. Details Franklin provided were checked out and found to be true.[13]

However, the information Franklin provided and the way he retracted his confession left the Gwinnett authorities in a quandary. Although they believed they had sufficient evidence to try Franklin, they simply did not have enough, they believed, to guarantee a conviction. Furthermore, the assault charges would always take second billing to the other murder charges against him.

Adding to the prosecution's frustrations, Larry Flynt was queering the pitch for any prospective trial. The magazine publisher did not help matters when he gave an interview to a news organization in which he alleged that Franklin was only one of three men involved in the assassination attempt against him and that he had a signed confession from one of the men involved. "They're using a guy who's in prison for the rest of his life and probably will never get out anyway," Flynt said.[14]

On July 11, the day before he was convicted of the Chattanooga bombing, an Atlanta television station broadcast a taped interview with Franklin in which he said he was paid by "a prominent Georgian" to shoot Flynt. Franklin was once again lying. No evidence has ever surfaced to corroborate Franklin's allegations, and he never repeated the charges.[15]

On June 12 District Attorney Huff presented evidence against Franklin to a grand jury, and Franklin was indicted for the shooting of Larry Flynt. He was charged on two counts of aggravated assault. Eventually the Gwinnett County indictment was left in abeyance as other authorities sought to bring Franklin to justice. Huff said he was "ready, willing, and able to go forward with the case," but he would defer to Madison, Wisconsin, authorities who wanted to try Franklin in the autumn of 1984 for the murders of Alphonse Manning Jr. and his girlfriend Toni Schwenn. "Based on the outcome there," Huff said, "I will re-evaluate the case. I cannot make that judgment until that's been done."[16]

In March 1984 Franklin had confessed during a telephone conversation with Madison police officers he had killed Alphonse Manning and Toni Schwenn. He told the officers he had shot a black man and a white woman at the shopping mall in 1977. Franklin was later identified from a photographic lineup as the person seen driving a car at the scene of the crime. Dane County, Wisconsin, district attorney Hal Harlowe said two first-degree murder charges would be filed against Franklin for the two murders. However, in the period before the 1986 trial, Franklin recanted his confession and said he faked the admission to win temporary release from Marion.

Franklin's first-degree murder trial began on Monday, February 10, 1986, in the Dane County Circuit Court, which was presided over by Judge William D. Byrne. The court employed security measures during the trial that included searching the jury for weapons, the use of metal detectors, and the stationing of armed guards throughout the courtroom. The court required the search of jurors because it had received information of a high security risk for persons inside and immediately outside the courtroom. Franklin acted as his own attorney with the assistance of stand-by counsel. He called no witnesses and did not testify. During the trial Franklin was shackled, but his shackles were hidden from the jury by protective drapes.

The prosecution played a tape of Franklin's confession. Prosecutor Hal Harlowe introduced the tape by telling the jury, "You will hear, in the defendant's own words, in the defendant's own voice, what drives someone to commit a murder of this sort." Jurors heard Franklin discussing checking into a Madison motel on August 6, 1977, using the name of former outlaw John Wesley Hardin. He said he planned the next day to kill a Dane County judge who he believed had been too lenient in sentencing blacks, but his plan went askew in a shopping mall parking lot. Franklin then proceeded to describe the details of the murders. After the tape had been played, Harlowe told the jury that the evidence showed how "various destinies impinged on one another and led to a horrible tragedy." He said Manning and Schwenn crossed Franklin's path as he attempted to flee a parking lot after spotting a police car. Harlowe continued, "His motive was they had gotten in his way and that was like a red flag in front of a bull."[17]

The judge Franklin had initially targeted, Archie Simonson, gave his testimony during the third day of the trial. Simonson said that he had been criticized for being too lenient with two young African American boys accused of assaulting a white girl. Simonson went on to tell the jury that the case had received national attention that brought him into Franklin's orbit. "I put him on my list," Franklin had said.[18]

In other testimony a former Columbus, Ohio, bank teller, Karen Thompson, identified Franklin as the man who robbed a bank there on August 2, 1977. She began to cry as she pointed to Franklin. "That one right there, that was him," she said in response to Harold Harlowe's request that she point out the robber. She said a .357 caliber Magnum pistol shown to her by Harlowe was similar to the gun the robber had used to steal $42,500 from the bank. When former state crime laboratory ballistics expert Richard Thompson testified, he said five bullets taken from the bodies of Schwenn and Manning could have been fired by a .357 magnum.[19]

Franklin, acting as his own attorney, began by telling the jury that he faked the confession to get out of prison and that some details in his confession statement were faked by police officers who were eager to solve the case. "The evidence in this case," Franklin said, "will show that the defendant was not the perpetrator of this crime." Franklin said he admitted murdering Alphonse Manning and Toni Schwenn in 1977 simply to get out of Marion Prison, "because of the brutal conditions there." He said his taped confession "was totally concocted by the defendant's imagination," with details gleaned from newspaper clippings and prompting from detectives.[20]

In closing arguments on Friday, February 14, Hal Harlowe called the killings "horrible, senseless, and pointless," and the "closest thing to killing for sport" he had ever seen. Harlowe added, "I am opposed to capital punishment but Mr. Franklin puts those beliefs to a sore test. Mr. Franklin is a pathetic creature who will be dangerous until the day he dies."[21]

Following the judge's instructions, the jury left the courtroom and deliberated for two hours before finding Franklin guilty of two counts of first-degree murder. Friends and family of the victims wept and held hands when the verdict was read. Franklin showed no emotion. When Byrne asked if he wished to comment Franklin replied "No, your honor." As the conviction carried a mandatory sentence of life imprisonment, Judge Byrne immediately sentenced Franklin to two consecutive life terms. Byrne said, "The defendant's history of violence, terror, murder prompts this court to do all it can so that he will never kill again."[22] Franklin showed no emotion when the sentence was passed.

When Franklin appealed the verdict, he cited the alleged bias of the judge, the high security measures employed at the trial, and the fact that a state witness was used to guard him for five to ten minutes as proof that his constitutional rights were abused. He also claimed the photo array given to a witness who had observed him in the parking lot seated in his Camaro was impermissibly suggestive. He argued that all the other subjects were much older, they had facial hair, and their photos were at least twice the size of his.

However, the appeals court dismissed all of Franklin's claims. From their review of the photos, they concluded that the trial court's finding was not "clearly erroneous" and that no one picture stood out. They considered Franklin's allegations that his inculpatory statements made to police officers over the telephone should have been suppressed since the officers did not give him Miranda warnings. However, the appeals judges argued that Franklin was not then in the officers' custody and that he could have terminated the calls at any time. The officers, they found, were not required to give Franklin Miranda warnings. It was also decided by the appeals court that the security measures did not abuse his rights and the trial court did not abuse its discretion with regard to the state witness guard as the witness did not connect Franklin to the crimes. The appeals court further judged that the trial judge, William D. Byrne, had shown respect to Franklin and did not exhibit partiality or bias. Accordingly, Franklin's appeal was rejected.

When the trial in Madison was over, Gwinnett County officials decided against trying Franklin for the Larry Flynt shooting. Even though Franklin had confessed to the shooting and had been indicted for it, plans for a trial were put on the back burner. The district attorney would come under severe criticism for this decision following the release of a Hollywood movie about the *Hustler* magazine publisher many years later. The movie, *The People vs. Larry Flynt*, highlighted the fact that Flynt's assailant had never been brought to trial.

In 1984 the FBI was also frustrated with the not-guilty verdict in the Vernon Jordan case. Even though accumulating evidence of Franklin's guilt may have acted in their favor in a second trial, the double jeopardy ruling determined that prosecutors could not try him again. Furthermore, it became increasingly unlikely that the state of Indiana would try him for the attempted murder, as their prosecutors did not believe they had a strong case. Authorities in Cincinnati, Indianapolis, and Oklahoma City were also hesitant to bring Franklin to justice due to the lack of sufficient evidence in their cases. Franklin's crimes in Johnstown and Atlanta would go undetected for another decade. In fact, it would take another ten years for the full truth about Franklin's sniper murders to emerge.

It would also be another fourteen years before the truth about the Rainbow murders came to light, despite the fact that Franklin had told Wisconsin special agent Ernest V. Smith, ATF agents, and West Virginia state trooper Debbie DeFalco in 1984 that he had murdered Nancy Santomero and Vickie Durian. However, Franklin did not supply the law enforcement officers with any details of the murders. Without any corroboration, West Virginia authorities dismissed Franklin's confession as not credible. They would eventually commit one of the biggest travesties of justice ever to occur in the state when another suspect was arrested, tried, and found guilty.

––––––––––––

Det. Michael O'Brien of the Cincinnati police never gave up his search for the person that killed Darrell Lane and Dante Brown. The investigation had become controversial in 1981 when city safety director Bert McGinnis appointed a new task force. Homicide detectives criticized the move and told local newspapers that the decision was unnecessary and politically motivated. They said over $100,000 was spent on the original investigation and that the new task force was a waste of money because their investigation had been as thorough as possible. After Franklin had been convicted in the Salt Lake City murders, Cincinnati police said they were interested in Franklin and could place him in the Cincinnati area at the time of the boys' murders, but there were other suspects in the case. They said they had been unable to recover the key piece of evidence—the .44 caliber Magnum rifle believed to be the murder weapon.[23]

O'Brien continued to build his case hoping to convict Franklin of the Cincinnati murders. But Frank Sweeney's testimony was judged by Cincinnati prosecutors to be insufficient to bring Franklin to trial. It was not until the late 1990s that O'Brien would be able to take the case forward, when Franklin decided he would talk with a Cincinnati prosecutor about the murders—as long as she was a beautiful woman.

FOURTEEN

Coming Clean

I don't have a death wish. I use my dreams for guidance.

—Joseph Paul Franklin, explaining why he confessed to
the murder of Gerald Gordon.

O n Sunday August 19, 1990, four years after the Madison murder trial, Franklin admitted to committing the Salt Lake City murders in an interview he gave for the Salt Lake City television station KUTV. The interview was held at Marion. Initially, Franklin balked at saying anything about the crimes. "No comment," he told Chris Vanocur, the television reporter. "Next question." However, an hour into the interview, when asked again if he had committed the Salt Lake City murders, Franklin sighed and answered, "Yes, the answer is yes. I won't discuss it any further." When the reporter made reference to David Martin's mother and her need to understand why her son had been killed, Franklin said, "Just for her, just to answer her question, I'll say that it was just because they were race-mixing. Had they not been race-mixing, you know, it would have been a totally different story."[1]

Franklin told Vanocur he spent most of his time in his cell reading the Bible and praying. He said he had no remorse for the Utah murders and repeated his white supremacist views. "No, I don't regret that," he said of the slayings. "Not to say there are not actions that I've done that I don't regret. I've sinned a lot in my life. Any sins that I've done I've repented of."[2]

In the early 1990s, John Douglas and Ken Baker interviewed Franklin in Marion as part of a joint Secret Service and FBI project to study assassination. Douglas noticed how Franklin wore "thick glasses and his eyes darted back and forth between Ken and me, trying to read us." After settling into the interview, he became more responsive and "animated." Douglas said Franklin was "not a super bright guy or a deep thinker," but he was "cooperative and articulate."[3]

During Douglas's visit, the FBI profiler learned that Franklin had become distraught because his ex-wife Anita had restricted his daughter's contacts with him. Douglas agreed to take some photographs of Franklin so he could send them to his daughter. Incredibly, given the nature of his crimes and the fact the photos were meant for his daughter, Franklin posed in various martial arts positions looking "macho and serious."[4]

Douglas sensed Franklin wanted to "get the proper credit and have us be impressed with him." When Douglas asked him about the Jordan shooting, he "just smiled" and said, "What do you think? I'll just say that justice was done."[5] Douglas believed this was not an admission of guilt, but noted that Franklin's ego did not allow him to deny it. In reality, Franklin did not want to confess outright to the Jordan shooting because he feared reprisals from black inmates. Douglas said Franklin never indicated any remorse or sense of contrition for his crimes. "It was all matter of fact," Douglas wrote.[6]

For ten years the FBI and the Richmond Heights police had suspected Franklin of killing Gerald Gordon in the 1977 sniper shooting outside the Brith Shalom Kneseth Israel Congregation. They had traced the rifle to him, but they did not have enough evidence to charge him until October 1994, when he made a confession to the FBI. The following month he gave incriminating statements to the Richmond Heights Police Department.

During the FBI interview Franklin said he had shot Gerald Gordon and William Ash, who was wounded in the left hand and lost his pinky finger. Franklin gave the FBI a detailed account of his preparation for and execution of the shootings, which included buying the 30.06 rifle in Texas, obliterating the rifle serial number, and wiping his fingerprints from the rifle and shell casings. He said he chose the Richmond Heights synagogue because it had bushes for cover and that he hammered nails into a telephone pole to use as a rifle prop, used a bicycle to flee the scene undetected, and monitored the police radio to determine if the police were looking for him. Later, when he repeated his confession to a Richmond Heights police officer, he said he wished he "had killed five Jews with the five bullets."[7]

Franklin also explained why he did not confess to the crime earlier. He said that in the mid-1980s, he refused to admit to the Gerald Gordon murder because he "knew it was a death penalty case and I wasn't anxious to be sentenced to the gas chamber." Franklin said he changed his mind in late 1994 after he had a dream in which he was told to confess. "I don't have a death wish," he said. "I use my dreams for guidance."[8] In an interview Franklin gave to the *Indianapolis Star* and the *Indianapolis News,* he told reporters he was not afraid of the death penalty anymore. "I am very pro-death penalty," he said, "especially because I consider it good. It is mentioned in the Bible."[9]

The state of Missouri indicted Franklin on one count of capital murder, two counts of assault with intent to do great bodily harm with malice aforethought, and three counts of armed criminal action. He was taken from Marion to the St. Louis County jail to await trial. Meanwhile, Franklin's court-appointed lawyer filed a notice of intent to rely on the defense of mental disease or defect and also requested a hearing on Franklin's mental fitness to proceed to trial. Franklin was evaluated separately by two psychiatrists, one chosen by the defense, the other chosen by the court.

On November 18, 1994, Franklin was brought before Judge Robert Campbell of the St. Louis Circuit Court so it could be determined whether he was fit to stand trial. The court needed to determine whether Franklin's mission to start a race war and his determination to rid America of African Americans and Jews was an act of mental illness.

When Franklin arrived in court, he was led into division 15 of the St. Louis County courthouse in Clayton, Missouri, wearing a pair of black shoes, an orange jumpsuit, and a pair of black rimmed spectacles. The identification marks on his arms, the Grim Reaper and eagle tattoos which had led to his capture, were clearly visible as Franklin was led to his seat surrounded by armed officers.

Franklin had already filed a motion to waive his right to counsel and proceed to trial pro se because he disagreed with his attorneys "in regards to the type of defense we want to use and other issues." The court denied his attorney's motion to withdraw and ordered defense counsel to serve as Franklin's advisory counsel. Before trial, Franklin signed and submitted a written waiver of counsel.

The prosecution, led by veteran prosecutor Doug Sidel, began by presenting two videotapes. The first video was his formal confession to police, and the second was an interview Franklin gave to a television news team. In both videos Franklin calmly and lucidly told the story of how he planned and executed the shootings at the synagogue. He spoke of how he got his Grim Reaper tattoo in Dallas and, incongruously, told of how much he admired the shock jock radio host Howard Stern, whom Franklin liked because of his honesty. In the news interview video, Franklin took issue with the media's characterization of his offenses as hate crimes, since he believed that "every murder is committed out of hate."

In his confession to the police, Franklin was asked if there was anything he would like to add to his story about the murder of Gerald Gordon. He replied, "I can't think of anything," then suddenly blurted out he had no remorse, adding, "The only thing I'm sorry about is that killing Jews isn't legal."[10] This would later become the cornerstone of his bizarre defense strategy; although he readily admitted to the killing, he didn't believe he was guilty because he thought killing Jews was morally acceptable.

The defense brought psychiatrist Dorothy Otnow Lewis of New York City's Bellevue Hospital to testify at the hearing. Lewis was an expert witness who had examined between 150 and 200 murderers over the course of twenty years. Some of her famous interviewees included John Lennon's killer, Mark David Chapman, and the notorious serial killer Ted Bundy. Lewis said she had spoken with Franklin twice, covering a period of six and a half hours, before concluding Franklin was a paranoid schizophrenic, "a psychotic whose thinking was delusional and confused." Lewis described Franklin's brutal childhood in which his mother beat him repeatedly, and she also described Franklin's bizarre beliefs, including his assertion he may have been a Jew in a previous life. She further concluded that Franklin was not fit to stand trial. Lewis said Franklin had brain impairment and had definite biological and psychological problems that diminished his responsibility for his murderous acts.

Dr. Sam Parwatikar, a state psychiatrist, conducted Franklin's pretrial chapter 552 examination. During the interview Franklin told Parwatikar that Jews were the cause of all evil in the world, that spirit guides spoke to him and guided him in various life decisions, and that the government, the media, and the film industry in the United States were "The Great Satan." Parwatikar diagnosed Franklin as suffering from "paranoid personality disorder," but concluded that he was competent to act as his own lawyer. He opined that Franklin suffered from "idiosyncratic" thoughts and found his behavior to be the result of a personality disorder rather than a mental illness. However, Parwatikar concluded that Franklin's "idiosyncrasies" did not rise "to the level of delusions associated with paranoid schizophrenia affecting his competence." Parwatikar found Franklin capable and competent to stand trial and assist in his own defense.[11]

The following day Franklin took the stand and confessed to a few "minor neuroses" but denied he was insane. He said the insanity defense that his lawyers were pursuing was "hogwash" because he "knew exactly" what he was doing when he committed the murder. Franklin said he respected Lewis but believed she "embellished" her statements "somewhat." He said he disagreed with Lewis's diagnosis of paranoid schizophrenia but admitted suffering from obsessive-compulsive disorder, attention deficit disorder, and social phobias. Franklin said he believed in reincarnation and was guided by dreams, numbers, letters, lights, astrology, common sense, and the Bible. He insisted his superstitions did not mean he was "psychotic or completely crazy or stark, raving mad." He added that he was instructed in a dream to give his confession, but he was never instructed to confess to a crime he did not commit. As evidence to show he was competent to act as his own lawyer, Franklin said that the state dropped the armed criminal action charges after he correctly advised his lawyers the state could not prosecute him because his crimes occurred in 1977, two years before the statute became law. Franklin said, "I am experienced in trial law, and although I've never been to law school, I've represented myself in two other murder trials, one of them a capital case." He did, however, request advisory counsel, and Karen Kraft was later appointed to represent him.

Concluding his testimony, Franklin also said he would prefer being sentenced to death in Missouri than being killed by unnamed persons in Marion who were "out to kill" him. He added that corrections officers at Marion were trying to kill him for exposing drug smuggling activities in the prison. However, he denied confessing to the crime of murdering Gerald Gordon because of these death threats. However, when he was expressly asked whether he confessed to Gordon's murder in order to facilitate a transfer out of the federal prison, Franklin emphatically denied it to be his motivation. His motivation came from his spirit guide, he said, who told him to confess and seek his own execution. The spirit guide, apparently, had also told Franklin to "seek castration for his sins."[12]

A week later the judge agreed that Franklin was competent to stand trial and also competent to act as his own lawyer. The court also noted that it found Dr. Parwatikar's testimony more compelling than that of Dr. Lewis and expressed disbelief in Dr. Lewis' diagnosis that Franklin was delusional.

The trial began on Wednesday, January 29, 1997. The court heard of how the twenty-seven-year-old Franklin drove to Dallas, Texas, in September 1977 after robbing a bank in Little Rock, Arkansas. While in Dallas, the jury heard, Franklin bought a 30.06 rifle through a classified ad and took it to a firing range to properly adjust his telescopic sight and practice firing. The prosecutors said Franklin spent a week in Dallas then drove to Oklahoma City. He became determined to murder numerous Jews and developed a plan to shoot congregants as they left a synagogue. Jurors heard of how Franklin abandoned his plan to kill Jews outside an Oklahoma City synagogue but instead chose St. Louis, which he believed had a larger Jewish community and thus provided a larger choice of targets. Prosecutors said that in late September or early October, Franklin drove to St. Louis and checked into a hotel under an alias. After reconnoitering numerous synagogues, he chose Brith Shalom Kneseth Israel Congregation in Richmond Heights. Prosecutor Doug Sidel told the jury that Franklin was "on a campaign to kill Jews."[13]

Although Franklin was defending himself against the charges, he paradoxically did everything possible to damage his case. Acting as his own advocate, Franklin had participated in jury selection, and during the trial, he cross-examined the state's witnesses but presented no evidence and urged the jury during closing arguments to sentence him to death. An appeals judge later described his monologue as "a sermon and a political polemic." Franklin had told the jury that if he did not get the death penalty, he would kill more people. Jurors believed him. They had deliberated for less than forty minutes. One day after the trial began, on Thursday, January 13, 1997, the jury found Franklin guilty. After the reading of the verdicts, Franklin smiled at them, gave the thumbs up sign, and said, "Right on!"[14] A sentence of life would almost certainly have sent him back to the federal prison in Marion.

Shortly after Franklin's conviction, he was interviewed by Kim Bell of the *St. Louis Post-Dispatch*. He told her he was not fazed by the conviction, saying he wanted it and that being executed was better than being slain in prison by inmates who despised him. "Being murdered by some punks is just a dishonorable way to die," he told Bell. "I got my name listed in encyclopedias on serial killers. They might just kill me for the notoriety. I'd rather be executed by the state . . . I would by far want a firing squad, and I barely missed out on that in Utah. They put a target over your heart and you die instantly, for one thing."[15]

Since the reinstatement of capital punishment, murder trials have consisted of two phases. In the first phase, the jury determines the guilt or innocence. The second phase is a presentation by the prosecution of "aggravating circumstances."

In other words, an explanation as to why the defendant deserves to die. In 1972 the United States Supreme Court had ended all executions following the case of *Furman v. Georgia*. The court had decided that death sentences were capricious and arbitrary and thus violated the Eighth Amendment's prohibition on cruel and unusual punishment. However, in 1976 the court reversed itself and declared that capital punishment was legal. In the interim period many states had enacted new capital punishment statutes to eliminate the capriciousness the court had objected to. States had introduced new rules to make sure there were "aggravating factors" that made the capital offense more than ordinary first-degree murder. The aggravating circumstances might include extreme cruelty, or murder while carrying out other crimes like burglary or rape.

The defense had the opportunity to present mitigating circumstances. Frequently, in murder cases, this became an overview of the offender's past life and the possible abuse he or she may have suffered while growing up. However, the prosecution could always point to the fact that many citizens had suffered a deprived childhood but they did not resort to murder. The defense might also contend that mental illness or brain damage was a mitigating factor. They would therefore have to use expert testimony to convince a jury. Likewise, the prosecution could use expert testimony to refute any suggestions of mental illness or brain impairment.

In the penalty phase of Franklin's trial, prosecutors presented evidence of his prior convictions, including the Salt Lake City murders, the Madison murders, and the Chattanooga bombing. Doug Sidel said Franklin's plan to kill more than one person during the sniper attack on the synagogue "exhibited a callous disregard for the sanctity of human life," and "the aggravating circumstances of the case justified the imposition of the sentence of death." He told the jurors, "If there was ever a case for capital punishment, it is this case and this man."[16]

In his own closing statement Franklin's argument was not designed to seek leniency but to provoke the jury into recommending the death sentence. Franklin told the jury about a fellow inmate's suggestion that if they did not recommend the death penalty, Franklin should "kill somebody to make sure they do the next time." Franklin told the jurors that after this conversation, he "decided that if you guys do not vote for the death penalty, that's what's going to happen. I'm already doing six consecutive life sentences already, plus some other time. And it would just be a total farce if you guys did not sentence me to death."[17]

The jury deliberated for sixty-five minutes. On Thursday, February 27, 1997, Judge Robert L. Campbell, following the jury's recommendations, imposed the death sentence along with two consecutive terms of life imprisonment for felonious assault. He sentenced Franklin to death by lethal injection. In reply Franklin told the court, "I'd just like to thank the court for a fair trial."[18] Franklin said, "I just felt safe when I got the death penalty. I just feel really secure now."[19]

Following sentencing, Franklin, having been advised by his spirit guide, executed a written waiver of appeal. However, Karen Kraft told reporters she would definitely appeal Franklin's conviction because she believed he was a paranoid schizophrenic who should not have been allowed to represent himself at trial. When Kraft told the court of her intentions, Franklin objected, insisting he did not want a new trial, and asked the court to "take [her] off the case so that [she] cannot try to file an appeal of this case." He refused to sign the appeal and wrote to the court in May 1998 stating, "I am a Missouri prisoner under sentence of death and am currently on writ of habeus [sic] corpus ad testificandum. This is to advise the court that I do NOT wish to appeal case no. 79735. Please set an execution date as soon as possible, either in July or August of this year [1998]."[20]

However, Franklin had once again attempted to fool the court. He initially said he automatically ruled out women from the jury panel because they were more compassionate than men and would not hand down a sentence of death. "In Utah, the jury was half women," he said in 1997, "and they voted for life. So here [in St. Louis] I deliberately struck all women. I used all nine strikes to strike women." However, years later he told Cincinnati police officer Michael O'Brien "I especially wasn't trying there [putting forward a good defense argument] . . . let me make one thing perfectly clear on this . . . I do not want to die . . . the only reason I told them to give me the death sentence, I knew that that was the only way I'd be sent from Marion to Potosi [prison], see . . . now I gotta try to wriggle outta this one . . . I told [my lawyer], I said fight this tooth and nail."[21]

In death penalty states, the appeal system is complex and prolonged—six higher courts might review a capital case. Initially, there is a direct review by the State Supreme Court. The court will take into account arguments by defense and prosecution lawyers who may have additional information or evidence. If the judges rule there was no error, then the next stage is to lodge a claim of habeas corpus,which states that the prisoner is alleging his detention is unlawful because his constitutional rights have been violated. The prisoner may file two habeas corpus claims with the federal courts. The federal court claim may go as high as the U.S. Supreme Court. If the Supreme Court rejects the appeal, the prisoner's lawyers may appeal to the Board of Pardons and Parole, which has the power to grant clemency. In Missouri the average time taken for the appeals process is ten years.

In February 1997, between Franklin's conviction for the Gordon murder and the later imposition of the death penalty, Franklin told *St. Louis Post-Dispatch* reporter Kim Bell he would not fight his punishment and that "appeals should last no longer than three years. . . . It disgusts me that these guys try to save their miserable lives."[22]

Two months after the trial had ended, Franklin had changed his mind about not wanting to appeal the case. In litigation, he said it was a spirit guide who wrongfully told him to waive his appeal and that his lawyers failed to present evidence at the trial of his obsessive-compulsive disorder. He also said his confession was motivated by threats to his life and that he would not have waived his right to a lawyer during the trial if his lawyer had agreed to tell the court about his mental disorders. Franklin did not appear to be aware that he had contradicted himself, as he had previously stated his mental disorders did not affect his competency to act as his own lawyer.

On June 16, 1998, the Missouri Supreme Court held that Franklin's sentence was "proper," and his appeal was rejected. The court said the punishment for Franklin matched his actions: buying a rifle with a sight and grinding the serial number off it, driving ten-inch nails into a telephone pole to steady the rifle, and then aiming that rifle and killing Gerald Gordon. The court said, "Franklin's punishment [was] neither excessive nor disproportionate in light of the crime and the strength of evidence against him." The court also said that the record refuted the notion that death threats while in federal prison motivated Franklin to seek his own death sentence in Missouri. The court acknowledged that Franklin did indeed suggest that he believed certain individuals at the federal prison in Marion were trying to kill him and that he would prefer being sentenced to death in Missouri than being killed at the federal prison. However, the court noted that when expressly asked during his competency hearing whether he confessed to the murder of Gerald Gordon in order to get out of the federal prison, he emphatically denied it to be his motivation. The court said, "Franklin has stated numerous times that his motivation for confessing came not from these death threats, but from a spirit guide who told him to confess and seek his own execution." The court also noted Franklin's shrewdness during questioning by defense attorneys trying to prove him incompetent against his wishes.[23]

After his appeals for a hearing to the U.S. Supreme Court and the Missouri Supreme Court were rejected, Franklin petitioned the District Court for the Eastern

District of Missouri, which granted his appeal in 2004 based on two grounds—Franklin's waiver of counsel was "not knowing, voluntary, and intelligent," and the trial court "erred in failing to give a penalty phase jury instruction." In 2004, in a surprise move, the district court required Missouri to release or retry Franklin for the Gordon murder. However, in July 2007 the Eighth United States Circuit Court of Appeals overturned the decision, arguing that Franklin was competent to represent himself during the trial and that since Franklin was competent to stand trial, the appeals waiver Franklin signed in 1997 barred the court from considering Franklin's appeal. "We conclude," the court said in its ruling, that "Franklin's voluntary waiver of his direct appeal resulted in procedural default and bars review of all of Franklin's claims raised in this appeal. . . . The district court, therefore, was without jurisdiction to grant relief on Franklin's claims."[24]

Even though Franklin had been sentenced to death, he had finally managed to extricate himself from Marion after spending nearly fifteen years there. Following the imposition of the death sentence in the St Louis court on Thursday afternoon, February 27, Franklin was taken to Potosi Correctional Center, Missouri where he would await a date for execution by lethal injection.

In June 1995, in an interview with the *St. Louis Post-Dispatch*, Franklin had admitted he shot Vernon Jordan, although he refused to elaborate. All Franklin would admit was that he "did it."[25] However, when he was taken from Marion to the St. Louis jail to stand trial for the Gordon murder, he decided to come clean about the murder attempt on Jordan. In February 1996 Franklin, now forty-five years old, agreed to an interview with *The Indianapolis Star* and *The Indianapolis News*.

Franklin began the interview by telling the reporters that the Vernon Jordan jury made a mistake. He then went on to tell the reporters in detail how he had committed the crime. He said he had acted on his white supremacist beliefs that, he said, he no longer held. "I was the executioner, the judge, and the jury," he said. "I was on a holy war against evildoers." Franklin said he arrived in Fort Wayne from Chicago after failing to kill Jesse Jackson. He had hoped to kill "race-mixers" in Fort Wayne, but after hearing a news broadcast that Jordan would be speaking at Fort Wayne's Marriott Hotel, he decided to go after the civil rights leader.

Franklin said he discovered Jordan was staying in a corner room of the hotel, waited for dark, and parked his car beside a nearby highway. He said he could not be sure if the man who exited a car near a corner room was Jordan, but he decided to shoot anyway, as he was enraged when he saw a black man with a white woman. After reading Franklin's confession, Fort Wayne prosecutors declined to file charges against him, stating he could not be retried because of the Constitution's protection against double jeopardy.[26]

Franklin also told the reporters he had renounced his racist views after taking up meditation in 1985. However, the reporters noticed he still peppered his conversations with anti-Semitic and racist remarks. He also said he had no remorse for his crimes and invoked the name of King David. "King David was a warrior," he said. "The prophets were not sissies. They were killers and warriors."[27]

At the time of the Gordon trial, Franklin continued to seek attention from the news media and hinted that he was responsible for many more murders than he had been convicted of or confessed to. State prosecutors were lining up to interview him.

Just two hours after his conviction for killing Gerald Gordon, Franklin finally made a full confession to the Larry Flynt shooting to the *St. Louis Post-Dispatch*. He had teased police for years. Now he was ready to come clean and give details of the shooting "only the gunman would know," according to Gwinnett County district attorney Danny Porter. He told Kim Bell he remembered what went through his mind when he saw one of *Hustler* magazine's explicit photographs of an interracial couple titled "Butch and His Georgia Peach." "I just saw blood," Franklin said. Although he confessed the shooting to Bell, he said he did not want to "discuss Larry Flynt at this moment."[28]

Franklin also told other news outlets that meditating on the Bible had led to a change of heart in his decision to confess fully to the Flynt shooting. "I was totally immersed in Nazi philosophy at the time," he said, "and I was obsessed with race-mixing . . . I figured the whole magazine would fold once I got rid of Flynt . . . I have nothing in my heart but love for Larry now. I really regret what happened. Larry has some faults but I don't hate him anymore. It's the only shooting I've committed that I've ever cried about." He said he no longer hated blacks and Jews and thought he might have been a Jew in a former life. "Before I used to blame Jews for all my problems," he said, "but I can see now how erroneous I was."[29]

Franklin told Cincinnati prosecutor Melissa Powers later that year, "I just became very upset . . . about, you know, not shooting, you know, killing Larry Flynt. And now I'm really, I regret actually even shooting him now, anyway."[30] Franklin was also regretful about shooting Flynt because he recognised the magazine publisher was just like him, "It's just the type of person he is . . . rebel . . . just basically what I am, you know."[31]

It appeared likely a new movie about Larry Flynt, Miloš Forman's *The People vs. Larry Flynt* (released in 1996), had a profound effect on Franklin's decision to give a full confession. Franklin was never named in the movie. When Kim Bell interviewed him in the St. Louis County jail, Franklin had asked, "with a child's curiosity," if she had seen the movie. He wondered how he had been portrayed in the film and "seemed preoccupied by the movie," according to Bell. He asked her to "check it out and tell me what you think." He was also clearly upset that he was not mentioned by name in the movie credits.[32]

The Forman movie, which sanitized Flynt's life and omitted character issues involving *Hustler*'s racism and misogyny, was shown in cinemas across America. Residents of Lawrenceville were upset that at the end of the movie, it was noted that Larry Flynt's would-be assassin was never brought to justice. They wanted to know why. Prosecutors in the county also took issue with the movie's epilogue. Officials said it was true Franklin was never tried. However, they insisted "justice had its hands full." They also said Franklin was indicted in the attack and had confessed to the shooting. He was already serving life sentences, prosecutors insisted, and Franklin would never get out of prison. They also said it did not serve the citizens of Lawrenceville well to go to the expense of a trial.

The district attorney at the time, Daniel J. Porter, said at the time of the movie's release, "We know who he is and where he is but we were sort of the least on the list in jurisdictions in terms of seriousness. He's been punished. Why add another notch to his stick? It's not a good use of our resources to bring him here. What would that accomplish?"[33] Porter added that Flynt had not pressed to have Franklin tried. Flynt said it was a waste of taxpayers' money. Gene Reeves, who had made a full recovery from his stomach wounds after the 1978 shooting, said he had never felt a need for revenge against Franklin. "He is apparently a very sick person to kill people like he's done," Reeves said. "I'm just glad he didn't shoot any better."[34]

Larry Flynt was also stoic about Franklin. "I never really looked at it as 'Who shot me,'" he said, "but rather, 'What shot me,' in terms of the mentality of someone that would kill someone else simply because they disagreed with their views. I'm in a wheelchair as a result of [the shooting] so it's not much consolation to me that he feels bad about it. But I don't have vengeance in this situation."[35]

During Franklin's St. Louis trial and after his transfer to Potosi, he had met with officials and news representatives from other states who wished to get to the bottom of the sniper attacks that occurred in their communities and were filed as unsolved. At Franklin's request, Det. Lesia Jones and Lt. Harry Reitze of the Falls Church, Virginia police department interviewed him in Potosi on March 10, 1997. In the videotaped interview, which was held in one of the prison assistant investigator's offices, Franklin admitted he had killed a black man in a Burger King restaurant in 1979. However, authorities judged it to be a futile exercise in bringing Franklin to trial for the murder of Raymond Taylor since he had already been sentenced to die.[36]

In early March 1998 Franklin had contacted Chattanooga authorities about a possible plea to the killing of William Tatum, who was shot outside a Chattanooga restaurant in July 1978. Chattanooga assistant district attorney general Joseph Rehyansky said that during the interview Franklin "rambled, sometimes showing remorse and other times expressing no regret." Rehyansky added, "I feel like I needed therapy after speaking with him."[37]

Franklin also made demands to Rehyansky that the court hearing be a Wednesday because it was the sixty-third day of the year and it corresponded with three, his favorite number. Later that month Franklin was taken to Chattanooga and tried for the murder. Under a plea bargain Franklin was sentenced to two concurrent life terms, one for the murder and another for an unrelated 1977 armed robbery. Although he had insisted on jury trials in his previous cases, he wanted to confess this one. Joseph Rehyansky, who prosecuted the case, said Franklin was a "homicidal moron . . . [who had] undergone some sort of bizarre religious conversion. At some point in the last years he decided pleading guilty was the right thing to do. I don't know why."[38]

Franklin had first confessed the Johnstown, Pennsylvania, murders to Melissa Powers, who interviewed him in Potosi in April 1997. Johnstown prosecutor Kelly Callihan and Det. Jeannine Gaydos, acting on information provided in the interview, contacted Franklin by telephone. For three months they discussed the case with him and established a rapport. Eventually, he invited them to visit him. The women arrived in Chattanooga in late January 1998 while Franklin was being held for the Tatum murder. Franklin refused to see them the first time they called but relented on the second day. They videotaped the interview in which he confessed to murdering Arthur Smothers and Kathleen Mikula.[39]

Cambria County assistant prosecutor David Tulowitzki and police chief Robert Huntley also interviewed Franklin about the Johnstown murders. Tulowitzki said, "He gave us information that could only be supplied by the perpetrator that was never in the paper that corroborated the physical evidence." Huntley said Franklin was "not remorseful. You could actually see him get excited when he described the murders. He gets louder and he gets a little fidgety in the chair." During the interview, which began in a "monotone," Franklin said he no longer held the white supremacist beliefs he once held. Tulowitzki added that it was unlikely Franklin would be tried for the killings because he was already serving life sentences and moving him would pose a security risk.[40]

Franklin also agreed to an interview with the *Johnstown Tribune-Democrat* when he was held in the high security cell of the Chattanooga jail. The reporters interviewed him on February 10. Wearing dark-rimmed glasses and a goatee, shackles inhibiting his hand gestures, Franklin told the reporters that if he had to commit the murders again, he would not do it. However, he said he was "glad a mixed-race couple was eliminated. I used to believe the only good interracial couple was a dead interracial couple. Now I realize that not even the dead ones are any good."[41]

During the same interview, Franklin said he had killed a white woman who had been traveling with a black truck driver in Tennessee in 1977 and read later that her class ring came from Johnstown. He went there, he said, looking for more interracial couples and spent several days cruising around the town, looking for secluded spots to shoot from. Franklin told them he climbed a hill overlooking the city and aimed his high-powered rifle at a black woman walking near the Washington Street Bridge. As he was about to shoot her, a "spirit" prevented him. Moments later Smothers and Mikula walked by and, "lo and behold, I see a mixed-race couple. At first I couldn't believe my eyes, I was so glad to see them." Franklin said he hit Smothers with the first shot, and as Mikula shouted at passing traffic, he fired at her but missed. Franklin said he reloaded his rifle and shot Mikula, then fired twice more at the couple before speeding away in his car. He also told the reporters, "I became really obsessed with the Nazi Party," and that he was upset at some news reports that characterized him as a "serial killer." "I don't consider myself a serial killer," he said. "King David was a serial killer. So was Samson. I would classify myself as just a killer."[42]

Franklin was on a roll. In March 1998, one year after his St. Louis death penalty trial, Franklin had informed DeKalb County prosecutors he might be willing to talk about the murders of fifteen-year-old Sandy Springs resident Mercedes Lynn Masters and twenty-seven-year-old Doraville Taco Bell manager Harold McIver. Franklin told police authorities his interview had to be conducted by "an attractive white female investigator." DeKalb County district attorney J. Tom Morgan said, "He would only talk to an attractive white female investigator . . . I directed one of my investigators, sort of like life imitating art, I mean Jodie Foster to interview Hannibal Lecter, but we prepared her to go to Missouri to interview Mr. Franklin. She was able to get a two-and-a-half-hour interview with him."[43]

Morgan, who believed Franklin was the most evil individual he had "ever come across," chose Assistant District Attorney Carol Ellis and DeKalb County police lieutenant Pam Pendergrass to interview Franklin at Potosi. In the March 26 interview, Franklin told them he had had a sexual relationship with Masters and killed her because she admitted to having sex with African American men. During the interview Franklin also said he had murdered Harold McIver. He said he had entered the Taco Bell restaurant earlier in the day and saw that McIver's colleagues were young white women. "I figured . . . he was using his position to hit up the young white women," said Franklin. He said he fired two shots at McIver from a wooded area off the rear parking lot, 150 feet away, with his 30.30 Savage rifle.[44]

Carol Ellis believed Franklin confessed to the two DeKalb County killings because "he likes attention. He told someone else he wanted to be known as the person with the most death sentences."[45] However, DeKalb County authorities decided against trying Franklin for the murders. Tom Morgan said the killings did not meet the standards for the death penalty. "There is no reason to bring him back here," Morgan said, "when I can't seek the ultimate punishment." Morgan added, "Mr. Franklin is the most evil individual I have ever come across."[46]

Meanwhile, Cincinnati prosecutors were working on a plan to elicit a confession from Franklin to the murders of Darrell Lane and Dante Evans Brown.

FIFTEEN

Justice in Cincinnati

Franklin was perturbed the media didn't pick up [the Jordan story] as a racial incident . . . and he was hell bent on making a statement in that fashion. He went [to Cincinnati] to kill preferably a racially mixed couple but in that absence, he was there to kill blacks. He was impatient waiting for somebody to shoot and after some length of time . . . these two kids walked in front of his gun sights. Joseph Paul Franklin fancies himself as this white supremacist, racial purist, and he would like to go down in history as that. The sad truth is, he enjoys killing people.

—Hamilton County district attorney Joseph T. Deters

For two decades, despite confessing to numerous murders and bombings, Joseph Franklin refused to discuss one particular crime. He kept denying he was responsible for the sniper murders of the two Cincinnati boys, Darrell Lane and Dante Evans Brown. Investigators had long suspected Franklin was guilty of the murders, but they did not feel they had sufficient evidence to charge him.

There had always been an ulterior motive behind Franklin's confessions. When some state authorities made the decision to try Franklin for his crimes, he was given the added bonus of relief from the monotony of prison life. He was also provided with new opportunities to escape from his custodians. However, confessing to the Cincinnati murders would place Franklin in a position he wanted to avoid. His motive in not previously confessing was his fear of the electric chair. "I didn't want to be on death row in Ohio," he said. "They have the electric chair there. I don't want to die in the electric chair."[1] However, Franklin's fears were unfounded. The death penalty was declared unconstitutional in Ohio in 1978 and not reinstated until 1981. He had apparently been ignorant of the fact that in 1980, when the Cincinnati murders were committed, Ohio's death penalty law was invalid, which meant he could only be sentenced to life imprisonment.

In February 1997 John Jay, an investigator in the Hamilton County prosecutor's office and a police officer in the investigative unit in Bond Hill when the shootings occurred, said the case was one of the most tragic and frustrating cases he had ever worked on. "We felt we had compiled substantial evidence against Franklin," he said, "but we couldn't nail him." Jay said police were able to establish that Franklin was in Cincinnati at the time of the shootings, but the case was categorized as open but inactive.[2]

After Franklin confessed to the murder of Raymond Taylor in March 1997, Hamilton County district attorney Deters noticed that Franklin had told Falls Church authorities he would only confess to the murder if he was interviewed by white female detectives or prosecutors. Deters decided Franklin might be ready to talk about the Cincinnati murders, but first he had to plan a strategy. He knew Franklin was unlikely to talk to any of his male assistant prosecutors because "apparently, he was abused by his father."[3] Deters summoned Assistant District Attorney Melissa Powers, who had been working in his office since 1991. Deters told Powers he had a job for her—interviewing Franklin—but added that she "could say no."[4]

Deters chose the blonde-haired Powers because she looked like a model. She was also familiar with Cincinnati's diverse communities, having grown up as part of a large Cincinnati family. Her parents valued "discipline, hard work, education, and strong moral values." Powers attributed her sense of fairness and equality to the example set by her parents.

Powers graduated from McAuley High School, the University of Cincinnati, and the University of Cincinnati Law School. She began her legal career in the Hamilton County prosecutor's office as an assistant prosecuting attorney in the Appellate Division, where she argued before the First District Court of Appeals. Thereafter, she was groomed and mentored for trial work. She advanced quickly through the litigation divisions of Juvenile, Municipal, and Common Pleas. As a prosecutor, Powers tried hundreds of cases in both jury and non-jury trials, including murder, rape, major drug trafficking, felonious assaults, DUI, and other felonies and misdemeanors.

Deters chose Powers because he knew that Franklin, after spending seventeen years in jail, wanted to see a "woman in makeup and smell her perfume." He also thought Franklin believed he could control a woman better than a man. "And he likes to be in control," Deters said.[5] Powers agreed to contact Franklin. Meanwhile, Cincinnati police chief Michael Snowden assigned two homicide detectives to assist Powers. Deters said asking Powers to take the assignment left a "bad taste" in his mouth but he knew it was the only way in getting Franklin to confess.

Powers first sent Franklin a handwritten letter with a photograph of herself attached. Franklin said it was "a really friendly letter. It was a woman, anyway, so I figured I'd discuss it. The omens seemed right." He wrote back and arranged a telephone call. During the conversation, Deters was listening in. Powers began by lying to Franklin, telling him her bosses were not very interested in the case and they were not giving her much time to solve it. She also said that she had to work on her own time. At one point Franklin told Powers, "You're so gorgeous. It'll be nice just sitting down face to face and talking with you, you know. A really pretty lady . . . [you are] a good-hearted person."[6]

Still centering his thoughts on his obsession with Nazism and mysticism, Franklin asked Powers if she was single and what her star sign was. He had already ruled out April 20 as a date for the meeting because it was Hitler's birthday and he always celebrated it. She asked if she could meet with him on Sunday April 13, his birthday. Franklin, impressed she had "done her homework," agreed to the meeting. Franklin was also taken with the fact that her name had thirteen letters in it. "It's a lucky number for me," he said. It was a good omen. Powers later said, "Well, first of all, the only reason he met with me was because of some crazy fixation with numbers . . . Something about the number of letters in my name. It all added up to thirteen. He kept asking me, 'You're not a witch, are you?' And I said, 'I don't know. What if I was?' And he said, 'If you were, I could tell you so much more.'" During the impending conversation, he promised, he would tell her if he had killed the two boys.[7]

Powers interviewed Franklin for five hours. He was shackled, and a single guard stayed in the attorney-client conference room at all times. They faced each other across a table and no glass separated them. She knew that she had to act "weak, quiet, and mousy" so she could elicit the confession.[8] According to Powers, the only thing she could remember that stood out so clearly was that she kept telling herself "to breathe, because I was holding my breath throughout the whole thing, and this desire to run, get me out of here, get me away from him."[9] Powers said, "He wanted to meet with me face-to-face. And I begged for that thing to be videotaped, but he'd only allow a tape recorder."[10]

She said he looked like he probably didn't weigh more than 140 pounds and was about five-nine in height. It didn't dent his confidence, however. "At one point, he stood up and said, 'I could kill you right here right now and you'd be dead because nobody could get in here fast enough. There's nothing to you.'" Powers thought Franklin was "very crafty, very manipulative. He's probably the ultimate of all manipulators."[11]

Powers said she began with "small talk" before she broached the subject of the murders of Lane and Brown. She gave him some incentive to confess by telling him that he could not be sentenced to death, as Ohio's death penalty law was invalid in 1980, meaning he faced only a life sentence that, of course, meant nothing to Franklin, as he was already not only under sentence of death but was also serving eight life sentences. Franklin responded by leaning into her and looking over the top of his spectacles. "You know I did it. I killed those dudes," he said.[12]

During the interview Franklin described the night of the murders and of how he crouched on a railroad trestle for hours before deciding to shoot the two boys as they walked along Reading Road in the Bond Hill area of Cincinnati. He told Powers he killed the boys because he wanted to start a race war that would eventually rid the United States of blacks and Jews. "I was trying to get rid of all the ugly people in the world," he said. "I considered the blacks the ugliest people of all." Franklin ended up telling her not only about the murders of the two Cincinnati boys but also the murders he committed in Johnstown and West Virginia.[13] "The Johnstown crime is the one he wanted to talk about in great detail, where he gave out his philosophy about preserving the white race," she said.[14]

Powers also believed Franklin was becoming sexually excited when he talked of his murders. "He literally went from a flat line personality and monotone . . . to this electrifying, charged individual who, before my eyes . . . looked like he was sexually turned on." Powers recalled, "Here's what I think. Yes, he's a racist. I asked him if there was a sexual component to his killing, he said never. But he was very weird about when it came to sex. He was very flat-lined when he was talking about everything, even the crime here [Cincinnati] where he killed the two boys. It didn't get him nearly as excited as when he was talking about killing the MRCs. . . . I think a sexual component was involved when he killed the interracial couples. That's when he came alive, like he was turned on. He became very animated, very excited. When I asked him about it, he denied it. The FBI thought he might possibly be impotent in some way. It was disgusting, very sickening."[15]

In fact, Melissa Powers said a key piece of evidence was missing that would suggest he killed a lot more women than he has been given credit for. "There was a scrapbook of Polaroid pictures," Powers said. "When they caught him here in Cincinnati, across the river in Florence, Kentucky, a scrapbook was one of the things that was taken from him. He was really surprised when it didn't show up in discovery when he was defending himself out in Salt Lake City. And nobody knows where that scrapbook is." She implied that a law enforcement agency, " . . . didn't exactly divulge everything that was requested." Powers added, "When I was involved in 1997 . . . we tried every angle we could think of to get that book. And we didn't get anywhere. . . . There were pictures of prostitutes posing naked with his guns in that book, that's what he told me. I'd be willing to bet the women in that book are dead."[16]

Documentary filmmaker Immy Humes later implied there were underlying sexual motives for Franklin's murders. However, Franklin insisted to Humes that, unlike other serial killers, he did not touch his victims or fantasize about his killings.

In an interview with the *Cincinnati Enquirer* on Wednesday, April 16, Franklin explained to reporters why he decided to confess. "All I can get," he said, "is two lifes and that ain't going to affect me at all. I already got eight life sentences." Franklin also gave an exculpatory answer as to why he shot the boys: "They didn't look like kids to me," he said. "They looked like grown men. It was dark out."[17] He told reporter Kristen Delguzzi, "To me that [the sniper attacks] was my mission. I just felt I was engaged in a war with the world. I just basically felt my mission was to get rid of as many evildoers as I could. If I did not, then I would be punished. I felt that God intended me to actually kill people." Franklin said he would have no objection to returning to Cincinnati to stand trial. He said he would not plead guilty but would act as his own lawyer and "basically throw the case."[18]

Deters and Powers announced the confession at a press conference on Tuesday, April 15, 1997. Deters called Franklin "an animal" and said he had asked a Hamilton County grand jury to indict Franklin. He characterized him as a man who would not "pick a fight in a bar room but would kick a dog," and that the murders were "an act of evilness we have never seen in this community." Deters added, "These two kids were citizens of this country when this derelict came into our community and snuffed out their lives. . . . The Evans family and the Lane family deserve justice here and it is our intention to bring Franklin back and try him for these murders . . . if there was ever a defendant who deserved to die it's Joseph Paul Franklin."[19]

Joseph Deters told the press that after nearly two decades, the murders still affected the citizens of Cincinnati, especially the relatives. "They're experiencing the same emptiness that you perceive with the families of any victims," he said.[20] Deters knew the confession was "huge. We were confident he had done this, and after the confessions, it was a very satisfying meeting with the families of the two boys to let them know for sure we knew who had done this." Dante Evans' younger brother LaVon told reporters, "I just want Joe Deters to get him."[21]

Deters was convinced he had a good case against Franklin. When the indictment was eventually handed down, he said the only problem was that it did not contain a specification that Franklin be put to death if he was convicted. When the Cincinnati prosecutor told the press that Franklin had initially been on the prowl for an interracial couple before he murdered Lane and Evans Brown, he was likely alluding to a mixed-race couple, twenty-five-year-old Cathy Knob Loch, who was white, and her forty-five-year-old African American boyfriend, Jesse Neal. On the day of the murders, the couple checked into the Gateway Motel at 7:00 p.m. Police interviewed them the night of the shooting thought nothing of the couple until Franklin's crimes were discovered and his motives discerned. The couple did not leave the motel until 4:45 a.m. on June 9. Police believed Franklin became impatient and shot the first African Americans he saw when the couple failed to exit the motel. To Franklin, it really did not matter if he failed to shoot the couple because he did not care who he killed or how old they were "as long as they were black."[22]

Following the news conference announcing Franklin's confession, Det. Michael O'Brien, who had worked on the case for nearly two decades said, "Yes, success . . . it's a good feeling. It's the feeling that a weight has been lifted off your shoulders. . . . It's a case that has always stuck in my mind, simply because of the age of the teenagers, the innocence. And the suspect was basically thumbing his nose at society. These kids deserved better. They deserved somebody to stand in their corner and fight for them."[23]

One year later, on Saturday, April 25, 1998, Franklin received a stay of execution and was taken from Potosi to the Hamilton County Justice Center in Cincinnati. Franklin was enjoying the attention. A year earlier when he had confessed, Franklin told a *Cincinnati Post* reporter, "Sometimes it helps, the publicity you get. It gets out my beliefs, my philosophy, which is different than most people's."[24]

For his part Franklin was surprised prosecutors were going to act on his confession as he was already serving multiple life sentences. "I didn't even expect them to indict me after I gave the confession," Franklin said. "I just figured that since I had one death sentence [in Missouri] and another one pending in Tennessee, plus doing multiple lifes, they wouldn't even bother."[25]

One of Franklin's fellow prisoners at the Hamilton County Justice Center was Ralph Lynch, who was accused of murdering a six-year-old girl. Before the trial began, a reporter asked Franklin whether he had made contact with Lynch. Franklin replied, "I don't fool with that sucker. I don't associate with that scumbag." One of Dante Evans Brown's relatives, Gary Trumbo, overheard the remark and told the press, "That's one scumbag calling someone else a scumbag."[26]

Law enforcement authorities had been extremely concerned with the transfer of the prisoner. They said Franklin was "high risk" and a desperate man who would do anything to draw attention to himself and his racist cause. "This guy is a screwball," St. Louis prosecutor Robert McCulloch said. "Given the opportunity, he would try something. Our . . . concern is security. Any time you have someone who's been sentenced to death they are an incredible security risk."[27] When he arrived in Cincinnati, Franklin caused some alarm when it was discovered he had hidden a piece of metal in a trouser leg. Judge Ralph Winkler decided not to use his own courtroom and chose an alternative that had better security arrangements.

On Tuesday, April 28, a forty-eight-year-old Franklin was arraigned in Hamilton County Common Pleas Court for the murders. Franklin's attorney was Dale Schmidt, a former state representative who had been elected in 1967 but went into private practice as a lawyer in 1972.[28] Security was tight, and five deputies escorted Franklin into the courtroom. Approximately a dozen more were stationed in the hall outside the exits. He was tightly handcuffed, and underneath his blue prison uniform, his legs were chained together. He also wore a device around his waist that could, if activated, deliver a jolt to his body similar to a stun gun.

As soon as Franklin sat down, he began to complain to the judge about his jail accommodation. He said his handcuffs were too tight and that he was forced to wear cuffs and leg irons in the shower. Franklin also complained about not having any privacy on the telephone and that his deputies were deliberately trying to hurt him. "I can't get through a locked door," he complained. "I'd like to go on record . . . and ask the court that I be transferred to another jail facility because these people are trying to kill me here."[29] Franklin also told the judge that deputies were trying to provoke him. "I just feel my life is in danger at this facility," Franklin told Judge Winkler.

Winkler asked Franklin's lawyer to look into his complaint. "It would seem to me," the judge said, "that the sheriff of Hamilton County could adequately provide facilities."[30] Franklin's complaints had extended the time expected for him to simply plead not guilty to the murders. The judge asked Franklin's defense attorney to look into the complaints and report back to the court. Winkler did not set a trial date but scheduled a conference with lawyers on May 12. Later that day sheriff's officers met with Schmidt and told him they would investigate Franklin's complaints. The jail spokesman, Col. Dan Wolfangel, said he knew of no harassment directed at Franklin.

For his part, Deters was swift to show his contempt for Franklin and said he was inclined to dismiss his complaints because he was "a professional prisoner . . . he's a punk. He's a coward. He's very brave when he's shooting little kids with a high-powered rifle . . . the fact that he's still alive says a lot about the criminal justice system."[31] Discussing the case with reporters after the hearing, Joseph Deters repeated his allegations that Franklin was "a coward. He has no concept of the lives he's taken. He's a cowardly punk."[32]

The families of the victims were also not impressed by Franklin's complaints. Thirty-four-year-old Gary Trumbo, who was eighteen when his nephew Dante was murdered, said, "He's an idiot. And he's crying the blues now about his treatment. He's getting it easy, real easy . . . what if it was your thirteen-year-old son who was gunned down while walking to the store just because of the color of his skin? Wouldn't you want closure? The Lord teaches us forgiveness. He also teaches an eye for an eye. Right now, I've got the eye-for-an-eye thing. Eventually, I'll forgive him. But I'd like to see him prosecuted first.[33] Prosecute him, then fry him." Trumbo added, "At least, it will give the family closure."[34]

Dale Schmidt entered pleas of innocence for Franklin during the arraignment. Franklin had initially pleaded not guilty by reason of insanity to two counts of aggravated murder but changed the plea to innocent. Sherry Baker, one of two psychologists who examined Franklin for the Cincinnati trial, said, "There was no indication he was suffering from a severe mental condition at the time of the alleged offense." Her report also noted there is no evidence Franklin "did not know what he was doing was wrong or would have consequences."[35] Both psychologists acknowledged that during the commission of his crimes, Franklin remained aware of his actions and the implications of getting caught. For an insanity defense to work, the defendant must show he was unable to recognize right from wrong.

When Joseph Deters was asked why he was bringing Franklin to trial when the convicted killer was already condemned to death, he told reporters that he did not have any faith in Ohio's justice system, "so why should I trust what might happen in Missouri? . . . If we can help make sure [Franklin] is never out walking around again that's what I want to do . . . [36] I've seen how the death penalty operates in this country, and I have no faith in it."[37]

Whenever he spoke of Franklin, Deters did not mince his words. As the trial got underway he told reporters, "This is a man who has confessed to multiple killings and the fact that this punk is still drawing breath is an insult. I don't think the cost of justice to these two families can be measured."[38] He said he did not expect insanity to be an issue. "The trial won't last long," Deters said.[39]

During an interview with a reporter in May while he was awaiting trial, said he would try to win a not-guilty verdict by claiming he had a "mental defect" at the time of the shootings. He also said he regretted his crimes and would like to get out of jail so he could work to improve race relations. "I oppose all violence," Franklin said. "It's a little too late now, though. They don't let you out of jail because you say you're sorry." He added, "This place is like being in prison over in communist China. I can tell these people want to kill me just because of what I'm charged with. Nobody presumes you innocent of anything anymore." Franklin said he was going to contact Jerry Springer to discuss on Springer's show how much he had changed his life. "I'm going to be contacting Jerry Springer soon," he said. "I read an article about him in *TV Guide*."[40]

In September Deters made it known he wanted to try the case himself but denied it had anything to do with his campaign for Ohio treasurer. "The last thing my campaign needs to do," he told reporters, "is get involved in a murder trial. This case touched me a great deal. If I have a chance to try it, I want to do it."[41] Deters added that he had made a promise to the parents of the boys he would try the case personally.

On Tuesday, September 15, at a court hearing Franklin asked the judge if the cameras could be pointed away from him during the forthcoming trial. He also asked to wear civilian clothes. Judge Winkler agreed to Franklin's requests and said he could wear street clothes and not be handcuffed in front of the jury. "Good," Franklin said. "I couldn't very well smuggle a machine gun through a shirt and a pair of pants." Franklin also asked the judge if he could be more involved in his defense, as he wanted to make sure he got a fair trial. "I had a couple of bad dreams about misrepresentation," Franklin said. "I took that as a bad omen." Winkler agreed to Franklin's request but cautioned him to follow the rules of the court. He asked Franklin if he had ever represented himself before. Franklin, without revealing any sense of embarrassment, said he had but lost both times. "It was close, though," Franklin said. "A lawyer is only as good as his case, you know."[42]

Franklin's attorney, Dale Schmidt, asked Judge Winkler to dismiss the statement Franklin gave to Melissa Powers in which he confessed to the murders because she had purportedly never informed Franklin of his constitutional rights. Schmidt also suggested that Franklin only confessed to Powers because he wanted to talk to a "pretty investigator." However, Powers responded by telling the court that Franklin knew exactly what he was doing when he confessed. "He knew his rights probably better than I did," she said. "He was in control of this. He could have terminated this at any time."[43] Judge Winkler agreed and told the court, "The defendant has also suggested that somehow Franklin confessed because Assistant Prosecutor Powers is attractive. The court dismisses this argument for the reason that, as far as I know, there is no constitutional right to an unattractive interviewer . . . Franklin was in total control of the course of the interview. That Franklin was anxious to voluntarily talk to Powers is evident." Winkler summed his conclusions up by stating that Franklin was willing to talk to Powers, invited her to visit him at Potosi, and knew that his statements could lead to criminal charges.[44]

Before the trial began, the jury and Franklin were taken to the crime scene and the parking lot the cousins walked through to reach the store to buy candy. Jurors were taken to the railroad trestle overlooking the road where Franklin fired his rifle, and they were also shown the convenience store the boys visited.

On Monday, October 19, Joseph Deters gave his opening statement and recounted the events of the murders but admitted he did not have any witness to the shooting nor did he have the murder weapon. He told of how the Bond Hill community was angered and distressed at the murders of the two boys and that the community was still feeling the effects. He said the Cincinnati police had up to twenty-seven investigators on the case, including fourteen homicide detectives. Deters concluded by telling the jury about Melissa Powers's interview with Franklin. As the trial broke for lunch and sheriff's deputies were handcuffing Franklin to escort him from the courtroom, Dante's uncle, Gary Trumbo, told Franklin, "You'll see this face every day. As long as this trial lasts, you'll see this face." Franklin gave no response.[45]

On the second day of the trial, the prosecution called eleven of its twelve witnesses, beginning with the testimony of Darrel Lane's older sister, Linda, who emotionally described how the boys left their grandmother's house to buy candy at a local store. Priscilla Richardson, the passing motorist at the scene of the murders, told the court how she stopped her car to give aid to the boys and how she called the police. Several police officers—including Jim Riley, the officer who arrested Franklin in Kentucky—also testified. The court heard how Franklin left behind his driver's license and a set of prints when he escaped from the custody of the Florence police and how the photo on the license ran in a Cincinnati newspaper, which prompted witness Susan Roudebush (Taylor) to come forward. Roudebush said she had bought a guitar and distortion unit from Franklin and that he had tried to sell her a rifle (not the murder weapon).

Cincinnati police criminologist Clarence Caesar gave testimony in which he related how he had matched fingerprints on the distortion unit and an instruction booklet to Franklin's prints. At this point in the trial, Franklin cross-examined Caesar, claiming that many fingerprints were found on the items therefore it did not prove anything. The court also heard of how on October 12, 1981, Paul Jacobs, an employee of the Brothers III store, contacted the Cincinnati police department and told investigators he had observed Franklin's photo on television. Jacobs said he told police that Franklin had come into the store on the afternoon of June 7, 1980, and on the morning of June 8, and Jacobs had waited on him both times.[46]

One of the last witnesses was Melissa Powers, who told the court of her interview with Franklin on April 13, 1997. Powers played the taped interview to the court and held up a photo of the murder scene, pointing out the place where Franklin waited for his victims.[47] Watching in the courtroom was Dante's brother, LaVon Evans. Listening to Franklin's hate-filled recorded comments, Evans could not control himself. He remembered seeing his brother's photo on television and how his mother wept when the police gave her the news of her son's murder. He made an obscene gesture to Franklin and after listening to the remainder of the tape, he walked out of the courtroom. "It was more than I expected," he said. "He just explained it like it was nothing. That right there just hurt me. He ain't sorry for what he did and I'll never forgive him anyway. He's going to be judged now, finally." Although Franklin had remained silent when the tape was played, he occasionally looked in Evans's direction.[48]

Franklin called no witnesses nor did he or his co-counsel make an opening statement. During the trial Franklin made repeated complaints. After one outburst in which Franklin claimed that he was being preyed upon by the county deputies guarding him, Winkler told the defendant, "If there is such a thing as a motion to whine, you would have filed it."[49]

In his closing argument, District Attorney Deters told the jury that even without Franklin's confession, the evidence of guilt was "overwhelming." He asked the jurors, "Do you know where you were eighteen years ago today? He [Franklin] knew it was dark. He knew where he did it, . . . How would he know that? There's only one way—he did it." He said Franklin had confessed to "the exact same type of murder" as in other cases and that the Cincinnati police had placed him in the city at the time of the murders. "Without his confession to Melissa Powers," Deters said, "he is guilty beyond a reasonable doubt." With the confession, he continued, Franklin was "guilty beyond all reasonable doubt." Deters then began to explain why Franklin had been brought to trial even though he was under sentence of death. "Justice for these two boys, for [their] families, for [their] communities, that's what matters," he said.[50]

Franklin and Schmidt did not make a closing argument, but after Deters had finished speaking, Schmidt once again objected to the pretrial decision to allow Franklin's confession. His complaint was rejected by Judge Winkler.

On Wednesday, October 21, before the jury began deliberating, Franklin thanked them. "Without you" he said, "I wouldn't have had even the semblance of a fair trial." The jury deliberated for less than an hour. After the jury's guilty verdict was read to the court, Franklin told the judge he would like to be sentenced immediately. However, Judge Winkler said he would wait until the next day in order to hear how the victims' families felt.

On Thursday, October 22, the trial came to an end when the judge handed down the sentences. Written impact statements submitted by relatives of the murdered boys were read to the court. Winkler, who had lost his own nineteen-year-old daughter to skin cancer, called them "heart wrenching." The judge also said that justice would be better served if the death penalty could be applied.[51] Although Dale Schmidt had given Franklin professional counsel, he had nothing but contempt for his client. As a way of showing it, he appeared in court wearing bright red suspenders under his suit jacket. He knew Franklin detested the color red.[52]

As soon as the court was brought into session and the judge began to address the court, Franklin, who was now wearing his blue county jail clothing, erupted. He was trying to provoke Winkler into citing him for contempt so he would not be sent back to Potosi's Death Row. There began a ten-minute heated exchange between

Franklin and the judge. Franklin repeatedly interrupted Winkler as the judge described the murders. "You're just a representative of this satanic system," Franklin shouted. "You'll be judged by Jesus Christ someday." The judge responded by telling him, "I won't have eighteen notches on my gun when I do." Winkler added that he was offended when Franklin told a television reporter earlier in the week that he was offering "his condolences" to the victims' families. "Is there something wrong with that?" Franklin responded. "I didn't even have to confess to this. I helped these people out in solving [the crime]. I think I should get at least some credit for that." Winkler told Franklin, "You gunned them down because of the color of their skin. You viewed yourself as some kind of grim ethnic cleanser."[53]

Judge Winkler continued by telling Franklin, "I look at you and I see the face of evil." He also called Franklin a "predator." Winkler then sentenced him to forty years to life in prison. "Does that make you happy, judge?" Franklin asked. "It's the right thing to do," the judge answered. "I have tried to find some good in you and I can find none." Winkler said he hoped the sentence would bring closure to the victims' relatives but admitted the sentence was only a formality as Franklin was already on Death Row in Missouri.[54] Later he described Franklin as having a "thinking pattern [that] made the hair on my neck stand up, not because I was scared but because he's truly evil and doesn't value human life."[55]

After Franklin was led away to the county jail where he would stay until his return to Potosi, Dale Schmidt told reporters he planned to appeal the verdict because the judge allowed Franklin's confession even though the prosecutors did not read Franklin his rights. However, responding to questions about Franklin's behavior in court, Schmidt said, "[He's] just not a normal person. He's been like that all along. It's tough to deal with."[56]

Some of the victims' families also spoke to the media after the trial was over. "He didn't get what he deserves, but it's over," Dante's mother, Abbie Evans, said. "He'll get what he deserves when he meets his maker."[57] LaVon Evans, Dante's brother, cried and hugged a friend in the hallway outside the courtroom.

SIXTEEN

Injustice in West Virginia

I committed the Rainbow murders, you know. The Rainbow killings were a little different . . . because I just picked them up hitchhiking.

—Joseph Paul Franklin to Cincinnati prosecutor Melissa Powers

On March 1, 1984, as he was being interviewed about the murder of Rebecca Bergstrom, Joseph Paul Franklin told Special Agent Ernest V. Smith of the Wisconsin Department of Justice that he had killed two white females in West Virginia and provided a hand drawn map depicting the location of the murders. The map showed his route from a bank robbery he committed in Burlington, North Carolina, on June 24, 1980, to the West Virginia murder scene. On the map Franklin located the place where he picked up Vickie Durian and Nancy Santomero, the store where he bought gas shortly before the murders, the location of the Rainbow encampment, a winding dirt road, and the smaller dirt road leading to the isolated area where he committed the murders. Franklin also correctly positioned the bodies after he shot the young women.[1]

Franklin later repeated his confession to agents of the Bureau of Alcohol, Tobacco, and Firearms. When West Virginia trooper Debbie DeFalco interviewed him in 1984, he initially denied involvement in the murders before taking responsibility for the killings. However, Franklin's eventual confession was omitted from the tape recording of DeFalco's interview. Later, when Franklin purportedly changed his story and admitted involvement, a recording device was not used.

Following these three instances in which he confessed to the Rainbow murders, Franklin refused to talk further about his involvement. Subsequently, Pocahontas prosecutors believed Franklin had been lying and that his confession was insufficiently reliable. They also believed his map was unreliable, as it lacked any route numbers or towns to indicate with certainty that the map referred to the area of the killings. Neither did prosecutors believe Franklin's account of how he shot the girls. He said he shot them from the front seat of his car while they sat in the back. However, prosecutors pointed to the ballistics evidence and the downward angle of the bullet wounds that conflicted with his account. No murder weapon or bullets were found. Prosecutors also believed that Franklin erroneously claimed he committed the murders in Berkley County.

The girls' murders remained unsolved for over ten years, despite Franklin's confessions. However, investigators believed they had a breakthrough in the case when a man confessed to seeing a friend, Jacob Beard, commit the murders. On April 16, 1992, police arrested Beard and six others—Johnnie Lewis, Arnold Cutlip, Gerald Brown, William McCoy, Richard Fowler, and "Pee Wee" Walton—for the murders. However, the charges were dismissed on July 17 by order of the Circuit Court of Pocahontas County because there were issues of credibility in the charge accounts. The state redrew the charges and prosecutors reindicted five of the original defendants on January 3, 1993. The two men who were not charged were "Pee Wee" Walton and Johnnie Lewis, who were granted immunity in exchange for their testimony against Beard. The charges against Cutlip, Fowler, and McCoy were later dropped when they decided to cooperate with the police.[2]

Jacob Beard was a mechanic at Greenbrier Tractor Sales in Greenbrier County, West Virginia. His employer described him as a good and dependable employee. His wife, Linda, described him as a hardworking husband who had a good job and a loving family. However, although he had no significant criminal record, Beard had a fearsome reputation in Pocahontas County, according to local residents and acquaintances. He was known for killing dogs with chain saws and going to parties with an ax in his hand, some community members alleged.

Beard had come to the attention of police investigators long before the indictment. The first inkling of Beard's involvement came two years after the murders, in July 1982, when police learned that Beard had called Vickie Durian's father to express his sympathy. According to investigators, Beard appeared to know a great deal about the murders but refused to identify himself to Vickie's father. A wiretap helped police track him down after a second phone call.

When questioned by police, Beard initially denied making the telephone calls but later said he did it out of concern for the families of the murdered girls. "I thought it was awful two girls had died in our home county and they hadn't found the killer," he said. "I told [my wife] Linda if this was our daughter I'd be on the police every day to find out what had happened. I thought maybe the parents could prod the police into doing something or bring in another law enforcement agency."

The police had no other evidence to go on, so the case remained unsolved. However, in the years that followed Beard would tell police increasingly bizarre stories. In one interview he implicated neighbors who police later learned had solid alibis. In another, he said the killer carried a third victim to his farm and put the body in a wood chipper. Police found no evidence to support his allegations. But police did begin to consider Beard a suspect.[3]

When Jacob Beard was arrested ten years later, following confessions secured from two of his friends, police believed they had solved the case. One of the two friends, "Pee Wee" Walton, had been arrested on another charge, and police allegedly used strong-arm tactics to eventually force him to confess to seeing Beard commit the murders. Walton claimed police beat him up before he made the statement incriminating Beard. By this time Beard had moved to Florida with his wife and daughter and was working as a service manager in an auto dealership. Neighbors and colleagues described him as a well-respected member of the community.

Prosecutors, led by Walt Weiford, claimed that three of Beard's friends—Fowler, McCoy, and Walton—were riding in a blue van at the time of the murders, picked up Vickie Durian and Nancy Santomero, and gave them a ride on the way to the Rainbow Festival in Monongahela National Park. The men allegedly told Durian and Santomero they had to stop at their boss's trailer to pick up a paycheck. After staying at the trailer for an hour, the three men told the women they would take them to the festival. However, prosecutors said, the men took the girls to a remote area in southern Pocahontas County called Briery Knob, where they met a group of friends, including Beard.

Prosecutors said all the men prevented the girls from leaving the area and demanded sex. Durian and Santomero allegedly told the men they would report them to the police if they were not allowed to leave. When they tried to flee, Beard shot them. Fowler then allegedly said to Beard, "My God, what did you do that for?" and Beard replied, "Because they were going to go to the law." Prosecutors said the bodies of the girls were then taken to another location and dumped. Beard reportedly returned home and he later attended a school board meeting in his neighborhood.

The trial of Jacob Beard was held in May of 1993. Weiford led the team of prosecutors. Steven Farmer and Robert Allen represented Beard. During the trial the defense argued that Beard had taken and passed several lie detector tests, but prosecutors dismissed them, saying the tests could be disputed, as Franklin also passed a test when he originally denied killing the girls. Furthermore, prosecutors said, two men had seen Beard kill the girls. When the press asked Walt Weiford why Franklin would have confessed to the Rainbow murders he said, "Maybe he just wants to be the king killer of all time."[4]

During Beard's trial, witnesses testified they saw Beard and the men with Durian and Santomero that night and then running away from the area where the bodies were found. The prosecution introduced a July 14, 1980, FBI analysis of paint chips that were found on Nancy's clothing. Sgt. Robert Alkire of the West Virginia State Police carried out the tests. Since the chips had originally been misplaced, Beard's defense team was unable to perform their own analysis in time for the trial.[5]

The prosecution argued that the paint chips came from Richard Fowler's blue van, which was destroyed for scrap in 1987. However, Sgt. John Giacalone—who had performed the original state police paint chip microscopic analysis on May 17, 1993—agreed that his report was not inconsistent with Beard's defense that the chips could have originated with a Chevy Nova, and some witnesses in the area of the murders had allegedly spotted the two girls exiting a Chevy Nova prior to their deaths.

Beard's lawyers argued that the jurors should ignore the testimonies of Cutlip, Fowler, McCoy, Walton, and Lewis because they were all drunk the night of the murders. Steven Farmer also argued there had been police misconduct with regard to "Pee Wee" Walton and Johnnie Lewis. He told the court that Walton was beaten at the police station and had been threatened and intimidated by a West Virginia police officer. Walton said that Sergeant Estep placed his foot on the back of his neck when he was in a prone position, threatened to strike his testicles, and referred to the type of sexual abuse he might suffer if he were sent to prison. Sergeant Estep denied Walton's allegations, and Corp. J. S. Tincher supported him.

Farmer related to the jury that Johnnie Lewis had also been threatened and intimidated by police. Lewis said that he first told his lawyer about the beatings and repeated the allegation many times, and that he was not present when Durian and Santomero were shot. He knew nothing about the murders, he said. The defense argued that Lewis only changed his story to incriminate Beard in order to cooperate with the police. The jury never heard about Franklin's confession, as the judge refused to admit it.

As the trial progressed Beard said he was not present at the scene of the crime and that he was at his mechanic's job on the day of the murders. Beard said he had left the office at 5:15 p.m. to go on a service call and make a delivery. His lawyers produced his time record as evidence to support his alibi. Beard said he returned home from work, had a meal, and then attended a school board meeting. His lawyers argued it would have been impossible for Beard to leave work at 5:15 p.m., drive to another county, and then go home and attend a meeting where several people saw him.

Despite having a credible alibi, the jury found Jacob Beard guilty of two counts of first-degree murder on June 4, 1993.The jury recommended he receive no mercy, meaning they wanted him to spend the rest of his life in prison. Beard was sentenced to two life sentences without the possibility of parole and sent to West Virginia's Mount Olive State Penitentiary. His lawyers were "shocked" by the verdict.[6]

Following the murder trial Jacob Beard appealed his conviction and introduced Franklin's 1984 confession and the detailed map he drew. His lawyers argued that the map corroborated Franklin's confession by showing a definite knowledge of the murder scene and surrounding area, including his route of travel from a bank robbery he committed in North Carolina to the West Virginia murder scene, the location in West Virginia where he picked up the girls, the store where he purchased gas shortly before the murders, the location of the encampment for the Rainbow gathering, a winding dirt road and the smaller dirt road leading to the isolated area where he killed the victims, and the parallel positioning of the bodies.

Additionally, Beard's lawyers argued that the court was in error because of a number of factors, including the trial court's refusal to admit polygraph test results, the exclusion of probative evidence regarding another individual's commission of the murders, the admission of scientific evidence not disclosed to Beard's lawyers until after trial began, and police misconduct with regard to police assaults on "Pee Wee" Walton.

Beard's lawyers also argued that the thirteen-year delay between the murders and his indictment constituted a violation of Beard's due process rights. They said Beard's rights were severely prejudiced by the lengthy time span between the commission of the murders and the indictment due to the deaths of several witnesses. They also argued that the destruction of his work records and the scrapping of Richard Fowler's van in 1987 harmed Beard's defense. They said the occurrence of a natural disaster that destroyed evidence in the state's possession constituted an infringement of Beard's rights. Additionally, Beard's lawyers said there had been significant changes to the crime scene and they were unable to challenge the credibility of the state's witnesses by investigating their activities on the date of the murder.[7]

The appeal was rejected in large part because of West Virginia Rules of Evidence. The appeals court judged Franklin's statements to be not credible and the polygraph evidence unreliable. The court reaffirmed the conclusion that "the polygraph test is simply not sufficiently reliable to be admissible. . . . We remain convinced that the reliability of such examinations is still suspect and not generally accepted within the relevant scientific community." The court judge decided that he was not going to allow Franklin's statements "because I don't think they have the degree of trustworthiness from a person who is incarcerated and makes one statement today and then won't talk to you after that about it, and then changes his mind when our own officers are there conducting the statement. That it lacks credibility." The judge said Beard did not meet the "formidable burden" imposed by the law and that Franklin's statement was "worthless."[8]

In a prison interview in November 1996, Franklin told Cincinnati's WKRC television station that he had killed Nancy and Vickie because "they dated black people." Franklin added, "I heard they got some guy locked up in the state pen in West Virginia for something I did. The only thing I can say is he's convicted just due to the sheer number of people lying about it."[9]

By 1997 Franklin was becoming increasingly annoyed that he had not been charged with the West Virginia murders. "They haven't done anything yet," Franklin said. "They are so slow. Are they going to charge me or not?"[10] Franklin was concerned about his image and how it would suffer if he were not charged. "I've become kind of obsessed about it," Franklin said. "I don't want it to ruin my reputation . . . [West Virginia] has got an innocent man." Franklin also repeated his motive for the murders, saying he killed the two girls because both admitted to dating African American men. "If I ever got the chance to kill any race mixers like that," he said, "I did it."[11]

Stephen Farmer responded to Franklin's statement by telling the press he would be asking for a new trial. "Franklin certainly has the résumé to have done what he says he's done," Farmer said. Farmer added that Beard had passed several lie detector tests and had no motive for the murders.[12] However, District Attorney Walt Weiford told the press that he had no plans to pursue Franklin and emphasized that two witnesses had seen Beard commit the murders. "I don't believe Franklin was the killer," Weiford said. "He has not given us anything to believe that he killed these two girls in West Virginia."[13] Weiford also said Franklin had failed two lie detector tests about the murders in the fall of 1996. "I don't know what would motivate him to [confess]," Weiford said. "It may be that he wants a few more notches on his gun or something."[14] Weiford conceded that police conduct may have been improper, but he believed Walton had been telling the truth.[15]

The case took a new turn in 1998 when CBS's *60 Minutes* television show devoted one of their stories to the Rainbow murders. The show broadcast parts of Franklin's November 18, 1996, interview with Deborah Dixon, the WKRC-TV reporter. Franklin told Dixon that Beard had been wrongly convicted. "Everything [he told me] matches all the evidence," Dixon said. The CBS crew also interviewed Beard in West Virginia's Mount Olive State Penitentiary. Weiford's response to the broadcast was to reiterate he had no intention to support a retrial and that he would fight any efforts to free Beard.[16]

On August 7, 1997, before *60 Minutes* was broadcast and after hearing arguments from both the defense and prosecution teams, appeals judge Charles M. Lobban ordered prosecutors to take a deposition from Franklin within sixty days. The judge said he would make a decision about Beard's request for a new trial once he had heard what Franklin had to say. Franklin provided a videotaped statement in October 1997 to prosecuting attorney Walt Weiford and defense attorney Brandon Simms. The new deposition contained many more details about the murders. Prosecutors said that a map Franklin had drawn in his 1984 confession was too general and lacked distinct features and landmarks. The initial confession was also too brief, they said, and when Franklin got to a certain point in his storytelling, he would simply stop talking. However, the new deposition gave police a "lot more details and specifics" according to State Police Col. Thom Kirk.[17]

It took Lobban more than a year to make a ruling, and he decided in favor of the defense. On January 22, 1999, the fifty-three-year-old Beard was granted a new trial. Lobban overturned the conviction based on Franklin's new confession, which was more detailed, and an affidavit by Arnold Cutlip, who said he was with Johnnie Lewis on the day the women were murdered and said they saw neither Beard nor the women. However, prosecutors and law enforcement officials were not pleased with the judge's ruling. Pocahontas County sheriff Jerry Dale said the evidence against Beard was clear and convincing. Walt Weiford said, "Franklin is someone who obviously would take a great deal of pleasure in confounding the system. I also think he'd like to be known as a great serial killer, to keep adding notches to his gun."[18]

Beard's new trial took place in Braxton County, West Virginia, in May of 2000, and a ten-man, two-woman jury was appointed. The venue was changed from Greenbrier County, the place where his first trial had taken place, because of the publicity the case had received. The 1993 trial had been moved from Pocahontas County to Greenbrier for the same reasons. Before the trial began, prosecutors visited Potosi, as Franklin had not been allowed to attend the trial for security reasons. Missouri officials also refused Franklin's request to be transported to St. Louis and be questioned by video teleconference.

Once more, Walt Weiford, assisted by Stephen Dolly, led the prosecution. Their case depended on key witnesses "Pee Wee" Walton and Johnnie Lewis. Lewis said he was seated in Arnold Cutlip's truck when he witnessed the murders. He said Beard, Brown, Fowler, McCoy, and Cutlip were together at Droop Mountain Battlefield State Park as well as Briery Knob. Lewis said he recalled Beard shooting the two girls. He heard gunshots and saw one girl fall and the second girl start running away from Beard. Lewis said Beard then shot the second girl, and he said he believed Beard shot the woman because he saw Beard's arm move at the same time he heard the shots. Lewis said he did not see a woman because Beard's back was to him. He said that after the murders, he and Cutlip went to a Hillsboro bar. Lewis recalled having only one beer, but Cutlip got drunk. Lewis said he had changed his story a number of times because he had been scared.

"Pee Wee" Walton told the court that he recalled being on Briery Knob and said Beard had had a weapon. However, Walton did not say Beard had shot the girls. Walton said he had been with Fowler and McCoy when they discovered that "two Rainbow Festival girls" were in Renick's Valley. Fowler drove to the area, Walton said, and saw the girls hitchhiking. Walton and Fowler picked the girls up and drove to Brown's trailer, where McCoy made telephone calls to invite others to the party they had planned. The group then left and drove to Droop Mountain, where they met Buddy Atkinson, Christine Cook, and Jacob Beard. Brown followed them to the park, and Cutlip arrived later with Lewis.

Walton said the group drank beer and spirits, then Fowler and McCoy announced they wanted to have sex with the girls. Their advances were rejected, however, so McCoy and Fowler held the girls in the van before deciding to leave them alone. They exited the van and began to "party." Walton said he was seated in Fowler's van behind the driver's seat and could see Beard coming down a hill with a rifle. Walton confessed to "being drunk by now." He then told a confused story of how everybody panicked and one girl started screaming and attempted to jump in the truck. Walton said he believed she was shot but could not recall who the shooter was. He said that after the shooting, he blacked out from the shock and the combination of liquor and marijuana, and when he came around, McCoy asked him why he had shot the girls. Walton denied he had done so. When Walton suggested they all call the police, McCoy became enraged and hit him. Walton said he could not recall seeing any bodies.

The prosecution called witness Odessa "Sis" Hively, who said she saw Beard at the entrance to Droop Mountain Park between 5:00 and 5:30 p.m. on the day of the murders. This statement contradicted her 1993 testimony, when she said she had seen Beard's truck along with Brown, Cutlip, and Fowler's trucks, but she said she did not see any people at the park. Now she said Beard was in his truck and Brown and Cutlip were standing beside the vehicle. Hively said her new testimony was the result of her having been scared of Beard in 1993. Hively also said she saw Beard at the school board meeting later, and he appeared to be intoxicated.

Steve Goode and Bill Scott gave testimony at the trial and said they had observed Beard at the entrance to the park between 3:30 and 4:00 p.m. They also said that Fowler and McCoy had been washing out the back of the van that allegedly had held the bodies of the girls. Dale Morrison said he had observed Fowler, McCoy, and two other men fixing bullet holes in the side of the van.

Betty Bennett Pritt, who was in a relationship with Fowler at the time of the murders, testified that Beard had threatened her and told her to say nothing of the murders. She had previously told police she knew nothing about the girls' deaths. "I was afraid to say everything I wanted to back then," she told the court, "because I didn't know if Jake [Beard] would be free to hunt us down." Speaking of Beard's threats, Pritt said, "He got down on the floor at my feet, laid his arms across my knees, and told me bluntly and coldly I was not to say anything at all. I was to keep my mouth shut. He said Stevie [her three-year-old son] would be easy to take to his farm to ride ponies and then disappear."[19]

Three witnesses gave testimony that challenged Franklin's confession. Robert Cassidy said he sold Franklin a Browning 30.06 rifle either on June 24 or June 25, 1980, in Nashville, which would have made it nearly impossible for him to be in West Virginia at the time of the murders. However, this contradicted an earlier statement made to the FBI in which Cassidy said he had sold the gun on July 25. Sgt. Dawson told the court that Franklin's map was not an accurate depiction and that Franklin said he traveled less than fifteen minutes from the interstate to the place where he shot the girls when it would normally have taken forty-five minutes to travel the distance of thirty miles. David Sterling, a convict in a federal penitentiary in Florence, Colorado, said Franklin told him he did not commit the murders.[20]

The defense team—now consisting of Stephen Farmer, Miles Morgan, and public defender George Castelle—built their strategy on destroying the credibility of the state's witnesses. They called on John Blake, who lived in Maxwelton. Blake had been driving home from work when he saw two women headed north on Route 219 just outside of Lewisburg. Blake said he stopped at the Little General Store in Maxwelton, saw the women enter the store, and then watched them leave with a tall thin man who had neither tattoos nor glasses. (Franklin had both.) Blake positively identified the red University of Iowa athletic department sweatshirt Santomero had been wearing when her body was discovered on Briery Knob. He said he could have seen the women as early as 3:30 p.m. or as late as 6:00 p.m.

Three police officers testified for the defense—Sgt. Mike Jordan, West Virginia State Police Bureau of Criminal Investigations (BCI) investigator; Dallas Wolfe; and State Police Corp. Gary Hott. Jordan stated Johnnie Lewis had told him he did not see the murders occur, which contradicted Lewis's other statements about the murders. Jordan believed Lewis had been telling the truth this time. Dallas Wolfe testified that Lewis told him he had been intimidated by the police and told them what they wanted to hear when he said he had witnessed the shooting. Wolfe also said that "Pee Wee" Walton had told him he did not know whether he had actually heard the shots or imagined them. Gary Hott testified that a smear of blood could have indicated that the bodies had been moved.

The defense argued that the jury should reject the testimony of Walton and Lewis for two reasons. First, Walton said he began to recall the murders five years later, but did not go to the police. Second, Walton and Lewis had been intoxicated on the day of the murders and might have taken drugs.

Dr. Elizabeth Loftus, professor of psychology at the University of Washington in Seattle, testified for the defense, telling the court about the traits of human memory. She said studies had shown how people could be suggestible when given inaccurate details about their childhood as well as when repeatedly told incorrect information. She said that alcohol, marijuana, stress, and trauma could all contribute to memory loss or inaccurately remembering details. Loftus said that Lewis's statements about seeing the murders then not seeing the murders was "unusual."[21]

Arnold Cutlip testified for the defense and said he was with Lewis all day on June 25, 1980, and they did not see Beard. Cutlip said Lewis had lived with him and was with him everyday cutting locust posts that they then delivered to a customer in

Buckeye. He said they drank liquor and beer all afternoon and were at Droop Mountain for a short period with Buddy Atkinson, but they did not see Beard, Brown, Fowler, McCoy, or Walton. Lewis had testified he was with Cutlip on Briery Knob when he saw Beard shoot the girls. Under cross examination, Cutlip admitted that he had originally said Beard may have committed the murders, but that he also speculated that Brown and a companion may have killed Santomero and Durian.[22]

Beard's lawyers attempted to destroy McCoy's credibility by telling the court he had been addicted to heroin when he made a false statement in 1999. At that time he told the police that he had observed Beard, Fowler, Cutlip, Brown, and Walton cleaning some blood out of the van and that he saw bullet holes in the rear of the vehicle. McCoy admitted that when he gave his statement to police, he was suffering from heroin withdrawal symptoms. He said the police had promised to get him out of jail and put him in a methadone program, and they gave him $500 for rent. McCoy also admitted he was never around Santomero and Durian nor did he ever see Beard with the women.[23]

Beard's wife, Linda, testified and said her husband came home around 5:30 p.m., ate supper, then attended a school board meeting later that evening. She said her husband had not been drinking and exhibited no unusual behavior at the meeting. Linda's cousin also testified and said that Beard had not been drinking and that her now-deceased husband, Roger had confirmed this. The defense also introduced Franklin's 1997 videotape in which he confessed to the murders. Beard's testimony included his account of his movements that day and said the ordeal had been difficult. "It's been very hard," he said. "It's destroyed my family."

In closing arguments Stephen Farmer alleged that Officer Alkire had orchestrated the case against Beard and coerced several witnesses into changing their stories to incriminate him. Farmer said several prosecution witnesses had changed their stories after spending time with Alkire, including Nancy and Vickie's traveling companion, Elizabeth Johndrow, who first said she left the women at 1:00 p.m. on June 25, 1980, the day of the murders. She then changed her testimony in 1993, saying she believed she parted from them in Richmond, Virginia, on June 24.[24]

Farmer told the jury, "If Jacob Beard goes to jail in this case, then none of us are free. Our families aren't free, our children aren't free. We'll all have to be scared that twenty years from now somebody is going to make up a story about us. The prosecution's case is like a puff of smoke. Every time you get hold of it, it slips through your fingers." Beard, Farmer told the jury, was just a man who worked hard as a mechanic and was taking care of a family. He said the state would "have you believe Mr. Beard, for no reason at all and totally out of character, shot these women."[25]

Farmer asked the jury to recall Franklin's confession. "Franklin," Farmer said, "had the résumé to do what he did. He traveled around the country doing it over and over." He said Franklin had confessed to the murders in 1984 and had drawn a map that detailed the area where the murders were committed. Farmer also introduced the defense's other theory of the case. He said that Beard's former codefendant, Gerald Brown, and his companion, Bobby Lee Morrison, could have killed Nancy and Vickie. Several people, Farmer said, had testified for the prosecution to protect Brown and Morrison. None of those people came forward when Brown and Morrison were arrested for the murders in 1983, the defense attorney said, and did not speak with investigators until 1992 when Beard was charged.[26]

Prosecutor Stephen Dolly took over closing arguments after Pocahontas County prosecuting attorney Walt Weiford was hospitalized with a lung infection. Dolly told the jury the premise of a conspiracy against Beard wasn't believable, noting that Alkire was "not out to get an innocent man." Dolly asked the jury, "For all that finger pointing at Bob Alkire, where's the evidence to back it up? We wouldn't be here today if it weren't for that phone call [Beard] made to Vickie Durian's father. And that's where he went too far. [Alkire] was put on to the defendant because of the defendant's own actions."[27]

Dolly told the jury that Franklin's confession was not credible and that his knowledge of the murders was based on information he had gleaned from the press. "He's just like the guys who tell fortunes and read palms," Dolly said. "He'll give you what you want to hear, but nothing you can verify."[28] He said Franklin's confession bought him more time on Missouri's death row. And if Franklin had been allowed to travel to West Virginia to testify in this case as the prosecution planned, Dolly said, he'd have some "windshield therapy." Dolly said Franklin was "not worth much belief," adding, "When you look at the face of Jacob Beard, you look at the face of a man who has already committed murder twice. There is not much that would stop him now to keep his freedom."[29]

The trial lasted nine days and ended May 31, 2000, after the jury had deliberated for two-and-a-half hours. They found Jacob Beard not guilty. Two members of the jury said a lack of evidence from the prosecution was important in arriving at the verdict. "We looked at all the points of contention," one jury member said. "We went on the basis of the evidence. We felt the defense was correct and certain things were not convincing enough from the prosecution to merit a guilty verdict."[30] And one overlooked fact in the case may have been decisive for some jurors when they concluded Beard was an innocent man. The women's backpacks were found nearly sixty miles from where their bodies were found, in a rhododendron thicket off Route 60 near Hico. Beard, who had attended a school board meeting that evening, would not have had the time to dump the bags so far away from his home.

Stephen Farmer was happy with the verdict. "It's a great day," Farmer said. "The system took a long time to work. It's been eight years and now [Beard] gets to go home and live with his wife." Beard was ecstatic. He had served six-and-a-half years in prison and was now a free man. "Truth wins in the end," Beard told the press. "I don't know if this will prove it to everyone. People who know me know I didn't do this. My conscience is clear."[31]

Walt Weiford was not so generous in his opinion of the jury's verdict. Unfortunately, he could not point to the prosecution witnesses as proof that the state's case had been correct all along, as they had either been contradicted by other witnesses or self-destructed on the witness stand. However, Weiford still claimed the testimony of two witnesses rendered Franklin's confession null and void. Weiford pointed to the fact that Robert Cassidy said Franklin could not have been in Pocahontas County at the time of the murders and ex-prisoner David Sterling's testimony that Franklin denied killing the girls.

In response, defense lawyer George Castelle said he compared the testimonies of ten prosecution witnesses and found "deeply troubling results." They had changed their testimonies, Castelle said. He also alleged there had been a "concerted effort by someone on the prosecution team" to elicit "massive coordinated perjury."[32]

The families of the two girls were confused about the verdict. Speaking for her father and herself, Nancy's sister, Kathy Santomero-Meehan, said, "I wish the evidence was strong enough the jury did not have any doubt. I hope the future brings us more enlightenment. Somebody killed her and it seemed like Beard was the one." Vickie's sister, Mary Kauffman, said that from the evidence she heard, the prosecution had the right man all along. "I feel a guilty man is now walking free," she said. "My hope is that we, the family, will now be able to remember Vickie for the loving, caring person she was and all the fun we shared with her in her twenty-six years of life. Now, maybe, we will not have to be constantly reminded of the fear and terror Vickie and Nancy must have felt in their last hours on earth." Mary said she had faith that God "knows exactly who was involved in this crime and the part they played. God's judgment and punishment for this act will be more severe than any punishment the courts could have."[33] Jacob Beard, who now lives in quiet solitude in Florida, has always maintained his innocence despite the concerns of Vickie's and Nancy's families.

In the years following the second Beard trial, Franklin never retracted his confession for the Rainbow murders. Nor have investigators found any additional evidence that would point the finger of guilt at Beard. Franklin's confession, Cincinnati prosecutor Melissa Powers said, was so detailed it should leave no one in doubt that he killed Nancy and Vickie. According to Powers, Franklin "said exactly where he dropped off the bag, that's where they were found; what was in their stomach; what they ate when they stopped at that little food store; how he laid the bodies, which he never told anybody. All of it matched. I mean this guy gave details like no other. This guy told me, 'You know, it's very traumatic to shoot somebody in your car.' There's still a power thing with it. When he talked, he can relive it. That's why he can remember the details he can. The details are just incredible."[34]

SEVENTEEN

Franklin's Demons

I did some stuff, I did a few things. I'm not totally a good guy, you know. But the end justifies the means.

—*Joseph Paul Franklin*

The individual whose world is falling apart is experiencing his own psychological apocalypse. From this state of ultimate powerlessness and meaninglessness, some create a world of meaning in their mind, a new world in which they have power and significance. Through this vision they have found personal redemption.

—*Robert S. Robins and Jerold M. Post, MD,* Political Paranoia—
The Psychopolitics of Hatred (1997)

P sychologists and psychiatrists have long debated why allegedly sane people like Joseph Paul Franklin commit acts of such incredible brutality. Is there a genetic predisposition to crime? Should mental illness be taken into account? Do family and social environments have a role? Do people become abusers because they have been abused? How can people who do terrible things consider themselves good people?

No one has been able to give the public definitive and conclusive answers. As Dr. Stanton Samenow wrote, "No factor or set of factors—sociological or biological—has proven sufficient to explain why a person becomes a criminal. So far, the search to pin down causation has been futile. But this does not stop people from coming up with ever more explanations, some seemingly plausible, some just plain kooky. We continue to be inundated by theories that offer excuses but explain nothing."[1]

Some psychologists believe the answer to the mystery of Franklin's psyche originates with the acts of abuse he suffered in his childhood and adolescent years. Others believe the ideology he embraced and the distorted Christian ideals he was taught led him to commit his criminal acts, and that the racially segregated Southern society he grew up in had some form of influence. Most sociologists would agree that growing up in the Deep South in the 1950s, the young Franklin would certainly have been influenced by the world around him as it would any child, and that he was especially susceptible to developing a racist mentality.

Some psychologists insist his inherited genes played a large role in his actions or his psychological makeup determined his life choices. Franklin himself once said that he was "more racist than the dumbass rednecks down South. I was born that way."[2] Additionally, the study of psychopathology has given new insight into the mind of murderers who kill at the drop of a hat. Experts say the distinctive personality features of a psychopath are common to people who commit crimes like Franklin's and that there is no cure.

Franklin described himself as "weird," which may be a rational personal insight into his own state of mind. His racism was visceral, and he left no one under the impression that his racism was benign. He wouldn't drive a Cadillac or a Lincoln because they were "nigger cars," and he told FBI special agent Robert H. Dwyer that he hated Mississippi because it was a "nigger-loving state."[3] "No one that I ever met in my life carried an aura of danger around with him like Franklin," one former Nazi said. "On one occasion he accidentally chose my work site as a place to apply for an engineer's position, and instantly I seriously considered changing jobs to distance myself."[4]

Franklin may have been suffering from some form of mental illness, as some psychiatrists have testified. And he obviously had a poorly constructed ego and low self-esteem. He once strutted around a courtroom shouting, "[I'm] a man, they [the prosecutors] are nothing but punk boys compared to me."[5] Or he may have been a sane individual, as he often stated in the many interviews he held with the press. He told one reporter he wanted to get the "record straight on what I did . . . I haven't forgotten anything I've done. I mean how you can forget when you kill somebody."[6] To Franklin these memories were a kind of trophy. Franklin's "insights" in which he insists he was sane are supported by a number of psychiatrists who examined him and concluded that he was not delusional and was fully cognizant of his actions when he committed his murders. Many judges concurred and pointed to Franklin's sensitivities to the contingencies of the law, and that if punishment had been certain, he probably would not have committed his crimes. As John Douglas has noted, no serial killer has ever felt so overcome with the compulsion to kill that he did so in the presence of a uniformed police officer.

Those who knew Franklin when he lived in Washington, D.C., support the notion that Franklin was sane, pointing to his cunning and manipulative nature as proof. They did not see him as a nut. Furthermore, although Franklin said spirits had guided him in his dreams, he did not hear voices or see visions—symptoms that would indicate psychotic patterns of thought.

Aside from Franklin's views with regard to race and his delusional idea that God condoned his murders, some of his ideological beliefs were anything but deranged and were compatible with a large segment of American society. The majority of people in Western nations prefer to associate with people of their own race and culture while holding the view that discrimination against other races and cultures should be condemned. The idea that homosexuality was unnatural, ungodly, and threatened the "sanctity of marriage;" the concern that third world immigration was destroying the fabric of American society; the view that immigrants are unable or unwilling to integrate into American society; protecting the unborn; and the belief that children require two parents, a male and a female—these are all fundamental to conservative Christian communities throughout the United States. Some Christian values, however, Franklin chose to ignore. His belief that he was fighting for a return to "true" American values was never reflected in his own behavior. He was unfaithful during his marriages, he frequented prostitutes, and except for a short period in his youth, he never attended church.

Nature versus nurture may be the wrong approach to take with regard to crimes that people like Franklin commit. Perhaps the approach should be nature *and* nurture. There are no simple answers to the bad versus mad debates, but there are clues in Franklin's personality, character, and life choices that provide answers as to why he acted the way he did, metamorphosing into an omnipotent, powerful, God-like individual that obliterated his previous self.

Dr. Dorothy Otnow Lewis, the psychiatrist at New York's Bellevue Hospital and professor at New York University School of Medicine who gave evidence at

Franklin's St. Louis trial, said her understanding of the racist killer led her to conclude he suffered from a mental illness and had a neurological dysfunction stemming from a brain injury and was therefore not responsible for his actions. Lewis based her conclusions on her wide experience in interviewing nearly two hundred murderers. She interviewed Franklin twice for a total of six and a half hours and concluded he was a paranoid schizophrenic, a psychotic whose thinking was delusional and confused.

Lewis said the head injury Franklin suffered as a child was directly related to the way he acted. Lewis based her conclusions on research she carried out with neurologist Jonathan Pincus. Lewis and Pincus testified for the defense in more than twelve criminal cases and published studies that outlined the medical and psychiatric histories of violent offenders. Lewis and Pincus believed that the most vicious criminals are nearly always people with some combination of abusive childhoods, brain injuries, and psychotic symptoms, especially paranoia. They also believe that these factors together somehow create a synergy that impedes these individuals' ability to control their behavior. In addition, newer studies have begun to explain the reasons why brain dysfunction and childhood abuse can have such negative effects.

Lewis's testimony at the Gordon murder trial was challenged by the prosecution psychiatrist, Dr. Sam Parwatikar, who diagnosed Franklin as suffering from "paranoid personality disorder," but concluded that he was competent to act as his own lawyer. In his opinion, Franklin suffered from "idiosyncratic thoughts," and Parwatikar found his behavior to be the result of a personality disorder rather than a mental illness. However, Parwatikar concluded that Franklin's "idiosyncrasies" did not rise "to the level of delusions associated with paranoid schizophrenia affecting his competence." The motions court found Dr. Parwatikar's testimony more compelling than Dr. Lewis's testimony, dismissing Dr. Lewis's diagnosis that Franklin was delusional. The court also noted Franklin's shrewdness during questioning by his defense attorneys as they tried to prove him incompetent against his wishes. The St. Louis judge also rejected Lewis's characterization of Franklin and concluded he was fit to stand trial.[7] In fact, in every one of Franklin's trials, he was never judged to be incompetent. No credible evidence of psychosis was discovered.

Franklin too was unimpressed with Lewis's testimony. He believed she was a "well-intentioned lady" who "seemed to embellish her statements somewhat." Franklin thought she was out of touch with the feelings of Midwesterners, "who didn't want a New York Jewish intellectual trying to tell people to feel sorry for a murderer."[8]

Additionally, those who argued that Franklin was sane pointed to his meticulous preparations for his crimes and his efforts to avoid detection, which proved that he knew what he was doing was illegal. They also pointed to his fear of judicial punishment. Franklin gave every indication of being sensitive to the contingencies of the law and was well versed in courtroom practice. During one trial, when asked whether he was capable of assisting his attorneys, Franklin described how he informed them that he did not believe he could be prosecuted for armed criminal action because the statute was enacted after his crime. He was correct, and the prosecution dropped the charges.

However, there is little disagreement among those who have studied Franklin that Lewis's perceptive remarks about his childhood are pertinent to understanding him. In her 1998 book *Guilty By Reason Of Insanity*, Lewis wrote about her study of fifteen adult murderers who had "limited, primitive, impulsive parents [who] had raised them in the only fashion they knew. They battered them . . . they neglected them. Sometimes they even tried to kill them. These brutish parents had set the stage on which our condemned subjects now found themselves playing out the final act. It was a drama generations in the making. The mothers and fathers of our subjects had held their children out of open windows of moving cars; they had set them on fire; they had shot at them; they had slashed them with knives and machetes . . . [the children] had lived to perpetrate on others the violence that had been visited upon them."[9]

Professor Kathleen M. Heide of the University of Florida at Tampa observed that child abuse had formerly been thought to have little long-term effect on the child. "We know now," she said, "and we didn't always know this, is that the brain is not developed until up to the age of twenty-five. What science is showing us is that there are changes in the brain of kids who have been abused and neglected. For example . . . the effect on the development of the pre-frontal cortex, which is the . . . higher center of the brain. That's very important in the area of judgement and decision-making. So kids who are abused . . . the brains are not developing normally in the sense of like a child who's raised under good conditions or ideal conditions. So when [the abused child] is in a stressful situation, they can't access those higher cortical functions. They can't stop and deliberate. They are much more likely to be driven by the old part of the brain, which is the limbic system, and here they're especially much more out of emotion."[10]

Franklin's rage leaves little doubt that it stemmed in part from the abuse he suffered from his parents. In fact, it can be argued the key to every violent criminal can be found in the file of his or her childhood abuse. He had little or no affirmation in life. He did not have any sense that people would care for him as a person, and he secretly sensed he was a worthless human being. In an insightful remark he made to Cincinnati detective Michael O'Brien, Franklin concurred that his crimes had their roots partly in his hatred for his mother. Franklin said when he killed, he was really killing his mother.[11]

There is also some evidence that Franklin's behavior was consistent with a psychopathic personality. Psychologists are not in agreement in conclusively establishing the root causes of psychopathic behavior. Some believe that psychopaths are born, not made, and their behavior may originate in the physical makeup of the brain. Others insist that psychopathic behavior lies in nurture, not nature. However, there is a growing consensus among experts that psychopathy is a specific biological condition, the result of a malfunction in the brain. Whatever the causes, there is agreement about common traits displayed by psychopaths—glibness, lack of empathy, shallowness, pathological lying and deception, callousness, remorselessness, manipulation, charm, narcissism, cunning, parasitic qualities, superficiality, egocentricity and grandiose feelings, promiscuousness, and an impersonal sex life. Emotionally, psychopaths are color-blind.

In his groundbreaking book *Without Conscience* (1993), Robert D. Hare, the world's leading expert on psychopathology, concluded that psychopaths lack a restraining mechanism. Most have the ability to kill at the drop of a hat, although it is also true that many psychopaths exist in society without committing criminal acts. A whole range of unsociable behaviors, unacceptable by the norms of society, is certainly consistent with a psychopathic personality, Hare concluded. The list includes multiple sexual relations bearing offspring, spousal abuse, and criminal behavior. It is commonly accepted that certain events in childhood can increase psychological vulnerability, which is manifested in a weak sense of self, a dysfunctional family, coercive or indifferent parenting, emotional abuse or neglect of others, low family income, and low academic achievement.

Joseph Paul Franklin's behavior is remarkably consistent with the conclusions reached by Hare as to what constitutes a psychopath. Throughout his life Franklin did not display the same emotions as others with regard to love, compassion, normal human interactions, or emotions, and he displayed a remarkable lack of remorse and a profound lack of empathy. Additionally, Franklin was unable to form close relationships and was egocentric and deceitful. Non-psychopaths have what may be called self-controlling behavior, in which they stop and think about an action before it is too late. In Franklin's case, emotions and a conscience did not inhibit him.

Franklin's grandiosity and pomposity, another trait, was evident in the courtroom. He criticized or fired his lawyers and took over his own defense at times, usually with disastrous results. Most relevantly, Hare has stated that psychopaths are not insane, even though they are capable of irrational behavior. Franklin showed a shocking lack of concern for the devastating effects his actions had on others–no sense of guilt or remorse for the pain and destruction he caused, and no reason to be at all concerned about the immorality of his acts. He was an expert in deception and lying, both of which are natural talents for psychopaths. He was also an expert in manipulation, as was seen when he interacted with his lawyers and in the way he tried to manipulate law enforcement officers into sending female investigators to interview him. According to Hare, manipulation is one of the psychopath's strongest traits. They believe it is legitimate to manipulate and deceive others in order to obtain what they see as their rights, and their social interactions are planned to outmaneuver the malevolence they see in others.[12]

Regardless of the confusing medical evidence about Franklin, he truly believed in his own mind that in order to fulfil his radical mission to rid the world of African Americans, Jews, and others who committed the cardinal sin of advocating or practicing race-mixing, he had to take matters into his own hands and commit immoral and illegal acts in furtherance of his cause. With Franklin, the whole surreal and sordid interweave of racism, intolerant Christianity, love of outlaw culture and guns, and personal bitterness that he developed as a child began to converge.

Joseph Franklin's life was molded in part by the society in which he grew up. and the conservative views that were held by most white Southerners in the 1950s and 1960s. He was raised in a society of Jim Crow laws that created separate public facilities for whites and blacks. As Jack Levin observed, "Sympathizers draw their hate from the culture, developing it from an early age. As a cultural phenomenon, racism is as American as apple pie. It has been around for centuries and is learned by every generation in the same way that our most cherished cultural values have been acquired: around the dinner table, through books and television programs, from teachers, friends, and relatives."[13]

In fact, Franklin's hatred and bigotry was located at the end of a continuum of cultural bigotry that began many years before his birth. The sense of grievance

Southerners felt at their treatment following the Civil War, real or exaggerated, led to the idea, held by most Southerners, that unjust laws had been imposed on the South, and they were justified in rebelling against them. Southerners also came to believe that violence against unjust laws could be legitimate. Some writers of the mid-twentieth century actually compared the KKK to the underground in World War II and the vigilantes of the Old West who, although they used uncivilized methods, actually benefited society.

As a young man Franklin loved guns, which was not exceptional in twentieth-century America but did reveal something about his fantasies. "Gunfighter Nation," a term introduced by Richard Slotkin, denoted an emotional involvement with guns as a peculiarly American characteristic, resulting in a heavily armed populace and a lack of satisfactory gun controls. The books and television Westerns that Franklin favored revealed the nineteenth-century West as a violent and romantic time and place. Ranchers, miners, deputy sheriffs, teenagers, old men, and occasionally even housewives and mothers carried a shotgun or a .38 revolver and killings were matter of fact. It was also a time of American radical individualism where lone riflemen take a stand against insidious forces. To many, however, it was "fascism in a ten-gallon hat." In a series of race wars sanctified under the auspices of civilization, Native Americans, African Americans, ethnic workers, labor agitators, and women were subsumed by the stampeding herds of capitalist advancement.

Franklin said that as a child, he always chose the role of the outlaw in his childhood games. Growing up, he had patterned his conduct after outlaws of the Old West. Throughout history outlaws have always been popular, particularly among young people who considered themselves as outside the norms of society, rebelling against their parents and the Establishment. He once told a reporter that he was a big fan of Jesse James and that William Quantrill, the Civil War guerrilla leader, "was my biggest influence." He said some of his crimes were based on Quantrill's Civil War exploits. "I knew Quantrill and his band killed men in Lawrence, Kansas," he said, "so I robbed a bank there in the seventies. It was a University of Kansas branch. I wore brown hunting clothes."[14]

Franklin became enamored with these fugitives, declared by the courts as outside the protection of the law, their rights and property forfeited, their lives endangered. To Franklin outlaws were a curious combination of victim and villain, violence and innocence, independence and depravity—a symbol of resistance to society's injustices and a major threat to society. They were fugitives who defaced the sanctity of the American Dream by extorting the capitalist system through crime. He became fascinated with America's train robbers and gangsters, and in his mind he juxtaposed the miserable, lonely, hunted, brutal, and dangerous real lives of outlaws with the idealizations that appeared in the films and television shows he watched. Besides William Quantrill and Jesse James, he also admired Billy the Kid and John Dillinger, outlaw heroes renowned for the toughness and energy with which they defied the system. In reality, they were nothing more than brutal and vicious men whose violent strains were likely the only identifying qualities that attracted Franklin. It is also not difficult to see how his views about race were reflected in Western mythology. The criminal justice systems of the Old West were weighted heavily in favor of defendants who were white and against those who were African American, Native American, or Mexican.

Franklin also adopted the victim mentality. In his mind he became the victim of a society in which everyone was corrupt, and he had been duped by an insensitive government. Similarly, Franklin believed his home, the South, had been under threat after the United States government passed civil rights laws that left men like him dispossessed. Like many uneducated and bigoted men before him, he came to believe he had every reason to fight Yankee-dominated society at the level of thievery and violence.

Hate is learned. It is not inborn, even though most criminals, as Dr. Stanton Samenow has argued, are different from normal people in the way they think. Franklin's first tutors were his parents, and their hatred of African Americans was transferred to their son. He also learned how to be a bigot and was taught from an early age which groups to associate with and which groups to reject, always taking his cue from his parents and the society around him. Franklin was therefore primed by a personal disposition that fostered a preference for his own racial group. William Brink and Louis Harris reported in their 1964 book *The Negro In America*, that a substantial proportion of white Americans in 1963—in some cases up to 70 percent—were willing to agree that African Americans had looser morals, were work-shy, wanted to live off government handouts, bred crime, and were less intelligent and inferior to whites. By 1966 their surveys still reported that 50 percent agreed African Americans had looser morals and wanted to live off handouts.[15]

Although Southern society affected Franklin in the way he interacted with people of other races, it was also true that most white Southerners did not identify with violent racists—but neither did they have sympathy for the civil rights movement. Most agreed that the civil rights movement was a "communist conspiracy." It allowed them to sit more easily on the fence when it came to taking a stand against

violent acts committed against African Americans. As one of Franklin's con-
temporaries said, "My parents raised me to be a segregationist or a racist . . . not
because they were hateful people or bad people. It's just the way that everybody
raised their kids."[16]

According to one Southerner who grew up in the South in the fifties and sixties,
"Racism permeated every aspect of our lives, from the little black Sambo . . . in the
first stories read to us, to the warning that drinking coffee before the age of sixteen
would turn us black. It was part of the air that everyone breathed."[17] Another white
Southerner of Franklin's era agreed that a minority of whites supported integration
or tolerated integration but, "In the back of your head from what came when you
were a child you had this idea. You still got that thing in there, that black boy, he's
trouble."[18] In the 1950s, 80 percent of whites believed "blacks should be kept in
their place."[19]

There were some Southerners who underwent epiphanies—they acknowledged
their own prejudices and decided to change. They were the ones who, although they
were comfortable with segregation and the old order and had no desire to change it,
were nevertheless disgusted at the violent mobs that took away the image of respect-
ability that pro-segregationists tried to maintain. They would have no truck with the
hate-filled mobs that ran rampant in the streets. Others decided they could live with,
but not embrace, integration, but they nevertheless concluded that whites and blacks
needed each other if the United States was to really become a nation. Although the
impact of the civil rights movement differed from family to family, some families,
mostly middle class and educated, testified to the benefits a "New South" would
bring—respect from their fellow Americans in the northern and western states, economic benefits, and a heightened sense of community based on mutual respect.

Most white Southerners did indeed reject the idea that violence was the answer to their problems. Some Southerners allowed their personal animosity toward
African Americans to reveal itself in support of segregationist mainstream politicians like Alabama's Governor George Wallace but rejected the idea that violent
responses to African Americans should be condoned. Others reacted to the civil
rights movement by retreating to their white enclaves, white private schools, and
all-white country clubs. However, many whites like Franklin, who came from a
"redneck" working-class background and had grown up without the benefit of a
stable childhood and supportive parents, were persuaded to channel their bitterness
into supporting extremist groups like the KKK and committing acts of violence in

furtherance of the white supremacist cause. And in many ways they were allowed to get away with it. State governments turned a blind eye to brutalities against African Americans and thus perpetuated a racial culture whereby white violent racists felt they could act with impunity. Franklin was only too aware that whites who committed hate crimes did not suffer the harsher sentencing that ordinary criminals were given—often they were acquitted. This idea was central to James Earl Ray's beliefs about wanting to kill Martin Luther King Jr. in a Southern state. Ray believed that if he was caught he would suffer the same fate as other racist killers of the era—the murderers of the civil rights workers in Meridian, Mississippi, and the murderers of Medgar Evers and Viola Luizzo, for example–and the jury would either acquit him or give him a lenient sentence. In other words his racially motivated crime would bestow a kind of immunity upon him.

Franklin was an adolescent boy when the civil rights movement began to change the United States and especially the Deep South. By the time Franklin entered manhood, he had been heavily influenced by events in his home state and surrounding states—events that he eventually came to believe were destroying the America he expressed to love. When he was eleven years old, a mob of whites in Alabama firebombed a Greyhound bus filled with Freedom Riders. In Birmingham whites attacked and beat the Freedom Riders, and local police looked on for fifteen minutes before they acted. When Franklin was thirteen, Birmingham police attacked civil rights marchers with dogs and fire hoses. When he was fourteen, Medgar Evers was assassinated, his accused killer went free, and the state of Mississippi refused to indict Klansmen for the murders of three civil rights workers. That same year, Klansmen near Colbert, Mississippi, murdered Lemuel Penn, a young African American Army officer, and an all-white jury acquitted his killers. When Franklin was sixteen, an Alabama jury acquitted the KKK murderer of Viola Luizzo and cheered him as he left the court. When Franklin was seventeen, NAACP leader Vernon Dahmer was burned to death by Klansmen. The same year, James Meredith was shot. When Franklin was nineteen Martin Luther King Jr. was assassinated in a Southern town.

Franklin's education and experiences were molded by the past. The history of the South had left a psychological imprint on him. He absorbed the historical memories that had been passed on from generation to generation. The Lost Cause myth became an ideological starting point and led Franklin to believe that America was a white nation that must be defended at any cost by the true sons of the South.

Franklin met the criteria for being a serial killer as determined by FBI profilers John Douglas and Robert Ressler. Throughout his life Franklin displayed common traits that are found among all serial killers, including having a rebellious nature, lying, stealing, living a lonely and isolated existence, and abusing animals. Franklin's sisters testified to the joy he experienced when harming animals he found in his backyard. As Franklin grew older, there were other signs he had in common with serial killers, including the inability to do well in school or hold a job, as well as family problems that indicated a developing aggression.[20]

Franklin also fit the assassin-type profile complied by Douglas and Ressler. "The assassin types," Douglas wrote, "came from dysfunctional backgrounds. Sometimes this was overt: physical abuse and /or sexual abuse; alcoholic parents or guardians; being shuttled—unwanted—from one foster home to another. In other cases it was more subtle; the absence of a loving or nurturing atmosphere; inconsistent or non-existent discipline; a kid who, for whatever reason, never adjusted or fit in."[21] In fact, Franklin suffered more than the absences of a parent—he experienced a long list of absences in his young life, including the absence of involvement at school, the absence of work or the hope of work, the absence of meaningful brother-sister relationships, and the absence of a role in the wider community.

Douglas had his own answers as to why men like Joseph Franklin embarked on their killing sprees. Douglas believed they felt "like a single grain of sand on a beach with billions and billions of grains." The killers believed they were "not as worthy as anyone else," and "inadequate," and that the only way they could become important was by "some great act that effects all those important people." A killer like Franklin, Douglas concluded, "sees himself as a real-life Lone Ranger or Shane."[22]

Douglas also believes that men like Franklin act in ways that are determined by their personalities and the individual skills and interests they develop. "Someone like [Texas sniper] Charles Whitman," Douglas wrote, "who had exceptional skills as a sniper, is going to fantasize his crime based on that ability. . . . Franklin was really adept at . . . sniping. This is significant because as the result of an injury, he had lost the vision in one eye . . . his expert marksmanship was a means of compensating for this handicap. In fact, if we look at everything in Franklin's background—the marksmanship, changing his name, joining hate groups—it's all about compensation for his own perceived inadequacies. Inadequate people have to try to feel worthy and one way to feel worthy is to find someone less worthy or inferior. If you can't find many people less worthy than yourself on individual merits, then you have to find them inferior by race or creed. Blacks and Jews have always been favorite targets for that."[23]

Former FBI agent Kathleen Puckett, who spent twenty-three years with the FBI studying the behavior of spies, serial killers, and terrorists, reviewed all the domestic terrorist and hate crimes cases the FBI had investigated and produced commonalities between the perpetrators. "They were all white males [who] were very different on the surface, but they all shared very similar psychological characteristics. Social isolation or rejection was a constant in the developmental history of all of them," she said. "They all desperately wanted to be part of a group, but because of some personality deficit, none of them was able to fit in. This was the crucial hallmark."[24] She also made other connections between the lives of the killers she studied that are pertinent to understanding why Franklin murdered. "Almost all of them," she said, "were quiet and withdrawn when they were kids. They were described as having few friends." Puckett noted they also had unsatisfactory relationships with women.[25] Like Franklin, the perpetrators all had "tremendous amounts of feeling. But they have a failure of empathy, an inability to put themselves in other people's positions. This is a hallmark of psychopathology. . . . Lone offenders . . . can idealize and identify until the cows come home. What they can't do is engage with real people. That's why their true affiliation is with ideas instead of with people. They trust ideas, they don't trust people."[26]

In their surveys and interviews with serial killers, Ressler and Douglas found they were all motivated to kill in different ways: some killed for the pure pleasure of killing, some killed for power, some killed for a mission, some killed because they believe they are told to, and some killed because they believed they had a responsibility to.[27]

Franklin objected to being equated with serial killers like Ted Bundy because he said he did not experience a deviant sexual need when he killed. He insisted he did not touch his victims and did not fantasize about his murders. Instead, he acted according to a higher ideal to justify his murders that places him in the category of the "missionary serial killer." This type often feels as if he or she has a responsibility or a special mission to rid the world of a certain specified group of people. Charles Manson, Ted Kaczynski, Timothy McVeigh, and Eric Rudolph are classified under this category.

Franklin's missionary zeal was often reflected in his statements to the press, including the time he espoused the idea that "America was founded by white men who were believers in Jesus Christ. They've been taken by atheists . . . the only way for the white man to survive is to get on their knees and pray to the Lord and accept Jesus Christ as their personal savior."[28] He also said that he was "engaged in a war with the world. I just basically felt my mission was to get rid of as many evildoers as I could. If I did not, then I would be punished. I felt that God intended me to actually kill people."[29]

The churches Franklin attended as a young man filled him with an indulgence of prejudice and paranoia that hid under the cloak of faith. Some of the churches he attended in Mobile preached that segregation was ordained by God. Others celebrated the "fact" that African Americans and Jews were "Satan's children." It is unlikely Franklin would have developed his biblical ideas about the Jews or African Americans without some form of tutoring, whether it was through sermons, literature, or the broadcasts he listened to on the radio.

The Bible has inspired many people with its words of love and justice, and it has also given rise to the greatest achievements of the human spirit. But the Bible has also inspired some believers into rejecting the majority view that the Bible is human interpretation of divine inspiration—not the actual word of God. This intolerant notion has led many into acts of hatred and aggression. The Association of Independent Methodist Churches (AIM) for example—which had established churches in Alabama, Tennessee, Louisiana, and Mississippi—issued its members with tenets to abide by, including "maintaining integrity of the races which is ordained by God, and to promote social separation of the races which is a rational, normal, positive principle, and is essentially constructive and moral."[30]

Franklin, committed to the literal word of God, was able to find ample justification in the Bible for a militant defense of his actions. The abandonment by the church of the charge that the Jews bore a historic and collective responsibility for the torture and murder of Christ (which appears in only one verse in one chapter of the Gospels: Matthew 27:24–25) only occurred in the latter part of the twentieth century. Most established Christian churches fell in line and embraced the idea that Jews were not to blame for Christ's death.

However, there were many fringe churches that held out against this liberal interpretation. The idea that the Bible supported the thesis that Jews were the literal offspring of Satan and that God's chosen people—Caucasians—were to serve as God's weapon in the battle against evil was resurrected in modern America in 1946 by Dr. Wesley A. Swift. Swift's teachings would later provide the religious underpinnings of the NSRP, the Minutemen, and later, Christian Identity and the Aryan Nations.[31]

It was not difficult for an emotionally damaged individual like Franklin to convert a religion of love into a religion of hate and to cherry-pick passages from the Bible to suit his mission. The Bible had plenty of passages that gave succour to Franklin's beliefs—temptation, retribution, hatred of enemies, dominance over women, and the duty to strike out at those who did not obey God's laws. It was not difficult for Franklin to find examples from the Old Testament as justification for his aggression. He frequently mentioned the lives of King David and King Solomon, who used destructive ferocity in attacking their enemies. In one interview he said, "King David was a warrior. The prophets were not sissies. They were killers and warriors."[32]

Franklin thought the Bible also supported his hatred of mixed-race couples. There was the Bible story in which Phineas slew an interracial couple having sex, which has been used in modern times to justify the violence and hatred that emanates from rightwing white supremacist and paramilitary groups throughout the United States. According to the Rev. Jarah Crawford, Phineas "took matters into his own hands, the one person who has the mind of God. There was no court trial, no judge, and no Supreme Court; just one man who knew the mind of God and acted upon it."[33] Today's Phineas Priesthood, which glorifies Franklin on Internet websites, is supposedly made up of like-minded lone killers who have taken it upon themselves to do God's will.

The idea of a Phineas Priesthood is spread by Christian patriot groups, a motley collection of tax protesters, Midwestern populists, doomsday prophets, New World Order critics, Christian Identity believers, and gun-toting fanatics who hate the United States government, the United Nations, and Jewish bankers and who are committed believers in all kinds of conspiracies. Their ideas have spread to millions through the Internet and have made their ideas sound plausible to tens of thousands of others who also have grievances and are eager to believe the worst. This has been done by seizing on myths and legends, then joining up all the wrong dots to create a monstrous fable that runs completely counter to the facts.

Franklin often repeated these myths—that white people were "the chosen people of God," and that the " niggers are just dupes to the Jews; the real enemies are the Jews."[34] In fact, Franklin's evocation of killing in the name of God was not all that unusual. Throughout the twentieth century, terrorists, governments, and anti-abortionists have killed in the name of God. In Franklin's case his violence was a striking out against those elements that challenged his ideas of a God-fearing white America. In this sense his acts of murder were a defensive reaction against the enemy within. And his belief that he was like a Biblical hero on a holy crusade was fueled by Nazi literature.

During the 1960s, when Franklin was growing up, a dramatic decline of traditional moderate forms of religion resulted in a spiritual void, and thus there was a need for people like Franklin to believe intensely in something. An unholy alliance between Southern racists, anti-Semites, Nazi believers, and fundamentalist preachers across America filled that void for Franklin.

As a young boy at home Franklin was relegated to the role of the dependent submissive underling. He was subjected to severe, even brutal discipline. Because of being maltreated at an early age, he grew up feeling a profound sense of powerlessness. And it is no coincidence he came to identify and look up to others who suffered from a physical disability—like Joseph Goebbels and J. B. Stoner—and his handicap may account for some of the rage he held. The famous psychoanalyst, Sigmund Freud, cited Gloucester in *Richard III,* who argued that since he cannot play the lover because of his hunchback, he will be the villain, intriguing and murdering as he pleases. For the physical wrong done to him, he claims the right to exemption from the scruples inhibiting others.

In order to compensate for his weaknesses, Franklin identified with powerful elements of society that reflected the bigoted views he was tutored in. The American Nazi Party and the Ku Klux Klan were facilitators who spurred him on through their violent hate-filled ideologies. Both organizations came to represent the family he never really had. He had loathed his parents, he was isolated at school, and his educational achievements only fit him for dead-end jobs. But in the Nazi Party and the KKK, he achieved what was missing at home—a sense of belonging and a vague feeling of his own importance. As Raphael Ezekiel noted in his study of neo-Nazi youths, there is a common experience extremist organization members have that makes them particularly susceptible to indoctrination. The men are usually in their teens when they are recruited, Ezekiel discovered, and they come under the influence of older leaders of the movement. Almost every member he studied was fatherless at a young age, most from divorce and only a few from the death of the father. Ezekiel said that a sense of abandonment and uncertainty followed the loss of the father if some support system was not present. As they grew up, they became exceptionally vulnerable.[35]

The paranoid leaders Franklin met appealed to his discontented soul; "It is not you who are the problem. It is they," extremist leaders exhorted their followers. The leader persuades them that the present society is corrupt and worthless, and he imbues in his members the idea they will be rewarded in the future. It is a powerful motivating force for misfits like Joseph Franklin. The leaders of the groups he joined persuaded him that society was out to get him, and counterattacks were justified for self-protection. The fantasy of a war between "us and them" was thus for Franklin transformed into reality.

Ezekiel expanded on the idea that parents were crucial in the development of a racist mind. "The absent parent," Ezekiel argued, "typically had no contact at all with the spouse or child; once out, he quickly vanishes. Stepfathers typically were cold, rough, and abusive, as were transient boyfriends . . . there was little sign of parenting in-depth through an extended family . . . church typically played no role in the family's life . . . a surprising number had been born with a childhood disease or deficiency."[36]

Ezekiel said that the white supremacist movement was a way to deal with this sense of "orphanhood," and that its young members have "a need to feel strong, masculine . . . tough guys."[37] The attraction to racism was about a "mood" and a "lonely resentment . . . and several ideas—white specialness, the biological significance of race, and the primacy of power in human relations . . . people will find some way to make their lives meaningful, and if nothing richer is at hand, racism [or religious fanaticism or nationalism or gang membership] will do."[38]

Franklin's repeated exposure to Nazi hate literature desensitized and indoctrinated him. And he may have suffered from what some have called the Fuhrerkontakt Effect—the oft-reported inspirational experience of exposure to Hitler's charisma. Franklin heard "facts" from his leaders, and they were repeated ad nauseum. The literature Franklin was exposed to included George Lincoln Rockwell's *White Power*, Gary Allen's *None Dare Call It Conspiracy*, and the Minutemen's *We Will Survive*, which spoke of the conspiracies against the white race. Many books, like Texas Klan leader Louis R. Beam's *Essays Of A Klansman,* set out the Klan's assassination point system that rewarded members for violence and assassination.[39]

Like many Americans in the late twentieth and early twenty-first centuries, Franklin was susceptible to conspiracy theories because there is a psychological need for them. Through the Internet, talk shows, books, and videos, conspiracy-mongers spread their fear and hatred and political paranoia—the forces of evil stalk the land, including the Jews, the Illuminati, and the United States government, which is controlled by Jews and Communists. The Nazi ideology Franklin learned combined the delusions of a worldwide Jewish conspiracy with that of a notion that the Jews are a satanic people. And, if Franklin believed that Jews and African Americans were subhuman, he would feel no guilt in exterminating them. The dehumanization of the Jews therefore justified acts of violence against them, and such acts could be committed without violating Biblical injunctions. As Morris Dees of the Southern Poverty Law Center observed, the Ku Klux Klan and American neo-Nazis share "moral responsibility" for Franklin's killings.[40]

Like the rest of us, Franklin obtained a reality check by comparing his beliefs with those of his associates. Wishing to belong, he never questioned Nazi or Klan ideology, and once a paranoid belief system is established in a group, it is nearly impossible to dislodge.[41] Furthermore, immersing himself in the American Nazi Party and the Ku Klux Klan made it much more likely he would commit murder, even if he were not predisposed to it. Franklin's sense of mission, which he repeated to anyone who would listen in the early days of his murder spree, was constantly reinforced by his fellow Klansmen and Nazis, and there was no one he came into contact with who could tell him his ideas were lunacy.

––––––––––––

Hate is a central emotion, and emotion is a very strong driving force, especially to those who have never discovered the world through education. Hatred also substitutes for money and power. Franklin was told everything he thought and did was right and the government was wrong and that it was legitimate to use violence for a just cause, and his tutors, the Nazis and the Klansmen, did it under the cloak of the First Amendment. Franklin responded to the call to arms by embracing violence as a form of "propaganda of the deed" and showed a real preference for spectacular and decisive action over the hard work of ideological contemplation. He could not assimilate with the groups he longed to be part of. But his desire to participate in their efforts remained with him. His ideology made him matter. And since his ideology was not dependent on a group, he had no fear he would be rejected by it. He also had no fear he would be challenged by other group members who may have diluted his ideology through reasoned debate. He could now focus his whole personality around his own interpretations of God's mission. He also felt safe because extremist groups are visible in society and attract the attention of law enforcement agencies.

Common among many murderers like Franklin is the build-up state, usually involving restlessness and anxiety. They need to show all the people who ignored them earlier on in life and treated them badly that they are to be reckoned with. They spend their time daydreaming of having power. In Franklin's case he was brainwashed by an unrelenting diet of Nazi propaganda and also guided by his quasi-religious beliefs and his beliefs in the occult that fueled his racism and gave it the imprimatur of scripture and fate.

Additionally, Franklin's use of a sniper rifle made it easier to kill because he was killing faceless objects and people he believed were the spawn of Satan and without souls. It was the type of killing many soldiers in World War II faced when confronted by Japanese troops. They were told the Japanese were an inhuman and brutal people; killing them became that much easier. And it is usually easier to harm a stranger than an acquaintance, and usually more comfortable to injure someone when his or her misery is not visible. As psychological experiments have shown, many ordinary people will obey the orders of a credible authority figure to do harm to others, but especially when they are able to distance themselves from the pain and the suffering of their victims. "He stops and shoots and doesn't hear the screams," said James Alan Fox, a professor of criminal justice at Northeastern University, in reference to sniper-killers. "Others enjoy squeezing the last breath from their victim. It makes it easier for [the sniper] psychologically to murder."[42] And when Franklin committed murders of unarmed individuals using his pistols, he had already killed by his sniper method. He had grown used to taking lives. Once a life is taken, it becomes easier to commit other murders despite the change in methodology that might be adopted.

Franklin knew what he was doing when he killed, but he didn't care. He lived by his own standards and believed he would get away with it. His hatred was visceral, personal, an irrational hatred that assumed the guise of an ideological antipathy. After his first few murders he became unrestrained and desensitized, losing all sense of morality, hiding behind the delusion that everything was all right because God condoned his actions and that he was helping to build a new America based on Nazi philosophy. His condition can best be described as "moral cretinism"—literally cut off from the norms of a moral society.

Franklin's acts were the product of a multiple of factors—his bitterness that life had dealt him a bad hand, the memories of the stories passed on to him that spoke of the "evil Jew" and the "no-good nigger," and the indoctrination by the leaders of the hate organizations he joined, all of which fed his hatred. However, in the end he alone was responsible for the murders he committed. He was convinced of his own rectitude, and his evil deeds were committed in the deluded, albeit sincere, belief that he was taking heroic measures to save his country.

EIGHTEEN

Death Row

I'm ready. From day one, I was prepared to die. Once you start something like this, you have to be prepared.

—*Joseph Paul Franklin*

When a vicious killer is sent to the electric chair or strapped onto a gurney for a lethal injection, society is condemning his crime with a seriousness and intensity that no other punishment achieves. By contrast, a society that sentences killers to nothing worse than prison—no matter how depraved the killing or how innocent the victim—is a society that doesn't really think murder is so terrible.

—*Jeff Jacoby, the* Boston Globe, *September 28, 2003*

The Potosi Correctional Center, which was built to hold the worst criminals in the state, is located on 140 acres approximately two miles east of the small town of Potosi in Washington County in southeastern Missouri. It is approximately sixty-five miles from St. Louis in one of the most forlorn parts of the state.[1]

Visitors can reach the prison from major Missouri cities by turning off I-44 at St. James and driving through thickly forested country. It is the first facility in the state to be built under the lease/purchase concept, and it received its first inmates in February 1989 shortly after opening. The prison is clean and well lit, and sits on a broad grassy plain from which every tree and bush has been removed. The main building is a stone structure with small window slots that resembles a suburban high school. It has recreational yards at one end, a large water tower off to the side, a concrete wall, and perimeter fences, and coils of razor wire enclose the buildings. The prison currently houses around 800 capital punishment, maximum-security, and high-risk male inmates. The average death row inmate is held in Potosi for approximately eleven years before execution.[2]

When it first opened, officials often described the prison as the cleanest, brightest, and best-equipped prison of its kind in the country. Potosi has a law library for inmates, a large gym, music rooms, well-kept visitor facilities, and central air-conditioning. The food, compared to many prisons in the United States, is nutritional and plentiful. In the late 1990s a 4H Club was started at the prison.

Still, despite the modernity of the place, it was "marked by a fundamental gloom," according to writer Michael W. Cuneo. "Everyone knew that Potosi was the end of the line," Cuneo observed. "Each and every one of its three hundred inmates had been sent there either to be executed or to rot away with no chance of parole. Brand spanking new, sure, but also the most forlorn of institutions—no exit, no mercy, no return ticket."[3]

———————

Prior to the acceptance of lethal injection as the primary method of execution, most states used hanging, the firing squad, the electric chair, and the gas chamber. Gradually the American public became shocked at the way such executions were carried out. The drop in a hanging was sometimes so badly miscalculated it resulted in either decapitation or slow strangulation. Electrocutions were sometimes so badly botched guards had to electrocute the condemned inmate more than once before signs of life had been extinguished. Marksmen sometimes missed the heart, and the inhalation of cyanide in the gas chamber produced some sickening results.

Before 1989, when Missouri chose lethal injection as the method of execution, the state used lethal gas. Before that, murderers were publicly hanged. The lethal injection procedure was judged to eliminate the shock value of capital punishment, which anti-death penalty advocates characterize as constitutionally cruel.

Potosi never had an actual Death Row where prisoners were sent after their convictions and remained there until they were executed. Prisoners condemned to death were held in the general population (GP) or the segregation wing until the date of execution. Prison executions were then carried out in the death chamber, an eighteen by twelve foot cinder block room located in the prison's hospital wing. A few hours before a prisoner was executed, he was kept in a cell near the infirmary and then escorted to the chamber and strapped onto a gurney before a lethal cocktail of drugs were pumped into his bloodstream.

Following criticisms about Missouri's execution protocol, the state now has a neatly typed, five-page public document setting out the procedures to be followed. A regular saline IV line is started in both arms. Upon the signal of the warden, a large dose of sodium thiopental (a common hospital anesthetic) is delivered, causing unconsciousness. This is followed by pancuronium bromide, which is a muscle relaxant that paralyzes the lungs and diaphragm. This causes the inmate's respiration to slow significantly. Finally, potassium chloride is introduced into the IV, which causes a fatal cardiac arrest. Death usually occurs approximately seven minutes after the lethal injection begins. According to the Texas Department of Criminal Justice, the cost for the drugs used in lethal injection is $86.08. Before Franklin's arrival at the prison, twenty-eight men were executed there by lethal injection. The following year three men were put to death. The peak year was 1999, with nine executions. Traditionally, executions were carried out at Potosi at just after midnight.[4]

In 2005 the execution chamber at Potosi was moved twenty-five miles east to the Eastern Reception, Diagnostic and Correctional Center in Bonne Terre, Missouri. Prisoners due to be exucuted are housed at Potosi before being taken to Bonne Terre on the execution date. Executions were moved to Bonne Terre because it has a specially designed holding cell to house the condemned prisoner in his final hours. The viewing area is bigger, allowing for additional state witnesses and relatives and friends of both the condemned killer and the victim of his or her crime. Another factor in the decision was the emotional toll executions took on the staff at Potosi. Despite the fact that around fifty to sixty men on Potosi's Death Row are convicted killers, prison staff tend to develop convivial relationships with the men. The first execution at Bonne Terre, in 2005, was thirty-eight-year-old Donald Jones, a drug addict who murdered his grandmother, sixty-eight-year-old Dorothy Knuckles, in 1993.

Potosi conducted all but one of the sixty-two Missouri executions between 1989, when capital punishment was reinstated, and 2005, when a moratorium was enacted. The exception was George "Tiny" Mercer who was put to death at the Missouri State Penitentiary in Jefferson City that year. He had raped and murdered a woman given to him by a biker gang as a birthday present.[5] Mercer was also the first to be executed by the brand-new, state-of-the-art lethal injection machine, invented by New Englander Fred Leuchter, who persuaded numerous state governments that his machine was more humane than other forms of execution. Leuchter's business motto was "Capital punishment, not capital torture."[6]

Capital punishment in the United States had stopped after the U.S. Supreme Court, in its landmark decision *Furman v. Georgia* (1972), ruled that the punishment had been unfairly applied, noting that it was the poor and African American prisoners who usually ended up in the execution chamber. For a number of years after the ruling, states attempted to bring in legal procedures whereby the punishment was more fairly exercised. In 1976 the Supreme Court said executions could resume because the revised laws of several states had eliminated bias and inequity. Missouri's revised Capital Murder Law was put into effect in 1977. Even then, it was not until twelve years later that the first execution was carried out.

By the late 1990s Missouri had the highest per capita rate of execution in the United States. When Joseph Paul Franklin arrived at Potosi, Mel Carnahan was the governor of the state before his tragic death in a plane crash in October 2000. Until that time Carnahan had presided over twenty-eight lethal injections. Only once, in the case of Bobby Shaw (who had committed two murders) had the governor commuted a death sentence. He did so in Shaw's case because he had been persuaded that the jurors at Shaw's trial had not been properly apprised of the defendant's mental retardation.

During his 2008 election campaign, a spokesperson for Missouri governor Jay Nixon told reporters that Nixon opposed a state bill that would halt executions until 2012 to study potential flaws in the state's death penalty system. Since 2005 a federal judge put the death penalty in Missouri on hold over concerns involving lethal injection. "[Jay Nixon] believes juries should have the option to sentence the harshest punishment for the most heinous crimes in a fair and just manner," the spokesman said. "There are brutal killers who have been sitting on death row in Missouri for years, and meanwhile, the families of their victims have not received the justice and closure they deserve. We must do everything to ensure that the death penalty is carried out in a fair and just manner, but we should not keep the victims' families from getting that closure."[7]

In 2007 oral arguments were heard in the case of *Baze v. Rees*, challenging the constitutionality of execution by lethal injection. On April 16, 2008, the U.S. Supreme Court issued its opinions. The constitutionality of the method was upheld on a 7–2 vote.[8]

In 2010 the U.S. Supreme Court cleared the way for executions to start again in Missouri. The court refused to hear the Missouri lethal injection case *Clemons v. Crawford.* The court dismissed the appeal because the dismissal complaint made no factual allegations suggesting any current or prospective member of Missouri's execution team would intentionally or unintentionally deviate from or ignore the written protocol. That meant lower court rulings would stand. The Supreme Court ruled lethal injection was permissible, and Missouri's attorney general stated executions would now start again. He also said he wanted Franklin to be the first to die.

———————

After receiving the death penalty for the murder of Gerald Gordon, Franklin soon became dissatisfied with his environment, even though he had tried for years to extricate himself from the loathed Marion prison. He began to feel that Potosi was just as bad as Marion. "It's a lot like Marion," he told Cincinnati detective Michael O'Brien. "I don't ever want to come back to this place again."[9] However, most prisoners agreed that Potosi was an altogether different and more advanced institution compared to Marion. The level of violence was less significant, and the facilities were good by prison standards, even though the atmosphere was poisoned by the debilitating effects of an institution that housed inmates who were never going to see the light of day or who had a death sentence hanging over them.

On arrival, Franklin spent the first two weeks quarantined and under observation in "One House"—standard procedure for any newly arrived death row inmate. Until 1994 each of Potosi's approximately 300 inmates had enjoyed the luxury of one-man cells. However, faced with prison overcrowding across Missouri, Department of Corrections officials decided that the answer to the shortage of space was for Potosi to convert many of the single man cells into double occupancy. The decision was put into effect in 1995, two years before Franklin's arrival, and capital punishment prisoners were doubled up. There were protests among the death row inmates, and they insisted on their right to a single cell. However, in May 1996 the Potosi warden issued an ultimatum to the prisoners—either double up or risk being sent to the isolation block. Most prisoners acceded to the threat, as they knew that inmates feared the isolation block, or "The Hole."

When lights were turned off at 10:00 p.m., the prisoners in the The Hole would shout and protest. The result was little sleep for those who ended up there. Lights were switched on at 5:00 a.m. Meals were served through slots in the cell doors. Lunch trays were brought to the unit at 10:30 a.m., and an early supper was delivered to the cells at 4:30 p.m. Prisoners were allowed no television and little reading material. Occasionally, they were allowed out of their cells for medical treatment or check-ups, but they were always chained and escorted. Prisoners were allowed visits but only on a non-contact basis behind glass in a cubicle off the main visiting area.[10]

During Franklin's time in the unit, he had conversations with a number of inmates, and one of them described Franklin as an "amusing conversationalist." "The guy could be civil," Darrell Mease said, "but he could also snap easy—hard and fast. Out on the street, you'd definitely want a gun on him at all times."[11]

Franklin whiled away his first few months by writing letters and working on his numerous appeals. He sought help from a *Cincinnati Post* reporter about how to place a personal ad for pen pals—"preferably of the female persuasion." But he didn't want any potential pen pals to know he was forty-eight years old. "Don't put that [his age] in there," he told the reporter. "I don't want any young women to know how old I am. If they think I'm twenty-five, they'll be more likely to send me a letter up here."[12]

As the years in Potosi passed, Franklin would repeatedly inundate prison authorities with complaints ranging from the prison food and his personal affects to his medical attention. For some of his offenses against prison discipline he was sent to what he described as the rubber room. He would frequently accuse prison staff of having some kind of animus towards him even while making demands on them. He said the most disparaging things about the prison system and staff. His arrogance was monumental and he displayed no remorse for his crimes or his insolent and disruptive behavior in prison.

———————————

The unwritten rules of racial identity for prisoners are as important in Potosi as they are in any American prison. New inmates quickly learn that the rules govern every aspect of their lives and that race determines whom prisoners take recreation with, whom they walk with, and whom they obey. The places of danger are the yard and the gym. During the summer months, hostilities inevitably boil over, and prison corrections officers are faced with outbreaks of conflict between inmates of the different racial groupings. Two of the important unwritten rules are that no inmate snitches (informs), and no inmate backs down when one of his group is threatened.

When he arrived in the Potosi segregation unit, Franklin quickly sent a note to one of the prison psychologists, Betty Weber, and asked if he could be transferred to a single man cell when he was eventually sent to general population. The request was denied by prison official Fred Johnson. Johnson told Franklin that when he was transferred to population, all the cells were two-man and "none of the population inmates are on any sort of a modified lock down status." The only possible way to guarantee Franklin's continued lock down status, Johnson said, was to leave him on administrative segregation (Ad-Seg), but he did "not meet the criteria at this time." Johnson said Franklin's only options were to ask for protective custody or to go to general population, both placements were double-cell occupancy.[13] However, the authorities soon realized that any inmate placed with Franklin in a two-man cell would be at risk, and Franklin was left in the segregation unit.

It was Franklin's choice to remain in Ad-Seg, according to one official, who noted that Franklin had "concerns for his safety" and that potential attacks by African American prisoners were "the reason he chose to stay in Ad-Seg." Prison official Richard K. Minard also noted that "Inmate Franklin stated to me that he felt the Administration set him up to be killed when he was assigned to general population. He based his suspicions on the high number of African Americans assigned to general population."[14] Franklin's choice left him with restricted access to personal property and "if the allowable limits are not sufficient for inmate Franklin to conduct his affairs, he is able to go to general population where he is allowed additional property."[15]

Franklin soon tired of his new housing unit and wrote to prison officials, saying he was "very dissatisfied here in 4-House." If he was not moved "soon," he informed prison officials, he would "flood the cell and/or go without food until I am moved."[16] His threats were not carried out. Two weeks later during a medical check up in the eye exam room, he vented his anger at the eye doctor and his assistant, shouting, "Who is asking questions you smartass bitch?" As he left the exam room, he turned to the doctor and said, "Now I know why they put the handcuffs on, you probably fucked them glasses up on purpose."[17]

Franklin whiled away his time in the drudgery of prison life by corresponding not only with his neo-Nazi fans but also the media, who were eager for interviews. Franklin told one newspaper reporter he had abandoned his racist views but then admitted he still had "friends in the KKK and with Nazi backgrounds."[18] In April and May of 1999, Court TV and *The Village Voice* interviewed Franklin. In 2001 he subscribed to *WAR*, the white Aryan resistance newspaper, but prison officials confiscated it. He also liked to read *Gallery* and *Penthouse* because he liked to visualize himself in the pictures with the "broads."

He also still kept in touch with his two sisters, Marilyn and Carolyn, and his brother Gordon Vaughn, as well as his daughter, who was eighteen years old when

Franklin arrived at Potosi. He spent his days cleaning his cell and listening to talk radio. Howard Stern, a controversial shock jock, became one of his favorites. Stern, who describes himself as "half Jew, half Italian," was known for his racial humor. Like Franklin, Stern suffered from obsessive-compulsive disorder. Franklin took a liking to Stern because the radio talk show host offered his honest opinions on subjects ranging from world affairs to American racial issues.[19] His fascination with Stern also appeared to center on the shock jock's abnormal persona.

In 1998, a year after his arrival, Franklin became fascinated with a television miniseries, *The Street Sweeper*, about a man who hunted down rapists and child molesters. When criminals were released from prison, the street sweeper would murder them. Franklin believed that the character in the movie, allegedly based on real events, was "trying to get public sympathy on his side. He's not denying the murders but he's trying to get public sympathy. And it turns out now that he's probably going to get out on a technicality cause the cop that searched his van and found one of the bodies and the guns made an illegal search. And so everything else is going to end up getting thrown out and he's going to be released." Franklin had been clearly comparing the events in the movie with his own circumstances. He was angry that police officials had lied about him and had done "anything, anyway they could use to nail me they did. . . . It didn't matter whether they violated my constitutional rights or not . . . got liars up . . . that testify against me and all that . . . my ex-wife and those jail birds out in Salt Lake City and all that, you know."[20]

Franklin spent a great deal of his time in Potosi reading works on numerology and spiritualism, and he subscribed to two spiritual periodicals, *Fate* and *Circle*. At his request this author bought him a subscription to a British periodical, *Psychic News*. Spiritualism postulates a belief in God but is distinguished from the Christian faith by a belief that spirits of the dead can be contacted, either by individuals or by gifted or trained mediums who can provide information about the afterlife. He told *Cincinnati Post* reporter Dan Horn about his spiritualist faith. When Horn asked Franklin how a religious man could justify his crimes, Franklin compared himself to flawed Biblical figures like Samson. He also said his sins explained why God allowed him to be captured. Apparently his spiritualist beliefs gave him strength to face his eventual fate. He said it would enable him to face lethal injection when the time came. "I'm ready," he told Horn. "From day one, I was prepared to die. Once you start something like this, you have to be prepared."[21]

Franklin has also kept up an interest in numerology—a mystical system associated with the occult that is said to divine truths from a person's birthdate and from the sum of the letters in a person's name. At the start of an interview with a *St. Louis Post-Dispatch* reporter, Kim Bell, he said he liked her first name because it had three letters.[22] Franklin's interest in the occult was in keeping with his Nazi ideology. In part, Hitler's program was aided by superstitious beliefs that evolved into an obsession with the occult. The SS researched the ancestral heritage of the Aryan race in the mid-1930s in an attempt to find proof that only the Aryan race was meant to rule the world and that mythic forces supported this idea.

Franklin said he was also influenced to confess to Melissa Powers because she had sent her ID to him as she was coaxing him to confess to the Cincinnati murders. "I began to see these little omens," he told Michael O'Brien. "As far as [Melissa Powers's letter] . . . on her ID there was a '23' written on there. She sent me a picture of her . . . a copy . . . of her ID. Picture ID. And there was a '23' on there which happens to be a very significant number to me . . . it's one of my lucky numbers like 2, 3, and 5, you know . . . I'm one of those really superstitious people . . . "[23] Franklin also liked the number 13, and if the letters in people's names added up to that number, it was a good sign, and he was more likely to have some kind of spiritual connection with them.

Franklin's thinking processes were also subjected to some bizarre system of reasoning. Shortly before he was tried for the murder of Gerald Gordon, he told *St. Louis Post-Dispatch* reporter Kim Bell that he thought he knew how to solve the world's ills and rid the planet of evil. "Abort all the male babies," he said. "And keep this up until the population is about 80 percent female. Most evil comes from males."[24]

Following his altercation with the prison eye doctor in 1997, Franklin appeared to have settled down to the routine of life in Potosi, and no conduct violations were reported. However, in April 1998, a prison search revealed that Franklin had torn his mattress. When questioned about it, the ever-rebellious Franklin said, "It is a false statement. The search team tore it up the last shakedown they had." A week later he told one of the prison nurses he was "getting tired of this shit, get out of here, bitch," when she asked him if he wanted a Medical Services Request form.[25]

April 1998 appeared to be a particularly upsetting month for Franklin. A week after insulting the prison nurse, he became enraged that a corrections officer in housing unit four had allegedly made a false statement about him. The officer had purportedly made the remark that Franklin wanted to kill one of the female officers. "I believe one or more of the white shirts put him up to it," Franklin complained in a letter to the prison authorities. "*Never* have I said that I want to take out a female officer, that is a bald-faced lie that I believe was made up by that officer and the homosexuals who work here, who want to make sure that women COs are not allowed to have any contact with me." Franklin offered to take a polygraph test to prove he was telling the truth, and he insisted that any inmates in adjoining cells be interviewed because he considered the accusations serious. He demanded that the corrections officer who was responsible take a polygraph test, and he said that if it were not done, he would "take this to the media and possibly even file a lawsuit."[26]

In a June 1998 telephone interview with Cincinnati police officer Michael O'Brien, Franklin said his life would be in danger if he were transferred to general population (GP). "My life could be at stake out there because [there are] so many blacks out there in GP . . . and just about every single one of them knows who I am." Franklin asked for a transfer to GP and to a cell with a white inmate whom he believed would protect him. "This is so tortuousness [sic] being in lock down like this all the time . . . you know I'd go out there and fight it out with them if I had this one guy . . . to stand beside me . . . he's telling me . . . he's been in some scraps himself here with them and there's a few others . . . like him around . . . and usually . . . they see the whites sticking together . . . they won't even make a move . . . and even with me they won't move on me when they're by their self. It's got to be a bunch of them." Franklin related to O'Brien how "there's a lot of violence out there . . . lot of fighting and shit."[27]

In another part of the conversation, Franklin appeared to have lost his sense of fear of being attacked by African American inmates. He bragged that he didn't fear black prisoners because "the Aryan brothers in here stick together, they don't have trouble with [blacks]."[28] He began to think about writing a book about his crimes and told O'Brien he was thinking about writing a letter to Bantam Books, which was his favorite publisher. O'Brien responded by telling Franklin, "Well . . . they've wrote books on people that have been a lot less . . . notorious than you."[29]

By the end of the year, Franklin was again upsetting the authorities with his demanding and insulting behavior, and it also appeared that Franklin was showing signs of having deviant sexual urges. As corrections officer Dennis W. Kirby was escorting Tara Willhite, Potosi's director of nurses, through the prison wing, they passed Franklin's open cell. According to Officer Kirby, Franklin was "stroking his penis vigorously." When Kirby stood in front of Franklin's cell to "protect Miss Willhite from the insulting thing Franklin was doing," Franklin said, "Would you mind moving, I'm trying to see the pretty lady." When he was asked to account for his behavior, the increasingly paranoid Franklin stated, "I feel that I have been set up."[30]

Whatever punishment Franklin received did not appear to have any effect, as he repeated this behavior the following month in front of corrections officer Elizabeth Pettus.[31] In August 1999 he told litigations officer, Brenda K. Gibson, he wanted to "hang out" with her "for awhile and get to know you, if that's alright with you."[32] In August of 2000 he wrote to her, asking, "Is there any way I can talk you into being my lover? I've kind of got a hard on for you. Thank you."[33]

The offense brought home the suspicions of Melissa Powers, who felt Franklin's crimes may have had a sexual aspect to them. In fact, during his time at Potosi, Franklin would frequently try to secure the assistance of female attorneys, no doubt his way of finding female companionship. In 1999 he tried to initiate correspondence with a woman who had worked at the Community and Diagnostic and Treatment Center in Cincinnati, Ohio. The center was responsible for evaluating Franklin during his trial for the murders of Dante Evans Brown and Darrell Lane. Teresa Izquierdo had contact with Franklin during this period. Franklin wrote Izquierdo a letter in which he asked if she remembered him and said he wanted to "swap X-rated letters" with her. "In other words," Franklin wrote, "have an 'affair' with me by mail, with phone calls?" He said his "dick gets hard just thinking about you. I'd love to stick it into that warm split between your legs."[34] Izquierdo was extremely upset with Franklin's letter and informed the prison authorities through the Cincinnati chief assistant prosecuting attorney. Senior staff at the prison warned Franklin never to make contact with Izquierdo again.[35]

During November 1998 Franklin also baited prison officials by telling them he was on a hunger strike until he was moved away from a nearby inmate whom he disliked. The hunger strike did not last longer than one missed meal.[36]

By 1999 Franklin had had enough of Ad-Seg and requested a move to protective custody. Prison official Michael J. Layden told Franklin and his caseworker, Sharon Gifford, that the application had been rejected on the basis that Franklin was not eligible.[37] Two days later Franklin defied authorities by covering the lower half of his cell door and refusing to give his name and number for the inmate count.[38] Three weeks later he created a disturbance by refusing to remove his T-shirt before he was taken to the shower room. The corrections officer gave Franklin a choice— remove his T-shirt or be refused a shower. When Franklin refused the officer's second order, his food port door was closed. Franklin then kicked the door of his cell and called the officer a "dick-sucking bitch."[39]

During an inmate count just over a week later, Officer Randall Wills approached Franklin's cell and told him to remove a blanket from his head. Franklin responded by screaming, "You bald-headed, dick-sucking motherfucker, stay away from my cell." Franklin's defiance prompted the other inmates on his wing to join in and began yelling also.[40] The next day Franklin showed his contempt for Officer Wills by ignoring him when the officer gave him several orders. When Franklin was interviewed regarding the offense, he told Officer Mike Lawson that Wills was "mentally deranged" and "he needs help."[41]

Franklin also used threats to try and influence prison staff. In May 1999, Franklin told his caseworker, Sharon Gifford, that if he did not get the cellmate of his choice that "one of them would end up dead." Gifford recommended that no one be celled with Franklin at that time.[42] Franklin responded to the concern over his death threats by writing a letter to Joe Hoffmeister, the functional unit manager, on the June 14, 1999. Franklin said he wanted to discuss a move to "3-House." He said that after nineteen years of living in a cell alone he would not be able to adjust to living with "another dude." "Besides," wrote Franklin, "most of the inmates [especially black inmates] here at Potosi would be afraid to cell with me . . . the statement I made to her was not a threat. It was simply reality. She is trying to say that my case is no different than anyone else's, that it is not a special case, and that I should be able to cell with anyone they choose (even though my case is a racial case that was classified as "broad publicity" by the U.S. Bureau of Prisons). Further, my life has been threatened numerous times by black inmates since I've been at Potosi, so my life would be in danger if I were put in a cell with a black inmate. During the most recent conversation I had with her about a move to 3-House, she leaned forward towards me, her nostrils flaring, and accused me of threatening to kill *any* inmate I was celled with, which was a flat-out lie, and she looked at me like a mad cow. . . . I would like any future conversations between me and her recorded."[43]

At the turn of the new millennium Franklin's behavior showed no signs of improving. In January 2000 he was once again in trouble with the prison authorities when he confronted Officer Coleman and shouted, "Shut up Coleman, you motherfucking son of a bitch, you fucking COs enjoy fucking with inmates, you keep messing with me and I'm going to fuck you up and all the rest of you fucking COs. If you don't believe me just keep it up." When he was asked to account for his actions, Franklin told the prison authorities, "I would not want to hurt the old bitch. I don't threaten old men his age."[44]

At various times during his incarceration at Potosi, Franklin was moved to different housing units for administrative purposes. In October 1999 Franklin's request to move back to housing unit four was denied. However, in March 2000 he got his wish and was transferred there. But there were concerns. In a memo from Linda Wilkinson, functional unit manager of housing units one and two, to Sharon Gifford, the caseworker in housing unit four, Wilkinson wrote, "Offender Franklin was one of the offenders chosen to move to housing unit four because of his current status. At this time, he is assigned to Ad-Seg. However, his institutional behavior is such that he should probably be considered for release from Ad-Seg (he has only one Conduct Violation Report in the past year). At this time, though, this is not considered an option. Offender Franklin has made statements that have indicated that he may intend to harm staff (especially female) and other offenders, in order to gain further notoriety. This fact, compounded by his (self-admitted) hatred of minorities, has resulted in his continuation of Ad-Seg assignment."[45]

Franklin remained in housing unit four, but by April 2000 he became such a problem for staff that he was transferred to housing unit two. According to Brenda Umpenhour, Franklin had been "continuously . . . a problem in housing unit four and it would be in the best interest of the unit for him to be removed as soon as possible. He is keeping the wing in turmoil on racial issues. He is keeping his peers awake to all hours of the night. He insists on being allowed more benefits than others are allowed, like an hour shower and anything else he can think of, or maneuver. He is uncooperative and threatening. In the best interest of and for the safety and security of the institution, I request Mr Franklin be removed from the unit."[46] The report contradicts Franklin's comments to the press about having modified his views about Jews and African Americans.

The move did not have any affect on Franklin, and his rebellion against prison rules and his insulting behavior toward prison staff continued. He exposed himself to female staff once again, and at every opportunity, he would make lecherous remarks to any passing female member of staff or prison visitor. In September 2000 he asked an officer to pass on a request to "nurse Marsha" that he wanted to "fuck her."[47] At one point he balked at taking a skin test because he believed the hospital staff was out to kill him and the hospital was run by a "homosexual."[48]

In the years that followed, Franklin would repeatedly complain about his cell searches and threaten the prison authorities with a call to the sheriff's office and the media. He threatened to sue the prison authorities for the misplacement of his mail and personal items and filed grievance charges against corrections officers. He repeatedly accused them of stealing personal items from his cell, including legal papers, legal letters, stationary, his ID card, journals, and magazines, and believed they were looking for any opportunity to Mace him. He was also paranoid about the staff at Potosi and made accusations of harassment. Jonna King, correctional case worker for housing units 2B and 2C, in a letter to Linda Wilkinson, functional unit manager for housing units one and two, wrote that on the February 28, 2001, during wing rounds, Franklin had requested he be transferred to another institution "due to constantly being harassed." King said she asked Franklin who was harassing him and he said, "Everyone." King added, "When I asked whether he meant staff or offenders he stated, 'Everyone in this institution.' When I asked him what 'everyone' was harassing him about he stated, 'Everything, mostly my case—its high profile.'" When King told Franklin he would not be transferred, he replied that his sentence would soon be overturned.[49]

Over the years Franklin had celebrated Hitler's birthday and he would always notify reporters or any law enforcement official that he would not be available for interviews on that important date in his calendar. The celebrations clearly took a toll on his emotions. In 2003 he shouted at a corrections officer, "You fucking bitch, you nigger-loving bitch. I can't get nothing because I'm white so fuck you, you fucking bitch." When he was asked to account for his behavior, Franklin told officials, "She treats the black inmates with respect but she disrespects the white inmates."[50]

Franklin's paranoia showed no signs of abating as the years passed. In February 2004 Franklin became enraged that Missouri's Department of Corrections was hiring homosexuals. He complained to prison officials that some guards whom he believed to be homosexual were "blowing kisses" at him and allegedly "feeling him up" during pat searches. With a tongue-in-cheek attitude towards Franklin, Don Roper, the superintendent of the prison, told Franklin that "some of your allegations are very vague. However, you have indicated that officers are mouthing you kisses through the door. If this is the case, please provide me with specific information so that I can have your allegations investigated."[51] Franklin was not satisfied with Roper's answer, so he wrote another letter in which he made allegations about a specific corrections officer whom he believed was homosexual. "What would you do if a homosexual guard was stalking you?" he wrote. "Is it possible that staff at Marion decided it would be best to recruit him and send him over here to target me, like intelligence services like the KGB recruit double agents . . . for whatever reasons?"[52] Roper's response this time was to advise Franklin that his conspiracy theory was "way out."[53]

In April 2006 Franklin continued to complain to officials about his record and wrote to the records office of Potosi. He had apparently taken offense at the mistakes made in his prison file. He enclosed some corrections to his face sheet. He wanted the authorities to know he had used "about 100 aliases, besides those listed," and that he would need to "get the list from the FBI because I've forgot most of them." Franklin said he was five-eleven not five-ten, as his records stated. He also informed the office that he had three siblings, plus one half brother and two half sisters. Still centered on his racial identity, he described his race as "white, Native American." He said his religion was "Christian Scientist/ Spiritualist." His hair, he said, was "three different colors, but basically medium brown." He wanted his record to state his occupation or trade as "cable assembler for Unicor, the Federal Prison Industries, for six-and-a-half years—making cables for the U.S. Military."[54]

Executions in Missouri had been on hold since 2005 as the courts decided whether lethal injection in general, and the state's three-drug method in particular, violated constitutional protections against cruel and unusual punishment. Some critics argued that if the initial anaesthetic did not take hold, the third drug that stopped the heart could cause excruciating pain and the inmate would be unable to communicate the pain because of a second drug that paralyzed him. In 2008, however, the U.S. Supreme Court upheld the process and a federal judge ruled in favor of Missouri's lethal injection method, opening the way for executions to begin again.

On May 20, 2009, under governor Jay Nixon, executions in Missouri resumed when forty-nine-year-old Dennis Skillicorn was put to death at Bonne Terre. He died within eleven minutes. In late August of 1994, Dennis Skillicorn, together with his friends, Allen Nicklasson and Tim DeGraffenreid, had just committed a burglary and were headed east from Kansas City to obtain illegal drugs when their car broke down. The next day, good samaritan Richard Drummond, a technical support supervisor for AT&T, saw the stranded motorists and offered to take them to a phone. Pulling a gun on Drummond, the men loaded the booty from their burglary into Drummond's car. Skillicorn watched as Nicklasson lead Drummond toward a wooded area. There, Nicklasson shot Drummond twice in the head. Tim DeGraffenreid, who was seventeen at the time of the killing, pleaded guilty to second-degree murder. Nicklasson is, at the time of this writing, condemned to die.

Now, more than half of Missouri's fifty death row inmates have been awaiting execution for a decade or longer, and in many cases, they are running out of appeals. In May 2009 state representative Scott Lipke, who chaired the House Crime Prevention Committee and witnessed Skillicorn's death, said he believed the state should move forward with executions. "If the appeals have run their course, the dates should be set," Lipke said. "We owe it to the victims and the victims' families not to prolong it anymore."[55] His comments were supported by a series of academic studies over the last half-dozen years that claim to settle a once hotly debated argument—whether the death penalty acts as a deterrent to murder. The studies count between three and eighteen lives that would be saved by the execution of each convicted killer.[56]

Today, Joseph Paul Franklin, whose last name ironically means "free man," continues to be held in what he describes as "Long Term Ad-Seg," extremely upset that he is "locked down 24/7/365 for my own protection . . . because the prison is wall to wall niggers and white homosexuals."[57] However, he may soon be free of his intolerable living conditions. In June 2009 Missouri attorney general Rick Koster asked the Supreme Court of Missouri to set a date for Franklin's execution because Franklin's "traditional appeals had been exhausted."[58] In the summer of 2010, after the Supreme Court had decided lethal injection was a lawful execution protocol in Missouri, Koster said he wanted Franklin to be the first to die when executions recommenced.

EPILOGUE

Looking Back

Joseph Paul Franklin represented everything my generation loathed and had tried to change in American society: racism, anti-Semitism, the cowboy myth, the love of guns, the sexism, the wife-battering. He was a twisted, demonic foot soldier who didn't like blacks and interracial couples any more than did the Night Creature, the Ratwoman, the Bag Lady of Sleaze, or Fuhrer Man.

—*Joe Eszterhas,* American Rhapsody

To understand Joseph Paul Franklin, you have to visualize a lonely young man, insignificant to his community and without friends that he could turn to in a moment of need. His parents beat him. He suffered a terrible accident as a young boy that left him handicapped. It made his isolation more complete and gave him an unrelenting bitterness. When he reached manhood, he presented himself as an ordinary, innocuous-looking man with no outstanding personality or looks and with no real purpose in life. He tried to identify with other Mobile citizens—without success. This "catastrophe of indifference," as psychoanalyst Dr. Stephen Grosz called it, may well have been the foundation for Franklin's growing paranoia, a feeling that society in general, and individuals in particular, had an animus towards him and that no one was *thinking* about him. The only people he could identify with were the outlaws of the Old West who became his role models in life. He began to look for something to believe in—something that would give him power and importance, which was a much more preferable goal than attempting to make a meager living without an education or any special work skills. He found his Holy Grail when he picked up Hitler's *Mein Kampf* from a local Mobile library. It was the answer to all his problems. Now he could understand why fate had relegated him to the bottom of the heap, and he discovered how he could attain meaning to his life.

Franklin was a bitter and twisted man who is angry with the world, a man who tries to elevate himself into a somebody with the only skills he has at hand—his ability to shoot. When he commits his murders, he feels powerful—"the executioner, the judge, and the jury."[1] He sees himself as a man chosen by God, a Biblical hero on a holy crusade. He is a nobody who tries to achieve the notoriety of James Earl Ray and Byron De La Beckwith, racists who believed they would be recognized as white supremacist heroes. Franklin is a man who believed that the American Nazi Party and the Ku Klux Klan hold the answers to America's racial problems.

Franklin's methods of killing tell us he knew right from wrong. He was fastidious in preparation of his murders, planning them down to the last detail and planning his escape routes. He was able to operate for three years before he was identified and arrested because he spaced his attacks apart in terms of geography and time and frequently changed his weapons and appearance. In a Jungian sense, and with reference to the famous psychotherapist's theory of synchronicity, the stars aligned for Franklin. Here was this huge opportunity for him to vent his racism, hatred, and rage and become a somebody. And he could carry out his murders with impunity because "God was on his side." This was not the modus operandi of an insane person, oblivious to the consequences of his acts.

At various times over the last decade, Franklin told various media people that he had renounced his white supremacist beliefs. In 1997 he told a reporter he no longer hated African Americans and Jews and thought he may have been a Jew in a former lifetime. "Before, I used to blame Jews for all my problems," he told a reporter, "but I can see now how erroneous I was."[2] In another interview he said he had come to appreciate the Jewish religion and regretted the murder of Gerald Gordon. "Now I would never kill anyone at a house of worship," he said. "I've come to respect the Jewish religion." He said he would not kill if he were a free man—which contradicted his comments at the Gordon trial, when he told jurors that if he were set free, he would continue on his killing spree. In the same interview, he said he no longer despised African Americans, but they were still not his "favorite people."[3]

Since his arrival at Potosi Correctional Center, Franklin has, at times, shown some remorse for his crimes. He once said, "I was misguided at the time. I did not know who . . . it never occurred to me that [the victims] would have families, and so I never really felt any sympathy for their families or for them, really. And . . . I was just on a mission to try to . . . start a race war, get a lot of blacks killed, and we would eventually have won the war and wiped them out. That was my goal."[4] At the end of another interview, given before he was sent to Potosi, Franklin was asked if he enjoyed committing the murders. Franklin said, "No, absolutely not." "Then do you ever feel sorry for what you've done?" the interviewer asked. Franklin hesitated, bowing his head. After a moment of silence, he raised his head and stared at the reporter before replying, "That's a hard question to answer."[5]

However, Franklin' prison file brings home the level of his internal rage and his shocking lack of any real remorse for his murders even to the present day. The file reveals that in conflicts with staff, he could go off on a rant with a hard, implacable, inhuman voice. He didn't care what anyone thought of him, and he didn't care much about showing his cold-blooded killer instinct. Franklin could kill because it made him feel better. And the real horror of Franklin's murders was that he could blow someone away without any passion.

Franklin has also never renounced his racist views despite his comments to various media organizations while in prison. He has repeatedly made statements implying he intended to harm staff, especially female corrections officers. He has also threatened other offenders as a way of gaining further notoriety. His hatred of minorities is a constant fixture in his dealings with others.[6] His present lawyer, Jennifer Herndon, is convinced he is severely mentally ill.

Former Chattanooga prosecutor Joseph A. Rehyansky, who tried Franklin for the William Tatum murder, has no doubt that Franklin would kill again if he were released. In a 2008 article, Rehyansky related how he met with Franklin during pretrial conferences and asked him if he would pick up where he left off if he were ever released from prison. "Oh no," Franklin told Rehyansky, "I'd start killing queers. Niggers and Jews are bad enough, but it's queers who are ruining this country now." Rehyansky also has his own ideas why men like Franklin spend so much time on death row. "The logjam in execution in most states," Rehyansky said, "is the result of federal judges with a liberal disposition granting stays of execution that bring the machinery of justice to a halt just long enough to allow the death warrant to expire. The result is that a new warrant will have to be applied for and signed by the governor, a new date set, and witnesses rescreened and renotified."[7]

Following interviews in which he insisted he was a changed man, it has not taken long for Franklin to lapse into his white supremacist refuge, no doubt egged on by his numerous supporters who give him succor through their letters to him and their website rants in which they characterize him as a hero for the cause. In his correspondence with me, Franklin vented his hatred of African Americans and complained endlessly about his incarceration. He wrote that he did not get the same visiting privileges that general population inmates get "with my lawyers or anybody else. With visits from family and friends I've got to speak through telephones and glass, while they're listening, so you've got to be careful what you say, while I've got to wear cuffs around my waist and legshackles when I get a visit from the media or from lawyers. It used to be different when I first got here back in 1997. At that time they would let me get contact visits alone without any retraints with the media and my lawyers, but they changed up, when they realized that wasn't causing any problems."[8]

Franklin's views about the Bible are unchanged, and his interest in the occult has not waned. In a 2008 letter he revealed how he was still immersed in Biblical myth. He called his critics "children of Belial" (Satan's children) and spends a large proportion of his time reading works on spiritualism and the occult. He even became fascinated with the life of gypsies. His Nazi sympathies are reflected in his letters, each page numbered in German. Dwelling on his tragic life, his racist ideology is perhaps the only thing he can turn to for meaning before he is put to death.[9] That, and the continuing links he has with his brother Gordon, his sisters, and his daughter, Sheryl, who is now in her thirties.

Since his trials in the late 1990s for the murders of Gerald Gordon, Darrell Layne, and Dante Evans Brown, he has revealed a startling lack of awareness regarding the seriousness of his crimes. In 1999 he told a documentary filmmaker that, depite being on death row, he may one day be released. "I've just got various streams of omens that way," he said. "I could be out there on the street. I mean, miracles do happen. With God all things are possible, the Bible says. And I've got a death sentence now and . . . I've been convicted and sentenced to twelve different life terms plus the death sentence. I mean, the odds of me ever getting out are slim to none, if you go by just man's standards but not by God's standards, see He can actually get me out if he wants to."[10] Even after his final appeals were rejected in 2009 and Missouri's attorney general asked the Supreme Court to set an execution date, Franklin had unrealistic hopes he would still be around in the future to "make money." He told me in August 2009, "I wish you would keep in touch even after the book is published, man—I've got plenty of ideas on how we could make some money, even more than you could make writing a book!"[11]

There are remaining mysteries surrounding Franklin's three-year crime spree. In 1997 he confessed to killing two African American men in Atlanta in 1978 and 1979. Both victims, Franklin said, were on Ponce de Leon, a main street in Atlanta, not far from the police station. It would appear that the 1978 killing was a reference to the murder of twenty-two-year-old African American Johnny Brookshire, who was murdered in February 1978 in a northeast Atlanta neighborhood. He had been walking down the street with his twenty-three-year-old girlfriend, Joy Williams. After a second admission, this time to Atlanta detectives in 1999, authorities took him seriously about the Brookshire murder. He was considered to be responsible but never charged or brought to trial.[12] Atlanta police did investigate the second alleged murder on Ponce de Leon but were never able to corroborate Franklin's confession after a search of their unsolved murders file.

In the same 1997 interview, Franklin also confessed to picking up a white woman at a truck stop along Interstate 65 near Nashville. According to Franklin the woman allegedly told him she had hitched a ride with an African American trucker from southern Illinois. Franklin purportedly drove her to a wooded area near a creek, pushed her in the water, and shot her with a .41 caliber Smith & Wesson, a rare handgun. Nashville police told reporters of a woman who had been pulled from a creek around this time, but she had been strangled.[13] In 2009 Nashville detective Patrick J. Taylor informed me that "I have checked out our unsolved homicides that occurred around the end of the 1970s and do not see anything that matches."[14]

Franklin also confessed to another unsolved shooting that allegedly occurred in Jackson, Mississippi, in 1979. In a 1998 telephone conversation from Potosi, Franklin told Cincinnati detective Michael O'Brien that he used a Black Hawk seven-and-a-half-inch barrel, single-shot pistol to shoot an African American police officer, not in uniform, who was standing next to a white cop on a Jackson street. He said his actions were "a little risky," but that after he shot the officer, bystanders thought the shot had come from someone in a passing car, and no one saw him standing in a darkened lot.[15] I researched officers killed in the line of duty in Mississippi within a five-mile radius of Jackson, but discovered no incident that would match Franklin's description of the handgun shooting or the date of the shooting. This still leaves open, however, the possibility that an officer had been shot by a handgun but then recovered from his wounds. Jackson authorities have never investigated or charged Franklin with the alleged shooting.[16] It also leaves open the possibility that Franklin's confession was a reaction to FBI profiler John Douglas's characterization of Franklin as a coward. Douglas had, according to Franklin, told the media that Franklin had been afraid "to actually stand right up next to somebody and shoot 'em face to face."[17]

Melissa Powers speculated that Franklin might have been responsible for the unsolved murders of a number of prostitutes. However, there is simply no way of knowing for sure. With the passage of time, Franklin is probably unable to remember crucial details that would be necessary for investigators because they would need corroborative evidence to pursue cold cases. Accordingly, for Franklin, the exercise would be pointless and unlikely to lead to further furloughs from Potosi. More likely, Franklin has already confessed to all the crimes he committed. This is the judgment of Cincinnati detective Mike O'Brien, who never knew Franklin to take credit for crimes he was not involved in. O'Brien said, "Knowing [Franklin] through the [Cincinnati] investigation . . . if [Franklin said] he did it, he did it." O'Brien told Franklin he had made his views known to investigating prosecutors. Franklin told O'Brien that the Cincinnati detective was correct in his assumptions—"I got enough notches on my belt already," Franklin told him.[18]

Reading Franklin's letters about his fascination with spiritualism and the afterlife, it struck me that Franklin may have really wanted to die when he told the St. Louis jury that he would kill again if they didn't hand down the death penalty. He seemed to be rolling the dice to see what was on the other side. Franklin has stated repeatedly that he is not frightened of dying and that he would rather be executed by the state than by "some punks," which he believes is a "dishonorable way to die." According to Melissa Powers, "He thinks it's honorable to be killed by the state, not by black men. Or in a shoot-out with the police officers."[19]

Shortly before he was sent to Potosi, he told one reporter he preferred a firing squad as his chosen method of death. " I barely missed out on that in Utah, he said. "They put a target over your heart, and you die instantly, for one thing." He also prefers to be executed by the state than slain in prison by inmates who despise him. "I got my name listed in encyclopedias on serial killers. They might just kill me for the notoriety. I'd rather be executed by the state," he said.[20]

But Franklin's braggadocio about wanting to die may have, after all, been a ruse. He told Michael O'Brien in 1998 that the only reason he told the St. Louis court to give him the death sentence was because he "knew that that was the only way I'd be sent from Marion to Potosi, see."[21]

What can be said is that Franklin's behavior during the past ten years suggests he has recovered the will to live, and he has fought to have his death sentence overturned. However, Franklin's pleas have not been met with any sympathy and, as of this writing, it appears that Franklin's rendezvous with death may be imminent. His appeals had no success at any level until June 15, 2004, when U.S. District Court judge Carol E. Jackson issued an order vacating Franklin's conviction and death sentence and giving the state ninety days to release or try him. Jackson said that Franklin's waiver of the assistance of legal counsel in the Gordon murder trial was "not knowing, voluntary, and intelligent," and that the trial judge failed to instruct jurors about aggravating and mitigating circumstances.

However, the Eighth Circuit United States Court of Appeals in St. Louis reversed that decision. The panel of three judges said Franklin had been competent to stand trial, and his lawyers presented no new evidence in the appeals process to question his competence. The judges also said that because Franklin waived his right to appeal his trial and conviction, all subsequent appeals were also barred. Following the decision, Scott Holste, a spokesman for the Missouri attorney general's office, said that no execution date has been set or sought for Franklin. He did say, however, "If there are additional attempts to have the conviction or sentence set aside, we will vigorously oppose those as well."[22]

In 2006 there was some hope that Franklin's death sentence might be revoked in favor of a life sentence. On June 26 Judge Fernando J. Gaitan Jr. of the United States District Court for the Western District of Missouri suspended the state's death penalty after lengthy hearings on the matter. Gaitan reasoned that the state's lethal injection protocol did not satisfy the Eighth Amendment because the written procedures for implementing lethal injections were too vague and the state had no qualified anesthesiologist to perform lethal injections. However, Jay Nixon, the Missouri attorney general who would later be elected governor of the state in 2008, promptly appealed to the United States Court of Appeals for the Eighth Circuit in St. Louis. On June 4, 2007, a panel of the Eighth Circuit reversed the district court's decision.

The matter of the constitutionality of the death penalty appeared to be settled with a U.S. Supreme Court decision. On April 16, 2008, the court decided that the current method of execution by lethal injection, by use of a three-drug cocktail, was constitutionally permissible, even though an alternative method such as a massive overdose of some other drug could be used and might be less painful or less uncomfortable for the condemned. As a result of the court's decision, some states that had instituted stays or moratoria announced a resumption of the practice. [23]

In July 2007, in what appeared to be his final effort to overturn the death sentence, a federal appeals court rejected his submission.[24] In June 2009 Missouri Attorney General Chris Koster asked the State Supreme Court to set an execution date. In 2010 the U.S. Supreme Court also cleared the way for executions to start again in Missouri. The court refused to hear the Missouri lethal injection case *Clemons v. Crawford.* The court dismissed the appeal because the dismissal complaint made no factual allegations suggesting any current or prospective member of Missouri's execution team would intentionally or unintentionally deviate from or ignore the written protocol. That meant lower court rulings would stand. The Supreme Court ruled that lethal injection was permissible, and Missouri's attorney general stated executions would now definitely start again.

Vernon Jordan recuperated from the attempted assassination and resigned from the Urban League, joining a major law firm in Washington, D.C., as a partner. His influence was sustained through positions on several major corporate boards, including American Express, Dow Jones, Union Carbide, and Xerox. From the vantage point of his influential law firm, Jordan continued to be an important behind-the-scenes operative and advocate for civil rights interests. In 1985 Jordan's wife of twenty-seven years, Shirley, died after years of battling multiple sclerosis.

Jordan's longtime friend Bill Clinton, who was elected president in 1992, chose Jordan to head his presidential transition team, and during Clinton's eight years as president, the former civil rights leader became very influential. However, in 1998 Jordan became embroiled in a Clinton sex scandal involving a White House aide. He was called to testify during the 1999 impeachment trial of the president regarding President Clinton's relationship with White House intern Monica Lewinsky. The *Washington Post*, ABC News, *Newsweek*, and *Time* reported that Lewinsky had implicated Jordan in an attempted conspiracy to get her to lie to the Paula Jones grand jury in return for Jordan's help in finding a job. The accusation was later found to be baseless. But suspicions remained. In 1996 former White House press secretary Dee Dee Myers said, "Vernon knows a lot of stuff about the president and his personal life, but he'll never trade on it. Vernon understands how power works better than anybody I know. He talks to the president about everything but it would diminish his power if he talks about it. He protects the president, his friend."[25]

Today, Jordan is a successful attorney and businessman living in New York with his second wife, Ann Dibble Cook, a business consultant.

In June 1980 the *Chicago Tribune* said African American women had been particularly outspoken in their criticism of Vernon Jordan and demanded to know why
he left his motel to drive twenty-five minutes to Martha Coleman's house around
1:00 a.m. Ethel Payne, a columnist for the Afro-American News Syndicate and
civic leader said, "If Jordan has a good answer to all the unanswered questions I am
sure everything will be forgotten. Surely he owes his constituency an explanation. It
must be remembered that black men who align themselves with white women strike
a very sensitive emotional nerve with black women. It's part of the whole pattern of
rejection of us by black men and it's not taken lightly."[26]

A year after the shooting, Martha Coleman was still hounded by an eager press
hoping to ask questions about her relationship with Jordan. She stonewalled every
request for an interview and angrily asked one reporter, "How much are you going
to pay me?"[27] However, within a few months the anonymity she craved finally came,
and she was never again subjected to press inquiries about her relationship with
Jordan.

Salt Lake City Detective Don Bell retired from the Salt Lake City Police Department several years ago, according to a spokesman for the police department.[28]
Following his retirement he worked for the Salt Lake City chief medical exam-
iner, Todd Grey, and teamed up with other investigators to solve murders. Later he
worked with the FBI's Violent Crime Apprehension Program, a computer-based
nationwide crime information network. He focused exclusively on serial homicides
and was on call for law enforcement agencies across the country.

Bell has his own ideas as to why killers like Franklin were so hard to catch.
He believes it is because "they were the ones who came across as . . . pretty normal. That's why they're so hard to catch. That's why they have so many victims—
because it takes so long for you to click on to who they are."[29] After Franklin's trials
for the murders of Ted Fields and David Martin, Bell became haunted by the case.
"I don't understand this type of killer," Bell said many years after the murders, "that
he would actually just take a complete stranger and because of their race and who
they were standing by or talking to, he would feel it necessary to kill them. He's one
of those few people that I have just absolutely no explanation for and it's still hard
for me to understand."[30]

Melissa Powers, who became a chief assistant prosecutor for the municipal division, left the Hamilton County prosecutor's office in 1999 to start a solo litigation practice. Her private practice primarily included criminal defense of adults and juveniles, domestic relations, and civil litigation. In May 2006 the governor of Ohio appointed Powers as a judge for the Hamilton County Municipal Court District 7. Her term will last until 2012. In 2008 she received a national honor, the "Heroes Against Hate" award from the Anti-Defamation League, for helping bring Franklin to justice. The award was presented at Washington's Kennedy Center.

Recalling the interview that was responsible for bringing Franklin to trial for the murders, Powers said that she remembered during the interview that she had to keep telling herself to breathe "because I was holding my breath throughout the whole thing, and this desire to run, get me out of here, get me away from him . . . he literally went from a flat line personality and monotone speaking with me, to this electrifying, charged individual who, before my eyes, to me he looked like he was sexually turned on."[31] Powers's suspicions that Franklin was sexually motivated in his murders gained currency when Dorothy Otnow Lewis revealed that once, while she was examining Franklin, he "sniffed her, in a grotesque, sexual way."[32]

Franklin continued writing to Judge Powers. She said that in the interest of justice, if he had new information to offer, she might visit him again and listen to his secrets. However, of all the people she has prosecuted, Franklin remains the one individual who would give her pause. "This guy scares me," she said.[33]

Franklin's crimes cast a long shadow over the families of his victims. Nearly twenty years later, LaVon Evans, Dante's brother, recalled the Bond Hill murders and how the memories never went away. "He took something special from us," LaVon said. "He said they [African Americans] were the ugliest people in the world. It was hard to hear him say the things he said [at the trial]. I mean, I just hold Franklin responsible . . . if he wants to believe in the Ku Klux Klan, he let them get in his head, that's on him, but he pulled that trigger. The Ku Klux Klan, that ain't never stopped . . . I can't hate all the white people just because one white person did this. I mean, I'm not, my momma didn't teach me that. You know, I just get on with my life."[34] Joe Deters, Hamilton County prosecutor, said, "After the confessions, it was a very satisfying meeting with the families of the two boys to let them know for sure we knew who had done this."[35]

Many years after his trial, Franklin still insisted he had no idea he had been shooting children but that it "didn't really matter" to him. In an interview with NBC, he said, "When you're a member of the Klan and you spend years around white supremacists you begin to think of blacks as nonhuman. Connie Lynch, who was a well-known Klan leader, said 'When I go out to kill rattlesnakes I don't make any difference between little rattlesnakes and big rattlesnakes because I know the little ones will grow up and bite me when they get big'—so I looked at blacks the same way."[36]

In May 1998 a neighborhood ballpark, formerly known as the Reading Road Ball Field, was dedicated to the memory of Evans Brown and Lane. The ballpark was renamed "The Dante Evans Brown and Darrell Lane Play Field." In addition to the victims' families, among those invited to the ceremony were the police and prosecutors who worked on the case. Mike O'Brien told reporters at the ceremony, "Anything we can do in these young kids' memories is great."[37]

Kathleen Mikula's father, Emil, declined to speak on the telephone with reporters in 1998 after the Johnstown murders had been solved. By that time Arthur Smothers's parents were dead. A brother, Rod Smothers of Johnstown, told the media he still felt the pain of his older brother's death, especially during holidays and on birthdays.[38]

On October 8, 2008, thirty-one years after Gerald Gordon's murder, a memorial garden at the Brith Shalom synagogue was dedicated to him. At the memorial service, the rabbi said that on the day Gerald was murdered, "the sanctity of the synagogue was violated." Gerald's friends spoke of their love for him. One of his friends described Gerald as a "gentle man, a sweet man, a family man," and told the congregants that he was "happy we finally realized that the world did not forget this tragic event."[39]

Franklin was never tried for the attempted assassination of Larry Flynt or the shooting of Gene Reeves. According to Joseph Rehyansky, who prosecuted Franklin for the Gerald Gordon murder, the confessed assassin was never tried because prosecutors feared that a jury in rural Lawrenceville, Georgia, would acquit him as a folk hero.[40]

Following the attempted assassination, Larry Flynt and his wife, Althea, re-treated to Bel Air, California, and hid in their bedroom behind a steel door. Flynt was diagnosed with manic depression and tried to take his life a number of times. He lived in excruciating pain and took large doses of painkillers to get through each day. He often overdosed. He underwent several operations over the years, but only the drugs seemed to help. Althea also began taking the medication—first rec-reationally, later habitually—and eventually developed an addiction to heroin. She contracted the AIDS virus, and on June 27, 1987, she drowned in her bathtub.

Following the release of the movie *The People vs. Larry Flynt* in 1996, many of the events in Flynt's past were reexamined by the media, and he appeared on many television shows. His oldest daughter, Tonya Flynt-Vega, also received attention when she publicly accused him of sexually abusing her as a child. Flynt, who fer-vently denied the allegation, stated that his daughter, whom he hardly knew, had a host of mental problems and was trying to "seize her fifteen minutes of fame." Flynt took a lie detector test concerning the allegations and passed.[41]

As the years passed Flynt ceased blaming faceless government agents for the shooting. He never had any proof to begin with. However, the irresponsible way he leveled charges against the FBI and the CIA provided succor to the American conspiracy industry, an amorphous group of individuals who use speculation, in-nuendo, and outright fakery to promote their lunatic theories that the United States government was behind the assassinations of President Kennedy, Robert Kennedy, and Martin Luther King Jr.

In the end Flynt came to accept that a lone individual misfit was responsible for the shooting, but he developed little interest in his would-be assassin. In 1997 Franklin told reporters, "I have nothing in my heart but love for Larry now. I really regret what happened. Larry has some faults but I don't hate him anymore. It's the only shooting I've committed that I've ever cried about."[42] The same year, when Franklin was sentenced to death for the murder of Gerald Gordon, Flynt said he could not care less. "I don't give it much thought," he said. Flynt said he was op-posed to the death penalty, "but I'm pretty sure they'll accommodate him and give him what he wants." Asked if he was angry with Franklin for shooting him, Flynt said, "Angry is a waste of time. I'm not the type of person to spend time dwelling on things I can't change."[43]

In 2000 Flynt published an ad in the *Washington Post* offering $1 million to anyone with documentary evidence revealing an adulterous affair by any prominent government official. He claimed his purpose was to expose the hypocrisy of politicians who pry into people's lives.[44] Later that year, Flynt was married for the fifth time, to his nurse, Elizabeth Berrios. In 2001 Larry Flynt stated his net worth was $400 million. In 2003 a recall in California of governor Gray Davis allowed Flynt to campaign as a replacement. He placed seventh out of 135 candidates, losing to Arnold Schwarzenegger. Flynt remains paralyzed from the waist down.

———————

After the shooting in Lawrenceville, Larry Flynt's lawyer, Gene Reeves, spent twenty days in a coma. After he came to, he ripped a breathing tube out of his throat in a panic when he couldn't breathe. He underwent surgery to repair damage to his esophagus. But Reeves made a full recovery and resumed his practice—divorces, estate cases, and petty crimes. He considered writing a book but dropped the idea.[45]

Larry Flynt paid Reeves's $18,000 medical bill and called to check on him even though the two had only known each other for about a week before the shooting. As the years passed, Reeves said Flynt would sometimes call him and ramble on about conspiracy theories. At one point, Reeves said Flynt was convinced they had been victims of a government plot. However, Reeves agreed with investigators that the gunman was Joseph Paul Franklin, and he also agreed with investigators that it would be a waste of taxpayers' money to prosecute Franklin for the shooting. Reeves, now in his late seventies and a senior magistrate in Gwinnett County, has put the shooting behind him. However, his friends said it had profoundly changed him. Before the shooting he gave only lip service to religion. Afterward he developed a deepened faith and became more involved in his community.

There was one negative consequence of Reeves's association with Flynt. He said that when he has run for public office, his opponents mentioned his representation of Flynt. Reeves said voters didn't seem to know or care that simply because he defended the publisher that did not mean he agreed with Flynt's views about pornography. Before he agreed to defend Flynt, he told the publisher he thought *Hustler* was "filth," but he agreed Flynt had a constitutional right to publish it. "I was forever tied to him," Reeves said. "Every time someone thought of something sleazy, they thought of me and Larry Flynt." However, Reeves said that, despite everything, he would still represent Flynt if he had to do it again.[46]

———————

Following Jacob Beard's second trial in May 2000, in which he was found not guilty, the West Virginia Board of Risk and Insurance awarded him nearly $2 million in installments.[47] He had served nearly six years in prison after being convicted of the murders of Nancy Santomero and Vickie Durian. After Beard was cleared of the slayings, he told reporters he was "glad it's over" then filed a lawsuit against prosecutors and police, alleging that police coerced witnesses and ignored physical evidence that did not support their case against him. "It was an investigation that was purposefully designed to accuse and convict Mr. Beard," said Beard's attorney, Charleston lawyer Stephen Farmer. "In order to do that, they had to create evidence that wasn't true and didn't exist . . . there are a whole lot of really good state police officers and prosecutors, but there are some bad ones who do bad things," Farmer said.[48]

Beard said he was pleased with the settlement. "I'll never forget the days in prison and the things I witnessed and experienced. There's no amount of money that could make up for it," he told reporters. Following his second trial, Beard moved to Lewisburg with his wife, Linda, to continue farming. He also said he would start working for Charlie Long and Bill Irons. Long and Irons posted Beard's $100,000 bond in 1992. "I'm not going to quit working and go out and buy new Corvettes. This money is for my family so we can get a new start," he said. Beard also said he and his wife were considering moving to Florida, where his two daughters resided.[49] In 2006 he was arrested on charges of driving under the influence of alcohol or drugs after he allegedly ran five vehicles off the road.[50]

Pocahontas County prosecutor Walter Weiford was never convinced of Franklin's guilt and opposed Beard's lawsuit. "If I wasn't convinced of his guilt, then I wouldn't have taken him to trial," Weiford said. Police Sgt. Steve Dawson, who testified at Beard's second trial, said Franklin's 1984 map was wrong. "I don't think it's an accurate depiction myself," he said. "It all took place on the other side of the road."[51] David Sterling—a former inmate of the federal penitentiary in Florence, Colorado—said he contacted the FBI after he saw Franklin on CBS's *60 Minutes II*. He told agents that Franklin's confession on the program was different than what Franklin told him. Sterling said Franklin began to talk about the Rainbow murders and said he got the information from newspapers. He said Franklin was busy talking about saving his own soul when he blurted out that he had nothing to do with the murders of Santomero and Durian. Franklin allegedly told Sterling, "I swear to God I didn't do that. I wasn't anywhere near there when that happened."[52]

For Beard the trial's end was a long-awaited relief. However, it did not end the grief that the two families, who still had questions about Nancy and Vickie's murders, had suffered. After the trial ended Kathy Santomero-Meehan was still confused about the jury's decision. "I wish the evidence was strong enough the jury didn't have any doubt," she said. "I hope the future brings us more enlightenment. Somebody killed her and it seemed like Beard was the one." She hoped that someone would come forward to shed more light on the circumstances of her sister's murder. She also said her father was disappointed with the jury's verdict.[53]

Mary Kauffman, Vickie's sister, said the jury's verdict left her in shock. Kauffman believed the evidence she had seen left her in no doubt as to Beard's guilt. She said she had faith that God knew "exactly who was involved in this crime and the part they played. . . . God's judgment and punishment for this act will be more severe than any punishment the courts could have."[54]

One of Franklin's heroes, J. B. Stoner founder and leader of the National States Rights Party—was a suspect in the June 29, 1958, bombing of the Bethel Baptist Church in Birmingham, Alabama, but was not indicted until 1977. He was not charged with planting the bomb but with conspiring to have the act committed. Prosecutors said he bragged to Alabama undercover officers that he masterminded the bombing. At his May 1980 trial, he was convicted in part on the venomous statements he made at the time of the bombing. When asked if he made a hateful quotation found in an old newspaper clipping, Stoner replied, "I don't think I said that, but I wish I had." A mostly white jury found him guilty in ninety minutes and sentenced him to ten years in prison, the minimum it could impose under Alabama law.[55]

Stoner appealed the verdict and vanished for several months in 1983 when his appeals ran out. Stoner ultimately turned himself in and served three-and-a-half years in prison before he was paroled in 1986. During the time he spent in prison, the NSRP imploded. On his release from prison, Stoner continued with his racist activities but was largely ignored by the media.[56] He died in 2005 at the age eighty-one. Until his death Stoner lived in northwest Georgia at a nursing home. His left side was partially paralyzed from a stroke. "History is written by the victors; you win it, you write it," he said in an interview with the *Atlanta Journal-Constitution* in

2004. "Society has changed. It was changed by defeat—defeat of the white people against race-mixing."[57] Stoner is buried at Forrest Hills Cemetery at the foot of Lookout Mountain in Chattanooga.

For years, black community leaders across the South and relatives of victims complained about the lack of action in both the more prominent and lesser-known unsolved civil rights murders of the 1960s and '70s. In the 1990s their urgings were taken more seriously because the political, social, and legal climate in the South had changed so significantly since the era of the killings. Their voices were heard in part because of the steadily growing political power of African Americans in the South and the fact that they pushed hard.

At the same time, more witnesses, perhaps with less fear of retaliation and hoping to unburden heavy consciences, were coming forward. And a new breed of prosecutors and investigators, feeling a sense of urgency as many witnesses and defendants in the cases grew old, were realizing the important role that resolving these cases could play in the South's efforts to move beyond its past of racial hate and terrorism.

As a result, law enforcement agencies during the 1990s made determined efforts to bring old civil rights violators to justice. Across the South, unresolved racially motivated killings of blacks, many of which were ignored by the authorities for years, were scrutinized and the perpetrators charged. The investigations into the long-ago killings were partly inspired by the well-publicized conviction in 1994 of Byron De La Beckwith in the 1963 assassination of the Mississippi civil rights leader Medgar Evers.

In 2005 Edgar Ray "The Preacher" Killen was sentenced to sixty years in prison for his part in the 1964 conspiracy to murder three civil rights workers (James Chaney, Andrew Goodman, and Mickey Schwerner) in Nashoba County, Mississippi. Killen was the local Kleagle, or organizer, of the Nashoba County, Mississippi Ku Klux Klan. In Alabama a former Ku Klux Klansman, Robert Chambliss, was found guilty of the 1963 racist bombing that killed four black girls in a downtown Birmingham church. In Louisiana the wife of one of the first black deputy sheriffs in a small parish met with a prosecutor who began reexamining the 1965 killing of her husband, Oneal Moore, in an ambush. And in the summer of 1999 in Mississippi, a white man pleaded guilty and three others went on trial for the 1970 killing of a black sharecropper who was beaten and found dead in a rural river.[58]

Following Franklin's arrest in 1980, America witnessed an unprecedented level of racial hatred by white supremacists. In the 1980s the Posse Comitatus, National Alliance, Christian Identity, and World Church of the Creator organizations became successful in promoting their white supremacist cause and recruited thousands of members to their ranks. However, courageous individuals and watchdog organizations in the United States matched their efforts by warning American citizens of the dangers of hate groups whose politicized hatreds, racial utopias, conspiracy theories, megalomaniacal misreading of historical reality, systematized religious delusion, and millenarian fantasies became deeply embedded within the social fabric of American democracy. At the forefront stood Morris Dees, the director of the Southern Poverty Law Center (SPLC) and Klanwatch. One of Dees's targets for exposure over the years has been William Pierce, founder of the National Alliance, who in 1978 wrote (under the pseudonym of Andrew MacDonald) *The Turner Diaries*. Dees describes *The Turner Diaries* as the *Mein Kampf* of white supremacists.

In 1989 Pierce published *Hunter*. The book opens with a description of the murder of an African American and his white girlfriend by Oscar Yeager, a white supremacist. The killer has already committed five similar murders because they had "therapeutic value" and could be "imitated by others." Pierce dedicated the book to Franklin and described him as "a lonely hunter who saw his duty as a white man and did what a responsible man of his race must do, to the best of his ability and without regard of the personal consequences."[59]

Pierce held a doctorate in physics and was a former college professor, but he left the world of academics to pursue a full-time career promoting white supremacy and anti-Semitism. In the 1960s he teamed up with George Lincoln Rockwell to try to attract more academics to the white supremacist movement. After Rockwell's assassination in 1967, Pierce became an executive leader of the American Nazi Party.

In *The Turner Diaries*, Pierce describes racist revolutionaries fighting, and eventually winning, a race war. One scene depicts the racists using a fertilizer-based truck bomb to blow up a federal building. Timothy McVeigh, the Oklahoma City bomber, used *The Turner Diaries* as a guide. The Order, a splinter group led by Robert Mathews and composed of National Alliance and Aryan Nations activists, also used the novel as a blueprint for a crime spree in the 1980s that included armored car robberies and the assassination of a Jewish radio host, Alan Berg, in

Colorado. Before his death in 2002, Pierce expanded his racist holdings to include a racist book publishing company (National Vanguard Books) and a white power music label (Resistance Records). He also hosted a radio program called *American Dissident Voices*, which combined current events with his racist and anti-Semitic commentary.

In April 2009 the Department of Homeland Security issued a new alert warning of the dangers posed by approximately 926 hate groups documented by the SPLC. The alert stated that "white supremacist lone wolves" and "small terrorist cells embracing violent rightwing extremist ideology" are currently the most significant domestic terrorism threat. A plot to kill Dees was thwarted in 2008 by an FBI informant. But according to the same informant, there are many other white supremacists bent on seeing Dees dead because of his courtroom victories against violent hate groups.[60]

The report "Rightwing Extremism: Current Economic and Political Climate Fuelling Resurgence in Radicalization and Recruitment" also warned of the recruitment of military veterans to extremist groups and said they were joining the armed forces to acquire combat training and access to weapons and explosives. The department's report was distributed to law enforcement agencies across the country to aid them in combating potential rightwing terrorism. The government report also noted that in the past five years, "various rightwing extremists, including militias and white supremacists, have adopted the immigration issue as a call to action, rallying point, and recruiting tool." The report said that veterans returning to the United States "possess combat skills and experience that are attractive to rightwing extremists." The department noted that it is "concerned that rightwing extremists will attempt to recruit and radicalize returning veterans in order to boost their violent capabilities."

In early 2009 the SPLC reported that white supremacist groups claimed a surge of new members and heavy traffic to their websites following the election of Barack Obama in November 2008. This surge came after scores of racially charged incidents—beatings, effigy burnings, racist graffiti, threats, and intimidation—were reported across the country following the presidential election.[61]

The link between the Internet and violent crimes is a concern for Dees now more than ever as websites proliferate and introduce new generations of youth to hate organizations.

The South has seen a resurgence of the Jewish faith in areas long thought inhospitable at the time Franklin embarked on his bombing campaign. Vibrant Jewish communities can be found in a number of large Southern cities. The situation looks even brighter if one goes by the Census Bureau's definition of the South. The South's Jewish population has tripled in size since 1970 from 382,000 to an estimated 1,200,000 in 2004. Atlanta is now one of the fastest growing Jewish communities in America, growing from 16,000 and three congregations in 1969 to well over 100,000 and thirty-seven congregations today. Austin, Texas, has grown from 500 Jews to nearly 18,000 today. However, there are still sporadic outbreaks of anti-Semitism in the South and other parts of the United States, sometimes resulting in bloodshed.

It would appear that the story of Franklin's stalking of President Carter, which gained currency through the retelling in various media accounts of his crimes, is a myth. There is no credible evidence on record that indicates he was bent on killing the thirty-ninth president, even though Kris Hollington, in his poorly sourced book *How to Kill,* asserts that Franklin laid in wait for the president in April 1980 at a fishing lake near Plains, Georgia. Hollington alleges that Franklin changed his mind about shooting Carter at the last minute.

For what it is worth, Franklin has denied stalking President Carter. In a letter Franklin wrote to me, he said, "I thought the story that Kris Hollington came up with was *hilarious!* I wish you would Xerox that and mail it to me. Stuff like that . . . is basically harmless, so I really don't trip on it, you know?"[62]

In an e-mail to the author, the Secret Service stated, "The United States Secret Service does not discuss protective intelligence cases. Do not make any inference that that means Franklin is/is not of record with us."[63] The Jimmy Carter Library has no information about Franklin's alleged stalking.

In one sense it was better that Franklin rejected the opportunity I gave him to give his own account of his crimes. All that he could possibly add to what has already been said would simply be additional, and probably uncorroborated, information about others he may have killed. However, as he has not revealed anything in over ten years, it appears unlikely he ever will. He is fond of prison furloughs, initiated through his numerous confessions, and he would most certainly avail himself of the opportunity again if he had any credible information law enforcement authorities could use. Furthermore, Franklin would have to supply corroboration for any further confessions he wishes to make, and that seems unlikely. As we have seen, Franklin's previous unsupported confessions of the murders he allegedly committed on Ponce De Leon Street in Atlanta lack credence.

It is also unlikely Franklin would have been able to provide any insight into his crimes that he has not provided already. In his previous interviews there was always something missing—his readiness to comment on himself was not there. His accounts of his murders fell into the same narrative style adopted by every psychopath—bland, matter-of-fact, episodic, and unstressed—with a refusal to attach value to any detail. When I was researching Franklin's life, I was reminded of comments made by a former Nuremberg prosecutor, Whitney Harris, who described the commandant of Auschwitz as "a normal person. That's the horrible thing about it. . . . He was cool, objective, and matter-of-fact. It was like, 'I had to go out and cut down so many trees.' He told what happened without emotion . . . and without sense of guilt."[64]

Joseph Paul Franklin was a man who really didn't think or feel the same way as normal people. Emotionless and not restrained by remorse, he cataloged and took stock of his crimes as if he were evaluating merchandise. "I have only confessed to, let's see . . . eleven . . . twelve . . . thirteen murders," he calmly told one reporter some years before the full extent of his crimes was known. As one might recount a favorite vacation trip, he added, "Put down eleven. That's how many I've been indicted or convicted of. And it happens to be a lucky number for me right now."[65]

JOSEPH PAUL FRANKLIN

Timeline

April 13, 1950: Franklin is born James Clayton Vaughn Jr. in Mobile, Alabama, to James Clayton Vaughn Sr. and Helen Rau.

1950s: James Clayton Vaughn Sr. and Helen Rau are divorced.

1955: James Jr. is enrolled in Arlington Elementary School in Mobile.

Late 1950s: An accident on his bicycle leaves James Jr. with severely impaired eyesight. He becomes blind in his right eye and partially blind in his left.

1965: James Jr. is appalled to see African American students join the student body of Murphy High School.

1966: James Jr. is given his first shotgun. He is attracted to fringe religions and joins the Sun Myung Moon church. Unimpressed with the church's teachings, he begins to attend other Christian churches in the Mobile area. He becomes obsessed with the Bible's purported messages about racial integrity. He is fanatical about the Bible because he uses it to prove his points about race. He quotes scripture word for word, but the bottom line is "whites are the master race."

1965–66: James Jr. steals a copy of Hitler's *Mein Kampf* from the Mobile Public Library and is in awe of Hitler's intelligence.

1967: James Jr. drops out of the eleventh grade despite having average to above-average intelligence. Due to the lack of vision in his right eye, Franklin is ineligible for the draft. He begins having brushes with the law, and his violent tendencies become worse. He is abusive toward his mother and is questioned by Mobile police officers.

1968: James Jr. meets sixteen-year-old Bobbie Louise Dorman. Two weeks later they are married. The couple divorces after four months. James moves to Arlington, Virginia, where he joins the American Nazi Party.

1969: James Jr. and his fellow Nazis travel to Washington, D.C., with the purpose of disrupting the New Mobilization Committee to End the War in Vietnam demonstration. The Nazis decide to attack the Mobe's headquarters. Alone, James storms the headquarters, setting off tear gas grenades that force an evacuation. He becomes a hero to Nazi supporters.

1969: James Jr. becomes enamored with Charles Manson and his plans to start a race war.

1970: James Jr. begins insulting mixed-race couples he sees on the streets of Washington, D.C., and neighboring towns.

1970: James Jr., protesting Israeli prime minister Golda Meir's visit, is photographed in a Nazi uniform.

1972: James Jr. is convicted of carrying a concealed weapon in Fairfax, Virginia.

1973: James Jr. moves to Atlanta and, at the age of twenty-three, joins the National States Rights Party, a racist organization led by J. B. Stoner. He sells the NSRP's racist newspaper *The Thunderbolt*.

1973: James Jr., now in his early twenties, moves from Atlanta to College Park, Maryland, just outside Washington, D.C. He earns a blue belt in karate and lives alone in an abandoned office building that he is hired to maintain.

1976: James Jr. joins the Ku Klux Klan in Atlanta. After a few months he leaves, claiming the racial organization is a joke and that his fellow Klan members are not violent enough.

Labor Day, 1976: James Jr. returns to the Washington, D.C., area. In Montgomery County, Maryland, he tails a black man and his white date for ten miles by car to a dead end and then sprays them with Mace. He is also angry that year after Jimmy Carter beats President Ford in the November election. James sends Carter a letter threatening his life.

1976: James Jr., now twenty-six years old, petitions to change his name from "James Clayton Vaughn Jr." to "Joseph Paul Franklin" in Prince George, Maryland. He develops plans to go to Rhodesia to fight for Ian Smith's racist government.

1977: Franklin joins the Alabama National Guard's 161st Medical Battalion. He attends regular meetings and is given training in weapons and armaments.

1977: Franklin commits his first major bank robbery in an Atlanta suburb.

1977: Franklin bombs the home of Morris Amitay, a Washington, D.C.-based American-Israel lobbyist.

1977: Franklin constructs a dynamite bomb, later characterized by ATF agents as "high grade and highly sophisticated," and plants it in a Jewish synagogue in Chattanooga, Tennessee. The bomb explodes shortly after services end.

1977: Franklin drives to Madison, Wisconsin, in hopes of killing Archie Simonson, a Jewish judge whom Franklin believed had been lenient towards black defendants in a juvenile rape case. He registers at a Madison motel and plans to kill Simonson the next day. On August 7, on the way to the judge's home, he sees an interracial couple and shoots them instead. Both victims die.

1977: Franklin robs a bank in Little Rock, Arkansas. He drives to Dallas looking for weapons. He purchases a Remington 30.06 for $200. He takes it to a rifle range to practice his skills and adjust the telescopic site.

1977: In a sniper shooting Franklin kills forty-two-year-old Gerald Gordon, and wounds thirty-year-old William Ash outside a synagogue in Richmond Heights, St. Louis.

1978: In a sniper attack, Franklin shoots twenty-two-year-old African American Johnny Brookshire, who is walking down an Atlanta street with his twenty-three-year-old white girlfriend, Joy Williams. Brookshire dies instantly from his wounds. Joy, who had been shot in the stomach, survives but is paralyzed from the waist down.

1978: Franklin paralyzes *Hustler* magazine publisher Larry Flynt by shooting him in Lawrenceville, Georgia. His attorney, Gene Reeves, is also shot but recovers from his wounds.

1978: Franklin robs a bank in Louisville, Kentucky.

1978: Franklin robs a bank Atlanta, Georgia.

1978: Franklin shoots an interracial couple—African American Bryant Tatum and his wife, Nancy—with a 12-gauge shotgun. Bryant Tatum is killed, but his wife survives.

1978: Franklin robs a bank in Montgomery, Alabama.

1978: Franklin returns to his home state of Alabama. He meets sixteen-year-old Anita Carden in an ice cream parlor in Montgomery. They begin dating.

1979: Franklin and Anita drive to Atlanta and are married in the DeKalb County Courthouse. The couple rent a duplex in Montgomery.

1979: Franklin drives to Doraville, Georgia, and shoots and kills twenty-nine-year-old African American Harold McIver with a high velocity 30.30 rifle.

1979: In Falls Church, Virginia, Franklin shoots and kills African American Raymond Taylor with his 30.30 rifle.

1979: Franklin telephones his wife and learns he has become a father. He visits Anita and their newborn baby in a Montgomery hospital.

1979: Franklin drives to Oklahoma City and shoots a mixed-race couple, forty-two-year-old African American Jesse Taylor and his thirty-one-year-old wife, Marian Vera Bressette. Both die.

1979: Franklin murders a girlfriend, Mercedes Masters, after she confesses she has dated African American men.

1980: Franklin shoots twenty-two-year-old Lawrence Reese with his 30.30 rifle as his victim stands inside an Indianapolis fast food restaurant. Reese dies at the scene.

1980: Franklin shoots nineteen-year-old African American Leo Thomas Watkins with his 30.30 rifle. He shoots through the plate-glass window of a convenience store situated in a small Indianapolis shopping mall. Watkins dies.

1980: Franklin murders student Rebecca Bergstrom in Mill Bluff State Park, Wisconsin. Bergstrom had been hitchhiking.

1980: Franklin seeks a new target when he fails to track Jesse Jackson's movements in Chicago.

1980: Franklin shoots Urban League president Vernon Jordan in the back as he gets out of a car in Fort Wayne, Indiana.

1980: Franklin shoots two young African American boys, fourteen-year-old Darrell Layne and thirteen-year-old Dante Evans Brown, as they walk to a convenience store in a Cincinnati suburb.

1980: Franklin shoots twenty-two-year-old African American Arthur Smothers and his sixteen-year-old white girlfriend, Kathleen Mikula, as they walk across a Johnstown, Pennsylvania, bridge. Smothers and Mikula both die at the scene.

1980: Franklin picks up ninteeen-year-old Nancy Santomero and twenty-six-year-old Vickie Durian, who are hitchhiking to the Rainbow Festival in Pocahontas County, West Virginia. He murders both girls after they confess to dating African American men.

1980: Franklin shoots and kills twenty-year-old Ted Fields and eighteen-year-old David Martin, both African American in a Salt Lake City park while they jog with two white women.

October 1980: Franklin is captured in Lakeland, Florida, after a nationwide search for the "Salt Lake City Sniper."

November 1980: Franklin is extradited to Salt Lake City and arraigned for the murders of Ted Fields and David Martin.

1981: In a federal trial, Franklin is convicted of violating the civil rights of Fields and Martin and sentenced to two consecutive life sentences.

1981: In a state trial, Franklin is convicted of killing Ted Fields and David Martin. During the sentencing phase of the Salt Lake City trial, Franklin tries to escape but is captured by guards. The jury can't produce a unanimous decision to send Franklin to a firing squad, so it recommends two more life sentences. He is sent to the Medical Center for Federal Prisoners in Springfield, Missouri.

1982: Franklin is transferred to the United States Penitentiary in Marion, Illinois, to begin serving his life sentences.

1982: Franklin is stabbed fifteen times in the neck and abdomen by a group of African American prisoners.

1982: Following a federal trial held in South Bend, Indiana, Franklin is found not guilty of violating the civil rights of Vernon Jordan.

1983: Franklin writes to Gwinnett police, saying he wants to talk to them. Lawrenceville police officers Capt. L. D. McKelvey and Sgt. Mike Cowart visit Franklin at Marion in September 1983. Franklin states he has a "good bit of knowledge about the [Larry Flynt] case."

1983: Franklin confesses to shooting Larry Flynt and bombing Morris Amitay's house in Washington, D.C.

1984: Franklin confesses to the murder of Rebecca Bergstrom.

1984: Franklin confesses to the Chattanooga synagogue bombing. He is tried in July 1984 and is sentenced to fifteen to twenty-one years for the bombing and six to ten years for possession of explosives.

1984: Franklin confesses to the Rainbow murders.

1984: Franklin confesses to shooting Alphonse Manning and Toni Schwenn.

1986: Franklin is convicted in Wisconsin of killing Manning and Schwenn and sentenced to two consecutive life terms.

1990: Franklin admits to killing Ted Fields and David Martin in Salt Lake City in 1980.

1993: Jacob Beard is found guilty of two counts of first-degree murder for the Rainbow murders of Nancy Santomero and Vickie Durian.

1994: Franklin confesses to killing Gerald Gordon.

1995: Franklin admits to shooting Vernon Jordan.

1996: Franklin tells Deborah Dixon, reporter for Cincinnati's WKRC that he killed Nancy Santomero and Vickie Durian because "they dated black people."

1997: Franklin is found guilty of Gerald Gordon's murder and in February 1997 is sentenced to death.

1997: Franklin admits to killing Raymond Taylor in Falls Church, Virginia, in 1979.

1997: Franklin confesses to the murders of Arthur Smothers and Kathleen Mikula in Johnstown, Pennsylvania, in 1980.

1997: Franklin confesses to the murders of Darrell Lane and Dante Evans Brown. He is tried in October 1997, found guilty, and sentenced to forty years to life in prison.

1998: Franklin admits to killing William Tatum in July 1978 outside a Chattanooga restaurant. Under a plea bargain, Franklin is sentenced to two concurrent life terms, one for the murder and another for an unrelated 1977 armed robbery.

1998: Franklin confesses to killing Mercedes Masters and Harold McIver in DeKalb County, Georgia.

2000: Jacob Beard is retried for the Rainbow murders and found not guilty.

2004: In a surprise move, a United States District Court requires Missouri to release or retry Franklin for the Gerald Gordon murder. However, in July 2007, a federal appellate court overturns the decision.

2006: A federal judge puts the death penalty in Missouri on hold over concerns involving lethal injection.

2008: The U.S. Supreme Court decides that the current method of execution by lethal injection is constitutionally permissible. As a result of the court's decision, some states that had instituted stays or moratoria announce a resumption of the practice.

2010: The U.S. Supreme Court refuses to hear the Missouri lethal injection case *Clemons v. Crawford.* Accordingly, lower court rulings stand. The Supreme Court rules that lethal injection is permissible, and Missouri's attorney general states executions will begin again. He also says he wants Franklin to be the first to die.

NOTES

INTRODUCTION

1. Wm. Bradford Reynolds, assistant attorney general, U.S. Department of Justice, Civil Rights Division, memorandum to William French Smith, attorney general, October 13, 1982.
2. Christopher Reed, "William Pierce," *Guardian* (Manchester), July 25, 2002, http://www.guardian.co.uk/news/2002/jul/25/guardianobituaries.booksobituaries1-.

CHAPTER 1. THE SHOOTING OF VERNON JORDAN

1. Kim Bell, "Convicted Killer, Avowed Racist Tells of a Life of Rage, Hatred," *St. Louis Post-Dispatch*, February 2, 1997, http://www.stltoday.com/stltoday/news/stories.nsf/stlouiscitycounty/story/F25292E229FE8D70862575D800420 228?OpenDocument.
2. "Economy Seen As Major Part Of Worry: Civil Rights Leaders Concerned About Summer," *Waterloo (IA) Courier*, June 1, 1980.
3. "Mugshots—The Story of Racist Serial Killer Joseph Paul Franklin," *Court TV*, http://www.trutv.com/library/crime/index.html. 2000.
4. "White Man Admits to 1980 Shooting of Vernon Jordan," *Jet*, April 22, 1996, 4.
5. Dan Horn, "Killer: It Was What God Wanted," *Cincinnati Post*, April 17, 1997.
6. "Denies Guilt In Slaying Blacks," *Syracuse Post-Standard*, October 30, 1980.
7. Joe Eszterhas, *American Rhapsody* (New York: Knopf, 2000), 243.
8. *Criminal Confessions* (1999; Santa Monica, CA: Live/Artisan, 2003), DVD.
9. "I Wasn't in Fort Wayne," *Syracuse Herald-Journal*, August 17, 1982.
10. Vernon Jordan with Annette Gordon-Reed, *Vernon Can Read!: A Memoir* (New York: Public Affairs, 2001), 237.

11. Malcolm Gladwell, "The Criminal Brain," *Independent* (London), May 3, 1997, http://www.independent.co.uk/life-style/the-criminal-brain-1259436.html.
12. Bill McClellan, "Death Means Life: Strange Truths of the Paranormal," *St. Louis Post-Dispatch*, November 20, 1996.
13. Bell, "Convicted Killer, Avowed Racist Tells of a Life of Rage, Hatred."
14. Joseph Paul Franklin, interview by Det. Michael O'Brien, transcript by Nancy Mynheir, June 17, 1998.
15. Joe Holleman and William C. Lhotka, "I Wanted to Kill at Least Two Jews Says Racist," *St. Louis Post-Dispatch*, June 19, 1995.
16. *Criminal Confessions.*
17. "Jordan, Assailant Goes On Trial," *Stars and Stripes*, August 11, 1982.
18. "I Wasn't in Fort Wayne," *Syracuse Herald-Journal.*
19. Joseph Paul Frank, interview by Melissa Powers, April 13, 1997, http://www.cincinnati-oh.gov/cpd/.
20. Ibid.
21. *Criminal Confessions.*
22. Melissa Powers interview.
23. Michael O'Brien, summary report, Cincinnati Police Department, June 8, 1980, 2.
24. "Conviction Motions After First Degree Murder/Death Penalty," Gordon Trial Appeal Records, *Missourinet*, www.missourinet.com/asp/asx.asp?listen=845.
25. Horn, "Killer: It Was What God Wanted."
26. Ibid.
27. "Ambush In The Night," *Time*, June 9, 1980, http://www.time.com/time/magazine/article/0,9171,952643,00.html.
28. "Urban League Head Shot in Fort Wayne," *Gettysburg Times*, May 29, 1980.
29. Jordan and Gordon-Reed, 280.
30. "Coleman Comes Out Of Hiding," *Chicago Daily Herald*, June 10, 1980.
31. *Chicago Daily Herald*, May 31, 1980.
32. "Coleman Comes Out Of Hiding," *Chicago Daily Herald.*
33. UPI, "Mrs Coleman Says Jordan Got Strange Calls Before He Was Shot," *Elyria (OH) Chronicle-Telegram*, June 10, 1980.
34. Jordan and Gordon-Reed, 281.
35. "Jordan Sniper Views Clash," *Syracuse Post-Standard*, May 31, 1980.
36. "Ambush In The Night," *Time.*
37. UPI, "Mrs Coleman Says Jordan Got Strange Calls Before He Was Shot."
38. "Vernon Jordan Shot, Not Racially Motivated, Official Says," *Syracuse Herald-Journal*, May 29, 1980.
39. Jordan and Gordon-Reed, 281.
40. Ibid.
41. Ibid.
42. Vernon E. Jordan Jr., "American Odyssey," *Newsweek*, October 29, 2001, http://www.newsweek.com/id/75713/page/12.

43. Jordan and Gordon-Reed, 281.
44. UPI, "FBI: Shooting a Part of Plot," *Chicago Daily Herald*, , May 30, 1980.
45. "Civil Rights Leader Testifies—He Didn't See Who Shot Him," *Chicago Daily Herald,* August 11, 1982.
46. "Ambush In The Night," *Time*.
47. "Vernon Can Read—A Memoir," Vernon Jordan, interview with 's *Booknotes*, C-SPAN, December 23, 2001.
48. Paul Delaney, "Civil Rights Committee to Feel Absence of Jordan," *Syracuse Herald-American*, June 8, 1980.
49. "Civil Rights Leader Testifies—He Didn't See who Shot Him," *Chicago Daily Herald.*
50. "Shooting Probe Continues," *Newport News (VA) Daily Press*, May 30, 1980.
51. UPI, "FBI: Shooting a Part of Plot."
52. *Marysville (OH) Journal-Tribune*, May 30, 1980.
53. *Waterloo Courier*, June 5, 1980.
54. "Police and FBI Look for another Shooter—Or Conspirators," *Chicago Daily Herald*, May 31, 1980.
55. "FBI Believes Metal Fence Helped Save Jordan's Life," *Philadelphia Sunday Intelligencer*, June 1, 1980.
56. UPI, "Mrs Coleman Says Jordan Got Strange Calls Before He Was Shot."
57. Mel Ayton, *A Racial Crime: James Earl Ray and the Assassination of Martin Luther King Jr.* (Las Vegas: Archebooks, 2005), 346.
58. "FBI To Question Ray Over Jordan Shooting," *Daily Sitka Sentinel*, June 25, 1980.
59. "Jordan Ambush Debated," *Post Standard*, May 31, 1980.
60. "Vernon Jordan is a Much-Needed Peacemaker," *Philadelphia Daily Intelligencer*, June 12, 1980.
61. "Police and FBI Look for another Shooter—Or Conspirators," *Chicago Daily Herald.*
62. UPI, "Mrs Coleman Says Jordan Got Strange Calls Before He Was Shot."
63. "Coleman Comes Out of Hiding," *Chicago Daily Herald.*
64. "Police and FBI Look for another Shooter—Or Conspirators," *Chicago Daily Herald.*
65. "Key Witness in Shooting of Jordan Now in Hiding," *Stars and Stripes*, June 1, 1980.
66. Ibid.
67. "Lawyer: Test Clears Coleman In Shooting," *Stars and Stripes*, June 9, 1980.
68. "Doctors Have Operated Again on Civil Rights Activist," *Syracuse Herald-Journal*, June 9, 1980.
69. UPI, "Mrs Coleman Says Jordan Got Strange Calls Before He Was Shot."
70. Melissa Powers interview.
71. Ibid.

CHAPTER 2. THE EARLY YEARS

1. James R. Gaines, "On the Trail of a Murderous Sniper Suspect: The Tangled Life of Joseph Paul Franklin," *People*, November 24, 1980, http://www.people.com/people/archive/article/0,,20077938,00.html.
2. "Serial Killer," *Weekend Edition*, NPR, September 20, 1998, http://www.npr.org/templates/story/story.php?storyId=1000716.
3. "Mugshots—The Story of Racist Serial Killer Joseph Paul Franklin," *Court TV*.
4. "Moving Target," *The FBI Files*, season 2, episode 15, aired April 9, 2000.
5. "Mugshots—The Story of Racist Serial Killer Joseph Paul Franklin," *Court TV*.
6. "Serial Killer," NPR.
7. Ibid.
8. Ibid.
9. *Criminal Confessions*.
10. Michael O'Brien interview.
11. "Serial Killer," NPR.
12. Bell, "Convicted Killer, Avowed Racist Tells of a Life of Rage, Hatred.
13. Holleman and Lhotka, "I Wanted To Kill At Least Two Jews, Racist Says."
14. "Serial Killer," NPR.
15. "Mugshots—The Story of Racist Serial Killer Joseph Paul Franklin," *Court TV*.
16. "Serial Killer," NPR.
17. Holleman and Lhotka, "I Wanted To Kill At Least Two Jews, Racist Says."
18. Joe Holleman and William C. Lhotka, "Inmate Recounts Twenty Murderous Years, Man Says Hatred and Anger Drove Him To Plot, Kill," *St. Louis Post-Dispatch*, June 5, 1995.
19. Kristen Delguzzi, "Sniper Feared The Chair," *Cincinnati Enquirer*, April 17, 1997. http://www.enquirer.com/editions/1997/04/17/loc_franklin.html
20. Ibid.
21. *Ultimate Crimes: Driven To Kill* (Leicestershire, UK: Odeon Entertainment, 2005), DVD.
22. Delguzzi, "Sniper Feared The Chair."
23. Terry D. Turchie and Kathleen M. Puckett, *Hunting the American Terrorist: The FBI's War On Homegrown Terror* (Palisades, NY: History Publishing Company, 2007), 253.
24. Reed Massengill, *Portrait of a Racist: The Man Who Killed Medgar Evers?* (New York: St Martin's Press, 1994), 276.
25. "Serial Killer," NPR.
26. "Mugshots—The Story of Racist Serial Killer Joseph Paul Franklin," *Court TV*.
27. "Warrant Out for Man in Sniper Attacks," *Deseret News*, October 6, 1980.
28. "Untitled," *Los Angeles Times*, October 7, 1980.
29. *"Serial Killer,"* NPR.

30. "Franklin: Dahmer, Bundy 'Not In My League,'" *Indiana (PA) Gazette*, February 13, 1998.
31. "Serial Killer," NPR.
32. "On the Trail of a Murderous Sniper Suspect," *People*.
33. "Untitled," *Los Angeles Times*.
34. "On the Trail of a Murderous Sniper Suspect," *People*.
35. "Racist Rifleman," *Time*, November 10, 1980, http://www.time.com/time/magazine/article/0,9171,949029,00.html.
36. Eszterhas, 324.
37. "On the Trail of a Murderous Sniper Suspect," *People*.

CHAPTER 3. LONGING TO BELONG
1. "Mugshots—The Story of Racist Serial Killer Joseph Paul Franklin," *Court TV*.
2. Martin Durham, *White Rage: The Extreme Right and American Politics* (New York: Routledge, 2007), 141.
3. "American Nazi Party Suffers From Deep Internal Division," *Fond Du Lac (WI) Commonwealth Reporter*, August 7, 1968.
4. "Mugshots—The Story of Racist Serial Killer Joseph Paul Franklin," *Court TV*.
5. "Serial Killer," NPR.
6. "Mugshots—The Story of Racist Serial Killer Joseph Paul Franklin," *Court TV*.
7. Jeffrey Kaplan, *Encyclopedia of White Power: A Sourcebook of the Radical Racist Right* (Lanham, MD: Alta Mira Press, 2000), 113.
8. Ibid., 112.
9. Rick Perlstein, *Nixonland: The Rise of a President and the Fracturing of America* (New York: Scribner, 2008), 440.
10. Kevin Lee, "Joseph Paul Franklin," 2006. http://www.lagniappemobile.com/articles/631-untitled.
11. Horn, "Killer: 'It Was What God Wanted.'"
12. "Serial Killer," NPR.
13. Horn, "Killer: 'It Was What God Wanted.'"
14. *Criminal Confessions*.
15. "Life Of Hate and Killing Began in '50," *Deseret News*, June 19, 1995.
16. Melissa Fay Greene, *The Temple Bombing* (New York: Ballantine, 1996), 415.
17. Joseph Paul Franklin, letter to author, August 31, 2009.
18. Durham, 132.
19. Greene, 408.
20. Fulton Lewis Jr., "The NSRP," *Traverse City (MI) Record Eagle*, January 25, 1965.
21. Ibid.
22. "On the Trail of a Murderous Sniper Suspect," *People*.
23. "Serial Killer," NPR.
24. Ibid.

25. Ibid.
26. Turchie and Puckett, 253.
27. "Accused Killer Tells Of Escape," *Marysville Journal-Tribune,* November 26, 1980.
28. Rhodri Jeffreys-Jones, *The FBI: A History* (New Haven, CT: Yale University Press, 2007), 172.
29. Massengill, 10.
30. Ibid., 219.
31. Letter from Joseph Paul Franklin to Potosi Prison Records Office, June 4, 2006.
32. Joseph Paul Franklin, letter to Potosi Correctional Center Records Office, June 4, 2006.
33. Raphael S. Ezekiel, *The Racist Mind* (New York: Penguin, 1996), xxx.
34. Turchie and Puckett, 252.
35. Salt Lake City Murders Appeal, U.S. Court of Appeals, Tenth Circuit, 704 F.2d 1183. April 12, 1983, http://cases.justia.com/us-court-of-appeals/F2/704/1183 /107287/.
36. Ibid.
37. Eszterhas, 324.
38. "On the Trail of a Murderous Sniper Suspect," *People.*
39. Cincinnati Police Department, summary report, 14.
40. Holleman and Lhotka, "I Wanted To Kill At Least Two Jews, Racist Says."
41. Turchie and Puckett, 252.
42. "Mugshots—The Story of Racist Serial Killer Joseph Paul Franklin," *Court TV.*
43. Eszterhas, 325.

CHAPTER 4. TARGETING JEWS

1. Greene, 60.
2. Durham, 68.
3. Ibid., 37.
4. Greene, 6.
5. Ibid., 153.
6. Melissa Powers interview.
7. *Criminal Confessions.*
8. Bryan Burrough, *Public Enemies: America's Greatest Crime Wave and the Birth of the FBI, 1933-34* (New York: Penguin, 2008), 18.
9. Eszterhas, 325.
10. Delguzzi, "Sniper Feared the Chair."
11. Bell, "Convicted Killer, Avowed Racist Tells of a Life of Rage, Hatred."
12. Roth W. Johnson, "Family of Five Escape Injury As Bomb Rips Lobbyist's Home," *The Post,* July 26, 1977.
13. Ibid.

14. "Police Continue Investigating Rockville Blast," *Post*, July 30, 1977.
15. Holleman and Lhotka, "I Wanted To Kill At Least Two Jews, Racist Says."
16. "Avowed Racist Convicted of Bombing Synagogue," *Post Standard*, July 13, 1984.
17. "Authorities Investigate Synagogue Explosion," *Gastonia (NC) Gaston Gazette*, July 17, 1977.
18. Hollemann and Lhotka, "I Wanted To Kill At Least Two Jews, Racist Says."
19. "Authorities Investigate Synagogue Explosion," *Gaston Gazette*.
20. "Dynamite Blast Hits Synagogue," *Corbin (KY) Times-Tribune*, August 4, 1977.
21. "Federal Officials Checking Blasts," *Lawton (OK) Constitution*, August 4, 1977.

CHAPTER 5. STALKING MRCS

1. Delguzzi, "Sniper Feared the Chair."
2. "Franklin: Dahmer, Bundy 'Not In My League,'" *Indiana Gazette*.
3. Lee, "Joseph Paul Franklin."
4. "Jury Hears Murderer Franklin's Taped Confession of Killings," *Tyrone (PA) Daily Herald*, February 14, 1986.
5. "Klansman Found Guilty of Murder," *Stars and Stripes*, February 16, 1986.
6. Delguzzi, "Sniper Feared the Chair."
7. "Mugshots—The Story of Racist Serial Killer Joseph Paul Franklin," *Court TV*.
8. David Rose, *Violation: Justice, Race and Serial Murder in the Deep South* (New York: Harper Perennial, 2008), 33.
9. Ibid., 63.
10. Greene, 149.
11. Gerard DeGroot, *The Sixties Unplugged: A Kaleidoscope History of a Disorderly Decade* (London: Pan Books, 2008), 24.
12. Rose, 142.
13. Greene, 150.
14. Ibid., 151.
15. Ibid., 149.
16. Massengill, 277.
17. Durham, 87.
18. George Lincoln Rockwell, *White Power* (Los Angeles: World Services, 1972), 444–48.
19. Durham, 84.
20. Lee, "Joseph Paul Franklin."
21. Ibid.
22. Ibid.
23. Holleman and Lhotka, "I Wanted To Kill At Least Two Jews, Racist Says."
24. "Police Say Synagogue Sniper Planned Attack," *Hagerstown (MD) Daily Mail*, October 10, 1977.

25. "Synagogue Sniper Kills One, Wounds One," *Gaston Gazette*, October 9, 1977.
26. Mike Sherwin, "Court Rejects Killer's Appeal," Brith Shalom Kneseth Israel, November 2006, http://www.e-bski.org/.
27. Joseph Paul Franklin v. Al Luebbers, U.S. Court of Appeals, no. 05-1043/1047, submitted November 13, 2006, filed July 24, 2007, www.Justia.com.
28. Gladwell, "The Criminal Brain."
29. "Sniper Kills One, Wounds One," *Big Spring (TX) Herald*, October 8, 1977.
30. "Synagogue Sniper's Work Premeditated," *Kittanning (PA) Leader Times*, October 10, 1977.
31. Ibid.
32. *Criminal Confessions*.
33. "Supremacist Admits To 1978 Murder," *Intelligencer Record*, November 2, 1999.
34. Melissa Powers interview.

CHAPTER 6. LAWRENCEVILLE, GEORGIA

1. Bell, "Convicted Killer, Avowed Racist Tells of a Life of Rage, Hatred."
2. *Criminal Confessions*.
3. *Larry Flynt: The Right To Be Left Alone*, directed by Joan Brooker-Marks (2007).
4. David Bowman, "Citizen Flynt," Salon.com, July 8, 2004, http://dir.salon.com /story/books/int/2004/07/08/flynt/index2.html.
5. Debbie Schlussel, "Larry Flynt's Former Lawyer Dismisses Hustler Chief's 'Conspiracy Theories,' Finds Faith," August 7, 2007, http://www.debbieschlussel .com.
6. Melissa Powers interview.
7. "Puzzling Aspects Mark Attempt on Flynt's Life," *Kingsport (TN) Times News*, March 12, 1978.
8. "Flynt On 50-50 Odds: 'I'm Going To Walk Again,'" *Chronicle-Telegram*, March 10, 1978.
9. "Flynt Shooting Suspect Faces Death Penalty for Killing," *Stars and Stripes*, February 18, 1997.
10. "Untitled," *Chicago Daily Herald*, March 8, 1978.
11. Melissa Powers interview.
12. *Larry Flynt: The Right to Be Left Alone*.
13. "Puzzling Aspects Mark Attempt On Flynt's Life," *Kingsport Times News*.
14. *Larry Flynt: The Right to Be Left Alone*.
15. "Flynt On 50-50 Odds: 'I'm Going To Walk Again,'" *Elyria Chronicle-Telegram*.
16. "Flynt Shooting Suspect Faces Death Penalty for Killing," *Stars and Stripes*.
17. Carl Williams, "Flynt Undergoes New Surgery, *Daily News*, March 9, 1978.
18. "Flynt On 50-50 Odds: 'I'm Going To Walk Again,'" *Elyria Chronicle-Telegram*.
19. "Flynt Shooting Suspect Faces Death Penalty For Killing," *Stars and Stripes*.

20. *Syracuse Post-Standard*, March 30, 1978.
21. "Flynt's Wife Won't Allow Police Questions," *Journal Tribune*, April 12, 1978.
22. "Puzzling Aspects Mark Attempt On Flynt's Life," *Kingsport Times News*.
23. *Larry Flynt: The Right To Be Left Alone.*
24. "Flynt's Spleen Taken out in Second Surgery," *Long Beach Independent-Press-Telegram*, March 7, 1978.
25. "Lack of Motive Stumps Cops in Flynt Shooting," *Chicago Daily Herald*, April 17, 1978.
26. Edward DiPierro, "Larry Flynt Says He Will Walk," *Moberly (MO) Monitor and Evening Democrat*, May 10, 1978.
27. "Flynt Says He'll Reveal JFK's Real Killer This Fall," *Chronicle-Telegram*, August 16, 1978.
28. "Flynt Physical and Emotional Wreck," *Chronicle-Telegram*, April 11, 1978.
29. "Several Suspected In Flynt Case," *Chicago Daily Herald*, May 26, 1978.
30. "Racist Convicted In Killings a Suspect In Flynt Shooting," *Chicago Daily Herald*, March 8, 1984.
31. Bill Thomas, "Larry Flynt: The Prisoner Of Bel Air," *Syracuse Herald-Journal*, March 14, 1983.
32. Ibid.
33. Ibid.
34. Melissa Powers interview.
35. *Criminal Confessions.*

CHAPTER 7. MRCS REDUX
1. Cincinnati Police Department, summary report, June 8, 1980.
2. Ibid.
3. "Bank Robbery Charges Filed Against Sniper," *Indiana Gazette*, November 5, 1980.
4. "On the Trail of a Murderous Sniper Suspect," *People*.
5. "Death Row Inmate Admits To Additional Racial Killings," *Chicago Daily Herald*, April 1, 1998.
6. *Criminal Confessions.*
7. John Douglas et al., *Crime Classification Manual* (New York: Jossey-Bass Inc., 1992), 190.
8. "Sniper Kills Two In Oklahoma City Shopping Center," *Post*, October 22, 1979.
9. Ibid.
10. "Two Killed by Sniper in Parking Lot," *Chicago Daily Herald*, October 22, 1979.
11. *Criminal Confessions.*
12. Lee, "Joseph Paul Franklin."
13. Melissa Powers interview.
14. "On the Trail of a Murderous Sniper Suspect," *People*.

15. Melissa Powers interview.

16. Cincinnati Police Department, "Joseph Paul Franklin: Homicides," summary report appendix.

17. "Sniper Wounds Third Victim," *Syracuse Herald-Journal*, January 16, 1980.

18. "Girl Found Shot to Death at Mill Bluff State Park," *Sparta (WI) Herald*, May 5, 1980.

19. "Few Leads Uncovered In Murder," *Sparta Herald*, May 19, 1980.

20. "Girl Found Shot To Death At Mill Bluff State Park," *Sparta Herald*.

21. "Homicide Victim Found At Mill Bluff," *Tomah (WI) Journal*, May 5, 1980.

22. "Few Leads Uncovered In Murder," *Sparta Herald*.

23. "Woman Found Dead," *Tomah Journal*, May 29, 1980.

24. "DA Issues Warning," *Tomah Journal*, May 29, 1980.

25. Christopher Hewitt *Political Terrorism and Violence in America: A Chronology* (Santa Barbara, CA: Greenwood Press, 2005), 125.

26. "Ambush In The Night," *Time*.

27. Ibid.

28. UPI, *Syracuse Post-Standard*, June 2, 1980.

29. Ibid.

30. UPI, "Black Possibly Shot At Jordan," June 9, 1980, http://www.upi.com/search /?sp=t&sLocation=sStories&ss=%22vernon+Jordan%22

31. "Ambush In The Night," *Time*.

32. Melissa Powers interview.

33. Michael Rutledge, "Need For Notoriety Drove Franklin," *Cincinnati Post*, April 16, 1997, http://www.cincypost.com/news/1997/frank041697.html.

CHAPTER 8. THE TRIANGLE MURDERS

1. Melissa Powers interview.

2. Ibid.

3. Cincinnati Police Department, summary report, June 8, 1980, 8.

4. Ibid.

5. Melissa Powers interview.

6. Ibid.

7. Cincinnati Police, "Timetable, Movements of Joseph Paul Franklin," page 3.

8. Melissa Powers interview.

9. Cincinnati Police Department, summary report, 9.

10. Melissa Powers interview.

11. Ibid.

12. Ibid.

13. Ibid.

14. Ibid.

15. Ibid.

16. Horn, "Killer: It Was What God Wanted."
17. Laura Pulfer, "Killer Tests Whine Reflex In Courtroom," *Cincinnati Enquirer*, April 30, 1998.
18. Melissa Powers interview.
19. Cincinnati Police Department, summary report, 15.
20. Melissa Powers interview.
21. Cincinnati Police Department, summary report, 5.
22. "Serial Killer Trial: Prosecution Witnesses Describe Horror of the Crime Scene," *Court TV*, October 20, 1998. http://www.courttv.com/archive/trials/franklin/102198.html.
23. Cincinnati Police Department, summary report, 1.
24. Cincinnati Police Department, summary report, 5.
25. Kristen Delguzzi, "Killer's Confession A Relief," *Cincinnati Enquirer*, April 16, 1997, http://www.enquirer.com/editions/1997/04/16/loc_wfranklin.html.
26. "Mugshots—The Story of Racist Serial Killer Joseph Paul Franklin," *Court TV*.
27. "Moving Target," *The FBI Files*.
28. Melissa Powers interview.
29. Ibid.
30. Ibid.
31. Ibid.
32. Cincinnati Police Department, summary report, 11.
33. Melissa Powers interview.
34. Ibid.
35. Ibid.
36. Ibid.
37. Ibid.
38. Ibid.
39. "Franklin: Dahmer, Bundy 'Not In My League,'" *Indiana Gazette*, February 13, 1998.
40. Melissa Powers interview.
41. Ibid.
42. Pamela Pritt, "Beard Denies Committing Murders, Can't Say Where He Was," *Pocahontas (WV) Times*, May 26, 2000, http://www.oranous.com/innocence/JacobBeard/nicely.html
43. "Man Takes Credit For Two Deaths," *Daily Register*, November 20, 1996.
44. Ibid.
45. Ibid.
46. Ibid.
47. Pamela Pritt, "Convicted Serial Killer Testifies In Rainbow Murder Case," *Pocahontas Times*, June 5, 2004, http://www.oranous.com/innocence/JacobBeard/nicely.html.

48. "Beard Grateful To Defense Team, Jury For Acquittal," *Pocahontas Times*, June 1, 2000, http://www.oranous.com/innocence/JacobBeard/nicely.html.
49. "Seeks Clerk's Help," *Journal-Tribune*, September 4, 1981, 9.
50. Lee, "Joseph Paul Franklin."

CHAPTER 9. THE SALT LAKE CITY MURDERS
1. Laurie Sullivan, "Tenacious Investigators Keep On Trail Of Serial Killers," *Deseret News*, November 1, 1990.
2. Salt Lake City Police Department, summary report, 47.
3. Ibid., 49.
4. Ibid., 45.
5. Ibid., 56.
6. Ibid., 36.
7. "Moving Target," *The FBI Files*.
8. Salt Lake City Police Department, summary report, 36.
9. Ibid.
10. Salt Lake City Murders Appeal, United States Court of Appeals, Tenth Circuit. http://cases.justia.com/us-court-of-appeals/F2/704/1183/107287/, 1186.
11. "Moving Target," *The FBI Files*.
12. "On the Trail of a Murderous Sniper Suspect," *People*.
13. Salt Lake City Police Department, summary report, case no. 80-67756—Homicides, David Martin and Ted Fields, 37.
14. Ibid., 56.
15. Ibid., 57.
16. Ibid.
17. Ibid., 21.
18. Ibid., 12.
19. Ibid., 21.
20. Ibid., 12.
21. Ibid., 10.
22. Ibid., 39.
23. Ibid., 9.
24. Ibid., 20.
25. "Moving Target," *The FBI Files*.
26. Salt Lake City Police Department, summary report, case no. 80-67756—Homicides, David Martin and Ted Fields, 25.
27. "Moving Target," *The FBI Files*.
28. Sullivan, "Tenacious Investigators Keep On Trail Of Serial Killers."
29. Michael Rutledge and Dan Horn, "Joseph Paul Franklin, Sniper Confesses," *Cincinnati Post*, April 15, 1997, www.KYPost.com.
30. Salt Lake City Police Department, summary report, 6.

31. Ibid., 15.
32. Ibid., 7.
33. Ibid., 35.
34. Ibid., 23.
35. "Moving Target," *The FBI Files*.
36. Ibid.
37. Ibid.
38. Ibid.
39. Ibid.
40. Elaine Jarvik, "Salt Lake Police Put Psychics on Hold," *Deseret News*, June 23, 2002, http://archive.deseretnews.com/archive/921469/SL-police-put-psychics-on-hold.html.
41. Mike Watkiss, "Hatred, Religion and a High-Powered Rifle," *Confessions of an Ambulance Chaser,* October 1, 2007, http://azfamily.beloblog.com/3tvTalks/2007/10/confessions_of_an_ambulance_ch_9.html#more.
42. Melissa Powers interview.
43. "Moving Target," *The FBI Files*.

CHAPTER 10. MANHUNT

1. Cincinnati Police Department, summary report, 5.
2. "Moving Target," *The FBI Files*.
3. Ibid.
4. Ibid.
5. Ibid.
6. "Manhunt Continues For Sniper Suspect," *Marysville Journal-Tribune*, September 26, 1980.
7. "Moving Target," *The FBI Files*.
8. "Mugshots—The Story of Racist Serial Killer Joseph Paul Franklin," *Court TV*.
9. "Manhunt Continues For Sniper Suspect," *Marysville Journal-Tribune*.
10. Cincinnati Police Department, summary report, 7.
11. "Manhunt Continues For Sniper Suspect," *Marysville Journal-Tribune*.
12. "Moving Target," *The FBI Files*.
13. Ibid.
14. "Mugshots—The Story of Racist Serial Killer Joseph Paul Franklin," *Court TV*.
15. The State of Utah, Plaintiff and Respondent v. Joseph Paul Franklin, Defendant and Appellant 735 P.2d 34. No. 18052 Supreme Court of Utah, 19 March 1987, 35.
16. "Mugshots—The Story of Racist Serial Killer Joseph Paul Franklin," *Court TV*.
17. "Accused Killer Tells Of Escape," *Marysville Journal-Tribune*.
18. Cincinnati Police Department, summary report, 7.
19. Ibid.
20. Cincinnati Police Department, "Timetable: Homicides of Joseph Paul Franklin," 5.

21. "Moving Target," *The FBI Files.*
22. "Manhunt Continues For Sniper Suspect," *Marysville Journal-Tribune.*
23. Salt Lake City Police Department, supplementary report, 55.
24. "Search Continues For Sniper Suspect," *Marysville Journal-Tribune*, September 29, 1980.
25. "Gun Linked To Jordan, Other Attacks," *Stars and Stripes*, October 6, 1980.
26. "Link Between Shootings," *Post Standard*, October 4, 1980.
27. "Moving Target," *The FBI Files.*
28. John Douglas, *The Anatomy of Motive: The FBI's Legendary Mindhunter Explores the Key to Understanding and Catching Violent Criminals* (New York: Simon and Schuster, 2001), 244.
29. "Moving Target," *The FBI Files.*
30. U.S. Court of Appeals, Tenth Circuit. April 12, 1983, 1186.
31. Cincinnati Police Department, summary report, 8.
32. "Racist Rifleman," *Time*, November 10, 1980.
33. UPI, "Police Fear Sniper Suspect On Way Back To Birmingham," October 29, 1980, www.upi.com.
34. "Vernon Jordan Sniper Suspect In Custody," *Daily Intelligencer*, October 29, 1980.
35. UPI, "Suspect in Race Killings Is Linked to Gun Deal Try," *Spokane Daily Chronicle*, November 1, 1980.
36. "Intensive Manhunt Ends At Blood Bank," *Waterloo Courier*, November 2, 1980.
37. Ibid.
38. Ibid.
39. Kristen Delguzzi, "Franklin: There Could be Surprises," *Cincinnati Enquirer*, April 18, 1997, http://news.cincinnati.com/apps/pbcs.dll/section?Category=NEWS.
40. "Franklin Said To Have Admitted Killings," *Stars and Stripes*, November 15, 1980.
41. Eszterhas, 325.
42. "Franklin Said To Have Admitted Killings," *Stars and Stripes*; Salt Lake City Police Department, summary report, 59.
43. United States of America v. Joseph Paul Franklin, United States Court of Appeals, Tenth Circuit. April 12, 1983, 1187.
44. Douglas, *Anatomy of Motive*, 245.
45. "Extradition to Utah Ordered For Suspect In Racial Ambushes," *Stars and Stripes.*
46. Salt Lake City Police Department, summary report, 59.
47. "Vernon Jordan Shooting Arrest Sniper Suspect," *Syracuse Post-Standard*, October 29, 1980, 1.
48. "Denies Guilt In Slaying Blacks," *Syracuse Post-Standard*, October 30, 1980.
49. *Criminal Confessions.*

50. "Vernon Jordan Shooting Arrest Sniper Suspect," *Syracuse Post-Standard*.
51. Salt Lake City Police Department, summary report, 59.
52. Ibid., 60.
53. "Murder Suspect Ordered Extradited," *Syracuse Post-Standard*, November 6, 1980.
54. Salt Lake City Police Department, summary report, 59.
55. Douglas, *Anatomy of Motive*, 245.

CHAPTER 11. DENIALS AND CONFESSIONS

1. Douglas, *Anatomy of Motive*, 245.
2. Ibid., 246.
3. Michael O'Brien interview.
4. "Sniper Suspect: U.S. Trying To Frame Me," *Elyria Chronicle-Telegram*, November 9, 1980.
5. "Pleads Innocent in Slaying of Black Joggers," *Pittsburgh Valley Independent*, November 11, 1980.
6. "Murder Charges Won't be Filed," *Marysville Journal-Tribune*, October 7, 1980.
7. "Pleads Innocent in Slaying of Black Joggers," *Pittsburgh Valley Independent*.
8. "Racist Convicted In Killings," *Chronicle Telegram*, March 8, 1981.
9. "Accused Killer Tells Of Escape," *Marysville Journal-Tribune*.
10. "Around The Nation; Judge Denies Trial Request For Suspect in Iowa Deaths," *New York Times*, January 16, 1980.
11. Cincinnati Police Department, summary report, 13.
12. Ibid.
13. U.S. Court of Appeals, Tenth Circuit, April 12, 1983, 1187.
14. "Moving Target," *The FBI Files*.
15. U.S. Court of Appeals, Tenth Circuit, 704 F.2d 1183, April 12, 1983, http://cases.justia.com/us-court-of-appeals/F2/704/1183/107287/, 1191.
16. Michael O'Brien interview.
17. Cincinnati Police Department, summary report, 14.
18. U.S. Court of Appeals, Tenth Circuit, 704 F.2d 1183, April 12, 1983, http://cases.justia.com/us-court-of-appeals/F2/704/1183/107287/, 1187.
19. "Moving Target," *The FBI Files*.
20. "Racist Convicted, Faces Murder Trial," *Syracuse Herald-Journal*, March 5, 1981.
21. "Franklin Case: Jury Begins Deliberation," *Syracuse Post-Standard*, March 4, 1981.
22. Ibid.
23. "Racist Convicted In Killings," *Chronicle Telegram*.
24. U.S. Court of Appeals, Tenth Circuit, 704 F.2d 1183, April 12, 1983, http://cases.justia.com/us-court-of-appeals/F2/704/1183/107287/, 1187.

25. George Tibbits, "Avowed Racist Berates Witness," *Ironwood (MI) Daily Globe*, February 28, 1981.
26. "Racist Convicted In Killings," *Chronicle Telegram*.
27. "Franklin Case: Jury Begins Deliberation," *Syracuse Post-Standard*.
28. "Avowed Racist Is Found Guilty," *Waterloo Courier*, March 5, 1981.
29. Ibid.
30. "Racist Convicted, Faces Murder Trial," *Syracuse Herald-Journal*.
31. UPI, "Franklin's Lawyers Cite Evidence For A New Trial," March 13, 1981, www.upi.com.
32. "Four More Charges For Avowed Racist," *Daily Intelligencer*, March 19, 1981.
33. "Charges For Racist Sniper," *Pittsburgh Valley Independent*, March 19, 1981.
34. "Accused Sniper Facing Murder Charges," *Tyrone (PA) Daily Herald*, March 19, 1981.
35. "Four More Charges For Avowed Racist," *Daily Intelligencer*.
36. "Accused Sniper Facing Murder Charges," *Tyrone Daily Herald*.
37. "Franklin Gets Life In Slaying Of Two," *Syracuse Post-Standard*, March 24, 1981.
38. "Racist Given Life Terms," *Syracuse Herald-Journal*, March 25, 1981.
39. "Franklin Gets Life In Slaying Of Two," *Syracuse Post-Standard*.
40. Ibid.
41. U.S. Court of Appeals, Tenth Circuit, 704 F.2d 1183, April 12, 1983, http://cases.justia.com/us-court-of-appeals/F2/704/1183/107287/, 1184.
42. "Racist Convicted In Killings," *Chronicle Telegram*.
43. "Franklin gets Life In Slaying Of Two," *Syracuse Pos- Standard*.
44. U.S. Court of Appeals, Tenth Circuit, 704 F.2d 1183, April 12, 1983, http://cases.justia.com/us-court-of-appeals/F2/704/1183/107287/.
45. Steven Long, *Every Woman's Nightmare: The True Story of the Fairy-Tale Marriage and Brutal Murder of Lori Hacking* (New York: St Martin's Press, 2006), 92.
46. Chip Parkinson, "Yocum's Been Guided By Luck, Timing," *Deseret News*, January 9, 1995.
47. "Untitled," *Waterloo Courier*, August 30, 1981.
48. "Ruling Paves Way For Sniper Suspect's Trial," *Ohio Chronicle Telegram*, June 11, 1981.
49. Michael O'Brien interview.
50. "Untitled," *Waterloo Courier*.
51. Ibid.
52. George Tibbits, "Woman Says Franklin Spoke To Her About Killing Blacks," *Syracuse Herald-Journal*, September 4, 1981.
53. Ibid.
54. "Accused Will Testify During Murder Trial," *Marysville Journal-Tribune*, September 9, 1981.

55. "Franklin Convicted In Blacks' Slaying," *Pittsburgh Valley Independent*, September 19, 1981.
56. Scott Snow, "Courtroom Art: A Twenty-Five Year Retrospective," Springville Museum of Art, November 28, 1997.
57. "Moving Target," *The FBI Files*.
58. "Convicted Racist Flees, Captured," *Galveston Daily News*, September 24, 1981.
59. Ibid.
60. "Franklin Gets Life, Escapes Into Elevator," *Tyrone Daily Herald*, September 24, 1981.
61. "Franklin Gets Two Life Terms," *Wisconsin Capital*, September 29, 1981.
62. "Convicted Murderer Requests Judge To Overturn Conviction," *Marysville Journal-Tribune*, September 24, 1981.
63. Jan Thompson, "Evidence, Not Race, Prompted Death Penalty, Prosecution Says," *Deseret News*, August 27, 1989.
64. Long, 91.

CHAPTER 12. THE STABBING

1. Marsha Hamilton, "Fort Wayne Agonizes Over Jordan Shooting," *Deseret News*, May 29, 1981.
2. Ibid.
3. Cincinnati Police Department, summary report, 14.
4. Ibid., 15.
5. Ibid., 15.
6. Ibid., 16.
7. "FBI Links Racist To Jordan Shooting," *Stars and Stripes*, March 29, 1981.
8. Pete Earley, *Hot House: Life Inside Leavenworth Prison* (New York: Bantam Books, 1993), 228.
9. "Marked Inmate," *Syracuse Herald-Journal*, February 5, 1982.
10. Earley, 93.
11. Jordan and Gordon-Reed, 287.
12. Pat Doyle, "Racist Murderer Stabbed 15 Times," *Chicago Daily Herald*, February 5, 1981.
13. "No Charges in Stabbing of Racist," *Chicago Daily Herald*, March 4, 1982.
14. Jordan and Gordon-Reed, 298.
15. Michael O'Brien interview.
16. Earley, 240.
17. "Jordan Undaunted by Shooting," *Syracuse Post-Standard*, September 10, 1980.
18. "FBI Discipline for News Leaks," *Pittsburgh Valley Independent*, November 21, 1980.
19. Ibid.
20. Louis Harris, "Convinced of Conspiracy," *Syracuse Herald-Journal*, July 9, 1980.

21. "Franklin-Jordan Link Reported," *Stars and Stripes*, March 27, 1981.

22. "Indictment in Jordan Shooting," *Chicago Daily Herald*, June 3, 1982.

23. "FBI Filmed Franklin Secretly for Line-up," *Chicago Daily Herald*, October 23, 1981.

24. Ibid.

25. Ibid.

26. Alan Zelfden, "Pit Bull Prosecutor Targets Skinheads," *Dallas Times Herald*, February 20, 1990.

27. "Indictment In Jordan Shooting," *Chicago Daily Herald*.

28. "Franklin-Jordan Link Reported," *Stars and Stripes*.

29. Jordan and Gordon-Reed, 237.

30. "Indictment Called 'Waste of Tax Money,'" *Waterloo Courier*, June 3, 1982.

31. "Suspect in Jordan Case Asks Transfer to Indiana," *New York Times*, July 25, 1982, http://www.nytimes.com/1982/07/25/us/around-the-nation-suspect-in -jordan-case-asks-transfer-to-indiana.html?scp=1&sq=Suspect%20In%20 Jordan%20Case%20Asks%20Transfer%20To%20Indiana&st=cse.

32. "Franklin Claims He Did Not Shoot Vernon Jordan," *Syracuse Herald-Journal*, August 17, 1982.

33. "Jordan To Tell Shooting Story," *Tyrone Daily Herald*, August 11, 1982.

34. Ibid.

35. Jordan and Gordon-Reed, 237.

36. "Acquittal Bid Reported in Jordan Case," *Stars and Stripes*, August 5, 1982.

37. "Franklin Testifies, Denies Shooting Jordan," *Chicago Daily Herald*, August 17, 1982.

38. "Avowed Racist Is Acquitted of Vernon Jordan Assault," *Stars and Stripes*, August 20, 1982.

39. "Media Fight Jury Ban," *Stars and Stripes*, August 31, 1982.

40. "Jurors Freeing Franklin Believe He Was Guilty," *Fredrick (MD) Post*, September 1, 1982.

41. "Despite Franklin Acquittal, Jordan Case Closed," *Waterloo Courier*, August 18, 1982.

42. "Jurors Freeing Franklin Believe He Was Guilty," *Fredrick (MD) Post*.

43. Cincinnati Police Department, summary report, 15.

44. "No Further Trials Expected For Acquitted Franklin," *Daily Intelligencer*, August 19, 1982.

45. Michael O'Brien interview.

46. Zelfden, "Pit Bull Prosecutor Targets Skinheads."

47. Jordan and Gordon-Reed, 238.

CHAPTER 13. GOING AFTER FRANKLIN

1. "Franklin Probe Spreading Wider," *Daily News*, March 8, 1984.

2. Homicide Charges Pending More Information, DA Says," *Sparta Herald,* "March 19, 1984.
3. Supreme Court of Tennessee, 714 S.W.2d 252, July 21, 1986.
4. "Avowed Racist Is Convicted Of Bombing Tennessee Synagogue," *Stars and Stripes,* July 14, 1984.
5. Supreme Court of Tennessee, 714 S.W.2d 252.
6. "Avowed Racist Convicted Of Bombing Synagogue," *Syracuse Post-Standard.*
7. Ibid.
8. Supreme Court of Tennessee, 714 S.W.2d 252.
9. Ibid.
10. "New Suspect? Police Think Larry Flynt's Attacker Was Racist Reacting To Nude Spread," *Indiana Gazette,* March 7, 1984.
11. Ibid.
12. "Franklin Probe Spreading Wider," *Daily News.*
13. Bell, "Convicted Killer, Avowed Racist Tells of a Life of Rage, Hatred."
14. "Racist Convicted in Killings a Suspect in Flynt Shooting," *Chicago Daily Herald.*
15. "Avowed Racist Is Convicted of Bombing Tennessee Synagogue," *Stars and Stripes.*
16. "Franklin Guilty in Flynt Shooting," *Chicago Daily Herald,* June 13, 1984.
17. "Double Slaying Confession Faked, Franklin Claims," *Syracuse Herald-Journal,* February 11, 1986.
18. "Ex-Judge Tells Jury in Franklin Trial about Ruling in Interracial Assault," *Milwaukee Journal Sentinel,* February 13, 1986.
19. Ibid.
20. Slaying Confession Faked, Franklin Claims," *Syracuse Herald-Journal.*
21. "Killing for Sport- Franklin Guilty of Interracial Couple Murder," *Casa Grande (AZ) Dispatch,* February 15, 1986.
22. Ibid.
23. "Cincinnati Task Force Appointment Draws Criticism," *Chronicle-Telegram,* 25 May 1983.

CHAPTER 14. COMING CLEAN

1. "Racist Admits to Killings Decade Ago," *Stars and Stripes,* August 23, 1990.
2. "Imprisoned Racist Admits to 2 Killings in '80," *New York Times,* August 21, 1990.
3. Douglas, *Anatomy of Motive,* 247.
4. Ibid.
5. Ibid., 246.
6. Ibid., 247.
7. U.S. Court of Appeals for the Eighth Circuit, no. 05-1043/1047.

8. Holleman and Lhotka, "I Wanted To Kill At least Two Jews, Racist Says."

9. "I Shot Vernon Jordan, Franklin Says," *Deseret News*, April 8, 1996.

10. Gladwell, "The Criminal Brain."

11. U.S. Court of Appeals for the Eighth Circuit, no. 05-1043/1047.

12. Ibid.

13. Ibid.

14. Bell, "Convicted Killer, Avowed Racist Tells of a Life of Rage, Hatred."

15. Ibid.

16. Anne E. Kornblut, "Flynt's Assailant Faces Death Penalty—Man To Be Sentenced For 5th Racist Murder," *New York Daily News*, February 23, 1997.

17. U.S. Court of Appeals for the Eighth Circuit, no. 05-1043/1047.

18. "Synagogue Sniper Gets Death Wish," *Post Standard*, February 28, 1997.

19. Delguzzi, "Sniper Feared the Chair."

20. "Synagogue Sniper Gets Death Wish," *Post Standard*.

21. Michael O'Brien interview.

22. Bell, "Convicted Killer, Avowed Racist Tells of a Life of Rage, Hatred."

23. U.S. Court of Appeals for the Eighth Circuit, no. 05-1043/1047.

24. Mike Sherwin, "Court Rejects Killer's Appeal."

25. "Sniper Admits He Shot Jordan," *Deseret News*, April 9, 1996.

26. "I Shot Vernon Jordan, Franklin Says," *Deseret News*.

27. Ibid.

28. Bell, "Convicted Killer, Avowed Racist Tells of a Life of Rage, Hatred."

29. "Larry Flynt's Assailant Has Left a Trail Of Bigotry And Murder," *New York Times*, February 16, 1997, http://www.nytimes.com/1997/02/16/us/larry-flynt-s-assailant-has-left-a-trail-of-bigotry-and-murder.html?scp=1&sq=Larry%20Flynt%E2%80%99s%20Assailant%20Has%20Left%20a%20Trail%20Of%20Bigotry%20And%20Murder&st=cse.

30. Melissa Powers interview.

31. Ibid.

32. Bell, "Convicted Killer, Avowed Racist Tells of a Life of Rage, Hatred."

33. "Flynt's Assailant Faces Execution," *Syracuse Herald-Journal*, February 20, 1997.

34. Ibid.

35. *Criminal Confessions*.

36. Gloria K. Gourley, Missouri Department of Corrections memorandum to Mike Bowersox, March 7, 1997.

37. Rachel Zoll, "Serial Killer Pleads Guilty To Murder In Chattanooga," *Indiana Gazette*, March 5, 1998.

38. "Serial Killer Admits To Tennessee Slaying," *Milwaukee Journal Sentinel*, March 5, 1998.

39. Claudia Coates, "Serial Killer Identified as Sniper in 1980 Deaths," *Daily News*, February 6, 1998.

40. "Serial Killer as Sniper Identified in '80 Deaths," *Titusville (PA) Herald*, February 6, 1998.
41. "Franklin: Dahmer, Bundy 'Not In My League,'" *Indiana Gazette*.
42. Ibid.
43. "Killer Admits Two More Slayings," *Milwaukee Journal Sentinel*, April 4, 1998.
44. "Death Row Inmate Admits To Additional Racial Killings," *Chicago Daily Herald*.
45. "Stone Killer Joseph Paul Franklin Indicted in Two 19-Year-Old Slayings," *Tennessee Oak Ridger*, April 3, 1998.
46. "Killer Admits Two More Slayings," *Milwaukee Journal Sentinel*.

CHAPTER 15. JUSTICE IN CINCINNATI

1. Delguzzi, "Sniper Feared The Chair." In an interview with Joe Holleman and William Lhotka of the *St. Louis Post-Dispatch* Franklin said, "I knew it was a death penalty case, and I wasn't anxious to be sentenced to the gas chamber." Holleman and Lhotka, "Inmate Recounts Twenty Murderous Years, Man Says Hatred And Anger Drove Him To Plot, Kill."
2. Tom O'Neill, "Hate Killer Sentenced To Die," *Cincinnati Enquirer*, February 28, 1997, http://www.enquirer.com/editions/1997/02/28/loc_franklin.html.
3. Cliff Radel, "High Fashion Prosecutor Gets Her Man," *Cincinnati Enquirer*, April 18, 1997, http://www.enquirer.com/columns/radel/1997/04/041897_cr.html.
4. Kristen Delguzzi, "Franklin Thought Message Missed," *Cincinnati Enquirer*, April 16, 1997, http://www.enquirer.com/editions/1997/04/16/loc_franklin.html.
5. Radel, "High Fashion Prosecutor Gets Her Man."
6. Dan Horn, "The Signs Pointed to Confession," *Cincinnati Enquirer*, September 16, 1998, http://www.enquirer.com/editions/1998/09/16/loc_franklin16.html.
7. Kevin Lee, "Mein Kampf Was His Map to Murder," Open Salon, June 12, 2009, http://open.salon.com/blog/kevin_lee/2009/06/11/mein_kampf_was_his_map_to_murder.
8. Radel, "High Fashion Prosecutor Gets Her Man."
9. "Joseph Paul Franklin," *Serial Killer Central*, http://www.skcentral.com/news.php?readmore=3239.
10. Kevin Lee, "Joseph Paul Franklin," *Lagniappe*, September 5, 2006, http://www.lagniappemobile.com/articles/631-untitled.
11. Ibid.
12. Horn, "The Signs Pointed to Confession."
13. Melissa Powers interview.
14. Lee, "Joseph Paul Franklin."
15. Lee, "*Mein Kampf* Was His Map to Murder."

16. Ibid.
17. Delguzzi, "Sniper Feared the Chair."
18. Ibid.
19. Rutledge, "Need For Notoriety Drove Franklin."
20. Kristen Delguzzi, "Killer Admits Slaying Two Boys Here In 1980," *Cincinnati Enquirer*, April 15, 1997, http://www.enquirer.com/editions/1997/04/15/loc_franklin.html.
21. Rutledge, "Need For Notoriety Drove Franklin."22. Cincinnati Police Department, summary report, 14.
23. Delguzzi, "Killer's Confession a Relief."
24. Rutledge, "Need For Notoriety Drove Franklin."
25. Kimball Perry, "Franklin Plots His Case—Won't Question County's Powers," *Cincinnati Post*, October 21, 1998, www.cincypost.com/news/1997/frank041697.html.
26. Ibid.
27. Dan Horn, "Caution Warned With Killer," *Cincinnati Post*, September 25, 1998.
28. Kimball Perry, "Franklin Murder Trial Remains Here," *Cincinnati Post*, September 16, 1998.
29. Kristen Delguzzi, "Franklin Pleads Not Guilty," *Cincinnati Enquirer*, April 29, 1998.
30. Ibid.
31. "Innocent Pleas Entered For Convicted Serial Killer," *Marysville Journal-Tribune*, April 29, 1998.
32. Delguzzi, "Franklin Pleads Not Guilty."
33. Ibid.
34. "Innocent Pleas Entered For Convicted Serial Killer," *Marysville Journal-Tribune*.
35. Dan Horn, "Mental Experts: Franklin Is Sane," *Cincinnati Post*, July 15, 1998.
36. Pulfer, "Killer Tests Whine Reflex In Courtroom."
37. "Convicted Serial Killer Back In Cincinnati Court," *Marysville Journal-Tribune*, April 28, 1998.
38. Delguzzi, "Franklin Pleads Not Guilty."
39. Tanya Albert, "Insanity Defense Unlikely," *Cincinnati Enquirer*, July 16, 1998.
40. Dan Horn, "Interview: Deluded Franklin Now Sorry," *Cincinnati Post*, May 8, 1998.
41. Dan Horn, "Determined to Have Role in Franklin Prosecution," *Cincinnati Enquirer*, September 25 1998.
42. Dan Horn, "Franklin Will Act As Own Co-Lawyer In Murder Case," *Cincinnati Enquirer*, September 16, 1998, http://www.enquirer.com/editions/1998/09/16/loc_fralaywer16.html.

43. Dan Horn, "Franklin Confession Stands," *Cincinnati Enquirer*, October 2, 1998, http://www.enquirer.com/editions/1998/10/02/loc_franklin02.html.
44. Ibid.
45. "Killing People For A Hobby," Kimball Perry, *Cincinnati Post*, October 20, 1998.
46. Cincinnati Police Department, summary report, 9.
47. "Serial Killer Trial," Court TV, October 20, 1998, www.courttv.com/archive /trials/franklin/.
48. Dan Horn, "Franklin's Taped Statement Hard On Victim's Families," *Cincinnati Enquirer*, October 21, 1998.
49. "Serial Killer Trial," *Court TV*, October 22, 1998, www.courttv.com/archive /trials/franklin/.
50. "Serial Killer Trial." *Court TV*, October 21, 1998, www.courttv.com/archive /trials/franklin/.
51. "Serial Killer Trial: Franklin Gets Two More Life Sentences" *Court TV*, October 22, 1998, www.courttv.com/archive/trials/franklin/.
52. Kimball Perry, "Defense Attorney Dale Schmidt," *Cincinnati Enquirer*, October 23, 1998.
53. Dan Horn, "Judge Shows Contempt For Franklin," *Cincinnati Enquirer*, October 23, 1998. 54.Ibid.
55. Kimball Perry, "Franklin Fascinated By Women," *Cincinnati Post*, October 24, 1998.
56. Ibid.
57. "Killer Convicted Again," *Stars and Stripes*, October 23, 1998.

CHAPTER 16. INJUSTICE IN WEST VIRGINIA

1. The Supreme Court Of Appeals Of West Virginia, January 1995 Term, no. 22504, 491.
2. Ibid.
3. "Jurors Find Beard Innocent In Rainbow Murders," *Iowa Daily Register*, June 1, 2000.
4. Dan Horn, "Franklin Confession May Re-Open Case," *Cincinnati Post*, April 18 1997, www.cincypost.com/news/1997/frank.
5. The Supreme Court Of Appeals Of West Virginia, January 1995 Term, no. 22504, 494.
6. "Jurors Find Beard Innocent In Rainbow Murders," *Iowa Daily Register*.
7. The Supreme Court Of Appeals Of West Virginia, January 1995 Term no. 22504, 495.
8. Ibid., 493.
9. "Man Takes Credit For Two Deaths," *Iowa Daily Register*.
10. Delguzzi, "Franklin: There Could Be Surprises."

11. Ibid.
12. Horn, "Franklin Confession May Re-open Case."
13. Delguzzi, "Franklin: There Could Be Surprises."
14. Ibid.
15. Horn, "Franklin Confession May Re-open Case."
16. John Kieseweiter, "60 Minutes May Shed Light On Two Killings," *Cincinnati Enquirer*, December 9, 1998, 6.
17. Ibid.
18. Dan Horn, "Franklin's Confession Frees Man," *Cincinnati Enquirer*, January 30, 1999, http://www.enquirer.com/editions/1999/01/30/loc_franklins_confession.html.
19. "Woman Testifies Against Accused Rainbow Killer," *Waterloo Courier*, May 21, 2000.
20. Pritt, "Beard Denies Committing Murders, Can't Say Where He Was."
21. Pamela Pritt, "Rainbow Defendant's Threats Kept Witness Silent," *Pocahontas Times*, May 19, 2000.
22. Pamela Pritt, "Key Defense Witness Testifies For Beard," *Pocahontas Times*, "May 25, 2000.
23. Pamela Pritt, "Former Co-defendant Wavers On Witness Stand," *Pocahontas Times*, May 22, 2000.
24. Pamela Pritt, "Braxton County Jury Finds Beard Not Guilty," *Pocahontas Times*, May 31, 2000.
25. Ibid.
26. Ibid.
27. Ibid.
28. Ibid.
29. Ibid.
30. Pritt, "Beard Grateful to Defense Team, Jury for Acquittal."
31. Pritt, "Braxton County Jury Finds Beard Not Guilty."
32. Pamela Pritt, "Rainbow Prosecutor Taken Ill, Judge Denies Defense Motion for Mistrial," *Pocahontas Times*, May 30, 2000.
33. Pritt, "Beard Grateful to Defense Team, Jury For Acquittal."
34. Lee, "Joseph Paul Franklin."

CHAPTER 17. FRANKLIN'S DEMONS

1. Stanton E. Samenow, *Inside The Criminal Mind* (New York: Crown Publishers, 2004), 11.
2. "No Further Trials Expected For Acquitted Franklin," *Daily Intelligencer.*
3. Douglas, *Anatomy of Motive*, 245.
4. "Should PLEs Carry Books About Serial Killers?" Stormfront.org, December 24, 2006, http://www.stormfront.org/forum/archive/index.php/t-352008.html.

5. "Franklin Brags Of Bombing Temple, Quickly Convicted," *Chicago Daily Herald*, July 13, 1984.
6. *Criminal Confessions.*
7. Gladwell, "The Criminal Brain." 8. Ibid.
9. Dorothy Otnow Lewis, *Guilty By Reason Of Insanity: Inside the Minds of Killers* (London: Arrow Books, 1999), 188.
10. "The Amityville Killings," *Killing Mum and Dad*, produced by Vivian McGrath, directed by Roger Thomas, 2005.
11. *Criminal Confessions.*
12. Robert D. Hare, *Without Conscience: The Disturbing World Of Psychopaths Among Us* (New York: The Guilford Press, 1993), 44.
13. Jack Levin, *The Violence of Hate: Confronting Racism, Anti-Semitism, and Other Forms of Bigotry* (Boston: Allyn and Bacon, 2002), 45.
14. Bell, "Convicted Killer Tells of a Life of Rage, Hatred."
15. Levin, *The Violence of Hate*, 11.
16. Jason Sokol, *There Goes My Everything: White Southerners In The Age Of Civil Rights, 1945-1975* (New York: Vintage Books, 2006), 106.
17. Ibid., 6.
18. Ibid., 15.
19. Ibid., 36.
20. Julietta Leung, "The Personality of a Serial Killer," BX Science, http://www.bxscience.edu/ourpages/users/villani/forensics/articles/psychologicalprofiles/killer.pdf.
21. Douglas, *Anatomy of Motive*, 31.
22. Ibid., 238.
23. Ibid., 239.
24. Maryanne Vollers, *Lone Wolf: Eric Rudolph; Murder, Myth, and the Pursuit of an American Outlaw* (London: HarperCollins, 2006), 314.
25. Ibid., 315.
26. Ibid., 318.
27. Burgess A., Douglas J., and Ressler R., "Serial Killer Characteristics," May 24, 2004, http://www.members.tripod.com/~Serialkillr/serialkillersexposed/characteristics.html. 28. "Franklin Brags Of Bombing Temple, Quickly Convicted," *Chicago Daily Herald.*
29. Delguzzi, "Sniper Feared the Chair."
30. Massengill, 262.
31. Ibid., 239.
32. "I Shot Vernon Jordan, Franklin Says," *Deseret News.*
33. Massengill, 303.
34. "No Further Trials Expected For Acquitted Franklin," *Daily Intelligencer.*
35. Ezekiel, 153.

36. Ibid., 154.
37. Ibid., 157.
38. Ibid., 321.
39. Massengill, 287.
40. "Mugshots—The Story of Racist Serial Killer Joseph Paul Franklin," *Court TV.*
41. Levin, *The Violence of Hate*, 87.
42. Patricia Davis and Carol Morello, "A Different Kind of Killer—Gunman Doesn't Conform to Usual Patterns, Experts Say," *Criminal Profiling Research*, October 9, 2002, http://www.criminalprofiling.ch/sniper.html#sniperdifferent.

CHAPTER 18. DEATH ROW

1. "Potosi Is Last Stop For Missouri's Condemned," *Intelligencer Record*, March 30, 1987.
2. "Potosi Correction Institution," Missouri Department of Corrections (MDC), http://www.doc.mo.gov/division/adult/pcc.htm.
3. Michael W. Cuneo, *Almost Midnight: An American Story Of Murder and Redemption*, 226.
4. Bob Herbert, "There's No Doubt, It's Cruel And Unusual," *Syracuse Herald-Journal*, March 12, 2001.
5. Jim Salter, "State Execution Location Changed," *Missourian*, March 30, 2005, http://www.columbiamissourian.com/stories/2005/03/30/state-execution-location-changed/.
6. Cuneo, 259.
7. "Nixon, Hulshof Oppose Death Penalty Moratorium," KY3 Blogspot, April 2, 2008, http://ky3.blogspot.com/2008/04/nixon-hulshof-oppose-death-penalty.html.
8. Joseph A. Rehyansky, "Panic In Needle Park-Listing To Starboard," Human Events.com, April 22, 2008, http://www.humanevents.com/search.php?keywords=missouri+death+penalty&author_name=&x=20&y=13.
9. Michael O'Brien interview.
10. Cuneo, 253.
11. Ibid.
12. Rutledge, "Need For Notoriety Drove Franklin."
13. Betty Weber, Missouri Department of Corrections (MDC) memorandum to Joseph Paul Franklin, April 30, 1997.
14. Richard K. Minard, MDC memorandum to Gloria K. Gourley, May 19, 1997.
15. Ibid.
16. Joseph Paul Franklin, MDC letter to Mr. Hofmeister, July 14, 1997.
17. MDC, Conduct Violation Report, July 25, 1997.
18. Rutledge, "Need For Notoriety Drove Franklin."
19. Michael O'Brien interview.

20. Ibid.
21. Horn, "Killer: 'It Was What God Wanted.'"
22. Bell, "Convicted Killer, Avowed Racist Tells of a Life of Rage, Hatred."
23. Michael O'Brien interview.
24. Bell, "Convicted Killer, Avowed Racist Tells of a Life of Rage, Hatred."
25. MDC, Conduct Violation Report, April 7, 1998, and April 14, 1998.
26. Joseph Paul Franklin, MDC letter to Ms. Vance, April 19, 1998.
27. Michael O'Brien interview.
28. Ibid.
29. Ibid.
30. MDC, Conduct Violation Report, November 5, 1998.
31. MDC, Conduct Violation Report, December 17, 1998.
32. Joseph Paul Franklin, MDC letter from Joseph Paul Franklin to Brenda Gibson, August 19, 1999.
33. MDC, Conduct Violation Report, August 22, 2000.
34. Joseph Paul Franklin, MDC copy of letter to Teresa Izquierdo, June 17, 1999.
35. Joe Hoffmeister, functional unit manager, MDC letter to Mark E. Piepmeier, Hamilton County prosecuting attorney, July 9, 1999.
36. COI Tommy Ivison, MDC memorandum to CSID. Taylor, third-shift supervisor, November 6, 1998.
37. Michael J. Layden, MDC memorandum to Joseph Paul Franklin and Sharon Gifford, February 1, 1999.
38. Officer Henry Boatright, MDC, Conduct Violation Report, February 3, 1999.
39. Officer Randall Wills, MDC, Conduct Violation Report, February 22, 1999.
40. MDC, Conduct Violation Report, March 2, 1999.
41. Officer Randall Wills, MDC, Conduct Violation Report, March 3, 1999.
42. Sharon Gifford, MDC memorandum to Linda Wilkinson, functional unit manager, June 4, 1999.
43. Joseph Paul Franklin, MDC letter to Joe Hoffmeister, functional unit manager, June 14, 1999.
44. Officer Richard Coleman, MDC, Conduct Violation Report, January 12, 2000.
45. Linda Wilkinson, functional unit manager, Housing Unit 1 and 2, MDC memorandum oto Sharon Gifford, CCW/II, Housing Unit 4, March 2, 2000.
46. Brenda Umpenhour, MDC memorandum to Sharon Gifford, April 17, 2000.
47. A. Butterworth, MDC, Conduct Violation Report, September 20, 2000.
48. D. King, MDC, Conduct Violation Report, July 24, 2001.
49. Jonna King, CCW, MDC memorandum to Linda Wilkinson, functional unit manager, March 6, 2001.
50. L. Brannum, MDC, Conduct Violation Report, April 20, 2003.
51. Don Roper, MDC letter to Joseph Paul Franklin, February 18, 2004.
52. Joseph Paul Franklin, MDC letter to Don Roper, April 19, 2004.

53. Don Roper, MDC, to Joseph Paul Franklin, February 19, 2004.
54. Joseph Paul Franklin, MDC, letter Potosi Correctional Center Records Office, April 6, 2006.
55. Jim Salter, "Many More Executions Possible In Missouri," *Kansas City Star*, May 20, 2009, www.kansascity.com/news/local/story,/1207901.
56. Lew Schucart, "Does the Death Penalty Deter Crime?" *St. Louis Post-Dispatch*, November 6, 2007, http://www.stltoday.com/blogzone/talk-of-the-day/talk-of-the-day/2007/06/does-the-death-penalty-deter-crime/.
57. Joseph Paul Franklin, letter to the author, December 8, 2008.
58. "Richmond Heights—Execution Sought," *STL Today*, June 17, 2009, http://www.stltoday.com/stltoday/news/stories.nsf/laworder/story/87870FEE9BBF0463862575D800193897?OpenDocument.

EPILOGUE
1. "White Man Admits To 1980 Shooting Of Vernon Jordan," *Jet*.
2. "Flynt's Assailant Faces Execution," *Syracuse Herald-Journal*.
3. Delguzzi, "Sniper Feared the Chair."
4. *Criminal Confessions*.
5. Holleman and Lhotka, "Inmate Recounts Twenty Murderous Years, Man Says Hatred and Anger Drove Him to Plot, Kill."
6. Linda Wilkinson, MDC memorandum to Sharon Gifford.
7. Rehyansky, "Panic In Needle Park-Listing To Starboard."
8. Joseph Paul Franklin, letter to the author, August 12, 2008.
9. Joseph Paul Franklin, letter to the author, September 4, 2008.
10. *Criminal Confessions*.
11. Joseph Paul Franklin, letter to the author, August 31, 2009.
12. "Supremacist Admits To 1978 Murder," *Doylestown (PA) Intelligencer Record*.
13. Kim Bell, "Serial Killer Franklin Adds 3 Names To His List," *Deseret News*, ", July 26, 1997, http://archive.deseretnews.com/archive/574345/Serial-killer-Franklin-adds-3-names-to-his-list.html.
14. Patrick Taylor, e-mail to the author, March 2, 2009.
15. Michael O'Brien interview.
16. E-mail sent to Jackson Police regarding Franklin's confession to Mike O'Brien; the shooting of a Jackson police officer, March 30, 2009.
17. Michael O'Brien interview.
18. Ibid.
19. Lee, "Joseph Paul Franklin."
20. Bell, "Convicted Killer, Avowed Racist, Tells of a Life Of Rage, Hatred."
21. Michael O'Brien interview.
22. Robert Patrick, "Court Rejects Appeal by Serial Killer," *St. Louis Post-Dispatch*, July 25, 2007.

23. "Thursday Editorial: The Quality of Mercy," *SLT Today*, http://www.stltoday.com/blogzone/the-platform/published-editorials/2008/08/thursday-editorial-the-quality-of-mercy/, August 20, 2008.
24. Patrick, "Court Rejects Appeal by Serial Killer."
25. Michael Rust and David Wager, "Mount Vernon," *Insight on the News*, February 16, 1998, http://findarticles.com/p/articles/mi_m1571/is_n6_v14/ai_20221606/.
26. Barbara Reynolds, "Attempt To Replace Vernon Jordan Fails," *Chronicle-Telegram*, June 15, 1980.
27. Hamilton, "Fort Wayne Agonizes Over Jordan Shooting."
28. Salt Lake City Police Department, e-mail to the author, March 2, 2009.
29. "Former Utah Investigator Turns Focus On Serial Killers Nationwide," *Deseret News*, March 31, 1991.
30. "Moving Target," *The FBI Files*.
31. "Judge Honored For Serial Killer Confessions," November 13, 2008, http://www.local12.com/.
32. "Something Borrowed," *New Yorker*, November 22, 2004, http://www.gladwell.com/2004/2004_11_25_a_borrowed.html.
33. Lee, "Mein Kampf Was His Map to Murder."
34. "Mugshots—The Story of Racist Serial Killer Joseph Paul Franklin," *Court TV*.
35. "Judge Honoured for Serial Killer Confessions."
36. *Criminal Mindscape: Words of a Serial Killer*, MSNBC Documentaries, 2008, http://www.msnbc.msn.com/id/21134540/vp/33687587#33687587.
37. "A Brief History of Paddock Hills," *Paddock Hills*, http://www.paddockhills.org/history.htm; also mentioned in *The Morgue Archives*, May/June 1999, http://www.mayhem.net/Crime/morg9906.html.
38. Coates, "Serial Killer Identified as Sniper in 1980 Deaths."
39. Emily Rasinski, "Remembering Gerald Gordon," *STL Today*, October 8, 2008,http://videos.stltoday.com/p/video?id=2263472.
40. Rehyansky, "Panic In Needle Park-Listing To Starboard."
41. Schlussel, "Larry Flynt's Former Lawyer Dismisses Hustler Chief's 'Conspiracy Theories,' Finds Faith."
42. "Flynt's Assailant Faces Execution," *Syracuse Herald-Journal*.
43. Kornblut, "Flynt's Assailant Faces Death Penalty—Man To Be Sentenced For 5th Racist Murder."
44. Schlussel, "Larry Flynt's Former Lawyer Dismisses Hustler Chief's 'Conspiracy Theories,' Finds Faith."
45. Ibid.
46. Ibid.
47. "State Agrees to Pay Man Cleared in Rainbow Killings Almost $2 Million," *Morgantown (WV) Dominion Post*, January 6, 2003.

48. Ibid.
49. Ibid.
50. Christian Giggenbach, "Former Murder Suspect Arrested for DUI," *Beckley (WV) Register-Herald*, October 25, 2006, http://www.register-herald.com/policecourts/local_story_298234305.html/resources_printstory.
51. Pritt, "Beard Denies Committing Murders, Can't Say Where He Was."
52. Ibid.
53. Pritt, "Beard Grateful to Defense Team, Jury for Acquittal."
54. Ibid.
55. *Alton Standard*, Aiken, SC. April 29, 2005, 6A.
56. Ibid.
57. Joe Holley, "Virulent Segregationist J. B. Stoner Dies," *Washington Post*, April 28, 2005.
58. Emily Yellin, "A Changing South Revisits Its Unsolved Racial Killings," *New York Times*, November 8, 1999, http://www.nytimes.com/1999/11/08/us/a-changing-south-revisits-its-unsolved-racial-killings.html?scp=1&sq=A%20Changing%20South%20Revisits%20Its%20Unsolved%20Racial%20Killings&st=cse.
59. Durham, 105.
60. Morris Dees, e-mail to the author, April 16, 2009.
61. "Homeland Security: Economic, Political Climate Fuelling Extremism," Southern Poverty Law Center, http://www.splcenter.org/news/item.jsp?aid=373&splcnewsletter=newsgen-041609.
62. Joseph Paul Franklin, letter to the author, August 31, 2009.
63. U.S. Secret Service, e-mail to the author, June 19, 2009.
64. *Auschwitz: The Nazis and the Final Solution; Liberation and Revenge*, written and produced by Laurence Rees, BBC/ KCET Hollywood Production, 2005.
65. Bell, "Convicted Killer, Avowed Racist, Tells of a Life of Rage, Hatred."

SELECTED BIBLIOGRAPHY

BOOKS

Ayton, Mel. *A Racial Crime: James Earl Ray and the Murder of Martin Luther King Jr.* Las Vegas: Archebooks, 2005.

Burrough, Bryan. *Public Enemies: America's Greatest Crime Wave and the Birth of the FBI, 1933-34.* New York: Penguin, 2008.

Cash, W. J. *The Mind Of The South.* New York: Random House, 1991.

Chalmers, David. *Backfire: How The Ku Klux Klan Helped The Civil Rights Movement.* New York: Rowman and Littlefield, 2003.

Clinton, Bill. *My Life.* New York: Knopf, 2004.

Cuneo, Michael W. *Almost Midnight: An American Story Of Murder and Redemption.* New York: St. Martin's Paperbacks, 2004.

DeGroot, Gerard. *The Sixties Unplugged: A Kaleidoscope History of a Disorderly Decade.* (London: Pan Books, 2008.

Douglas, John and Mark Olshaker. *The Anatomy of Motive:The FBI's Legendary Mindhunter Explores the Key to Understanding and Catching Violent Criminals.* New York: Simon and Schuster, 2001.

Douglas, John, Anne W. Burgess, Allen G. Burgess, and Robert K. Ressler. *Crime Classification Manual.* New York: Jossey-Bass Inc., 1992.

Durham, Martin. *White Rage: The Extreme Right and American Politics.* New York: Routledge, 2007.

Earley, Pete. *Hot House: Life Inside Leavenworth Prison.* New York: Bantam Books, 1993.

Eszterhas, Joe. *American Rhapsody.* New York: Knopf, 2000.

Ezekiel, Raphael S. *The Racist Mind: Portraits Of American Neo-Nazis and Klansmen.* New York: Penguin, 1996.

Fest, Joachim and M. Bullock. *The Face of the Third Reich: Portraits of the Nazi Leadership.* New York: Penguin, 1979.

Greene, Melissa Fay. *The Temple Bombing.* New York: Ballantine, 1996.

Hare, Robert D. *Without Conscience: The Disturbing World Of Psychopaths Among Us.* New York: The Guilford Press, 1993.

Hewitt, Christopher. *Political Terrorism and Violence In America: A Chronology.* Santa Barbara, CA: Greenwood Press, 2005.

Jeffreys-Jones, Rhodri. *The FBI: A History.* New Haven, CT: Yale University Press, 2007.

Jordan, Vernon with Annette Gordon-Reed. *Vernon Can Read!: A Memoir.* New York: PublicAffairs, 2001.

Kaplan, Jeffrey, ed. *Encyclopedia of White Power: A Sourcebook of the Radical Racist Right.* Lanham, MD: Alta Mira Press, 2000.

Langer, Elinor. *A Hundred Little Hitlers: The Death of aBlack Man, the Trial of a White Racist, and the Rise of the Neo-Nazi Movement in America.* New York: Picador, 2003.

Levin, Jack and Jack McDevitt. *Hate Crimes Revisited: America's War on Those Who are Different.* Boulder, CO: Westview Press, 2002.

Levin, Jack. *The Violence of Hate: Confronting Racism, Anti-Semitism, and Other Forms of Bigotry.* Boston: Allyn and Bacon, 2002.

Lewis, Dorothy Otnow. *Guilty By Reason Of Insanity: Inside The Minds Of Killers.* London: Arrow Books, 1999.

Long, Steven. *Every Woman's Nightmare: The Fairy-Tale Marriage and Brutal Murder of Lori Hacking.* New York: St Martin's Press, 2006.

Mailer, Norman. *The Executioner's Song.* New York: Vintage Books, 1979.

Marable, Manning. *Race, Reform and Rebellion: The Second Reconstruction and Beyond in Black America, 1945–2006.* New York: Palgrave Macmillan, 2007.

Massengill, Reed. *Portrait of a Racist: The Man Who Killed Medgar Evers?* New York: St Martin's Press, 1994.

Perlstein, Rick. *Nixonland: The Rise of a President and the Fracturing of America.* New York: Scribner, 2008.

Reimann, Victor. *Goebbels.* New York: Doubleday, 1975.

Ressler, Robert K. and Tom Shactman. *Whoever Fights Monsters.* New York: Pocket Books, 1993.

Robins, Robert S. and Jerrod M. Post. *Political Paranoia: The Psychopolitics of Hatred.* New Haven, CT: Yale University Press, 1997.

Rockwell, George Lincoln. *White Power.* Los Angeles: World Services, 1972.

Rose, David. *Violation: Justice, Race and Serial Murder in the Deep South.* New York: Harper Perennial, 2008.

Samenow, Stanton E. *Inside The Criminal Mind.* New York: Crown Publishers, 2004.

Schmaltz, William H. *Hate: George Lincoln Rockwell and the American Nazi Party*. Washington, DC: Brassey's, 1999.

Sokol, Jason. *There Goes My Everything: White Southerners in the Age of Civil Rights, 1945–1975*. New York: Vintage Books, 2006.

Turchie, Terry D. and Kathleen M. Puckett. *Hunting the American Terrorist: The FBI's War On Homegrown Terror*. Palisades, NY: History Publishing Company, 2007.

Waldrep, Christopher. *Racial Violence On Trial: A Handbook with Cases, Laws and Documents*. Oxford, UK: ABC-CLIO, 2001.

Wade, Wyn Craig. *The Fiery Cross: The Ku Klux Klan in America*. New York: Oxford University Press, 1987.

Williamson, Joel. *A Rage For Order: Black and White Relations in the American South Since Emancipation*. New York: Oxford University Press, 1986.

Vollers, Maryanne. *Lone Wolf: Eric Rudolph; Murder, Myth, and the Pursuit of an American Outlaw*. London: HarperCollins, 2006.

GOVERNMENT DOCUMENTS

"American Nazi Party." Federal Bureau of Investigation. http://foia.fbi.gov/foiaindex/anazi.htm.

"Aryan Brotherhood." Federal Bureau of Investigation. http://foia.fbi.gov/foiaindex/aryanbro.htm.Cincinnati Police Department. *Timetable: Homicides of Joseph Paul Franklin*. Supplied to the author by Stephanie R. McKenzie, Cincinnati Police Department Records Section, 2007.

Franklin, Joseph Paul. Interview with Det. Michael O'Brien, Cincinnati Police Department. Transcribed by Nancy Mynhier. June 17, 1998. Supplied to the author by Stephanie R. McKenzie, 2007.

Franklin, Joseph Paul. Interview with Melissa Powers, Cincinnatti Police Department. April 13, 1997. http://www.cincinnati-oh.gov/cpd/.

Missouri Department of Corrections. Joesph Paul Franklin prison file. DOC ID 990133. Supplied to the author by Brian Hauswirth, chief public information officer, Missouri Department of Corrections, September 10, 2007.

"National States Rights Party." Federal Bureau of Investigation. http://foia.fbi.gov/foiaindex/national_states_rights_party.htm.

O'Brien, Michael. *Summary Report*. Cincinnati Police Department. June 8, 1980. Supplied to the author by Stephanie R. McKenzie, 2007.

Oklahoma Police Department. *OCPD Crime-Incident Report on the Murders of Jesse Taylor and Marian Bressette*. October 2, 1979. Supplied to the author by Lucy Rains, OCPD Records Department, September 6, 2007.

Salt Lake City Police Department. *Summary Report Case No: 80-67756–Homicides, David Martin and Ted Fields*. February 20, 1981. Supplied to the author by

Sandra Stranger, GRANMA coordinator, Salt Lake City Police Department, October 12, 2007.

U.S. Department of Justice, Civil Rights Division. Memorandum to William French Smith, attorney general, from William Bradford Reynolds, assistant attorney general. October 13, 1982.

AUDIOVISUAL MATERIALS

"The Amityville Killings," *Killing Mum and Dad*, DVD, produced by Vivian Mc-Grath, directed by Roger Thomas (Northern Territory, Australia: Redback Films Productions, 2005).

Auschwitz: The Nazis and the Final Solution; Liberation and Revenge, DVD, written and produced by Laurence Rees (BBC/ KCET Hollywood Production, 2005).

Criminal Confessions, DVD (1999; Santa Monica, CA: Live/Artisan, 2003).

Larry Flynt: The Right To Be Left Alone, DVD, directed by Joan Brooker-Marks (New York: Midtown Films, 2007).

"Moving Target," *The FBI Files*, Discovery Channel (season 2, episode 15, 2000).

"Mugshots—The Story of Racist Serial Killer Joseph Paul Franklin," *Court TV* video, 2000. http://www.trutv.com/library/crime/index.html.

Ultimate Crimes—Driven to Kill, DVD (History Channel, 2002).

INDEX

ABOUT THE AUTHOR

MEL AYTON is the author of many highly acclaimed books, including *A Racial Crime*, the story of Dr. Martin Luther King's assassin, and *The Forgotten Terrorist: Sirhan Sirhan and the Assassination of Robert F. Kennedy* (Potomac Books, 2007). Ayton has a master's degree in history from Durham University and is a former Fulbright teacher, deputy principal, and college lecturer. Ayton has appeared in documentaries produced by NBC News, the National Geographic Channel, and the Discovery Channel, and has worked as a historical consultant for the BBC. Ayton is also the author of numerous articles for various print and online publications, including *History Ireland*, *Crime Magazine*, David Horowitz's *FrontPage Magazine*, *Washington Decoded*, and George Mason University's *History News Network*. He lives in County Durham, England.